I
LOVE
CHICAGO
GUIDE

Marilyn J. Appleberg

Drawings by **Albert Pfeiffer**

COLLIER BOOKS
Macmillan Publishing Company
New York

COLLIER MACMILLAN PUBLISHERS
London

10654718

Acknowledgments

To Page Philips, thank you for a job well done. To Jane Herman and Sharon L. Gonzalez, gratitude once more for patience and aid.

Map credits: The Downtown Street Plan and House Number Map are reprinted courtesy of Rand McNally & Company, © copyright by Rand McNally & Company, RL-87-S-3. The Neighborhoods map is adapted from material supplied courtesy of the City of Chicago, Bureau of Maps and Plats.

Copyright © 1982, 1988 by Marilyn J. Appleberg

All rights reserved. No part of this book may be reproduced or transmitted in any form or by any means, electronic or mechanical, including photocopying, recording or by any information storage and retrieval system, without permission in writing from the Publisher.

Collier Books
MACMILLAN PUBLISHING COMPANY
866 Third Avenue, New York, N.Y. 10022
Collier Macmillan Canada, Inc.

Library of Congress Cataloging-in-Publication Data

Appleberg, Marilyn J.
  I love Chicago guide.

  Includes index.
  1. Chicago (Ill.)—Description—1981-   —Guidebooks. I. Title.
F548.18.A66   1988   917.73'110443   87-30923
ISBN 0-02-097191-5

Macmillan books are available at special discounts for bulk purchases for sales promotions, premiums, fund-raising, or educational use. For details, contact:

Special Sales Director
Macmillan Publishing Company
866 Third Avenue
New York, N.Y. 10022

10 9 8 7 6 5 4 3 2 1

Printed in the United States of America

Extreme care has been taken to see that all information in this book is accurate and up to date, but the publisher cannot be held responsible for any errors which may appear.

CONTENTS

Contents

INTRODUCTION

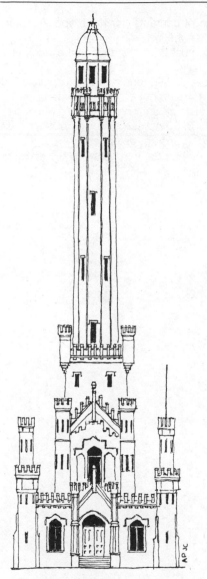

The Water Tower

Chicago! It's never idle, it bustles, it bristles. As the hurly-burly image of the past recedes, what's taking its place is just as exciting, just as energetic, albeit more polished, more sophisticated. I have no doubt that Chicago will surprise you. Fine restaurants, excellent museums, innovative galleries, chic shops, and exciting theater will all vie for your attention. Alluring still is the splendid historic architecture of Adler, Sullivan, Holabird, Burnham, Root, and Wright, side by side—ofttimes literally—with contemporary architectural wonders. The in-city parks and beaches are much-beloved Chicago givens but are *never* taken for granted. The omnipresent Lake Michigan provides innumerable opportunities for the city to reflect upon itself, and it obviously likes what it sees—and *so will you.*

Whatever your interest, Chicago can satisfy. If you are here on business look up, literally and figuratively, and take advantage of the fact that you are in one of America's most dynamic cities. If you are here on vacation, plan your time carefully or you won't see all there is before you have to leave, and that would be a shame. If you are lucky enough to live here, then you already know—*Chicago is second to none in so many ways.*

HOW TO USE THIS BOOK

General categories are listed in the table of contents; for more specific information on what is included in the book, use the index.

To save space, abbreviations have been used for the days of the week and for the months.

Small shops, if in busy shopping areas, usually conform to the policies of their larger neighbors; the hours of the department stores are listed, as the only major change occurs during the Christmas shopping season, when they are all open every evening. Others conform to the eccentricities of their area of town; if they are unusual they are listed. If unsure, call ahead.

Where a shop or restaurant accepts credit cards, the following key is used:

AE	American Express
CB	Carte Blanche
DC	Diners' Club
MC	MasterCard
V	Visa

BASIC
INFORMATION

HELPFUL HINTS

Chicago's streets are laid out in a grid pattern. In the Loop (south of the Chicago River), State Street (which runs north-south) and Madison Street (which runs east-west) are the central dividing points. So north and south street numbers ascend as you move away from Madison, east and west ascend as you move away from State. Each block is represented by a hundred number; eight city blocks (or 800 numbers) equal one mile. Michigan Avenue (north of the Chicago River) is downtown Chicago's main thoroughfare. One more helpful hint: The Lake is east—*always*.

GETTING AROUND

Though the city of Chicago covers an area of approximately 25 miles to the north and south and 15 miles to the west, the major sites are located in a relatively concentrated area: the Loop with the financial district and retailing giants, and Michigan Avenue and the Near North Side with shopping and dining delights. If you have a car, my suggestion is to park it. Given good weather and an unhurried schedule, walking is the best way to discover all that is special about Chicago.

The next-best way to get around is by the *very* extensive mass-transit system. Buses may be slow, but the el (elevated trains) may be too fast for some; both offer a view while getting you to your destination. Taxis are expensive, and they charge extra for each additional passenger.

The Mayor's Office of Inquiry & Information, City Hall, Room 100, Chicago IL 60602, 744-5000, will supply a map of the city's Bikeway System and its rules, if you would like to get around on two wheels.

WEATHER

The best time to visit Chicago from a weather standpoint is autumn—when it's dry and the temperatures are in the high 50s. Spring tends to be wet, and summer is hot and humid (average temperature 73°), but the presence of city beaches mitigates this fact. What can one say about winter? It's cold. The weather is 30°, but remember, Chicago is known as the Windy City, and despite claims that that refers to the long-windedness of former city-boosters, the wind-chill factor can be painful. Dress for the season. Layering of clothing is best, because in any season the weather can be unpredictable. In winter, outerwear should include hat (with ear covering), gloves, and boots, which will be suitable for—did I forget to mention it?—snow.

CAVEAT

First, about the city. True love is never blind. Chicago, like any city, can be unsafe in certain areas at certain times. Common sense *must* prevail regarding when you go and at what time you get there. Be sure of your destination in the evening and how you are going to get to it and back again. Secure your wallet or purse, and do not flaunt cash or gold jewelry.

Second, about the book. There is little about Chicago that is stagnant. Change is inevitable *and* desirable. Though at press time all information contained herein is correct, there will surely be changes. Phone numbers are included, and it is recommended *always* to call ahead.

INFORMATION CENTERS

These are the main information sources for tourists (and natives) concerning places, events, and travel.
Chicago Convention & Visitors Bureau, Inc.
McCormick Place-on-the-Lake. 567-8500. Guides, brochures, maps, and listings of current events. Helpful staff. *OPEN Mon-Fri 8:30am-4:30pm. CLOSED Thanksgiving, Christmas, New Year's Day.*
Chicago Tourism Council Visitors Information Center
163 East Pearson. 280-5740. Brochures, maps, guides, monthly listings of current events. *OPEN 7 days 9am-5pm. CLOSED Thanksgiving, Christmas, New Year's Day.*
Chicago Council on Fine Arts
Chicago Public Library Cultural Center, 78 East Washington at Michigan, 2nd fl. F-I-N-E-A-R-T (346-3278). Information and pamphlets on museums, galleries, music; a monthly calendar of cultural events. *OPEN Mon-Thurs 9am-5pm; Fri 9am-6pm; Sat 9am-5pm. CLOSED Sun.*
Chicago Public Library Cultural Center
78 East Washington at Michigan. 269-2837. Pick up a calendar of cultural events, most of which take place at the Center, all of which are FREE. *OPEN Mon-Thurs 9am-7pm; Sat 9am-5pm. CLOSED Sun. (See also HISTORIC & NEW CHICAGO, Historic Buildings & Areas.)*
Event Line
225-2323 (recording) *24 hours a day, 7 days a week.* Entertainment tips presented by the Chicago Convention & Visitors Bureau: theaters, symphony, museums, sports, special events, and shows, some of which are free.
Illinois Tourist Information
310 South Michigan. 793-2094. Brochures and a six-month calendar of events for Chicago and the state of Illinois. *OPEN Mon-Fri 8:30am-5pm.*
Illinois Traveline
1-800-252-8987 (recording). Events for both Chicago and the state of Illinois.

International Visitors Center
520 North Michigan. 645-1836. Helpful information especially geared to the international student. *OPEN Mon-Fri 9am-5pm.*

PARKING

Parking is allowed on most Chicago streets, though finding a spot is usually difficult. Be sure to read the signs carefully, your car may be ticketed or towed if illegally parked. Meters require a variety of amounts for a variety of times. Please note: In winter many streets are designated snow routes and are so indicated by red-white-and-blue signs. Parking is not allowed on these streets when it snows.

Municipal Parking
Park District General Information. 294-2437.
East Monroe Underground, 250 East Monroe. 294-4740.
Grant Park Underground: North, 25 North Michigan, 294-4598; South, 325 South Michigan, 294-4593.
McCormick Place Underground, 23rd & the Lake. 294-4600.
Chicago City Parking: 744-4501.
Navy Pier Lots
600 East Grand.
601 East Grand.
555 East Illinois.
553 South State.
875 North Rush.
820 North Marshfield.
In addition there are privately owned parking lots in Chicago, with rates varying according to location and time of day and week.
NOTE: *A right turn on red is permitted unless otherwise noted.*

BUS & SUBWAY INFORMATION

Information and directions to anywhere in the city or suburbs via rapid transit or bus, available 24 hours a day, 7 days a week. Call the Travel Information Line, 836-7000; *in the suburbs,* (1-800) 972-7000.

CTA
Chicago Transit Authority, 836-7000: bus, subway, and elevated (el) train information for Chicago.

RTA
Regional Transit Authority, 836-7000: bus and train information for Chicago-area suburbs.

CTA Buses
Basic bus fare is $1. Reduced rate (50¢) for senior citizens, handicapped, and children age 7-11 (under age 7 may ride free when accompanied by fare-paying passenger). Exact fare or CTA tokens.

Monthly passes are available for unlimited riding on any regular CTA service, $50 (senior citizen/handicapped rate $25). A 14-day pass is also available for $25.

Bus stops are marked with blue-and-white signs. Glass-enclosed bus shelters are provided at many stops. Board in the front of the bus and deposit fare, exit in the rear. Smoking is not allowed. Animals (except Seeing Eye dogs and pets in carrying cases) are not permitted to travel on buses. Most buses run 24 hours, 7 days a week, albeit on reduced schedules in nonpeak hours and days. Try to avoid rush hours.

Standard Transfer
A transfer is required when changing buses or between bus and rapid-transit service. The transfer is 25¢ and must be purchased upon boarding. It is valid for a period of two hours (or three rides) for a trip in the same general direction if presented at transfer points only.

Rapid Transit
Fare is $1. Reduced rate (50¢) for senior citizens, handicapped, and children age 7-11. A transfer is necessary when changing train lines. Rapid-transit trains run both above (the el or elevated) and below ground; there is only one class of train. Smoking is not allowed on the train. Animals (except Seeing Eye dogs and pets in carrying cases) are not permitted to travel on trains. Most trains run 24 hours, 7 days a week, although on reduced schedules in nonpeak hours and days. Booth employees can make change up to a $20 bill.

Super Transfer
See CTA Buses.

Evanston Service
Train information for Evanston: 836-7000.

Skokie Swift
Train information for Skokie: 836-7000.

RAILROAD INFORMATION

For long-distance train information:
Amtrak (Union Station): 558-1075.
Burlington Northern, Milwaukee Road, Norfolk & Western (Union Station): 207-6577.
Illinois Central Gulf (Randolph Street Station): 836-7000.
Chicago & Northwestern (Northwestern Station), Rock Island (La Salle Station), South Shore (Randolph): 836-7000.
If you're not sure which line you need, call the RTA Travel Center: 836-7000; (1-800) 972-7000 (suburbs).

LONG-DISTANCE BUSES & TERMINALS

Greyhound
General information: 781-2900. Greyhound Terminal, Clark & Randolph. 346-5000.

Chicago Neighborhoods

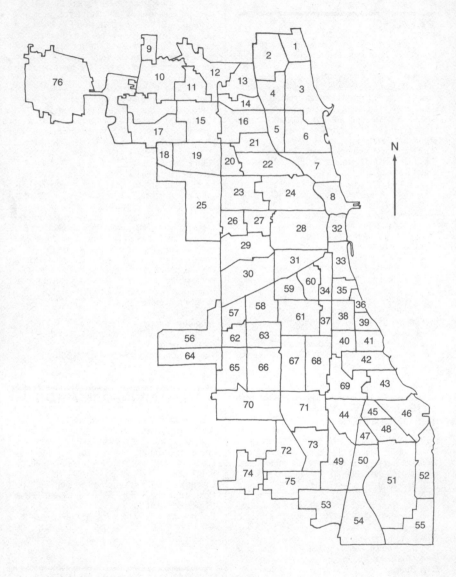

Key for Chicago Neighborhoods

1	Rogers Park	39	Kenwood
2	West Ridge	40	Washington Park
3	Uptown	41	Hyde Park
4	Lincoln Square	42	Woodlawn
5	North Center	43	South Shore
6	Lake View	44	Chatham
7	Lincoln Park	45	Avalon Park
8	Near North Side	46	South Chicago
9	Edison Park	47	Burnside
10	Norwood Park	48	Calumet Heights
11	Jefferson Park	49	Roseland
12	Forest Glen	50	Pullman
13	North Park	51	South Deering
14	Albany Park	52	East Side
15	Portage Park	53	West Pullman
16	Irving Park	54	Riverdale
17	Dunning	55	Hegewisch
18	Montclare	56	Garfield Ridge
19	Belmont Cragin	57	Archer Heights
20	Hermosa	58	Brighton Park
21	Avondale	59	McKinley Park
22	Logan Square	60	Bridgeport
23	Humboldt Park	61	New City
24	West Town	62	West Elsdon
25	Austin	63	Gage Park
26	West Garfield Park	64	Clearing
27	East Garfield Park	65	West Lawn
28	Near West Side	66	Chicago Lawn
29	North Lawndale	67	West Englewood
30	South Lawndale	68	Englewood
31	Lower West Side	69	Greater Grand Crossing
32	Loop	70	Ashburn
33	Near South Side	71	Auburn Gresham
34	Armour Square	72	Beverly
35	Douglas	73	Washington Heights
36	Oakland	74	Mount Greenwood
37	Fuller Park	75	Morgan Park
38	Grand Blvd	76	O'Hare

Trailways (Continental)
General information: 726-9500. Continental Trailways Depot, 20 East Randolph. 726-9500.

TAXIS

The following have taxis available 24 hours a day, 7 days a week.
American United Cab Association: 248-7600.
Checker Taxi and Yellow Cab: T-A-X-I-C-A-B (829-4222).
Flash Cab: 561-1444.

If you have any complaint about a fare or a driver, call City of Chicago, Department of Consumer Service, Public Vehicles Operations. 744-6227. *OPEN Mon-Fri 8:30am-4:30pm.*

GETTING TO & FROM THE AIRPORTS

CTA Train

To O'Hare International via CTA train from the Dearborn Street subway station, arrive at the new ultramodern CTA transit terminal 35 minutes later, the cost, only $1. (From the Michigan Avenue area, take the #151 [Union Station] or #146 bus to Dearborn Street subway station or via train from the State Street subway station. From the South Loop, take the #1 or #146 bus or the train from the State Street subway station. NOTE: The subway and bus fare is $1; the price of a bus transfer is 25¢. *CTA trains run 24 hours a day.* For travel information, call 836-7000.

Bus

Continental Air Transport
454-7800. Scheduled airport express buses to O'Hare and Midway airports from 22 city locations and 23 suburban locations. Buses depart O'Hare every 15 minutes for each airline terminal for Loop and Gold Coast hotels, as well as for Sears Tower and the Merchandise Mart. Buses depart from Midway approximately every hour to downtown and Near North hotels. Call for times and locations. Cost, approximately $9.

Taxicabs

Available at the lower level curb front of each terminal on a first come, first served basis or by phone dispatch. Cost, approximately $20 from O'Hare to downtown.
American United Cab Association: 248-7600.
Checker Taxi and Yellow Cab: T-A-X-I-C-A-B (829-4222).
Flash Cab Co.: 561-1444.
Jiffy Cabs: 487-9000.
  Pay only the rate on the meter plus 50¢ per extra passenger and 50¢ per bag or trunk.

TELEPHONE SERVICES

Emergency calls: 911.
Telephone Information
Unless otherwise mentioned, the area code is 312. The cost of a local call is 25¢.
Local information: 411.
Operator assistance: 0.
Out-of-town: area code + 555-1212.
International Calls
Many countries can now be direct-dialed. Dial 0 (operator) for information concerning the code number of a particular country. Otherwise have the operator assist in placing the call.
Telegrams
Western Union: 435-0200.
Cablegrams
ITT World Communications: 263-4712.
RCA Global Communications: (1-800) 842-7224).
Recorded Services
Consumer-FDA: 353-7126.
Curtain Call: 977-1755.
Dial-a-Poem: 346-3478.
Dial-a-Prayer: 736-1166.
Event Line: 225-2323.
F-I-N-E-A-R-T: 346-3278
Jam's rock concert hotline: 666-6667.
Jazz Hotline: 666-1881.
Road Conditions, Midwest: 283-6204.
Ski Report: 236-SNOW.
Time: 976-1616.
Weather, Chicago: 976-1212.
Weather, nationwide: 298-1413; 686-2155.
Sports Information
Sports phone: 976-1313.
Cubs (NL): 281-5050.
White Sox (AL): 924-1000.
Bears (NFL): 663-5100.
Bulls (NBA): 943-5800; 733-5300.
Black Hawks (NHL): 733-5300.
Stock Market
939-1600.
Board of Trade Hotlines
939-2268: important news affecting the exchange or the industry current bid and asking prices, last sale of memberships, changes in margin requirements, results of membership votes, and actions taken by its Board of Directors.
  922-7885: futures and asking prices, including market commentary and market statistics for the exchange's contracts.
  341-1214: information on Board of Trade deliveries; estimated sales available at approximately 4pm daily.
Chicago Public Library
269-2800: Library Information Center. The quick-answer telephone reference service will try to answer any question or refer you to the proper agency. For the same service for the Spanish-speaking, call 269-2940.
Dial-Law
644-0800. A library of brief tape-recorded mes-

sages of general information concerning legal questions.
Tel-Med
670-3670. A library of brief tape-recorded messages containing health information.

POSTAL INFORMATION

Post office locations and general information: 765-3210.
Zip codes: 765-3585.
Express mail: 765-3527. Guaranteed 24-hour delivery of any mail brought to one of the specially designated post offices before 5pm: to major cities only. Call for location of nearest post office that features the service.

CHICAGO MAPS & GUIDES

Available at most large Chicago bookstores (see SHOPPING, Specialty Shops & Services: Books).
Chicago on Foot (Bach)

Chicago's Famous Buildings (Bach)
Chicago Street Guide (Rand McNally)
Flashmaps (Lasker)
Norman Mark's Chicago (Chicago Review Press)

CHICAGO PUBLICATIONS

Chicago *Tribune:*
Daily. 222-3232. Home turf of columnist Mike Royko (need I say more).
Chicago *Sun-Times:*
Daily. 321-3000. A Rupert Murdoch tabloid. Home base for Roger Ebert, music critic and half of TV's ubiquitous duo. Gene Siskel is at the *Tribune.*
Chicago *Magazine:*
Monthly. Packed with information on Chicago activities and entertainment.
Chicago *Reader:*
Weekly (Friday). Alternative paper available FREE at various shops and restaurants. Good for extensive arts and nightlife listings.

HOTELS

Drake Hotel

RESERVATIONS

Chicago is one of the country's top convention and exhibition towns, hence reservations are a must—in a sense Chicago has no off-season. The Greater Chicago Hotel and Motel Association can give you current room availability for over 100 Chicago hotels, ranging from moderate to deluxe, though they do not make reservations. Call (1-312) 236-3473 for their daily update. In addition, nearly all of the hotels listed in this chapter offer a toll-free 800 number for making reservations.

WEEKEND PACKAGES

Nearly all of the hotels in the Deluxe, Expensive, and Moderate categories offer a variety of weekend packages and/or greatly reduced rates with or without tempting amenities. If such a package is available it is indicated at the end of the entry. Also, the Illinois Hotel Motel Association, P.O. Box 395, Springfield, Il 62705, (1-217) 522-1231, offers a seasonal Metro Chicago Hotel guide detailing weekend getaway packages and their cost. With planning and advance booking, bargains may be found in any season in Chicago, even at the best hotels.

TAXES & TIPS

A tax of 10.1% is added to the price of your hotel room, and in most cases the price quoted to you either on the telephone or in a brochure will not reflect the final total.

Remember that tipping is a reward for good service; never tip if you have been treated shabbily or if the service is either inadequate or unpleasant. Bellhops should be given 50¢ per bag, with an extra 50¢ if you have really loaded him down. For the maid, $5 per week, per person, is standard; for less than a week, $1 a day is the norm. The doorman should get 50¢ for hailing a taxi and $1 if he has helped with the bags. For room service give 10–15% of the bill, for laundry or valet, 15%.

DELUXE

Each of these hotels tends to add up to more than just a sum of its parts.

The Drake
140 East Walton Place, Chicago, IL 60611. 787-2200; (1-800) 445-8667. Old-time elegance at this venerable 65-year-old *grande dame* now under Vista International ownership. A dream location at the top of the Magnificent Mile with Lake views across the Oak Street Beach. Spacious, high-ceilinged accommodations. Upper lobby with fireplace, European air for afternoon tea. Winston Churchill and Queen Elizabeth II have been guests. Cape Cod Room for fish (*see* RESTAURANTS, Fish & Seafood). Shoppers' arcade. Children under age 12 in parents' room free. Late checkout. Valet parking. Convention facilities. 530 rooms. Weekend packages available. Women execs: do ask about their special accommodations.

Mayfair Regent
181 East Lake Shore Drive, Chicago, IL 60611. 787-8500. Old-world amenities and charm accompany a grand restoration of the Former Lake Shore Drive Hotel (ca. 1924). Elegant is the word—from the luxurious oversized lobby with fire ablaze in winter, where high tea is served every afternoon, to use of telephone-equipped limo, as well as complimentary umbrellas and terry robes for guest use. With 19 stories on the Drive, obviously a Lake-filled view is what to have. The Palm for steak priced sky-high, and Le Ciel Bleu for sky-view dining at the top (*see* RESTAURANTS, Rooms with a View *and* Steak). Multilingual staff, foreign-currency exchange, and news kiosk carrying foreign newspapers and

periodicals. Valet parking. 24-hour room service. Children under age 18 in parents' room free. Small pets allowed. Meeting facilities. 200 rooms. Weekend packages available.

Omni Ambassador East
1301 North State Parkway, Chicago, IL 60610. 787-7200; (1-800) 843-6664. Now an Omni hotel, this Gold Coast *grande dame,* a luxury landmark built in 1926, has been refurbished wisely—many of the old, still luxurious appointments have been retained in the update. Quiet, large rooms have a traditional feel; amenities include a sweet-dreams Godiva mint with turndown. The hotel, and its famed Pump Room (*see* NIGHTLIFE, Dinner/Dancing), were and still are elegant celebrity draws. VIP executive services; eight meeting rooms. Courteous multilingual staff; valet parking; airport shuttle. Children under age 12 in parents' room free. 278 rooms. Weekend package available.

Park Hyatt Hotel
800 North Michigan, Chicago, IL 60611. 280-2222; (1-800) 228-9000. Very un-Hyatt—a "small hotel" where the emphasis is on *very* personal service and understated elegance, evident from the moment you check in: concierge escort to your room, maid's aid in unpacking, and richly decorated rooms filled with the "little things" that count, from Perrier to sachet. The Drawing Room, facing Water Tower Square, a library-sitting room for reading (*great* Chicago book selection), board games, or a drink. Tea and coffee served in the posh lobby starting at 10am daily accompanied by piano and harp music; La Tour (*see* RESTAURANTS, Rooms with a View) for very fine dining. In-room movies available. Concierge; 24-hour room service. Valet parking. Multilingual staff. Graciously appointed conference rooms. 255 rooms. Weekend packages available.

The Ritz-Carlton Chicago
160 East Pearson, Chicago, IL 60611. 266-1000; (1-800) 268-6282. This location is a shopper's dream come true. On floors 13-31 of the deluxe 74-story Water Tower Place complex, this is an elegant full-service cosmopolitan hotel (now a Four Seasons property) with the amenities of a small one: nightly turndown, complimentary shoe shine, terry robes for guests' use. Rooms are wonderfully spacious, with 9-foot ceilings! Duplex suites also available. The Spa with heated swimming pool; athletic facilities, massage, sauna. A kennel for four-legged guests. High tea is served in the skylit Greenhouse Restaurant with atrium fountain lounge and there's a bar and café (*see* RESTAURANTS, Afternoon Tea). 24-hour room service; round-the-clock valet service; multilingual staff. Parking available. Children under age 18 in parents' room free. 382 rooms, 29 suites. Weekend packages available.

The Tremont Hotel
100 East Chestnut, Chicago, IL 60611. 751-1900; (1-800) 621-8133. Just off Michigan Avenue, old-world traditional elegance and personal service (a multilingual staff of 170!). The Tudor-style lobby *cum* living room immediately sets the mood. Rooms are small, but impressively decorated with English antiques and king-sized beds. The three penthouse suites have Michigan Avenue-filled views. Nightly turndowns accompanied by a Godiva mint. On the premises, Cricket's Hearth Bar and the popular clubby Cricket's restaurant (*see* RESTAURANTS, American). Privileges at the McClurg Court Sports Center. Children under 18 in parents' room free. 24-hour room service. Valet parking. Four conference rooms. 139 rooms. Weekend package available.

Whitehall Hotel
105 East Delaware Place, Chicago, IL 60611. 944-6300; (1-800) 621-8295. Since opening in 1975, this has become world renowned as *the* small hotel in Chicago. Consistently impeccable European-style service and an air of stability (that not even former guests the Rolling Stones could shake). Amenities include large rooms with king-sized beds and refrigerators; the *Trib* and *Wall Street Journal* in the am; access to the exclusive members-only Whitehall Club for breakfast, lunch, and dinner; and McClurg Court Sports Center facilities privileges. High tea is served in the lovely lobby, and there's the wonderful Whitehall Bar (*see* RESTAURANTS, Afternoon Tea *and* Bars & Burgers). Children under age 12 in parents' room free. 24-hour room service; concierge services. Valet parking. Six function rooms. 222 rooms. Weekend package available.

EXPENSIVE

Ambassador West
1300 North State Parkway, Chicago, IL 60610. 787-7900; (1-800) 621-8090. Fine Gold Coast residential location, but within walking distance of Michigan Avenue. Luxurious accommodations. Use of nearby health club facilities, including tennis and racquetball, for nominal fee. Children under age 18 in parents' room free. Convention meeting rooms and facilities available. Restaurant. Airport shuttle. Valet parking. 217 rooms. Weekend packages available.

The Barclay Chicago
166 East Superior, Chicago, IL 60611. 787-6000; (1-800) 621-8004. At North Michigan Avenue, this 29-story hotel (under the same management as the Knickerbocker-Chicago) contains luxury suites *only* and caters to the busy corporate executives. All accommodations have wet bars, some have kitchen facilities. Secretarial and office services available. Room service; Benihana of Tokyo restaurant. Outdoor swimming pool and sun deck on 29th floor. Guest arrangements with nearby McClurg Court Sports Center. Children under age 12 in parents' room free. Valet parking. 120 rooms. Weekend packages available.

The Chicago-Hilton Hotel and Towers
720 South Michigan, Chicago, IL 60605. 922-4400; (1-800) H-I-L-T-O-N-S (445-8667). Built in 1927 as the Stevens, it became the Conrad-Hilton in 1945; in 1985, following a $180 million restoration, it reopened as the grand Chicago Hilton. Wonderfully situated across from Grant Park and near Chicago's great museums. From the upper of its 28 floors the views of the Lake are unmatched. Each floor has its own lounge, and some suites have woodburning fireplaces. Indoor swimming pool; health club facilities. Children in parents' room free. Buckingham's, a contemporary American restaurant and lounge with entertainment. A sumptuous brunch is served in the Normandie Lounge (see RESTAURANTS, Breakfast/Brunch). 1,620 rooms. Weekend packages available.

Chicago Marriott Hotel
540 North Michigan, Chicago, IL 60611. 836-0100; (1-800) 228-9290. A bustling convention hotel downtown, right smack on the Magnificent Mile: 46 stories of Marriott-modern accommodations enhanced by Lake Michigan views. Health club with exercise, steam, sauna, and sun rooms; indoor swimming pool and tennis. In-room first-run movies. Children under age 18 in parents' room free; pet-care facilities. The Concierge Level: two floors dedicated to the tender loving care of business executives. Lobby Galleria of shops. Six restaurants, lounge with entertainment. 1,175 rooms. Weekend packages and family plan available.

Congress Hotel
520 South Michigan, Chicago, IL 60605. 427-3800; (1-800) 826-0900. Formerly the Pick-Congress. Built in 1893, and updated in 1902 and 1956, it's now under new management and has been recently renovated once again. Opposite the Art Institute. Understated elegance with views of Grant Park and Lake Michigan; handsome lobby; three restaurants and two bars. Popular convention site. Children under age 18 in parents' room free. Garage facilities. In-room first-run movies. 800 rooms. Seasonal Weekend packages available.

Executive House Hotel
71 East Wacker, Chicago, IL 60601. 346-7100; (1-800) 621-4005. A good no-nonsense hotel, in terms of location and quality aimed at the business person. Many rooms have wonderful Chicago views. Sports club privileges available at reduced rates. Newly renovated rooms are Chicago's largest; all have stocked mini bar area, king-sized double beds. Color TV and first-run films. The 71-Club Restaurant on 39th floor (see RESTAURANTS, Rooms with a View). Children under age 18 in parents' room free. Valet parking. Meeting and banquet facilities; corporate rates available. 415 rooms. Weekend packages available.

Holiday Inn Chicago City Center
300 East Ohio, Chicago, IL 60611. 787-6100; (1-800) 465-4329. Just off Michigan Avenue, 26 stories with a skylit lobby. Popular with executive travelers. Large rooms; reduced-fee access to the private McClurg Court Sports Center with tennis, racquetball, exercise room, sauna, steam room, massage, indoor pool. In summer, outdoor pool perched on fifth-floor rooftop. Lounges, restaurants, shopping. Free parking. Meeting facilities. Children under age 18 in parents' room free. 500 rooms. Weekend packages available.

Holiday Inn Mart Plaza
350 North Orleans, Chicago, IL 60654. 836-5000; (1-800) 465-4329. On the bank of the Chicago River, perched atop the Apparel Center on floors 14 to 23; nine-story skylit atrium. Indoor swimming pool, free in-room films. Children under age 18 in parents' room sleep free, under 12 eat free. Pets allowed in room. Shopping arcade; lounge with entertainment. Convention facilities. 525 rooms. Weekend packages available.

Hyatt Regency Chicago
151 East Wacker, Chicago, IL 60601. 565-1234; (1-800) 228-9000. East of the Michigan Avenue Bridge, part of the Illinois Center complex, America's most expansive urban retail/commercial/residential development. One of the country's largest luxury convention/exhibition hotels, with the kind of lobby for which Hyatts have become famous (infamous?): this one is a four-story atrium complete with huge lagoon. Everything is big: the rooms, the beds, the baths. For exclusivity, the Regency Club Penthouse with fireplace-equipped suites away from the roar of the crowd. Pluses include Chicago River/Lake Michigan views, health club privileges, full-length in-room movies, 24-hour room service. Nine restaurants and bars, including the 24-hour Scampi's (see RESTAURANTS, Late-Night/24-Hour); shopping arcade; multilingual staff. Children under age 18 in parents' room free. 2,019 rooms. Weekend packages available.

Knickerbocker Chicago Hotel
163 East Walton Place, Chicago, IL 60611. 751-8100; (1-800) 621-8140. Forty-nine years old and the Playboy Towers no longer, this hotel is restaking its claim to a wonderful piece of real estate at Michigan Avenue (near the Lake, John Hancock Center, and Water Tower Place) and to a reputation for gracious service and elegant surroundings. Rooms are large, some with canopied beds, some with two baths; and small amenities abound. The Walton Place Cafe and the Prince of Wales restaurant (where a harp and piano music are played during dinner) as well as the Limehouse Pub. Health club available nearby. Children under age 18 in parents' room free. Conference facilities. Valet parking. 256 rooms. Weekend package available.

McCormick Center Hotel
Lake Shore Drive & 23rd, Chicago, IL 60616. 791-1900; (1-800) 621-6909. New 23-story modern hotel facility across the street from McCormick Place-on-the-Lake. Busy and bright. Indoor swimming pool; health club facilities include sauna, steam room, Nautilus equipment. Children under age 14 in parents' room free. 30,000

square feet of meeting, banquet, or exhibition space. Maxie's, their "room with a view" for dining (see RESTAURANTS). Valet parking. Airport bus. 650 rooms. Weekend packages available.

Midland Hotel
172 West Adams, Chicago, IL 60603. 332-1200; (1-800) 621-2360. Built in 1929 as a private men's club right in the heart of downtown Chicago—the Loop—this few frills hotel is perfectly located for business travelers or theatergoers. Service is courteous and efficient. The Exchange Restaurant is an opulent jewel. Free in-room cable TV. Children under age 12 in parents' room free. Convention facilities. 300 rooms. Weekend packages available.

Palmer House and Towers
17 East Monroe at State, Chicago, IL 60690. 726-7500; (1-800) 445-8667. This distinguished landmark hotel in the Loop, built in 1925, is a tribute to the way it was and is part of what makes State Street such a great street. A link in the Hilton chain redecorated in 1983, it's still a grand downtown Chicago hotel. The Towers, 181 rooms, 15 suites, and a penthouse on the 22nd and 23rd floors, are devoted to luxury executive accommodations. Barber and beauty shops on premises. Seven restaurants, including the restored beauty of the Empire Room and the world-famous Trader Vic's (see RESTAURANTS, Polynesian). Children in parents' room free. In-room first-run movies; wet bar available. Year-round indoor swimming pool and health club facilities. Baby-sitting service, currency exchange, international telex. Convention facilities. Airport bus service from hotel. 1,750 rooms. Weekend packages available.

Sheraton-Plaza Chicago
160 East Huron, Chicago, IL 60611. 787-2900; (1-800) 325-3535. Located just off Michigan Avenue. Built as condominium apartments, the rooms are large and nicely decorated. Excellent choice for business people looking for personalized VIP services: The Distinguished Corporate Service Club offers guaranteed room with only one day's notice based on availability, late (up to 4pm) checkout, free local phone calls, and a spouse stays at no extra charge. Rooftop (40th floor) open-to-the-sky sun deck and swimming pool, with poolside service. Health club privileges at Downtown Club. Some suites overlook Lake Michigan. Bentley's Restaurant, Tiff's Bar. Children under age 17 in parents' room free. Small pets allowed. Valet parking. Multilingual staff. Meeting facilities. 334 rooms. Weekend packages available.

Westin Hotel Chicago
909 North Michigan, Chicago, IL 60611. 943-7200; (1-800) 228-3000. Good Magnificent Mile choice, formerly the Continental Plaza. Luxurious, spacious accommodations with period furnishings as well as health club facilities and rooftop swimming pool with poolside service. 24-hour room service. Valet parking; airport shuttle. Popular Lion Bar, Chelsea Restaurant,

and the Lobby Bar. Convention facilities. Children under age 18 in parents' room free. No-smoking floors available. Small pets allowed. 754 rooms. Weekend packages available.

MODERATE

The Allerton Hotel
701 North Michigan, Chicago, IL 60611. 440-1500; (1-800) 621-8311. Well located on the Magnificent Mile, just two blocks from Water Tower Place, and though one of the city's oldies, recently refurbished and well priced for the location. Gucci in the lobby and the fine L'Escargot restaurant (see RESTAURANTS, French) on the premises. Convention facilities available. Children under age 12 in parents' room free. 450 rooms. Weekend packages available.

Best Western Inn of Chicago
162 East Ohio, Chicago, IL 60611. 787-3100; (1-800) 528-1234. One block east of Michigan Avenue (formerly the St. Clair Hotel), a renovated affordably priced hotel with pleasant service. All rooms have been modernized and contain double-sized beds and in-room movies. No-smoking rooms upon request. A 24-hour deli-restaurant will provide room service till midnight. Health club facilities nearby. Four meeting rooms available. Valet parking. Children under age 12 in parents' room free. 336 rooms; 18 suites. Weekend packages available.

Best Western River North Hotel
125 West Ohio, Chicago, IL 60610. 467-0800; (1-800) 528-1234. In the heart of Chicago. Indoor pool with skyline view, outdoor sun deck (in season), sauna. Pleasant service; restaurant, lounge, room service. Free parking. Meeting room. Children under age 18 in parents' room free. 150 rooms. Weekend packages available.

Bismarck Hotel
171 West Randolph, Chicago, IL 60601. 236-0123; (1-800) 643-1500. A bit past its prime but in the process of upgrading the rooms, it's nonetheless a good-value downtown hotel. The lobby is lovely and so is the Walnut Room restaurant. Also, the Chalet, a popular spot for Swiss-German specialties. Accommodations are comfortable, service attentive. Health club facilities are available at reduced rates for guests, including tennis and racquetball. Children under age 10 in parents' room free. Garage available for a fee. Convention facilities. 500 rooms. Weekend packages available.

Blackstone Hotel
636 South Michigan, Chicago, IL 60605. 427-4300. This hotel was built in 1910, and the French Renaissance exterior and the wonderfully ornate lobby are reflections of a bygone era. Often political headquarters during the major parties' nominating conventions. Faces Grant Park and the Lake. The hotel is open but is

presently in the process of renovating the rooms. Children under age 16 in parents' room free. 300 rooms. Weekend package available.

Chicago Downtown TraveLodge
1240 South Michigan, Chicago, IL 60605. 427-4111; (1-800) 255-3050. Small motor hotel in downtown Chicago. All rooms are air-conditioned and have private bath. Restaurant nearby. Children under age 17 in parents' room free. 62 rooms. Weekend package available.

The Claridge
1244 North Dearborn Parkway, Chicago, IL 60610. 787-4980; (1-800) 245-1258. This Gold Coast newcomer (opened May 1987, it is actually a gut rehab of the old Tuscany Hotel) boasts a quiet elegance and modest prices, even though it caters to a corporate and business clientele. Pluses include complimentary morning newspapers, continental breakfast served in the lobby level restaurant, and a no-smoking floor. Concierge service; in-room movies. Children under age 18 stay free in parents' room. On-premises dining room, café, and lounge; small meeting facilities and an intimate ballroom. Adjacent parking. 174 rooms.

Days Inn Lakeshore Drive
644 North Lake Shore Drive, Chicago, IL 60611. 943-9200; (1-800) 325-2525. Thirty-three stories right on Lake Michigan, and all rooms have views, half of them of the Lake. Outdoor swimming pool. On the 33rd floor, the revolving Pinnacle Restaurant (see RESTAURANTS, Rooms with a View). Meeting facilities. Children under age 18 in parents' room free. Free parking facilities. Airport shuttle to and from O'Hare. 580 rooms. Weekend packages available.

Delaware Towers
25 East Delaware, Chicago, IL 60611. 944-4245; (1-800) 621-8506. Good Near North location. Efficiencies and one-bedroom suites, comfortably furnished; hotel services. Same management as The Elms and The Talbott Hotel. Daily, weekly, and monthly rates. 145 units. Weekend packages available.

The Elms
18 East Elm, Chicago, IL 60611. 787-4740; (1-800) 621-8506. Fully appointed suites available for daily or monthly stays. All with equipped kitchens and wet bar; hotel services. Same management as the Delaware Towers and The Talbott Hotel. Weekend packages available. 145 rooms.

Essex Inn
800 South Michigan, Chicago, IL 60605. 939-2800; (1-800) 621-6909. Newly renovated downtown motor inn with modern accommodations; meeting facilities. Well located for McCormick Place Convention Center attendees. Outdoor swimming pool and sun deck. Free parking and free bus service to the Loop. Piano bar. 275 rooms. Weekend packages available.

The Hilton at Hyde Park
4900 South Lake Shore Drive, Chicago, IL 60615. 288-5800; (1-800) 445-8667. Located on 4 acres overlooking the Lakefront in the prestigious Hyde Park historic area; nearby, the University of Chicago and the Museum of Science and Industry (the Midwest's largest tourist attraction). Large outdoor swimming pool and sun deck; health club facilities available. Chartwell House restaurant; café and lounge with weekend entertainment. Free shuttle bus to McCormick Place, the Loop, North Michigan Avenue, and the airports. Children free in parents' room. Meeting facilities. 320 rooms. Weekend packages available.

Lenox House
616 North Rush Street, Chicago, IL 60611. 337-1000; (1-800) 445-3669. The former Croyden, completely refurbished and now catering to a business clientele. Just one block west of the shops on the Magnificent Mile, accommodations consist of executive studios and one-bedroom suites, all equipped with kitchen/wet bar and a sleeper sofa for extra family member. Amenities include in-room movies and health club facilities nearby. On premises, Houston's restaurant and a coffee shop. Room service; laundry and valet service. Corporate plan available. 330 suites. Good-value weekend rates.

Oxford House Hotel
225 North Wabash, Chicago, IL 60601. 346-6585; (1-800) 344-4111. Near the Chicago River, convenient to the Loop and convention facilities. All large rooms with kitchen/bar facilities; color TV. Free indoor parking. Café Angelo restaurant; The Library dining room; The Wine Room bar. Meeting rooms available. 175 rooms. Weekend packages and reduced weekend rates available.

Raphael Hotel
201 East Delaware Place, Chicago, IL 60611. 943-5000; (1-800) 821-5343. Another of Chicago's "small hotels." This one, just a block from Michigan Avenue, offers comfortable, very spacious, newly redecorated rooms and pleasant, personal service: nightly turndown and filled ice buckets; complimentary Godiva chocolates and Perrier. Health club facilities available. Excellent choice for location and price. Children under age 12 in parents' room free. 172 rooms. Weekend package available.

Richmont Hotel
162 East Ontario, Chicago, IL 60611. 787-3580; (1-800) 621-8055. A charming hotel with a European feel and no pretensions. Completely renovated oldie (formerly the Eastgate), with small but very pleasantly decorated rooms. Extremely helpful, courteous management; excellent service and complimentary continental breakfast (coffee, juice, croissants) complete with *Wall Street Journal* and *Trib* in the pleasant Rue St. Clair café, are strong pluses. For location (just a block away from North Michigan Avenue's shops, galleries, *boîtes*) and ambiance, the rates are hard to beat. Appeals to "frugal executives," but it's a great base for "frugal tourists" too. Access to McClurg Court Sports Center. Children under 19 in parents' room free. 193 rooms. Weekend packages available.

Rodeway Inn—Chicago Downtown
506 West Harrison, Chicago, IL 60607. 427-6969. Three blocks from Sears Tower. Outdoor swimming pool. Restaurant, lounge with entertainment. Room service. Parking available. Meeting facilities. 155 rooms.

Talbott Hotel
20 East Delaware, Chicago, IL 60611. 944-4970; (1-800) 621-8506. Same management as The Elms and The Delaware Towers, similar accommodations. Residential feel, hotel services. All-suites accommodations with fully equipped kitchens and wet bars. Daily and monthly rates available. 149 units. Weekend packages available.

BUDGET

Ascot Motel
1100 South Michigan, Chicago, IL 60605. 922-2900; (1-800) 621-4196. Large downtown motor inn across from Grant Park, south of the Art Institute. Meeting facilities. Outdoor swimming pool and sun decks. Pets welcome. Free parking. Wine Cellar Lounge with entertainment. All rooms are air-conditioned; color TV; valet service. 175 rooms.

Avenue Motel
1154 South Michigan at 12th, Chicago, IL 60605. 427-8200; (1-800) 621-4196. Overlooking Grant Park. All rooms are air-conditioned; color TV. Free parking. Use of the outdoor swimming pool at either the Ascot or the Essex. Waffle Shop restaurant. Meeting facilities. 75 rooms. Tour package available.

Chicago East Apartment Hotel
11 West Division, Chicago, IL 60610. 944-4560. Efficiency apartments, all with kitchenettes, air-conditioning, and color TV. Daily, weekly, and monthly rates.

Harrison Motor Motel
65 East Harrison, Chicago, IL 60605. 427-8000. Restaurant, coffee shop, bar. Low-priced choice. Some rooms not air-conditioned; all have private bath. Garage parking for a fee. 350 rooms.

La Salle Motor Lodge
700 North La Salle, Chicago, IL 60610. 664-8100. Highly affordable motor hotel located downtown. Restaurant; room service. Parking included. 70 rooms.

Ohio East
15 East Ohio, Chicago, IL 60611. 644-8222. Between State and Wabash, downtown budget, bare essentials; no air-conditioning. 212 rooms.

Ohio House Motel
600 North La Salle, Chicago, IL 60610. 943-6000. Two-story, motel-basic right on the Expressway in downtown. Budget accommodations. Color TV; air-conditioning; room service—coffee shop. Free parking, also free courtesy transportation to the Loop. 50 rooms.

BED & BREAKFAST

Bed & Breakfast Chicago
P.O. Box 14088, Chicago, IL 60614. 951-0085. An alternative to the traditional hotel stay. Comfortable, reasonably priced lodgings in homes and apartments in Chicago and the near suburbs; with or without hosts at home. Some hosts multilingual, all are carefully selected. Rates vary with the season. Send for their brochure with over 90 listings. Stipulate any special needs, such as private bath, no pets, no steps, etc. There is a minimum stay of two nights in private homes and three nights in no-host furnished apartments. Weekly and monthly rates are available. Phone reservations must be guaranteed with a credit card.

HOSTELS & Y's

Austin YMCA
501 North Central, Chicago, IL 60644. 287-9120. West Side. Men only. 297 rooms.

International House of the University of Chicago
1414 East 59th, Chicago, IL 60637. 753-2280. For men and women faculty or students. Only in summer. Reserve three to seven days in advance. Cafeteria on premises. Over 500 rooms available.

Irving Park YMCA
4251 West Irving Park Road, Chicago, IL 60641. 777-7500. North Side. Men only. 200 rooms.

Lawson YMCA
30 West Chicago Avenue, Chicago, IL 60610. 944-6211. Downtown Chicago. Co-ed. 615 rooms; mostly shared baths.

Lincoln Belmont YMCA
3333 North Marshfield, Chicago, IL 60657. 248-3333. North Side. Men over 18 only. Private rooms, shared bath. Reserve one week in advance in person. 200 rooms.

11th Street YMCA
4 East 111th, Chicago, IL 60628. 785-9210. South Side. Men only. 168 rooms.

Washington Park YMCA
5000 South Indiana, Chicago, IL 60615. 538-5200. South Side. Co-ed.

HOTELS AT & NEAR THE AIRPORTS

By virtue of their location some of these accommodations may tend to be frenetic.

Air Host Motel
4101 North Mannheim Road, Schiller Park, IL 60176. 678-4470. Budget-rate motel with outdoor swimming pool. Shuttle bus to O'Hare. Restaurant on premises. 67 rooms.

Chicago Marriott O'Hare

8535 West Higgins Road, Chicago, IL 60631. 693-4444; (1-800) 228-9290. Seven minutes from O'Hare, pleasant rooms, all with in-room first-run movies. Resort facilities include indoor/outdoor pool, sauna, sun room, tennis, ice skating in winter; game room. Three restaurants and a lounge. Children under age 18 in parents' room free. Courtesy limo to and from airport. Free outdoor parking. Small pets allowed. Conference and meeting facilities. 697 rooms. Weekend packages available.

Embassy Suites O'Hare

6501 North Mannheim Road, Rosemont, IL 60018. 699-6300; (1-800) EMBASSY. An all-suites national chain geared to the business traveler. Accommodations that overlook a central atrium include a refrigerator and wet bar. Indoor swimming pool, whirlpool, exercise equipment available for guest use. Room service; restaurant, lounge with entertainment. Free parking. Conference facilities. 300 units. Weekend packages available.

The Hamilton

400 Park Boulevard, Itasca, IL 60143. 773-4000; (1-800) 468-3571. A Stouffer Hotel, 3 miles south of Woodfield Mall and 20 minutes west of O'Hare Airport. Twelve-story atrium; seven restaurants including the Danish café overlooking the lake, and a lounge with entertainment. Swimming, tennis, golf, fitness center; racquet club; jogging course. Complimentary morning coffee and newspaper. Children in parents' room free. Conference facilities. 409 rooms. Weekend packages available.

Hotel Sofitel O'Hare

5550 North River Road, Rosemont, IL 60018. 678-4488; (1-800) 221-4542. Accommodations with a French accent. Indoor swimming pool and health club facilities. Restaurant, lounge with entertainment. Pets allowed. Free parking. Conference facilities. 305 rooms. Weekend packages available.

Hyatt Regency O'Hare

O'Hare International Airport, 9300 West Bryn Mawr Avenue, River Road at Kennedy Expressway, Rosemont, IL 60666. 696-1234; (1-800) 228-9000. Large modern convention facility at the world's busiest airport. A glittering Hyatt, this lobby is a 12-story-high atrium with glass-enclosed elevators. Rooms are elegantly appointed, some with terraces, and all are gratefully soundproofed. Indoor year-round swimming with poolside service; health club with sauna, steam and sun rooms; as many restaurants as in some small towns, and a shopping arcade. Children under age 18 in parents' room free. In-room first-run films. Pets allowed. Shuttle to airport takes 5 minutes; downtown Chicago is a half hour away. Meeting facilities. Free parking. 1,100 rooms. Weekend packages available.

O'Hare Hilton

O'Hare International Airport, P.O. Box 66414, Chicago, IL 60666. 686-8000; (1-800) 445-8667. Right *in* O'Hare Airport is this Hilton hotel, connected to the terminals by enclosed "moving sidewalks." Rooms are attractive and, in spite of locale, quiet. "Office Away": a complete business service for the corporate traveler, including secretarial services; multilingual staff. Shopping promenade and seven restaurants including the membership Gaslight Club. Conference facilities. 886 rooms. Weekend packages available.

O'Hare Plaza Hotel

5615 North Cumberland, Chicago, IL 60631. 693-5800; (1-800) 654-2000. Pleasant accommodations. In-room first-run movies; outdoor swimming pool. Restaurant, lounge. Courtesy van to and from O'Hare Airport. Executive section with special amenities including complimentary wine and breakfast. Access to fitness center nearby. Small conference facilities. 245 rooms. Special weekend rates available.

Ramada Hotel O'Hare

6600 North Mannheim Road, Rosemont, IL 60018. 827-5131; (1-800) 228-2828. Five minutes to the airport, 20 minutes from downtown. Ramada clean and efficient. Three restaurants. Indoor and outdoor swimming pools; 9-hole par-3 golf course and two day or night tennis courts; sauna and whirlpool. Meeting rooms; exhibit and convention space. Free parking. Courtesy limo to and from the airport. Children under 18 in parents' room free. Family Bonus Plan: Up to four people in same room (Monday to Thursday) stay for single adult rate. 723 rooms. Weekend packages available.

Sheraton International at O'Hare

6810 North Mannheim Road, Rosemont, IL 60018. 297-1234; (1-800) 325-3535. Sheraton-pleasant rooms and suites. Swimming pool and health club facilities. Restaurant, lounge with entertainment. Pets allowed. Meeting facilities. 460 rooms. Weekend packages available.

TraveLodge Chicago O'Hare

3003 Mannheim Road, Des Plaines, IL 60018. 296-5541; (1-800) 255-3050. Eight minutes to O'Hare Airport; half hour to downtown Chicago. Unpretentious, clean accommodations for reasonable rates. Outdoor swimming pool. Shuttle bus to the airport. Meeting facilities. 95 rooms. Weekend packages available.

The Westin Hotel O'Hare

6100 North River Road, Rosemont, IL 60018. 698-6000; (1-800) 228-3000. Four minutes from O'Hare. Amenities include swimming pool, health club facilities, and racquetball courts. Restaurant, lounge with entertainment. Banquet and convention facilities. Courtesy bus to O'Hare. 529 rooms. Weekend packages available.

Woodfield Hilton and Towers

Euclid at Rohlwing Road, Arlington Heights, IL 60006. 394-2000; (1-800) 445-8667. A Hilton with resort facilities just 40 minutes from O'Hare Airport; 30 miles from the Loop and only minutes from Woodfield Shopping Mall, one of the world's largest indoor shopping centers. On premises, Olympic-size indoor pool; outdoor tennis, day or night; Swedish sauna. Adjacent to the Arlington Park Race Track and a private 18-hole golf course. Four restaurants and bars. Bus shuttle to and from the airport. The conference center boasts 19 meeting and board rooms. 421 rooms. Reduced weekend rates and packages available.

SIGHTSEEING

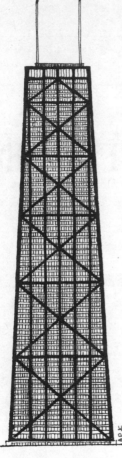

John Hancock Center

VIEWPOINTS

*The natural flatness of Chicago (the "mountains"
and "canyons" are man-made) and the omnipresent beauty of Lake Michigan provide limit-
less opportunities for eye-pleasing, spirit-lifting
views. The following afford some of the best,
including some from the top—which also double
as orientation points. (See also SIGHTSEEING,
Lake & River Trips.)*

Burnham Park
Achsah Bond Drive at 1300 Lake Shore Drive.
From this vantage point you have Lake Michigan
on both sides of you.

Field Museum
Lake Shore Drive at Roosevelt Road. From the
top of the north steps: a wonderful view of the
famed Chicago skyline.

John Hancock Observatory
875 North Michigan. 751-3681. The building itself (the fifth tallest but the world's tallest for
mixed residential/office use) is 1,127 feet high
(not counting the TV antennas). The observatory, on the 94th floor, is 1,030 feet high. You
reach it in 39 seconds! On a clear day the 60-
mile visibility affords fantastic views of Lake
Michigan and the states bordering it. *OPEN 7
days 9am-midnight.* Admission charge, discount for senior citizens and children age 5-15;
children under age 5 FREE. Call in advance for
group rates and reservations. (*See also* HIS-
TORIC & NEW CHICAGO, Modern Architecture.)

Images
See RESTAURANTS, Bars & Burgers.

Lake Shore Drive
5700 North to 5900 South. Drive along the Lakeshore with its parks, marinas, and beaches on
one side and the high-rises, skyscrapers, and
mansions on the other. By day or night an urban delight—except, of course, during rush
hour.

Le Ciel Bleu
See RESTAURANTS, Rooms with a View.

Lincoln Park
Fullerton at the Lagoon. Look to the skyline from
this bucolic setting.

Michigan Avenue Bridge
400 North Michigan. Look around: In any direction a treat for the mind's, or camera's, eye.

Navy Pier
East end of Grand Avenue. 744-6450. In summer, along the tree-lined East Promenade of the
pier, take a ¾-mile walk out onto Lake Michigan
and soak up the views. (*See also* ANNUAL
EVENTS, May, and check local listings for special
city-sponsored happenings here.) *OPEN June
1-Labor Day.*

The Ninety-Fifth
See RESTAURANTS, Rooms with a View.

Oak Street Beach
Oak & North Lake Shore Drive. Lovely Chicago:
the Lake, the Gold Coast, and in summer lithe,
tanned Chicagoans—what better view could there
be? Only a sunrise from here.

One & Two Illinois Center
North Michigan & South Water. A dramatic view
from the north terrace, across the Chicago River.

Pedestrian Walkway
From Wabash Avenue along the north bank of
the Chicago River. Take a look at the Loop from
here.

The Pinnacle Restaurant
See RESTAURANTS, Rooms with a View.

The Ravenswood El
A ride on one of Chicago's roller-coaster-like
elevated Loop trains is very much a part of this
city's experience. So hop on this particular one
even if you're without destination, 'cause on the
Ravenswood the getting there is all the fun,
getting close to Loop buildings and seeing the

skyline and the back porches of Chicago's neighborhoods.

Sears Tower Skydeck
233 South Wacker. 875-9696. A view from the top of the world's tallest (1,454 feet) building is a must. The enclosed Skydeck Observatory on the 103rd floor is 1,353 feet above the streets of Chicago, and the nonstop elevator gets you there in one minute! You have a 360° view and, on a clear day, 60-mile visibility—wave to your friends in Indiana, Wisconsin, and Michigan. *OPEN 7 days 9am-midnight (last ticket sold 11:30pm).* Admission charge, discount for children under age 16; children under age 5 FREE. Fully accessible to disabled visitors. Call for group rates. (*See also* HISTORIC & NEW CHICAGO, Modern Architecture.)

Standard Oil Building Plaza
200 East Randolph Drive. From here you can see the Loop, the Lake, and the Art Institute.

CHICAGO TOURS

CTA Culture Bus
836-7000. A wonderful and inexpensive way to tour Chicago. Three culture bus routes, north, south, west, are operated *every Sun and all holidays from early May through Sept 10:30am-5pm.* All buses start and end at the Art Institute, Michigan & Adams, or you may board at any stop, or get off at any stop and catch a later bus at no extra cost. Fare is $2.50 ($1.25 for senior citizens, children age 7-11, and the handicapped), exact change is required; a commentator points out cultural and architectural sights on the route. Culture bus passes are also valid on all regular CTA service that day.

By Coach

American Sightseeing Tours
530 South Michigan. 427-3100. An interesting variety of day and night bus tours with commentary, lasting 2, 4, or 8 hours. Some include lunch or dinner. "Ladies' Program" for wives of visiting businessmen (*see* SIGHTSEEING, Chicago Tours, Specialized Tours). Courtesy service from many downtown hotels. *Call 7 days 8:30am-5:30pm; Memorial Day-Labor Day 8:30am-7:30pm. CLOSED Christmas, Thanksgiving, New Year's, Easter Sunday.* (*See also* SIGHTSEEING, Day Trips: Escorted.)

Chicago Motor Coach Co.
5601 North Sheridan, Chicago, IL 60660. 989-8919. Old-fashioned open-top Double Deckers—replicas of buses that ran the Boulevard route in Chicago from 1917 to 1937. The coaches wend their way along the Lakefront, Michigan Avenue, and the Loop. Tours lasting from 1 to 1½ hours leave at 10am from the Sears Tower, Franklin Street side. Call for exact schedule and other boarding points. Also available for charter.

NOTE: Neither rain nor cold will stop them—some of the buses have tops.

Gray Line Tours
33 East Monroe. 346-9506. An assortment of lectured tours lasting 2, 4, 5, or 7 hours. Some include Lake and river trips (in season), views, and other Chicago highlights. Key hotel pickup points. Reservations recommended. *OPEN 7 days 8am-4pm; not in operation Thanksgiving, Christmas, New Year's Day, or Easter Sunday.*

Highlights Bus Tour
Chicago Architecture Foundation, Archicenter, 330 South Dearborn. Recorded tour information 782-1776. Survey the best of Chicago's architecture. This 4-hour tour covers 30 miles, including the Loop, the Gold Coast, three university campuses, and Frank Lloyd Wright's Robie House. Every Saturday at 9am (from the west side of the Old Water Tower, 806 North Michigan) and at 9:30am (from the Archicenter, 330 South Dearborn). Reservations are required, call 922-3432.

Keeshin Tours
615 West 41st. 254-5333. They offer two different tours, lasting either 2½-3 hours or 3½-4 hours. These narrated bus tours concentrate on Chicago as a whole, making some stops along the way. Reserve a day in advance. Several pickup points at different hotels. Tours Monday to Friday 10:30am and noon; Saturday and Sunday 9am and 1pm. Fare lower for senior citizens and children age 5-11; children under age 5 FREE. *OPEN Mon-Fri 8am-5:30pm; not in operation Thanksgiving, Christmas, New Year's Day, or Easter Sunday.*

Specialized Tours

Adventure in Art & Architecture
111 East Wacker, Suite 1212. 346-7784. Custom-designed tours of Chicago's artistic and architectural aspects, for groups and individuals. The narrated bus tours usually include a visit to the Art Institute, galleries, and artists' homes. Performing arts tours also available. Call for rates and additional information. *OPEN Mon-Fri 8:30am-5pm.*

Art Encounters
927 Noyes Street, Evanston, IL 60201. 328-9222. Every Saturday, regularly scheduled gallery walks and a Wednesday evening series provide an opportunity to visit private collections. (Sign up for a series or an individual day or evening.) Also, tailored tours and art programs for businesses, organizations, and schools. There are twice-a-year trips throughout the country, all with an art agenda. Membership available. Write or call for specific information.

Art Safari Tours
2953 West Devon. 338-7310. Bus tours to art galleries, museums, private collectors, and cultural attractions. In depth, expertly escorted by trained guides. Bilingual guides upon request.

Champagne Nite-Life Tours
525-3762. A choice of several nights on the

town. Includes transportation, champagne en route, food, drinks, top entertainment, taxes, and tips. Reserve. *Every Fri & Sat 7pm-1:30am.* Call for information Monday to Saturday 9am to 9pm.

Chicago Is . . . , Inc.
151 North Michigan. 565-1550. The 6-hour narrated "Inside Chicago Tour" highlights the best of this toddlin' town, from the Loop to the Magnificent Mile, with time on your own for shopping and lunch at Water Tower Place. Service to and from O'Hare hotels. Specializes in programs for spouses of busy executives in town for conventions. Custom-designed activities and tours for groups. Bilingual guides available. Reservation required. Call Monday to Friday 9am to 5pm.

Chicago's Haunted City Tours
20130 Ash Lane, Lynwood, IL 60411. 895-5750. Ghost hunter and paranormal investigator Norman Basile leads bus tours of Chicago graveyards and other ghostly sites. Year-round, Saturdays and Sundays, lasting from 5 to 8 hours. Write or call for current schedule. There are also mini-tours for 8 to 14 people lasting 3 hours. Happy haunting!

Chicago Supernatural Tours
Richard T. Crowe, Chicago Fortean Society, Box 29054, Chicago, IL 60629. 735-2530. Take a guided 5-hour bus tour of 12 local "haunts" and legendary places. Leave from De Paul University Lincoln Park Campus. .Two different tours weekend afternoons and evenings. Price includes snacks. Private tours anytime by appointment only. Write or call for reservations well in advance.

Falicia, Inc.
815 South We-Go Trail, Mt. Prospect. 640-5404. For groups. "Feast your senses on the Chicagoland area." A repertoire of tours custom-designed to appeal to a variety of interests, be it architecture, theater, or art. Via motor coach, escorted; lunch or dinner can be included.

FANtastic Tours
1971 Loomes, Downers Grove. 964-4141. The energetic Lee Gibbs has a tour for every interest, be it a special event, an art exhibit, or a coordinated ethnic evening on the town. She provides a private tour for one person or any size group. She *obviously* loves Chicago. She will even supply a guide for your coach. Call for information.

Ladies' Program
American Sightseeing Tours, 530 South Michigan. 427-3100. For the busy visiting executive's wife—tailored packages that can include shopping, theater, and dinner.

My Kind of Town
2100 Linden Avenue, Highland Park. 432-4966. From a choice of 30 custom-designed creative tours for groups only, focusing on historic, ethnic, architectural, or financial aspects of Chicago. *OPEN Mon-Fri 9am-5pm.*

On the Scene Tours
505 North La Salle. 661-1440. A VIP tour for one particular place of interest, or an escorted motor-coach tour touching on all aspects of Chicago

attractions, lasting anywhere from 1 to 8 hours, day and evening. One choice is a tour to the Merchandise Mart (otherwise closed to the public), *every Tues and Thurs 10am except during marketing conventions.* Call Monday to Friday 9am to 5pm for reservations.

Walking Tours

Abbie Adventures
823 Lake, Oak Park, IL 60301. 383-4348. In Chicago and the suburbs, art talks and tours by Lynn Abbie for groups of 12 or more. The walking tours emphasize the art deco period. Reserve in advance. She will also advise your group on what to see on your own in Chicago or will provide step-on guide service for your bus.

ArchiCenter
330 South Dearborn. 782-1776 (recorded tour information). Downtown headquarters of the Chicago Architecture Foundation, which is dedicated to developing public awareness of Chicago architecture—past, present, and future. There are permanent and changing exhibits, lectures, and tours—walking, biking, or bus. Year-round tours include a 2-hour Loop Walking Tour, *Mon-Fri 1pm; Sat & Sun 2pm;* the Glessner House Museum, *Tues-Sun noon, 1, 2 & 3pm;* the Clarke House Museum, *Tues-Sun 12:15, 1:15; 2:15 & 3:15pm;* and a Frank Lloyd Wright Oak Park Tour *every Sun at 1 & 2:30pm.* The bookstore is very well stocked with Chicago architectural and historical publications. *OPEN Mon-Fri 9:30am-5:30pm; Sat 9am-3pm.* (*See also* HISTORIC & NEW CHICAGO, Historic Buildings & Areas: Clarke House *and* Glessner House.)

Art Safari Tours
2953 West Devon. 338-7310. *Every Sat 10:30am-1pm,* a continental breakfast followed by a walk to five or six outstanding art galleries. For groups of six or more only. Reservations are necessary.

Chicago Historical Society
North Clark at North Avenue. 642-4600, ext 42. In the spring, summer, and fall: historical walking tours of Lincoln Park, the Gold Coast, and the Old Town area. Also, some bus and el tours.

Chinatown Tour
Chinese American Civic Council, 2249 South Wentworth, 2nd floor. 225-0234. An educational group walking tour of Chinatown with visits to the Chinese Community Center, the Chinese Christian Union Church, and St. Therese's Catholic Mission. Shops may be visited, but dining is on your own time before or after. Tours *Mon-Fri between 10:30am and 3pm.* Reserve ten days in advance. Call weekdays after 1:30pm.

Frank Lloyd Wright Walking Tours
Oak Park Visitors Center, 158 Forest, Oak Park. 848-1978. A guided walking tour of the celebrated architect's structures. Orientation *every Sat & Sun at 1:45pm.* Tour *begins at 2pm. OPEN Mar 1-Nov 30, 7 days 10am-5pm.* Other times tickets available at the Frank Lloyd Wright Home & Studio at 951 Chicago Avenue. (*See also*

HISTORIC & NEW CHICAGO, Historic Buildings & Areas: Oak Park.)

ON YOUR OWN

The Atrium
State of Illinois Center, 100 West Randolph. 917-6660. In a stunning marble, tinted glass, and steel setting the mall offers three levels of shops and services, including apparel, gift, and jewelry boutiques; a currency exchange; and a U.S. Post Office. On the concourse level is the 900-seat food court, The Great State Fare.* Every Wednesday throughout the year there is entertainment and special events, and the dazzling building is a spectacle in and of itself. Mall *OPEN Mon-Fri 8am-6pm. Between Thanksgiving and Christmas, Sat 10am-4pm as well. *OPEN for breakfast at 6:30am.* (See also HISTORIC & NEW CHICAGO, Modern Architecture: State of Illinois Center.)

Auditorium Theater
50 East Congress. 922-4046. Tours for groups of 10 or more of this Sullivan and Adler masterpiece are offered *Mon-Fri 10am to 4pm.* Advance reservations are required. Admission charge. (See also HISTORIC & NEW CHICAGO, Historic Buildings & Areas.)

Buckingham Fountain
Grant Park at Congress Parkway. Beautiful fountain displays *May 30-Labor Day 7 days 11:30am-9pm;* Major color displays *9-10pm, on Grant Park concert nights till 10:30pm. July-Aug 12:30-1pm daily.* (See also HISTORIC & NEW CHICAGO, Historic Buildings & Areas.)

Central Water Filtration Plant
Navy Pier, 1000 East Ohio. 744-3692. Forty-five-minute guided tour of the world's largest water-filtration plant. See the chemical and microbiology labs, roller pump room, control room, chemical disposal, and a terrific view to boot. Tours *Tues & Thurs at 9, 9:45, 10:30, 11:30am, 1:30, 2:15 & 3:30pm.* Reserve. No children under fourth-grade level. Maximum group: 40 people. *Call for information Monday-Friday 8am to 4pm. FREE*

Chapel in the Sky
Chicago Methodist Temple, 77 West Washington. 236-4548. This is the world's tallest church building. From the 22nd floor, climb 173 steps to the small chapel located in the spire, 400 feet above street level. Start at the second-floor reception desk. *Mon-Sat at 2pm; Sun after the 8:30 & 11am services.* Reserve for ten or more: call Monday to Friday 9am to 5pm; Saturday 9am to 3:30pm. FREE. (See also HISTORIC & NEW CHICAGO, Churches & Synagogues: Chicago Methodist Temple.)

Chicago Board of Trade
Board of Trade Building, 141 West Jackson at La Salle. 435-3590. Glimpse a fascinating aspect of the free enterprise system. The world's largest (17,000 members) commodities futures trading market (in grains, wood, silver, and gold)

is a blur of activity and *very* high drama. You're above the roar of the crowd in the fifth-floor glass-enclosed visitors' gallery, but nonetheless you will be caught up in the trading frenzy. There is a film and slide presentation and a CBT guide will help you understand what you are viewing. (Visitors' Gallery *OPEN Mon-Fri 9am-2pm. CLOSED holidays.* For group tours of from 10 to 50 persons, reserve several weeks in advance; call 435-3721. No children under age 16. FREE. (See also HISTORIC & NEW CHICAGO, Historic Buildings & Areas, and BASIC INFORMATION, Telephone Information: Board of Trade Hotlines.)

Chicago Fire Academy
558 West De Koven. 744-4728. On the spot where the Great Chicago Fire of 1871 started (in Mrs. O'Leary's fabled barn) now stands the academy where firefighters train. During half-hour tour see training, apparatus, and exhibits. *Mon-Fri at 10 & 11am, 1 & 2pm.* Reserve 2 weeks in advance. FREE.

Chicago Mercantile Exchange
30 South Wacker. 930-8249. The frenzied commodity futures exchange may be observed from the Visitors' Gallery. Staffers explain the activity. *OPEN Mon-Fri 7:30am-3:15pm.* Private tours for groups must be reserved a week in advance, minimum of 10, maximum of 60. No children under age 14. FREE.

Chicago Police Department
1121 South State. 744-5570. Tour one of the world's most advanced police headquarters. For groups of 15 to 30 people only. No children under age 12. Reserve 2 weeks in advance. *Tues-Fri 10am & 2pm.* FREE.

Chicago Post Office
433 West Van Buren. 765-3009. A two-hour guided tour of the world's largest post office building (handles approximately 8 million letters a day); includes a slide presentation. *Mon-Fri 10:30am-12:30pm (except Dec).* Reserve a week in advance. Group maximum of 40; no children below fifth-grade level. FREE.

Chicago *Sun-Times*
401 North Wabash. 321-2032. One-hour, in-depth tour of newsroom, photo lab, composing room, and printing facilities. *Mon-Fri at 10:30am.* Reservations necessary; group maximum of 40. No children under age 10. FREE. (See also HISTORIC & NEW CHICAGO, Historic Buildings & Areas.)

Cook County Criminal Court Building
2600 South California. 443-3985. See the courts, a trial in progress, perhaps talk to a judge. NOTE: You *will* be searched. Tours last 2 hours, *Tues, Wed, Thurs at 9:30am.* Reservations requested. No students below high-school level.

Federal Reserve Bank
164 West Jackson. 322-5112. See a film overview of this central bank, then tour some of the departments, including check, cash, as well as a "money museum." Reserve in advance. Group tours (maximum of 20 people) by appointment only. *OPEN Mon-Fri 9am-1pm.* FREE.

First National Bank
1 First National Plaza, Monroe & Dearborn. 732-6037. See the retail services and commercial operations, and an otherwise inaccessible view from either the 57th or 39th floor of the world's tallest bank. Tour lasts an hour *Mon-Fri at 10am.* Reserve in advance. Group maximum of 25 people. No children under age 12. FREE. (*See also* HISTORIC & NEW CHICAGO, Modern Architecture: First National Plaza.)

Here's Chicago!
163 East Pearson, Chicago, IL 60611. Recorded information 467-5304. Located in the landmark Water Tower Pumping Station, a unique sound-and-light show introduction to Chicago. *Heartbeat Chicago* is a 63-projector slide show starring the people of Chicago, and *City of Dreams* is an exciting 70mm grand tour with a bird's-eye view on a giant screen. Also, a narrated walk through the still-operating pumping station; original artifacts illustrating the Great Chicago Fire. Gift shop for souvenirs, gifts, and books. The first show is at 10am; shows every 30 minutes on the hour and half hour. *OPEN May-Thanksgiving, Sun-Thurs 9:30am-6pm; Fri & Sat 9:30am-7pm. Balance of the year, Sun-Thurs 9:30am-4pm; Fri & Sat 9:30am-6pm.* Admission charge lower for senior citizens and children age 12 and under. There is a savings for a family ticket. Groups reserve in advance, call 467-7114.

Horse & Carriage Rides
Stand located at the Old Water Tower at the west side of Michigan at Pearson. For 1-6 people, an old-fashioned treat: ride through the streets of Chicago in a horse-drawn carriage. *Year-round, 7 days 10:30am-3:30pm & 6:30pm-2am. 6:30pm-1am; Sat & Sun 6:30pm-2am.* For information call 266-7878.

Merchandise Mart Tour
350 North Wells at the Chicago River. 661-1440. A 90-minute tour of the world's largest wholesale market center, which is not normally open to the public. Start at the information desk in the lobby. Tour includes a brief history of the building, concentrates on the home furnishings floors and

Merchandise Mart

showrooms. Individual tours *Mar-Dec 1, Tues & Thurs 10am.* Call day before tour. Group tours for 20 or more are available Monday to Friday by reservation. Group tours last approximately 2 hours. Admission. (*See also* HISTORIC & NEW CHICAGO, Historic Buildings & Areas.)

Moody Bible Institute
820 North La Salle. 329-4400. Twenty-minute multimedia show; tour of the building and of WMBI radio station. Tours *Mon-Fri at 11 & 2pm.* Reserve in advance. FREE.

State Street Shopping Mall
State Street in the Loop. Planned as the nation's largest pedestrian shopping mall. Bus traffic only, and covered bus shelters. Wide sidewalks—a window shopper's delight. Entertainment in summer months. (For individual store listings *see* SHOPPING, Large Stores.)

Under the Picasso
Daley Civic Center Plaza, Washington & Dearborn streets. For recorded information, call F-I-N-E-A-R-T. (346-3278). Under the once controversial, now classic, Chicago Picasso (*see* HISTORIC & NEW CHICAGO, Outdoor Artwork & Sculpture), noontime entertainment programs and exhibits outdoors on the Plaza or indoors in the east lobby. Presented by the Chicago Office of Fine Arts. *Year-round, 7 days a week at noon.* FREE.

Water Tower Place
835 North Michigan. 440-3165. A modern residential, professional, and commercial urban complex. Houses the Ritz-Carlton Hotel, movie theaters, and a seven floor-atrium shopping mall that includes Marshall Field's and Lord & Taylor. The gleaming interior—waterfalls, chrome-and-glass elevators, several restaurants, and some of the choicest shops in town—constitutes a major Chicago attraction. Mall *OPEN 7 days 9am-midnight.* Shops *OPEN Mon & Thurs 10am-7pm; Tues, Wed, Fri & Sat 10am-6pm; Sun noon-5pm.* (*See also* SHOPPING, Shopping Malls.)

LAKE & RIVER TRIPS

Chicago River Boat Tour
Departs: North Pier Terminal, 501 East Illinois Street. Recorded tour information 782-1776. This Chicago Architecture Foundation tour, a 1½-hour cruise, is a perfect way to view Chicago's famed riverfront architecture. Coffee and croissants are included. Boat tour *June-Sept, Mon-Sat at 10am.* Reservations required, call 922-3432. Private group charter available.

Mercury Sightseeing Boats
Wacker Drive & Michigan Avenue, lower level. 332-1353. For more information write: P.O. Box 68, Palatine, Il 60078-0068. Tour Lake Michigan and the Chicago River for 1, 1½, and 2 hours. Narrator on board. *Early May-late Sept 7 days 10am-7:30pm, later on Fri & Sat.* Fare lower for children under 12. For group rate call 332-1368.

Shoreline Marine Sightseeing
3721 Foster Street, Evanston, Il 60203. 427-2900. A 30-minute boat trip on Lake Michigan north to Navy Pier, then on to the Lighthouse. *May 30-Sept 15,* weather permitting. Boats leave from Shedd Aquarium (1200 South Lake Shore Drive) *every hour 12:15-5:15pm;* from Buckingham Fountain *at 8:15, 9:15 & 10:15pm;* and from the Planetarium (near Aquarium) *every hour 1:15-9:15pm.* Fare lower for children under age 10.

Wendella Sightseeing Boats
400 North Michigan at the Wrigley Building. 337-1446. Take a delightful 1½-hour narrated cruise on the Chicago River, through the Chicago Locks out to Lake Michigan for fabulous views. Soft drinks available. Reserve. *Apr-Oct 7 days at 10 & 11:30am & 1:15, 3 & 7:30pm.* Fare lower for children under age 12. Special rates available for groups of 30 or more.

DAY TRIPS

Escorted

American Sightseeing Tours
530 South Michigan. 427-3100. Air-conditioned motor coach tours include the following (many are seasonal): *Brews & Cruise:* brewery tour and cruise down Milwaukee's waterways; *Historic Galena & Mississippi Cruise:* sightsee and have a colorful excursion on a paddlewheeler on the Mississippi; *Stonecroft Port Washington:* charming lakeshore village; *Honey Bear Farm:* country-style shops, restaurants, pet farm; *Wisconsin Adventure:* Lake Geneva, Honey Bear Farm, and dinner. Call for information and reservations.

On Your Own

Argonne National Laboratory
9700 South Cass Avenue, Argonne. 972-2773. Located on 1,700 acres approximately 28 miles southwest of Chicago. Operated by the University of Chicago for the Department of Energy. Great for those interested in computers, physics, chemical engineering, and environmental research among other scientific pursuits. The 3½-hour tours that are given on *Sat at 9am & 1:30pm* begin with an orientation. No children under age 16. FREE. Advance reservations necessary.

Aurora Historical Museum
Oak & Cedar streets, Aurora. 897-9029. A 125-year-old Victorian mansion, 45 minutes from downtown Chicago. Exhibits trace the history of Aurora from prehistoric times to the 1920s. Restored carriage house open in summer (nominal admission fee). *OPEN Wed, Sat & Sun 1-5pm.* Group reservations accepted Monday to Friday. FREE. Donations accepted. (*See also* Blackberry Historical Farm Village.)

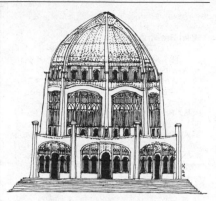

Bahi'a House of Worship

Bahi'a House of Worship
112 Linden Avenue, Wilmette. 256-4400. Forty-five minutes from downtown, a beauty overlooking Lake Michigan. Built in 1929, it is North America's only Bahi'a (Persian) house of worship. The number 9, symbol of perfection and unity, recurs throughout: nine doors (welcoming all people from all directions), a nine-sided dome, nine sculptured gardens. The inscribed ornamentation represents the world's major religions. *OPEN Oct 15-May 15, 7 days 10am-5pm:* balance of the year 10am-10pm. Guides are available; call in advance for groups of more than 15 people. FREE.

Blackberry Historical Farm Village
Galena Boulevard, Aurora. 892-1550. Forty-five minutes from downtown Chicago, this restored 19th-century village includes a working blacksmith shop, a schoolhouse, a carriage shop, and charming shops. *OPEN Apr-Labor Day,7 days 10am-4:30; Labor Day-mid Oct, Fri, Sat & Sun only 10am-4:30pm. Closed mid Oct-Mar. Call for Special Event Days.* Admission charge, lower for senior citizens and children age 2-12; children under age 2 FREE. Family fee available. (*See also* Aurora Historical Museum.)

Bradford Museum of Collector's Plates
9333 North Milwaukee Avenue, Niles. 966-2770. A unique museum of limited-edition collector's plates in a lovely setting. Pretty as it is, it's also big business, as evidenced by the number of transactions handled daily at the Bradford Exchange. Guided tours Monday to Friday at 10am by appointment. Museum *OPEN Mon-Fri 9am-4pm; Sat & Sun 10am-5pm.* Admission charge, lower for senior citizens; children under age 12 FREE.

Brewery Tours
Milwaukee, Wisconsin. The average Milwaukee resident drinks seven times more beer per year than residents of other cities (42 gallons versus 6 gallons). Perhaps that's because Milwaukee

has two of America's largest breweries. Free tours of each are available.

Miller Brewing Company
4251 West State Street, Milwaukee. (1-414) 931-2153. Fifty-minute tours *Mon-Fri 9am-3:30pm (9, 10, 11, 12, 1, 2, 3 & 3:30); Apr-Oct Sat as well.* For group tours of 15 or more call (1-414) 931-2151. Children under age 19 must be accompanied by an adult.

Pabst Brewery
901 West Juneau, Milwaukee. (1-414) 223-3500. Tours *first Sat in June-Sat after Labor Day, Mon-Fri 9am-3pm on the hour; Sat 9, 10 & 11am. Balance of the year, Mon-Fri only at 10 & 11am & 1, 2 & 3pm.* Reservations required for groups of 20 or more.
NOTE: *If you are in the vicinity just prior to Thanksgiving, Milwaukee has a Holiday Folk Fair that is the largest ethnic fair in America, with foods, crafts, entertainment. Call* (1-414) 933-0521 *for information.*

Contigny
Roosevelt & Winfield roads, Wheaton. 668-5161 The 500-acre estate of the late Colonel Robert R. McCormick. Named for the French town where a bitter WWI battle took place. There is a museum dedicated to the history of the First Battalion; the McCormick Museum, the *Chicago Tribune* owner's home, reflecting his tastes and interests; a formal garden as well as acres of woodlands for picnics and nature walks. Gardens *OPEN Feb-Dec 7 days 9am-dusk. CLOSED Jan.* First Division Museum *OPEN Memorial Day-Labor Day Tues-Sun 10am- 5pm; Labor Day-Memorial Day, Tues-Sun 10am-4pm. CLOSED Jan.* McCormick Museum *OPEN Memorial Day-Labor Day, Tues-Sun 10am-5pm; Labor Day-Memorial Day, Tues-Sun 10am-4pm. CLOSED Jan.* Gardens and museums FREE. Free chamber-music concerts by local musicians every Sunday from 3 to 4pm (except in January). By reservation only.

Frankfort, Illinois
(1-815) 469-3356. A restored 1890s village, 45 minutes from Chicago, with some original pre-Civil War buildings and German *Gemütlichkeit* reflecting early town patriarchs. Two German restaurants. Gas lamps. Country stores and crafts emporiums. Historical buildings, now businesses, are open to the public to explore. Replica of old train station in park in center of town. Historical museum *OPEN Sun only 1-4pm.* Times of other buildings vary; call for specific information. Group tours of 10 or more by arrangement. FREE.

Green County, Wisconsin
Known as "Little Switzerland" and only 2½ hours from Chicago. Monroe, one of the county's charming towns, is the Swiss-cheese capital of America. In New Glarus is a Swiss Historical Village, (1-608) 527-2317. Replicas of 12 old Swiss-American buildings including cheese factory, blacksmith shop, firehouse, and print shop, all housing authentic artifacts from the 19th century. Admission charge, lower for children age

6-13. Group tours by reservation. *OPEN May-Oct 7 days 9am-5pm. CLOSED Nov-Mar.*

Illinois Railway Museum
Olson Road, Union. (1-815) 923-2488. An outdoor museum on 46 acres to make a railroad or nostalgia buff's heart beat faster. Over 150 cars and locomotives as well as Chicago streetcars. On weekends ride a steam train out of an 1851 station; weekdays ride an electric streetcar. Snacks or picnic facilities available. *OPEN late Apr/early May-Labor Day Mon-Fri 10am-4pm; Sat & Sun 11am-5pm.* Admission charge, lower for children and senior citizens; children under age 5 FREE. For group tour information write P.O. Box 431, Union, IL 60180.

Long Grove Village
Routes 83 & 53, Long Grove. 634-0888. Forty minutes from downtown, this restored town, originally settled in the early 1800s by German farmers, retains its charming old-fashioned ways. Shops, a covered bridge, and an 1847 church that still holds Sunday services. The Village Tavern, which has been operating since 1849, features an old-fashioned fish fry every Friday pm. The Sunday after Labor Day is "Turn O' the Century Day," a festival including a parade, a water fight, and a great deal of food and beer. *OPEN Mon-Sat 10am-5pm; Sun noon-5pm.* FREE.

Naper Settlement
201 West Porter, Naperville. 420-6010. Approximately 25 miles west of Chicago on the 11-acre site of the Caroline Martin-Mitchell mansion. A settlement that portrays life as it was in a northern Illinois town ca. 1830-70 is presently being created. There are 17 buildings on the site; 11 are fully restored and open to the public, including an 1843 log cabin, Judge Murray's 1842 Greek Revival house, an old smokehouse, and a wood-frame Gothic church. Restoration continues. *OPEN May-Oct Wed & Sun 1:30-4:30pm.* Admission charge, lower for children and senior citizens; children under age 6 FREE. Group tours year-round Monday to Friday by arrangement.

Paramount Arts Centre
23 East Galena, Aurora. 896-7676. Opened in 1931 at a cost of $1 million, this, the premier art deco vaudeville/movie house of the Midwest, has a new lease on life. Reserve in advance for a free tour behind the scenes of this superbly restored 1,888-seat theater. Deco fans will be delighted. Tours *Mon-Fri 10am-4pm.* Subscriptions to performances are available. Box office: 896-6666.

Rialto Square Theater
102 North Chicago Street, Joliet. (1-815) 726-7171. This splendid theater opened in 1926 as a venue for vaudeville and motion pictures. Restored in the 1970s, it is now listed in the National Register of Historic Places. Public guided tours are offered every Wednesday at 12:45pm. No reservations are required. Suggested donation. Groups may tour at any time by prior arrangement. (For groups of 40 or more there is also an organ concert on the Barton Grande Pipe Organ.)

Svoboda's Nickelodeon Tavern
Routes 83 & 30, Lynwood. 755-1838. Tavern doubles as a unique museum of coin-operated musical instruments, all antique, most in working order: nickelodeons, zithers, music boxes, Victrolas, etc. Live, presumably non-coin-operated Dixieland jazz every Saturday night. Fun for those who don't mind the decibels. Children must be accompanied by adults. Admission charge during entertainment only. *OPEN 7 days noon-1am.*

Volo Antique Auto Museum & Village
Route 120, Volo. (1-815) 385-3644. On 14 acres, over 100 vintage autos (many of which are for sale at not-so-vintage prices) and motorcycles. Re-created 1920s town with shops keep the mood. Sports car store. Arcade with antique amusements. *OPEN year-round Wed-Mon 10am-5pm.* Admission charge, lower for children and senior citizens; children under age 4 FREE. Group rates available.

Windy City Balloonport
100 Ski Hill Road, off Route 22, Fox River Grove. 639-0550. Close by in suburban Fox River Grove, your spirits will soar even if you only watch balloonists as they prepare to go up, up, and away in their beautiful balloons. Early morning at sunrise or early evening (2 hours before sunset) with the proper weather conditions. Rides and lessons, too. Bring your camera.

Woodfield Shopping Mall
Golf Road & Route 53, Schaumburg. 882-0220. More than 200 stores and restaurants comprise this, one of the largest enclosed shopping centers in the world. (Will a day be enough?) *OPEN Mon-Fri 10am-9pm; Sat 10am-5.30pm; Sun 11am-5pm.*

ANNUAL EVENTS

Buckingham Fountain

CALENDAR

These are some of the great and little events that reflect Chicago's energy, creativity, diversity, and humor.

January

Chicago Boat, Sports & RV Show
McCormick Place, 23rd & the Lake. Early January for five days. Hands-on displays of sporting goods, boats, motor homes, and recreational vehicles. Call 836-4740 for information. Admission charge, lower for children under age 12.

Chinese New Year
Wentworth from Cermak to 24th. Late January to mid February, depending on the lunar calendar. A parade, firecrackers, and a paper dragon dance through the streets of Chinatown to banish evil spirits and uplift some good ones. Call 225-0234 for particulars. FREE. NOTE: Many Chinatown restaurants serve traditional banquet feasts during this time.

National Housewares Show
McCormick Place, 23rd & the Lake. Mid January for five days. All that's new in appliances and kitchenware. Trade show—closed to the general public. Call 644-3333 for information.

Annual Chicago Jazz Fair
Blackstone Hotel, 636 South Michigan. Mid January, sponsored by the Jazz Institute of Chicago. Local groups feature all that's jazz: traditional, swing, bebop, and avant-garde. Films and tapes of past greats too. Call 664-4069 for details. Admission charge.

University of Chicago Folk Festival
Mid to late January for three days. A midwinter musical must. Sponsored by the university's Folk Lore Society, this down-home tradition has blues, gospel, country, and bluegrass music; workshops too. Friday and Sunday music performances at Mandel Hall, 57th & South University. Saturday workshops at Ada Noyes Hall. Call 962-7300 for information. Tickets may be purchased in advance.

Old-Time Street Market
Century Shopping Center, 2828 North Clark. 929-8100. Last two weekends in January (starting on Friday). Sidewalk sale and old-fashioned banjo strumming. FREE.

Chicagoland Sportfishing, Travel & Outdoor Show
O'Hare Exposition Center, 5555 River Road, Rosemont. 692-2220. Late January for nine days. A good cure for cabin fever—start making those vacation plans. Admission charge.

Mostly Music Lunchtime Concerts
First Chicago Center, Dearborn & Monroe, plaza level. 732-4470. Beginning at the end of January, every Tuesday for ten weeks. Classical chamber-music concerts from 12:15 to 1pm. Admission charge.

February

Black History Month
Chicago Public Library Cultural Center, 78 East Washington. 346-3278. A month-long, citywide celebration of the Black American's life, times, and art, with films, dance, lectures, music, theater, and exhibits. FREE. Similar events: Museum of Science and Industry, 57th & Lake Shore Drive, 684-1414; Daley Plaza, Randolph & Washington, 346-3278.

Black Creativity Festival
Museum of Science & Industry, 57th & Lake Shore Drive. 684-1414. Beginning of February for approximately ten days. In the museum auditorium the annual arts-and-performance festival by local and national Black artists. FREE.

Azalea Flower Show
Lincoln Park Conservatory, 2400 North Stockton Drive; 294-4770. And Garfield Park Conserva-

tory, 300 North Central Park Boulevard; 533-1281. Mid February to early March. Thousands of spring flowers—a magnificent display *just* when you need one. *OPEN Sat-Thurs 10am-6pm; Fri 9am-9pm.* FREE.

Lake Shore Loppet
Lincoln Park, Waveland Golf Course. Mid February for one day. Part of the Dannon series, a 10-kilometer cross-country race. Usually attracts several hundred city skiers. Call 294-2493 for information.

Chicago Auto Show
McCormick Place, 23rd & the Lake. Begins the last week in February and runs for nine days. The largest commercial show in the world. All the new models, some classics, race cars also. Call 791-7000 for information. Admission charge, lower for children under age 12 and senior citizens on certain days and at certain times.

March

Chicago Schools Science Fairs
Museum of Science and Industry, 57th & South Lake Shore Drive. 684-1414. A fair with winning science exhibits from public, parochial, and independent schools in Chicago. FREE.

Women's History Week
Early March. Activities in and around Chicago and the state of Illinois. Films, theater, lectures, dance, and more, all to celebrate the achievements and talents of women. Multifaceted events. Call 922-8530 for information. Many events are FREE.

Shrine Circus
Medinah Temple, 600 North Wabash. 266-5000. Beginning of March for three weeks. Longstanding Chicago tradition. The Shriners' one-ring circus comes to town. A little dusty but for a good cause—children's hospitals. Tickets may be bought in advance.

Ice Capades
Chicago Stadium, 1800 West Madison. 733-5300. Mid March for approximately ten days. Artistry on ice; colorful and entertaining. Admission charge, lower for children (and senior citizens for selected shows). Tickets may be purchased in advance.

St. Patrick's Day
Dearborn & Wacker. It may be a bit of blarney, but *everyone* in Chicago is Irish today. Forty pounds of vegetable dye turns the Chicago River

Medinah Temple

green! Honest. Mass at 9:30am at Old St. Patrick's Church at Adams & Des Plaines begins the official celebration. The parade, along Dearborn Street, starts at 11am. Floats, marchers, marching bands, and several hundred thousand spectators. FREE.

Festival of Chicago Poets
Loyola University, Damen Hall, 6525 North Sheridan Road. Late March for one afternoon. A celebration of Chicagoland poets: readings and other related activities. Call 508-2240 for information. FREE.

March-April

Depending on when Easter falls.

Spring & Easter Flower Show
Lincoln Park Conservatory, 2400 North Stockton Drive; 294-4770. And Garfield Park Conservatory, 300 North Central Park Boulevard; 533-1281. Mid March to mid April for two weeks, depending upon when Easter falls. An eyeful of spring. *OPEN Sat-Thurs 10am-6pm; Fri 9am-9pm.* FREE.

Balzekas Museum
4012 South Archer. 523-5523. One Saturday, two weeks before Easter Sunday, learn the Lithuanian way of decorating eggs—the ancient symbol of renewed life. Two 2-hour classes. Bring your own eggs and supplies; call 847-2441, and they will tell you what is required. For children age 10 and up. Small fee.

Easter Parade at Brookfield Zoo
Brookfield Zoo, 8400 West 31st Street, Brookfield. Easter weekend, Saturday and Sunday around noon. See the animals in their Easter finery. The public is invited to participate in its finery as well. Call 242-2630 for information. FREE.

April

Smelt Fishing
Early April to mid May. Lights, lanterns, and nets along Lake Michigan. Call 294-2493 for information.

Chicago Pipe-Smoking Contest
The Sirloin Inn, 1528 North Wells. One Sunday at noon in mid April, men and women in a smoke-filled room. The idea is for participants to try to keep their pipes going using only 3.3 grams of tobacco and two matches. The person who stays lit the longest is the winner. Call 337-8025 for information. FREE.

O'Hare National Antique Show & Sale
O'Hare Exposition Center, 5555 River Road, Rosemont. Mid April for four days. Large semi-annual show of antiques and collector's items. Call 692-2220 for information. Admission charge.

The Chicago Sports Health & Fitness Fair
O'Hare Exposition Center, 5555 River Road, Rosemont. Held mid April for three days. Exhibits devoted to helping the whole family enjoy a healthy, more active life. Demonstrations, lectures, seminars. Admission charge, lower for

children under age 12; children under age 5 FREE. Call 692-2220 for information.

May

America's Marathon
Held one Sunday in early May. Starts at 9:30am from Daley Center. Approximately 7,000 men, women, and children run this 26.2-mile route through Chicago's neighborhoods. The finish line is in Grant Park. Come cheer them on.

Beverly Art Center
2153 West 111th. 445-3838. One Saturday in early May from 9:30am to 6pm. An art auction—from antiques to "junque" donated for fund-raising.

Historical Preservation Week
Always beginning on Mother's Day and lasting for a full week, this national event is enthusiastically celebrated in Chicago. Local groups plan many special activities. Tours of old, new, and renovated neighborhoods; house tours too. Party in an el train, dance in a ballroom, or go antiquing. Held in various parts of the city. Call the National Trust at 353-3419 for information.

Echo Blo-Bowl for Easter Seals
Grant Park near the old band shell. One Saturday in May at 10am. An interesting mix of teams including the Chicago Police Department. A single elimination tournament played with power blowers and a Nerf ball. Great spectator sport. Call 732-5473 for information.

Arts & Crafts Expo
American Indian Center, 1630 West Wilson. 275-5871. Second weekend in May. Fashion, entertainment, and arts and crafts of the Native American. Some events are FREE, others have admission charge.

Art Chicago
Navy Pier, Grand & the Lake, Grand Ballroom and East End Complex. Mid May for three days. Art, both past and present at the Chicago International Art Exhibition, draws artists, curators, and collectors. Features 100 prestigious art galleries from the U.S. and abroad, representing approximately 1,500 international artists (everything is for sale). Large-scale outdoor sculpture promenade; video and performance art too. Call 787-6858 for information. Admission charge, lower for students and senior citizens; children under age 12 FREE. Tickets available through Ticketron.

CTA Culture Bus
From mid May through September, every Sunday and all holidays starting at 10:30am. Departure point: the Art Institute, Michigan & Adams. Three routes take you north, south, or west. Call 836-7000 for information. (*See also* SIGHTSEEING, Chicago Tours.)

Buckingham Fountain Display
In Grant Park, at Congress Parkway. May 30 to Labor Day. Spectacular water display (colorful at night). Daytime from 11:30am to 9pm, Monday to Sunday. Color shows from 9pm to 10pm every evening and later on Grant Park concert nights (till 10:30pm). Call 294-2493 for information. FREE.

Spring Carnival
Lincoln School, 615 West Kemper Place. Third weekend in May. On Saturday a fire engine leads the parade down Geneva Terrace to Fullerton then to Clark to Webster to Lincoln and then to Orchard, where the carnival starts. Garage sales, food, books, and lots of activities for kids and adults. Call 549-2474 for information. FREE.

Wright Plus
Frank Lloyd Wright Home & Studio Foundation, 951 Chicago Avenue, Oak Park. 848-1976. One day in May. Tour the interiors of ten homes designed by Frank Lloyd Wright and his contemporaries. The once-a-year time to get inside—don't miss it. Admission charge. Tickets go on sale March 1. Reserve in advance, tickets are limited.

June

Summer Dance
The city's fine companies dance their way through the parks and plazas all summer long.

Brandeis Used-Book Sale
Edens Plaza, Wilmette. For one week in June. Over 300,000 books. Good hunting for the rare as well as first editions. The closing weekend is bargain time. Call 251-0690 for information. Donation requested on opening night only.

Neighborhood Festivals
Every Saturday & Sunday in June. Chicago neighborhood ethnic fairs with headline entertainers, ethnic foods, and fun in celebration of Chicago's heritage. They include a Polish Festival on the Northwest Side, a Greek Festival in Lincoln Square, a Puerto Rican Festival in Humboldt Park, an Asian Festival in Albany Park, a Mexican Festival in Little Village Pilsen, a Black Festival on the West Side, an Italian Festival in Belmont-Cragin, a Jewish Festival in Rogers Park. Call 744-3370 for information.

The Plaza Lunchtime Concerts
The following have free lunchtime outdoor concerts on various days, from June through August. Call for specifics.

Cathedral of St. James
Huron & Rush. 787-6410. On the Cathedral Commons, every Wednesday from June to August, from noon to 1pm. Outdoor concerts, primarily classical. Box lunches for sale benefit Cathedral Counseling Center. FREE.

First National Bank Plaza
Dearborn, Monroe & Clark. Beginning the first Tuesday in June to late August, every Tuesday and Thursday from noon to 1:45pm. Some evening concerts. All Chicago-area artists. Call 732-4470 for recorded information. FREE.

Plaza of the Americas
430 North Michigan. From the end of June to late July, on Tuesday and Thursday at noon. A variety of jazz, blues, pop, classical,

baroque, and folk. Call the Uptown Federal Bank, the sponsors, at 822-9300, for information. FREE.

State Street Mall
State between Randolph & Van Buren. The State Street Council sponsors many outdoor street activities; call them at 782-9160 for information. FREE.

Sandcastle Competition
North Avenue Beach, just north of the Beach House. Held one afternoon during the first weekend in June. Build your own condo-sandcastle. Hand tools are permitted; no bulldozers, please. Judges are Chicago architects. Sponsored by the Chicago AIA; call them at 663-4111 for information. FREE.

WLS-AM Run for the Zoo
First Sunday in June at 8am. Starting point is the Grant Statue on Cannon Drive in Lincoln Park. WLS-AM sponsors this 8.9-mile run through the park to Foster Avenue and back to the finish line at the east entrance to the zoo. The lion's share of the runner's fees are donated to the zoo. Call 984-0890 for information. FREE for spectators.

Body Politic Lincoln Avenue Festival of the Arts
Lincoln between Belden & Webster. Early June for one weekend, from noon to dusk. Art, crafts, food from local restaurants, bands from local clubs, and street entertainment. The Body Politic runs evening events at the theater, 2261 North Lincoln, 525-1052. Call them for information. FREE.

Chicago Children's Choir Gala Concert
Held in the Hyde Park Area. One weekend in early June, Saturday night at 8pm and Sunday at 3pm. One hundred and thirty members of the group sing their little hearts out. Call 324-8300 for information. Admission charge; lower for children, students, and senior citizens.

Beaches
The city's beaches are open from mid June through August, 7 days 9am to 9 pm. Call 294-2334 for information.

Theater on the Lake
Lincoln Park Fullerton Pavilion, Fullerton Parkway & North Lake Shore Drive. Mid June for 12 weeks. Twelve plays—a mix of comedy, mystery, drama, and musical—performed by amateur groups. Call 294-2375 for information. Admission charge.

Chicago Fies (Festival)
Mid June—the annual Gaelic festival. Young Irish step dancers compete for prizes and an opportunity to go on to an international contest in Ireland. Call 636-8241 for information.

Old Town Art Fair
1800 North block on Lincoln Park West & Orleans. Second weekend in June, from noon to dusk. Sponsored by the Old Town Triangle Art Center. Emphasis on painting, watercolor, printmaking, graphics, and photography; some crafts. Call 337-1938 for information. Suggested donation, lower for children under age 12 and senior citizens.

JuneFest
K.A.M.-Isaiah Israel Congregation, 1100 East Hyde Park Boulevard. 924-1234. Mid June for one weekend. A festival with a different theme each year. Always art objects, bargains, entertainment, and food. Tours of landmark buildings also. Admission charge; children under age 12 FREE.

Chicago's Farmers' Market
Season begins approximately the third week in June and lasts till mid October. Fresh produce at reasonable prices in a pleasant outdoor environment. Large variety direct from farms in Illinois, Michigan, and Indiana. Downtown and in the neighborhoods.

Beverly Art Center Art Fair & Festival
Beverly Art Center, 2153 West 111th. 445-3838. Third weekend in June for two days, from 11am to 6pm. Juried art exhibits; costumed craftsmen demonstrating medieval and colonial skills; local and professional performing artists. On the grounds of Morgan Park Academy. Food for sale, including freshly baked breads. FREE.

Ravinia Festival
Ravinia Park, Ravinia Park Road, Highland Park. 728-4642 (box office). From late June to late August. One of summer's joys: A 12-week season of the Chicago Symphony Orchestra, dance, jazz, ballet, folk, and comedy in a beautiful picnic setting. There are five or six shows a week. Starting times are either 7:30pm or 8:30pm; call 433-8800 for information. Admission charge to lawn and pavilion. For travel information call 836-7000.

Fine Arts & Selected Crafts Fair
Plaza of the Americas, 430 North Michigan. Late June for two days, Thursday and Friday from 8am to dusk. Arts and crafts from local and midwestern artists are displayed and sold. Call 895-3710 for information. FREE.

Custer's Annual Last Stand
Custer, Washington, Main & Chicago streets, Evanston. Second to last weekend in June, on Saturday and Sunday from noon to dusk. Block fair with merchants, artists, craftspeople, and antique dealers. Music, food, and entertainment. Call 475-3187 for information. FREE.

Water Tower Art & Craft Festival
Chicago Avenue & adjacent streets between Michigan & Lake Shore Drive. Last full weekend in June, Friday and Saturday from 11am to 7pm. Arts and crafts including some unusual art forms and one-of-a-kind pieces by individual artists. Demonstrations of art forms (if the winds permit). Call 280-5740 for information. FREE.

Grant Park Concerts
James C. Petrillo Music Shell, Grant Park. From the end of June to August 30 every Wednesday, Friday, and Saturday at 8pm; Sunday at 7pm. Chicago's free Lakefront musical festival. With Michigan Avenue in view, you can't forget you're in a city—but evenings like these make you glad

you are. A loaf of bread, a bottle of wine, the Grant Park Symphony, and you. The music on-stage and the stars up above are FREE. Draws crowds. Call 294-2420 for information.

Evanston Farmers' Market
University Place, west of Benson Street, Evanston. From June 30 to the end of October every Saturday from 8am to 3pm. Forty trucks brimming over with farm-fresh produce.

July

Check the May and June listings for ongoing summer events.

—Independence Day (July 4th) Weekend Celebrations

Concert & Fireworks
Grant Park, Petrillo Music Shell. July 3 at 8pm. The first Grant Park concert was performed July 4, 1934, in a temporary music shell that had been built for the 1933 Chicago World's Fair. It was used until 1978, when a modern James Petrillo Music Shell was built at Jackson Boulevard and Columbus Drive. Grant Park Symphony presents a classical program in what has become Chicago's traditional start of the July 4th celebration. Fireworks too. Bring a picnic to the park lawn or Monroe Harbor beaches and listen to the simulcast on WFMT. Call 294-2420 for information.

Taste of Chicago
Grant Park, Columbus Drive & the Lake. The July 4th weekend, Friday to Monday from noon to midnight. A fabulous al fresco food festival with over 100 of Chicago's restaurants participating. A wide variety of musical entertainment as well, including performances by the Grant Park Symphony at 7:30pm each night. Children's entertainment too. A charge for the food only. Call 744-3315 for information. FREE.

Old-Fashioned Fourth of July
Chicago Historical Society, Clark at North. 642-4600. Gather at the East Portico at 10:30am for an old-fashioned celebration with a reading of the Declaration of Independence, speeches, music, and fireworks. FREE.

The Chicago Park District
The outdoor swimming pools are open from early July to Labor Day, 7 days from 1pm to 9pm. Call 294-2334 for information.

Park District Concerts
July 4 to Labor Day. The Chicago Park District and the Chicago Federation of Musicians present a series of 70 free concerts in the city's parks. Well-known conductors, big-band leaders, and musicians perform a wide spectrum of music from semiclassical to jazz to blues and pop. A free schedule of times and places is available early spring, call 294-2320 or write to Music Supervisor, Department of Recreation, Chicago Park District, 425 East McFetridge Drive, Chicago, IL 60605.

Art & Craft Festivals
At several city and suburban locations during July, August, and September. Call 744-3315 for locations and times.

Troubadours
Daily in July and August. On nearly every downtown street corner, street entertainers will perform and delight.

The City Child in Summer
The Chicago Public Library Cultural Center, 78 East Washington. 346-3278. From July to August, in the theater. A series of fantasy-based films inspired by children's literature. The aim: to challenge curiosity and imagination. Suitable for preschool to junior high level. Call for information. FREE.

Court Theater
University of Chicago, 57th & South University. 753-4472. Beginning in early July, a nine-week summer schedule of classic plays outdoors. Every evening plus a Sunday matinee. Tickets may be purchased in advance.

Bastille Day Celebration
Ontario between St. Clair & Fairbanks; St. Clair between Ohio & Erie. Held on the Saturday closest to July 14 at approximately 6pm. French food, wine, and dancing in the streets. Call 337-1070 for information. Admission charge.

Garden Clubs of America
Chicago Horticultural Society, Lake Cook Road, Glencoe. 835-5440. In mid July for two days. Theme flower arrangements and plants on display. FREE.

Chicago-to-Mackinac-Island Yacht Race
In mid July, one Saturday at noon. The most popular inland yacht race starts just east of Navy Pier, off the Monroe Street lighthouse. Good viewpoints from the shore or aboard cruise ships on the Lake. Call 861-7777, the Chicago Yacht Club, the race's sponsor, for information.

Felician Art Festival
3800 West Peterson. 539-2328. In mid July for one day. An outdoor art fair on the lovely and spacious college grounds. FREE.

Sheffield Garden Walks
Corner of Sheffield & Webster at St. Vincent's Church. Held the third weekend in July, Saturday and Sunday from 11am to 6pm. Self-guided walking tour of the Sheffield-area private gardens. Enjoy garage sales, food, and entertainment along the way. Call 477-5100 for information. Admission charge, lower for senior citizens.

Air & Water Show
Chicago Avenue at the Lake. Held late July, Saturday and Sunday from noon to 3pm. A dazzling aerial display in the sky over Lake Michigan. An exciting summer tradition. Call 294-2200 for information. FREE.

Chinatown Festival
Centered around Wentworth & Cermak. Held the last Sunday in July. Starts at 9am with a fun-run, followed by a parade at noon and a carnival the rest of the day. Call 633-1500 or 326-4255 for information. FREE.

August

Check the May, June, and July listings for on-going summer events.

Bud Billiken Day Parade
Second Saturday in August at 10:25am. From Lake Meadow Shopping Center at 39th & Martin Luther King, Jr., Drive south to Washington Park. The South Side Black community's fun-filled event for kids and grown-ups.

Festa Italiana
Mid August for three days. A cultural festival featuring food, entertainment, and exhibits. Call 346-8448 for location and information. Admission charge.

Ginza Festival
Midwest Buddhist Temple, 435 West Menomonee. 943-7801. Mid August for three days and nights. Indoors and outdoors, a celebration of Japanese culture featuring food, dance, mime, martial arts, music, origami, painting, and sculpture. Admission charge, lower for children and senior citizens.

O'Hare National Antique Show & Sale
O'Hare Exposition Center, 5555 River Road, Rosemont. In mid August for four days. Antiques and collector's items in air-conditioned comfort. Call 692-2220 for information. Admission charge.

Midwest Bonsai Show
Chicago Horticultural Society, Lake Cook Road, Glencoe. 835-5440. In mid August for two days. The exquisite miniatures. FREE.

O.W.P.G.F. (Old Wicker Park Green First)
Damen & Schiller. In mid August for one weekend, from noon to 5pm. View some of Chicago's finest restored mansions (a fee is charged for tours of the interiors). There's also food, entertainment, arts and crafts, garage sales. Call 342-1966 for information. FREE.

Annual Chicago Jazz Festival
Grant Park, Petrillo Music Shell. Held during the week prior to Labor Day, a seven-night jazz marathon from 6:30 to 10:30pm. It's the world's largest free jazz festival—features most of the greats from traditional and swing to bebop, blues, and avant-garde. Call 294-2420 for information.

Venetian Night
Along Monroe Harbor, from Navy Pier to the Planetarium. Late August for one evening, at dusk, a grand annual tradition: fireworks, the Grant Park Symphony, and the parade of animated floats and illuminated yachts. A stunning spectacle. Call 744-3370 for information. FREE.

Arlington Million Week
At the end of August, a week-long equine festival consisting of 14 major events, sponsored by a variety of groups, held in and around Chicago. Included are an international polo tourney, speed jumping derby, $500,000 steeplechase competition, equine parade down Michigan Avenue, horse show, Ambassador's Ball, and thoroughbred race at Arlington Park Race Track for the world's richest purse: $1 million. Call 255-4300 for specific dates and times.

September

—Labor Day Weekend

Frankfort Fall Festival
Frankfort, Illinois (45 minutes from Chicago). (1-815) 469-3356. Labor Day weekend for three days, this entire town closes to traffic and instead fills up with arts-and-crafts booths and beer tents; corn roasts and a carnival. Tour the town in a horse-drawn carriage for a nominal fee. Sunday parade: horses, antique cars, fire engines, and lots more. FREE.

Golden Arts
Museum of Science and Industry, 57th & South Lake Shore Drive. 684-1414. In early September, arts and handicrafts by Chicago's senior citizens. FREE.

Fine Arts & Selected Crafts Fair
Plaza of the Americas, 430 North Michigan. Held mid September for two days, Thursday and Friday from 8am to dusk. Local and midwestern artists and craftspeople display and sell their works. Call 895-3710 for information. FREE.

Mostly Music Lunchtime Concerts
First Chicago Center, Dearborn & Monroe, plaza level. From September through mid December for ten weeks. Classical chamber music concerts Tuesday from 12:15 to 1pm. Admission charge.

Alley Walk
Two blocks west of Kimball; entrance to the alley is at 5300 North Berwyn. Held every other year on the last weekend in September, Saturday from 10am to 4pm. Antiques, food, entertainment, and little white elephants. Call 463-0055 for information.

October

New theater season begins.

Fall House Walk
Old Town Triangle Association, 1016 North Wells. 337-1938. In early October for one Sunday afternoon. A guided tour through eight homes: four modern and four renovated Victorian gems. Admission fee.

Amlings Haunted House
8900 West North Avenue, Melrose Park. 344-0770. For the whole month of October, a traditional Halloween "treat." Outdoor carnival too. *OPEN 7 days 4-9pm; longer hours as Halloween gets closer.* Admission charge.

Annual Pullman House Tour
Historic Pullman Center, 614 East 113th. Second weekend in October, Saturday and Sunday from 11am to 5pm. The Historic Pullman Community's annual fall tour; includes homes and historic buildings. Refreshments are available. Admission charge. Call 785-8181 or 660-1276 for information.

Chicago International Film Festival
Usually in mid November for two weeks. Exciting new international films, directors, and stars.

Screenings at theaters throughout the city. Call Cinema/Chicago at 644-3400 for information. Admission charge. Hot line: 644-5454.

Brookfield Children's Zoo
Halloween party, on or near October 31 from 11am to 3pm. Kids are invited to wear their costumes to be judged in a contest. Old-fashioned events like bobbing for apples and a treasure hunt. All activities divided by age group. Animals out on walkways with keepers. Zoo admission charge, but children's zoo is free for the day. Call 242-2630 for information.

Annual Poetry Day
Late October or early November, a one-day celebration of English and American poets. Held at various places in the city. Call 413-2210 for information. Admission charge.

November

Chrysanthemum Show
Lincoln Park Conservatory, 2400 North Stockton Drive; 294-4770. And Garfield Park Conservatory, 300 North Central Park Boulevard; 533-1281. First weekend in November till the end of November. Mums is definitely the word. OPEN Sat-Thurs 10am-6pm; Fri 9am-9pm. FREE.

Virginia Slims Championships of Chicago
Mid November for seven days. America's best women tennis players compete for a hefty purse. Call 782-6553 for dates and location. Admission charge.

International Folk Festival
McCormick Place West, Donnelly Hall, 411 East 23rd. In mid November, on Saturday and Sunday from 11am to 7pm. Longtime annual festival celebrating Chicago's ethnic communities and traditions. Over 100 countries are represented. Continuous entertainment with audience participation encouraged. Ethnic food, music, boutiques, and cultural exhibits. Admission charge; seniors, children under age 12, and any folks arriving in ethnic dress are admitted FREE. Call 744-3370 or 744-3315 for information.

Ringling Brothers/Barnum & Bailey Circus
Chicago Stadium, 1800 West Madison. 733-6300. In mid November, for two weeks, the legendary circus comes to town. For children of all ages. Tickets may be purchased in advance.

Art for Young Collectors Sale
The Renaissance Society, Goodspeed Hall, 1010 East 59th. 962-8670. Third week in November for three weeks. Drawings, prints, paintings, sculpture for sale for $10 to $1,000. Proceeds help support the gallery. FREE.

The Annual Latke-Hamantash Symposium
Cloister Club, Ida Noyes Hall, 1212 East 59th. The Tuesday before Thanksgiving at 7:30pm. "Learned" University of Chicago scholars debate the relative merits of the potato pancake (latke) versus the prune or poppy-seed Danish (hamantash). Earth-shaking. Call 752-1127 for information. FREE.

Christmas Festival on the Mall
State between Randolph & Van Buren. From the Thursday before Thanksgiving till January 1. The shopping season on the shopping street. Ethnic Christmas trees and the animated store window displays are fabulous. Stores have special indoor events as well. Call 782-9160 for information. FREE.

A Christmas Carol
Goodman Theater, Main Stage, 200 South Columbus Drive. 443-3800. From late November to early January. A lavish production of the Dickens classic.

Ice Follies & Holiday on Ice
Chicago Stadium, 1800 West Madison. 733-5300. Late November to early December for two weeks. A colorful fantasy on ice. Tickets may be purchased in advance.

Holiday Season Chicago
Third week in November till January 2. Thousands of little lights adorn the already Magnificent Mile. State Street is aglow, and on that great street a parade heralds the arrival of Santa on the Sunday following Thanksgiving, at 1pm. Call 782-9160 for information.

Christmas Around the World Festival
Museum of Science and Industry, 57th & South Lake Shore Drive. 684-1414. From late November till January 4—approximately six weeks. A display of thirty-four 18-foot-tall trees and Nativity displays from as many countries give Christmas in Chicago an international flavor. Ethnic concerts and performances as well as an international buffet and brunch offering for sale such goodies as Swedish meatballs and Hungarian chicken make this a yuletide tradition worth savoring. FREE.

American Indian Pow-Pow
Last weekend in November from Friday to Sunday. Various American and Canadian Indian tribes present ceremonial rituals and dances. Sponsored by the American Indian Center, 1630 West Wilson, 275-5871. Call for exact location and date. Admission charge.

December

See the November listings for ongoing holiday events.

Cultural Center Christmas Program
Chicago Public Library Cultural Center, 78 East Washington. 346-3278. All of December till January 6. Ethnic Christmas traditions—Hanukkah too—through crafts demonstrations, theater productions, exhibits, films, music, dance concert. For adults and children. Call for information or pick up a program. FREE.

Daley Plaza Tree
From early December to early January. A giant tree on display in the southwest corner of Daley Plaza.

Marshall Field's
State Street. 781-4555. In the Randolph Street

light court, the perfect setting for a tradition: a huge, beautifully decorated Christmas tree.

Evanston Art Center Holiday Market
2603 Sheridan Road, Evanston. 475-5300. Handmade quilts, gingerbread houses, herb wreaths, other arts, crafts, and imports.

Martin D'Arcy Christmas Tree
6525 North Sheridan Road. 274-3000, ext 2679. From the beginning of December till December 25. A magnificent, ceiling-high tree decorated with 1,100 lights and 800 intricately handcrafted ornaments. Christmas music and the setting make this a special holiday treat as well as a respite from the bustle. *OPEN 7 days noon-4pm; in addition Tues-Thurs 6:30-9pm.* FREE.

Holiday Festival
Chicago Horticultural Society, Lake Cook Road, Glencoe. 835-5440. From early December to early January. Christmas trees decorated by various area garden clubs. An unusual display. FREE.

Adler Planetarium
1300 South Lake Shore Drive. 322-0300 (recording). From early December to early January, a Christmas-season tradition: "Star of Wonder" Sky Show. The sky over Bethlehem at the time of Christ's birth—the traditional and scientific views. Admission charge.

Nutcracker Ballet
Arie Crown Theater, McCormick Place, 23rd & the Lake. 791-6000. Mid December for two weeks (not Christmas or New Year's Day). Tchaikovsky's Christmas gift to us all. Tickets may be purchased in advance.

Do-It-Yourself Messiah
Orchestra Hall, 220 South Michigan. In mid December for two evenings at 8pm. Professional soloists and directors lead an enthusiastic chorus of amateurs in Handel's *Messiah.* For details and ticket information call Talman Federal Savings, the sponsor, at 434-3322, Communications Department. Hallelujah! FREE. NOTE: Usually broadcast on WFMT-FM, 98.7.

Chicago Bank of Commerce Carolers
Chicago Bank of Commerce lobby in the Standard Oil Building, 200 East Randolph. 861-1000. For two weeks before Christmas, school choirs perform in the lobby daily from 11am to noon. FREE.

Chicago Children's Choir Christmas Concert
One weekend in mid December, Saturday at 8pm and Sunday at 3pm. Angelic voices celebrate the season. Concerts are held in the Hyde Park area. Call 324-8300 for information. Admission charge; lower for children, students, and senior citizens.

Christmas Flower Show
Lincoln Park Conservatory, 2400 North Stockton Drive; 294-4770. And Garfield Park Conservatory, 300 North Central Park Boulevard; 533-1281. From the weekend before Christmas to the first week in January. Nature's contribution to the holiday season. *OPEN Sat-Thurs 10am-6pm; Fri 9am-9pm.* FREE.

Brookfield Zoo
First Avenue & 31st Street, Brookfield. 242-2630. The Saturday before Christmas from 11am to 3pm. Santa Claus arrives at the Safari Lodge and then at the Children's Zoo. Kids get stocking stuffers. Bring good-condition used toys for Toys for Tots, or contributions of food for the birds. Zoo admission charge; Children's Zoo FREE for the day.

Caroling to the Animals
Lincoln Park Zoo, 2200 North Cannon Drive. On the Sunday afternoon before Christmas, at 3pm, Santa arrives at the Sea Lion Pool and leads the carolers to the zoo mall. Entertainment, cocoa and cookies for the kids. Call 294-2492 for information. FREE.

A Victorian Christmas
Aurora Historical Museum, Oak & Cedar streets, Aurora (45 minutes from Chicago). 897-9029. The Sunday before Christmas; if that day is Christmas Eve, it's the preceding Sunday. The museum, a Victorian mansion, takes you back to Christmas in Victorian times, featuring an elaborately decorated tree. History-of-Christmas theme is made cheerier with the sale of Victorian-style homemade breads and cakes. FREE.

New Year's Eve
State & Randolph. December 31, from 11pm to 12:30am. A giant New Year's Eve bash on the Mall. With music, dancing, street vendors, cider, and roasting chestnuts. Fireworks at midnight. A footrace down State Street as well. Call 871-6557 for information.

HISTORIC
&
NEW
CHICAGO

Glessner House

HISTORIC BUILDINGS & AREAS

Arthur Aldis House
1258 North Lake Shore Drive. (Holabird & Roche, 1906.) This three-story town house is a Venetian Gothic charmer.

Alta Vista Terrace
1054 West between Byron & Grace. (Attributed to J. C. Brompton, 1900-4.) A unique and charming oasis out of time and space, also known as "the street of 40 doors." Real-estate developer Samuel Eberly "low down payment, low monthly installments" Gross is responsible. He re-created this English row with a variety of architectural façades including Georgian, Gothic, Palladian, Ionic, and Doric—20 in all, each facing its twin on the opposite side of the street.

American Furniture Mart
666 North Lake Shore Drive. (N. Max Dunning, 1923-26.) When built, this massive 16-story structure was the *largest* building in the world! Past home to furniture wholesalers, with an English Tudor exposition hall of baronial proportions. Now converted to residential/commercial/retail use.

Andersonville
North Clark at Foster. The beginning of Chicago's old Swedish community. Stop for a smorgasbord lunch.

Archbishop's Residence
1555 North State Parkway. (Alfred F. Pashley,

Alta Vista Terrace Doorways

1880.) This three-story Victorian mansion has been home to Chicago's Roman Catholic archbishop since 1880. Children have fun counting the chimneys (19 of them).

Art Institute of Chicago
Michigan at Adams. 443-3600. (Shepley, Rutan & Coolidge, 1892; McKinlock Court: Coolidge & Hodgdon, 1924; North Wing: Holabird & Root, 1956; Morton Wing: Shaw, Metz & Associates, 1962; East Wing: Skidmore, Owings & Merrill, 1976.) Flanked by Kemey's two lions, the original building is in the Classical-Renaissance style. Its purpose was to make art accessible and familiar to the people of the city. Its classes in art, and in more practical subjects like lithography, stained glass, and magazine illustration, were incredibly popular. Today its collections are world renowned. For hours, *see* MUSEUMS & GALLERIES, Museums: General Art Museums.

Arts Club of Chicago
109 East Ontario, 2nd floor. 787-3997. (Club interior done by Mies van der Rohe, 1955.) Private club open to the public during special exhibits. (*See* MUSEUMS & GALLERIES, Art Galleries.)

Astor Historic District
North Astor between East Division & East North Boulevard. Everyone's idea of a grand street. Within the Gold Coast, named for early fur trader John Jacob Astor, a street of grand mansions, many in the most fashionable late-19th-century architectural styles. Charming and elegant still. (*See also* HISTORIC & NEW CHICAGO, Historic Buildings & Areas: Charnley House, Court of the Golden Hands, *and* The Gold Coast.)

Auditorium Building
430 South Michigan at Congress. 341-3623. (Adler & Sullivan, 1890.) This modified-Romanesque building was designed as a multipurpose ten-story office, hotel, and opera house—a novel idea when conceived in 1886. It was dedicated by President Benjamin Harrison and, though unfinished, was the site of the Republican party's national nominating convention in June 1888. When completed, its 17-story tower, then the highest in Chicago, was topped by a weather station and observatory. It was also, at 110,000 tons, the heaviest and most massive building in the world. The engineering problems faced and solved by Dankmar Adler reflected his brilliance. The lobby, with its mosaic floors, marbleized columns, and stenciled ceiling ornamentation, is testimony to Louis Sullivan's decorative-design genius. The building was purchased by Roosevelt University in 1946; restoration and remodeling proceed. An exhibit and model of the building is in the lobby. Lobby *OPEN Mon-Fri 7:30am-10:30pm; Sat & Sun 8:30am-5pm.* Group tours by appointment, call in advance. (*See also* Auditorium Theater.)

Auditorium Theater
70 East Congress Parkway. 922-4046. (Adler & Sullivan, 1889.) "Fifty years ahead of its time," declared Frank Lloyd Wright. A monument to the engineering skill of Dankmar Adler and the

design genius of Louis Sullivan. Famed for its excellent acoustics and unimpeded view from all 4,000 seats. The largest permanent theater in its day, it was equipped with hydraulic stage lifts and a unique air-conditioning system. The elliptical arches are strikingly dotted with carbon filament light bulbs. Its large stage has been graced by such luminaries as Caruso, Pavlova, Lillian Russell, Sarah Bernhardt, Isaac Stern, Pavarotti, and Baryshnikov. Group tours by appointment only; admission charge. Call for reservations. (*See also* Auditorium Building.)

Emil Bach House
7415 North Sheridan. (Frank Lloyd Wright, 1915.) One of the few Wright residences within the city limits. Small rectangular with strong horizontal lines. The windows demonstrate the classic Wright view of privacy.

Beverly
Longwood Drive (1850 West). This fine 100-year-old Far Southwest Side residential neighborhood is the largest listed in the National Register of Historic Places. English Manor, Carpenter Gothic, and Prairie School architecture are represented. (Combine with a visit to nearby Pullman Historic District.)

Biograph Theater
2433 North Lincoln. 348-1350. A colorful piece of Chicago history—where gangster John Dillinger was shot, July 22, 1934.

Bismarck Hotel
La Salle & Randolph. (Rapp & Rapp, 1926.) Early office building/theater/hotel complex (*see* HOTELS, Moderate).

Blackstone Library
4904 South Lake Park Avenue. 624-0511. (Solon S. Beman, 1904.) This Neoclassical stone and marble structure was the city's first branch library. Recently modernized, but its original design remains intact. Group tours by appointment only. *OPEN Mon-Thurs 9am-9pm; Fri & Sat 9am-5pm.*

Brewster Apartments
2800 North Pine Grove at Diversey. (R. H. Turnock, 1893; remodeled Meiko Hayano, 1972.) A nine-story, roughhewn granite apartment building with a rectangular central light court topped with skylight. Early use of steel-frame construction. See the lovely grillwork elevators and staircase in the lobby if you can. Recently, tastefully, updated to condos.

Bridgeport
Between Halsted & Lowe, 30th to 37th. The emerald-green aisle to the mayor's office had traditionally (since 1933) started here (*see* HISTORIC & NEW CHICAGO, Historic Buildings & Areas: Mayor Richard J. Daley Home). But within this South Side area live not only Irish but Croatians, Germans, Poles, Italians, Lithuanians, and Mexicans.

Buckingham Fountain
Grant Park at Congress Parkway. (Edward H. Bennett, Marcel Loyau, 1927.) Fashioned after Versailles' Latona Fountain, though it's twice as big—280 feet in diameter with a 1.5-million-

Carson Pirie Scott & Company Store

gallon capacity. Said to be the world's largest, with jets reaching 135 feet into the air, it's certainly one of the most beautiful. An interesting though unromantic footnote: Its operation is computer controlled. Fountain displays: May 30 through Labor Day, seven days from 11:30am to 9pm. Color displays: 9 to 10pm; on Grant Park concert nights till 10:30pm. From July to August 7 days 12:30 to 1pm.

Bughouse Square
Dearborn & Walton. Really Washington Square, it's Chicago's former corner of soapbox oratory à la London's Hyde Park.

Carson Pirie Scott & Company Store
1 South State at Madison. 744-2000. (Louis H. Sullivan, 1899, 1903-4; addition: Daniel H. Burnham & Co., 1906; addition: Holabird & Root, 1960.) At the "World's Busiest Corner," Sullivan's last major commission is graced with his stunning cast-iron ornamentation. Architecturally one of America's most highly regarded commercial structures. Extensions follow Sullivan's original plan. Lovingly restored and preserved. *OPEN Mon & Thurs 9:45am-7:30pm; Tues, Wed, Fri & Sat 9:45am-5:45pm. CLOSED Sun.* (*See also SHOPPING,* Large Stores.)

Century Shopping Center
2828 North Clark. 929-8100. Success story: aging, dark vaudeville, then movie, house regains new lease on life as lively skylit atrium shopping mall. Retained: the wonderful terra-cotta façade—spotlighted at night à la Hollywood premiere. Shoppers become spectators/performers whether ascending in elevators or descending on ramps. More relaxed and plebeian than Water

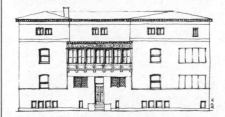

Charnley House

Tower Place. Note the whimsical neon sign of the adjacent parking garage. Mall *OPEN Mon-Fri 10:30am-9pm; Sat 10:30am-6pm; Sun noon-5pm.*

Charnley House
1325 North Astor. (Adler & Sullivan, Frank Lloyd Wright, 1892.) Located in the Astor Historic District, this three-story, 11-room private residence was built for James Charnley, lumber-dealer friend of architect Sullivan. A pre-Prairie Wright was the chief draftsman; Sullivanian embellishments are evident on the façade.

Chicago Board of Trade Building
141 West Jackson. (Holabird & Root, 1930.) Dominating La Salle Street's southern end is this 45-story, 526-foot-high skyscraper—a stunning example of richly decorated art deco architecture. The three-story lobby is a deco-delight not to be missed. The 23-story addition designed by Chicago architectural wunderkind Helmut Jahn is a glass echo of the stepped-back form of the original. Lobby *OPEN Mon-Fri 9am-5pm.* Visitors' Gallery *OPEN Mon-Fri 9:15am-2pm.* Reserve for groups of ten or more, 435-3721. No children under age 16 in bookings. (*See also* SIGHTSEEING, On Your Own.)

Chicago Fire Academy
558 West De Koven. (Loebl, Schlossman & Bennett, 1960.) Built, appropriately, on the site of Mrs. O'Leary's house and barn where, allegedly, that infamous cow kicked over that lantern that set the whole town ablaze (1871). In front of the building is a bronze flame by Egon Weiner. Tours are available (*see* SIGHTSEEING, On Your Own).

Chicago Portage
Harlem Avenue, south of 47th, in the Salt Creek Forest Preserve Division. This 87-mile portage route formed a land bridge between the St. Lawrence and Mississippi waterways when the Des Plaines River was too low. Now a National Historic Site.

Chicago Post Office
433 West Van Buren. 765-4352. (Graham, Anderson, Probst & White, 1932.) America's largest post office! Burnham's plan of 1909 envisioned a roadway running through the center of the post office; the space was left in 1932, and the Eisenhower Expressway was built in 1956. Not bad. For tours *see* SIGHTSEEING, On Your Own. *OPEN Mon-Fri 7am-5:30pm; Sat 8am-5:30pm.*

Chicago Public Library Cultural Center
78 East Washington at Michigan. 269-2900. (Shepley, Rutan & Coolidge, 1897; restored Holabird & Root, 1977.) The Chicago Public Library was established in 1872 to handle books sent from England to replace those destroyed by the Great Fire of 1871. After being housed in a water tank (*see* HISTORIC & NEW CHICAGO, Historic Buildings & Areas: The Rookery), in 1897 it acquired this home. Now a cultural center (the old Goldblatt's Department Store is the new headquarters of the Public Library), the elaborate Italian Renaissance palazzo-style interior features a stunning Tiffany stained-glass dome

(third floor), as well as wood wainscoting and marble and mosaic embellishments, including a white Carrara marble grand staircase. Soldiers Memorial Hall (second floor, north) displays Civil War mementos; there is a Fine Arts division, an exhibition hall, a theater, a children's library (*see* KIDS' CHICAGO, Libraries: Thomas Hughes Children's Library). Scene of exhibitions, civic events, free entertainment. *OPEN Mon-Thurs 9am-7pm; Fri 9am-6pm; Sat 9am-5pm. CLOSED Sun.* Free tours of the Cultural Center are conducted by the Friends of the Chicago Public Library every Thursday at 11am and 1pm. Begin at the fourth-floor Washington Street vestibule. For groups of ten or more (maximum 80 high school students or adults) call 269-2922 for reservations at least two weeks in advance.

Chicago River
Another Chicago engineering feat: The river's current was reversed in 1900 in order to better serve the city: it flows *from* Lake Michigan *to* the Mississippi. Not only does it run backward, but on March 17 each year it runs green! (*See* ANNUAL EVENTS, March: St. Patrick's Day.)

Chicago Sun-Times Building
401 North Wabash. (Naess & Murphy, 1957.) A modern newspaper printing plant facing the river. Cut through the lobby and view the plant through windows on your way. An elegant plaza runs along the river's edge. Tours available (*see* SIGHTSEEING, On Your Own).

Chicago Theater
175 North State at Lake. (C. W. and George Rapp, 1921.) Called the "world's wonder theater" when it originally opened in 1921, it was the first major movie palace to be built in a downtown area. Nearly claimed by the wrecker's ball in 1982, an energetic restoration and pres-

Chicago Theater

ervation plan has transformed the theater into a splendid performance center. Frank Sinatra headlined the reopening in 1986; big names, touring orchestras, and stage shows will play the 3,800-seat theater.

Chinatown
Cermack & Wentworth near 23rd. Covering a relatively small area, the South Side home of Chicago's Chinese-American community. Good restaurants. Oriental boutiques, pagoda telephone booths.

City Hall-County Building
121 North La Salle. (Holabird & Roche, 1907, 1911.) Huge twin Classical Revival edifices. Interior renovation.

Chicago News Bureau
35 East Wacker, Suite 792. 782-8100. Since it began, it has remained open 24 hours a day, 7 days a week, 365 days a year (366 in leap years)

Clarke House
1855 South Indiana. Dating from 1836, Chicago's oldest house (aka the Widow Clarke House) and only remaining example in Chicago of the Greek Revival-style residence architecture popular in the early 19th century. This is its third site; it was moved "to safety" just after the Fire, now it's back near its original site. Restored to be the focal point of the Prairie Avenue Historic District, it is now a museum with period furnishings. (See also HISTORIC & NEW CHICAGO, Historic Buildings & Areas: Prairie Avenue Historic District.)

Clark Street
Follow this street, which goes north through Swedish, Korean, Jewish, Indian, Irish, and German neighborhoods—now *that's* a taste of Chicago.

Coleman House
1811 South Prairie. (Cobb & Frost, 1886.) Romanesque Revival built for hardware scion Joseph Coleman. Part of Prairie Avenue Historic District.

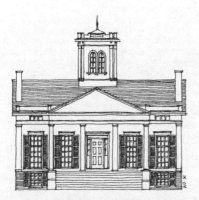

Clarke House

Detail, Court of the Golden Hands

Continental Illinois National Bank & Trust Company
231 South La Salle. (Graham, Anderson, Probst & White, 1924.) When all the mergers are traced back, this is Chicago's oldest bank. The interior: Neoclassical design on a grand and glorious scale.

Court of the Golden Hands
1349-53 Astor. The entranceway to the courtyard of this apartment complex is embellished with ornamental golden hands, each holding an apple. (See also HISTORIC & NEW CHICAGO, Historic Buildings & Areas: Astor Historic District *and* The Gold Coast.)

Cow Path in the Loop
100 West Monroe. The path was reserved for farmer Willard Jones's cow to walk to water when the farmer sold his property (now in the Loop) in 1844. No longer used even though a 1938 City Council ordinance states that cattle *can* still be driven over Loop streets daily between 7am to 7pm.

Crilly Court
Eugenie near Wells. In the Old Town Triangle area. A private street of attractive row houses with lovely rear gardens, the result of one of the first attempts at urban renewal (post-WWII). (See also HISTORIC & NEW CHICAGO, Historic Buildings & Areas: Old Town Triangle.)

Mayor Richard J. Daley Home
3536 South Lowe. In the Bridgeport area, the brick bungalow residence of the late mayor. An unassuming little castle for a "kingmaker."

Dearborn Street Station
47 West Polk. (Cyrus L. W. Eidlitz, 1883-85.) Romanesque Revival-style train station. Being restored and recycled as a mixed-use mall.

Delaware Building
36 West Randolph at Dearborn. (Wheelock & Thomas, 1874.) Typical post-Fire Chicago com-

mercial building. The original skylit atrium lobby remains.

Francis J. Dewes House
503 West Wrightwood. (Adolph Cudell and Arthur Herez, 1896.) The lavish Baroque spare-no-expense quality reflects the old-world taste of wealthy brewery owner Dewes and his European architects. Note the egalitarian use of both male and female caryatids. Now the Swedish Engineers Society of Chicago headquarters.

East Lake Shore Drive
Michigan Avenue to 999 North Lake Shore Drive. A harmonious grouping of eight elegant buildings designed by Marshall and Fox, and Frigard and Knapp, erected between 1912 and 1929.

The El
What is 20 feet off the ground and moves at right angles as it loops around the city? Right—the Chicago elevated train system. One of the city's top amusements for daredevils.

Melissa Ann Elam House
4726 South Martin Luther King, Jr., Drive. (Harry L. Newhouse, 1903.) Commissioned by Simon Marks, clothing manufacturer. The Marx family—including sons Groucho, Harpo, Chico, and Zeppo—lived here until 1919. Bought in 1930 by Miss Elam for use as a Black women's residence. Now devoted to social and cultural functions.

Elbridge House
1900 South Prairie. Three-story mid-Victorian mansion. Part of the Prairie Avenue Historic District.

Elks National Memorial Building
2750 North Lake View. 477-2750, ext 213. (Egerton Swartout, 1926; Magazine Building: Holabird & Root, 1967.) Constructed as a memorial to Elks members who died in WWI. The central rotunda is 75 feet in diameter and 100 feet high. The two bronze elks are serene sentinels (by Laura Gardin Fraser). There are no formal tours but the public may have a look at the interior. *OPEN Mon-Fri 9-4pm.* FREE.

Federal Reserve Bank of Chicago
230 South La Salle. 322-5322. (Graham, Anderson, Probst & White, 1922; addition C. F. Murphy & Associates, 1960.) The Midwest's central bank. (*See also* SIGHTSEEING, On Your Own.)

Marshall Field's
111 North State. 781-1050. (Daniel H. Burnham & Co., 1893, 1902, 1906, 1907.) Enormous world-famous department store that occupies an entire city block. Founded by the man who revolutionized retailing with money-back guarantees and if-we-don't-have-it-we-will-order-it merchandising. The earliest part resembles a Renaissance palazzo. In the south rotunda of the State Street building: a light court with a Tiffany-glass mosaic dome. Note the ornate clocks on the exterior at State & Randolph and at State & Washington. They're 80 years old, weigh 7¾ tons each, and, best of all, they *work*! NOTE: Meetings "under the clock" for some reason always refer to the one at Washington. *OPEN Mon & Thurs 9:45am-7:30pm; Tues, Wed, Fri & Sat 9:45am-5:45pm.*

Fine Arts Building

CLOSED Sun except for special monthly sales. Check newspapers. (See also SHOPPING, Large Stores.)

Fine Arts Building
410 South Michigan. 939-0181. (Solon S. Beman, 1885.) Originally the Studebaker Building. Built to house the Studebaker carriage and wagon showroom (the reason for the large windows on the lower floors). In 1898 it was converted into artists' studios, craft shops, concert halls, and theaters, becoming an important performing-arts center. In the lobby entrance the motto "All passes—ART alone endures"; happily, so does this building.

Fisher Building
343 South Dearborn. (Daniel H. Burnham & Company, 1896.) Early, Gothic-inspired, 20-story steel-frame structure. Now an architectural landmark. Aquatic embellishment in honor of Mr. *Fisher* (get it?). Addition built in 1907.

Fort Dearborn Site
875 Michigan at Wacker. Bronze tablets indicate the site of the first non-Indian settlement in Chicago, 1803. Strategically positioned for Great Lakes traffic and portage to the Mississippi. Burned by the Indians in 1812; a second one was built in 1816.

Gage Building
18 South Michigan. (Holabird & Roche, Louis Sullivan, 1898.) Cited for design excellence; especially for Sullivan's contribution—the imaginative decorative façade.

Glessner House
1800 South Prairie. 326-1393. (Henry H. Richardson, 1887.) The sole remaining building in Chicago by famed Boston architect Richardson. Built for International Harvester Co. founder John J. Glessner. Simple and graceful despite its massive proportions and heavy masonry façade. The tiny windows on the street side and

the L-shaped construction, allowing a large private interior courtyard (onto which large windows faced), made the realistic best of city dwelling. Since 1966, owned by the Chicago School of Architecture Foundation; also houses the Chicago Chapter of the AIA. It was Chicago's first designated landmark. Tours *Tues-Sun noon-3pm on the hour.* Group tours by appointment. Admission charge; free for foundation members. (*See also* HISTORIC & NEW CHICAGO, Historic Buildings & Areas: Prairie Avenue Historic District.)

The Gold Coast
Lake Shore Drive from Oak (1000 North) on the south to North (1600 North). It wasn't this coast that was lined with gold—it was merely the pockets of its residents. Eclectic architecture with one thing in common: these Queen Anne, Tudor Revival, and Romanesque mansions, and the elegant apartment buildings of the 1920s, were home to the city's wealthy. Good perspective from the Oak Street Beach pedestrian walkway (via the pedestrian tunnel at Lake Shore & Michigan). (*See also* HISTORIC & NEW CHICAGO, Historic Buildings & Areas: Astor Historic District.)

Goose Island
At Chicago & Halsted. In the 1860s a landing point for Irish immigrants. Here they squatted with their cows and geese—hence the name. Site of Armours's grain elevator, tanneries, and now rail yards. Spawning ground for some of Chicago's toughest citizens. Nostalgia only.

Harris & Selwyn Theaters
180-190 North Dearborn. (Crane & Franzheim, 1923.) The white terra-cotta English Renaissance exterior remains though they were renovated in 1960 (Bertrand Goldberg & Associates). Another one the wrecker's ball will miss this time around with the North Loop development project.

Heald Square
East Wacker, one block west of Michigan. Named for the commandant of Fort Dearborn who had the misfortune to preside over the ill-fated evacuation that left half the settlers dead. Site of a Revolutionary War monument (*see* HISTORIC & NEW CHICAGO, Statues & Monuments: Heald Square Monument).

Heller House
5132 South Woodlawn. (Frank Lloyd Wright, 1897.) Part of the Kenwood Historic District. This private residence, built for Isidore H. Heller, is an early Wright with just hints of what was to come.

Ernest Hemingway Home
600 Kenilworth. Hemingway spent his childhood in this home, where his doctor father had his offices as well.

Hull House & Residents' Dining Hall
800 South Halsted at Polk. 996-2793. (Reconstruction: Raftery, Orr & Fairbank, 1967.) Originally the home of Charles J. Hull; in 1889 it became the famed settlement house of pioneer social worker Jane Addams. The majority of Hull House's 13 buildings were torn down in 1963 as part of the Near West Side's urban renewal.

Hull House

Now the reconstructed mansion and dining hall, containing many of the original furnishings, serve as a museum of Addams's life and work. The dining hall exhibits depict the immigrants (German, Irish, Greek, Bohemians, and Jews) who came to this port-of-entry neighborhood and used Hull House facilities. A part of the University of Illinois at Chicago. *OPEN Mon-Fri 10am-4pm; in summer Sun noon-5pm as well.* FREE.

Hutchinson Street District
West Hutchinson (4232 North) from North Maine Drive to Hazel. Residences designed mainly by George Maher, constructed between 1894 and 1913, reflect a variety of styles. A glimpse of residential architecture in transition.

Hyde Park
Borders the Lakefront from 51st to 59th west to Washington Park. This area contains the University of Chicago campus and to a certain extent vice versa. The work of the 19th and 20th centuries' major architects is well represented. (*See also* HISTORIC & NEW CHICAGO, Historic Buildings & Areas: Robie House.)

International House
1414 East 59th. (Holabird & Root, 1932.) Rockefeller-endowed social and cultural center for international students and staff at the University of Chicago. Founded in 1932.

Jackson Boulevard Bridge
700 West Jackson over the I-94 Dan Ryan Expressway. Beneath the bridge, the heaviest traffic flow in the country.

Jackson Boulevard Historic District
The 1500 West block between South Ashland & South Laflin. A remnant of the way they were. A tranquil enclave of 19th-century residential architecture in a variety of styles. Chicago's former most fashionable area, ca. 1870, where prominent Chicagoans, including five-time Mayor Carter Henry Harrison, lived. Renovation in progress. Designated a historic landmark in 1976.

Jeweler's Building
15-17 South Wabash. (Adler & Sullivan, 1882.) Small loft building is the oldest surviving design by this famed team.

Keith House
1871 South Prairie. Three-story brick house with

elegant interior detailing. Built for Edgar G. Keith, banker. Part of the Prairie Avenue Historic District.

Kemper Insurance Building
20 North Wacker at Madison. (Graham, Anderson, Probst & White, 1929.) This 45-story skyscraper was originally the Civic Opera House. The 3,500-seat auditorium is now home to the Lyric Opera of Chicago.

Kenwood Historic District
Boundaries: 47th, Blackstone, 51st & Drexel. A former wealthy suburb before being incorporated into the city of Chicago in 1889. Its residents could afford the time's best architects, including Howard Van Doren Shaw, George Maher, and Frank Lloyd Wright. Still an upper-middle-class area retaining an aura of elegance as well as a wonderful variety of impressive architectural styles.

Kimball House
1801 South Prairie. (Solon S. Beman, 1890.) Prairie Avenue's French château designed by the Pullman architect and built for *$1 million* for piano company head W. W. Kimball. Now owned by R. R. Donelley & Sons, printers. Part of the Prairie Avenue Historic District.

Krause Music Store
4611 North Lincoln. (William C. Presto, Louis H. Sullivan, 1922.) Terra-cotta façade was Sullivan's last commission; he died in 1924. Now the Aruntzen-Coleman Funeral Home.

Lake Shore Club
850 North Lake Shore Drive (Jarvis Hunt, 1929.) A remnant of another time.

Lakeview
Diversey to Irving Park, from the Lake to Ashland. Runs the gamut: rich, poor, ethnic—Mexican, Korean, German, Filipino, and Japanese. (Includes New Town.)

La Salle Street
From Jackson to Washington. This famed canyon is the Midwest's Wall Street. (*See also* HIS-

TORIC & NEW CHICAGO, Historic Buildings & Areas: Chicago Board of Trade.)

Lathrop House
120 East Bellevue. (McKim, Mead & White, 1892; remodeled Perkins & Will, 1972.) Chicago real-estate man Lathrop commissioned the famed New York architectural firm to design this elegant three-story Georgian Revival mansion. Now houses the Fortnightly of Chicago, a private women's club.

Leiter II Building
403 South State. (William Le Baron Jenney, 1891.) Exemplary of the Chicago School of Commercial Architecture. Former Sears Roebuck store, now being converted to commercial office space.

Lexington Hotel
2135 South Michigan. (Clinton J. Warren, 1892.) Early high-rise; steel-frame construction. Built to receive visitors to the World's Columbian Exposition of 1893. It played host to Al Capone, who set up headquarters here, from 1928 to 1932. (The live televised proceedings of the opening of his vault beneath the hotel was a bust—it was empty!) The building, now a landmark, is being restored for residential use.

Lincoln Tower Building
75 East Wacker. (Herbert H. Riddle, 1928.) Formerly the Mather Tower, this narrow 24-story commercial structure has the dubious distinction of offering the *least* amount of floor space per story of any ever built in Chicago.

Little Italy
This Near West Side area, heavily ethnic Italian, is undergoing a renaissance. Now that the wrecker's ball is stilled, this "new" West Side is drawing young professionals to where Alphonse Capone once lived. Taylor Street is main.

Logan Square
Boundaries: Diversey on the north, Fullerton on the south, Western on the east, Kostner on the west. A large-area Northwest Side neighborhood with up-and-down sides; undergoing rehabilitation. Historically a Polish area, but the Spanish-speaking population is on the increase. So, too, is the number of returning suburbanites.

The Loop
Van Buren to Lake, Wabash to Wells. The elevated transit system (el), with destinations north, south, and west, *loops* around this, the commercial heart of Chicago, with its business and shopping centers. Much is presently being done to breathe new life into the area, especially in the pm. (*See also* HISTORIC & NEW CHICAGO, Historic Buildings & Areas: State Street.)

Madison Park
Woodlawn to Dorchester, between Hyde Park & 50th. Through the iron gates, a three-block residential enclave within the Kenwood Historic District.

Madlener House
4 West Burton Place. (Richard E. Schmidt, 1902; interior remodeled Brenner, Danforth & Rockwell, 1963.) Chicago meets Prairie in this austere though elegant mansion, which boasts some

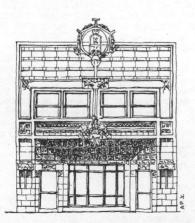

Krause Music Store

attractive decorative elements around the entrance. Present home of the Graham Foundation for Advanced Studies in the Fine Arts.

Magerstadt House
4930 South Greenwood. (George W. Maher, 1906.) In the Kenwood Historic District by a Wright-influenced contemporary. Nicely renovated in 1968.

Mandel Hall
Reynolds Club Building, University of Chicago, 5706 South University. 753-3568. (Shepley, Rutan & Coolidge, 1903.) Funded by Chicago merchant Leon Mandel. The exterior was patterned after the English Gothic manor house of Sir John Crosby. The auditorium provides seating for 1,000 for a variety of entertainment events.

Manhattan Building
431 South Dearborn. (William Le Baron Jenney, 1890.) An engineering feat: the first commercial building completely supported by a steel frame, and the first 16-story building in the world. Converted to residential use.

Marquette Building
140 South Dearborn. (Holabird & Roche, 1894.) Built around a central court for natural light, this 17-story building was typical Chicago School of Architecture: steel skeleton and wide windows. The bronze ornamental details are a Sullivan influence. Inside, the mezzanine balcony is graced by brilliant Tiffany glass mosaics depicting episodes from the life of Jesuit missionary and explorer Father Marquette. Worth a visit. Lobby OPEN Mon-Fri 9am-5pm.

Maxwell Street Market
Maxwell near Halsted. A colorful area, especially early on Sunday mornings, when a ragtag army of flea marketeers sets up shop outdoors (even in winter, with bonfires providing warmth) to sell anything from tires to diapers, to used refrigerators, to fruits and vegetables, to antiques and collectibles, to anything-but-plain-junk. Weather permitting, for added color there's live blues from 8am to 3:30pm at 14th & Halsted.

McCarthy Building
Dearborn & Washington. (John Mills van Osdel, 1872.) Italianate commercial building by Chicago's first practicing architect, who did this and the Page Brothers Building in the same year following the Great Fire.

McClurg Building
218 South Wabash. (Holabird & Roche, 1900.) A simple nine-story Chicago landmark. Its "Chicago window" treatment is the most striking architectural feature.

McCormick Row-House District
Between Belden & Fullerton, Halsted & the el. Developed in the 1880s by the McCormick Theological Seminary to house faculty. Now the 19th-century row houses, situated around a serene private park, Chalmers Place, are individually owned.

Medinah Shriners Temple
600 North Wabash. (Huehl & Schmid, 1912.) Large Moorish-style building houses auditorium, offices, and drill halls. Site of an annual circus presentation (see ANNUAL EVENTS, March: Shrine Circus).

Merchandise Mart
350 North Wells at the Chicago River. (Graham, Anderson, Probst & White, 1930.) "The store for storekeepers." With 4 million square feet housing 5,000 manufacturers, it's one of the world's largest wholesale market centers and the fifth largest commercial building in the world. Site of the twice-annual, very-well-attended housewares show. Owned by Boston's Kennedy clan. (See also SIGHTSEEING, On Your Own.)

Michigan Avenue
North of the Chicago River to Lake Shore Drive. The Magnificent Mile, aka "Boul Mich." Chicago's chief center of chic: boutiques, boîtes, galleries, restaurants. Even the McDonald's is tasteful (architecturally speaking).

Monadnock Building
53 West Jackson. (Burnham & Root, 1891; south side addition Holabird & Roche, 1893.) Sixteen stories, 197 feet. When built it was the world's tallest office building, and it is still the tallest wall-bearing structure. To support the weight, the base walls are 6 feet thick! The addition, built two years later, has a steel frame. The lack of ornamentation on the original—very un-Chicago School—is said to have come from the developer's insistence on simplicity and a desire to cheat pigeons out of a roosting place.

Museum of Science and Industry
South Lake Shore Drive at East 57th, in Jackson Park. 684-1414. (Charles B. Atwood, 1893; restored Graham, Anderson, Probst & White, 1929-40.) Typical of the Neoclassical style of architecture popular at the World's Columbian Exposition of 1893, where this structure housed the Palace of Fine Arts. Details of the edifice are copied from Athens's Parthenon and Erectheum. Since 1929, home of one of the world's best and best-loved museums (see MUSEUMS & GALLERIES, Museums: Science Museums).

Navy Pier
600 East Grand. 744-6450. (Charles Sumner Frost, 1916; restored Jerome R. Butler, Jr., 1976.) Part of Daniel H. Burnham's Chicago Plan of 1909. A 3,000-foot-long peninsula originally built to handle commercial maritime activities. Subsequently used by the navy in WWII, then became part of the University of Illinois. The pier provides a unique setting for special events, such as the Art Chicago (see ANNUAL EVENTS, May).

Newberry Library
60 West Walton. 943-9090. (Henry Ives Cobb, 1892; remodeled Harry Weese & Associates, 1968.) This research library, endowed by Walter Loomis Newberry, early Chicago businessman, has been called "an uncommon collection of uncommon collections," including Indian-language grammars; genealogical records; and rare bound and unbound manuscripts in the fields of literature, history, and music. Houses a

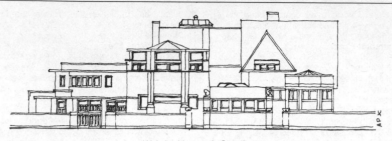

Wright Home & Studio

superb conservation department. Lectures, exhibitions, classes, musical events. Membership available. *OPEN Tues. Wed & Thurs 11am-7:30pm; Fri 11am-5pm; Sat 9am-5:30pm. CLOSED Sun & Mon. Tours Thurs at 3pm & Sat at 10:30am,* call (ext 310) for information.

New Town
Vicinity 2400 North to 3400 North on Clark and on Broadway. An area still in transition. Broadway's the main street, elegant residences grace the side streets.

Nickerson Mansion
40 East Erie. (Burling & Whitehouse, 1883.) Now owned by the College of Surgeons, this solid three-story mansion was built for financier Samuel M. Nickerson, founder of Chicago's First National Bank. Known as the "Marble Palace" in its time because of the lavish opulence of the interior: alabaster staircase, marble floors, onyx wall panels. When built it was valued at $450,000!

Oak Park
The square-mile Frank Lloyd Wright Historic District (just ten miles west of downtown Chicago) contains the largest collection of Wright buildings in the world: a concentration of 25 houses, including his own, designed by the famed architect and built between 1895 and 1915, providing a visual record of his evolvement of the Prairie style. Several of the buildings are open year-round, but the interior of all the houses may be viewed once a year only in May (*see* ANNUAL EVENTS, May: Wright Plus).

Oak Park Visitors' Center
158 Forest Avenue at Lake Street. 848-1978. The best place to start. Tour information, exhibits, 2½-hour guided tours (Saturday and Sunday only, at 1:45pm) or recorded self-tours (7 days). *OPEN Mar 1-Nov 30, 7 days 10am-5pm, otherwise see below.* Admission coupons available here for entry fees and tour.

Frank Lloyd Wright Home & Studio
951 Chicago Avenue at Forest Avenue. (Frank Lloyd Wright, 1889-1911.) Designed for his bride in 1889, when he was 22 years old. Wright remodeled it constantly while experimenting with his Prairie style of design. His successful practice demanded a new studio, which he built in 1898. Here he lived and worked for 20 prolific years during which he designed and built 120 buildings, including the noted Robie House, after which his place in the forefront of American architecture was assured. A *must* visit! Guided tours: *Mon-Fri 11am, 1pm & 3pm; Sat & Sun 11am-4pm continuous.* Admission charge. Also here, the Ginkgo Tree Book Shop (848-1606), *OPEN Mon-Sat 10am-5pm; Sun 1-5pm.*

Unity Temple
875 Lake Street at Kenilworth Avenue. (Frank Lloyd Wright, 1905.) This Unitarian-Universalist church is Oak Park's only public Wright. Built in cubic form with natural light entering through skylights and windows under the eaves, and with a pulpit surrounded by seats on three sides, it was truly a revolu-

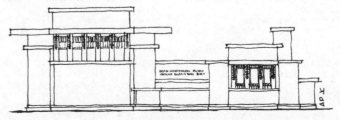

Unity Temple

tionary masterpiece. (Interior and exterior renovation.) *OPEN year-round, self-guided tours Mon-Fri 2-4pm; Sat & Sun a guided tour at 2pm.* Admission charge. Discount for students under age 18 and senior citizens. Children under age 10 FREE. Check at the Visitors' Center, 158 North Forest, for combination admission.

Also the following Wright-designed Oak Park houses:

Harry S. Adams House
710 Augusta Boulevard. (1913.)
O. B. Balch House
611 North Kenilworth. (1911.)
P. A. Beachy House
238 Forest. (1906.)
Edward H. Cheney House
520 North East Avenue. (1904.)
Dr. W. H. Copeland House
400 Forest. (Remodeled 1909.)
E. Arthur Davenport House
559 Ashland. (1901.)
William G. Fricke House
540 Fair Oaks. (1902; remodeled 1907.)
George Furbeck House
223 North Euclid. (1897.)
Rollen Furbeck House
515 Fair Oaks. (1898.)
Mrs. Thomas H. Gale House
6 Elizabeth Court. (1909; renovated 1962.)
Thomas H. Gale House
1019 Chicago Avenue. (1892.)
Walter Gale House
1031 Chicago Avenue. (1892.)
H. C. Goodrich House
534 North East Avenue. (1896.)
Arthur Heurtley House
318 Forest. (1902.)
E. R. Hills House
313 Forest. (Remodeled 1902.)
W. E. Martin House
636 North East Avenue. (1903.)
Nathan G. Moore House & Stable
333 Forest. (1895; rebuilt 1924.)
R. P. Parker House
1027 Chicago Avenue. (1892.)
Charles E. Roberts Stable
317 North Euclid. (1896.)
Isabel Roberts House
562 Keystone. (1909.)
George W. Smith House
404 Home. (1898.)
Frank Thomas House
210 Forest. (1901.)
Chauncey L. Williams House
530 Edgewood Place. (1895.)
Francis Wooley House
1030 Superior. (1893.)
H. P. Young House
334 North Kenilworth. (1895.)
Off Center Shopping
300 West Grand. A vertical discount-shopping center housed in the former Red Cross spaghetti factory, which now sports a high-impact Richard Haas *trompe l'oeil* mural (*see also* HISTORIC &

NEW CHICAGO, Outdoor Artwork & Sculpture: La Salle Towers)—this one affording "X-ray vision." *OPEN Mon-Fri 10am-6pm; Sat till 5pm; Sun 11am-5pm.*
Old Colony Building
407 South Dearborn. (Holabird & Roche, 1894.) Very much a product of the Chicago School of early commercial architecture. Seventeen stories (210 feet) with distinctive bays and, to the delight of engineers, a portal bracing system for flexibility and strength.
Old Greek Town
Vicinity: South Halsted at Jackson. A popular area within *Opaa!*-shouting distance of the Loop for belly dancing, bouzouki, and baklava. For where to eat in this area, *see* RESTAURANTS, Greek.
Old Town
Wells from 1200 to 1700 North. The heart of Old Town is a half mile area for very casual dining and shopping. The section has seen several heydays in its time: from 1950s "bohemian" to 1960s psychedelic sideshow. Home of the famed Second City Improvisation troupe (*see* ENTERTAINMENT, Theaters).
Old Town Triangle
North Avenue, Lincoln Park, Ogden Avenue extension north to Armitage. The homogeneous quality of this charming neighborhood historic district is the result of a highly successful urban-renewal project in the 1940s. Among some 500 residences of interest, it contains some lovely Victorian homes, Sullivan row houses (1826-34 North Lincoln Park West—1885), and "Chicago cottages" with wooden balloon frames (developed in 1874 following the Fire).
Orchestra Hall Building
220 South Michigan. 435-8122. (D. H. Burnham & Co., 1905; restored Harry Weese, 1969.) This fine hall has been home to the world-renowned Chicago Symphony Orchestra since 1898. The entrance design contains the names of Bach, Mozart, Beethoven, Schumann, and Wagner. Soon to be remodeled once again—the fourth time in its 82-year history.
Paderewski House
2138 West Pierce. In the old Wicker Park area. Acquired its name because in the 1930s the famed Polish pianist played a concert on the front porch of this house, which was, at the time, the Polish Consulate in Chicago. (*See also* HISTORIC & NEW CHICAGO, Historic Buildings & Areas: Wicker Park.)
Page Brothers Building
State at Lake Street. (John Mills van Osdel, 1872.) By Chicago's first architect, this last surviving cast-iron façade in the city *just* squeaked past the wrecker's ball in the debate over what goes and stays in the North Loop development project. Listed in the National Register of Historic Places.
Patterson House
20 East Burton Place. (Stanford White, 1900; David Adler, 1927.) Part of the Astor Historic District, this large mansion was designed by the

famed New York architect for socialite Mrs. Robert W. Patterson. Elegant interior included winding staircases and marble bathrooms. Lovely exterior wrought-iron gate.

Pilsen
Ashland & 18th. In the Near Southwest Side, once a firmly entrenched Czech community. Now home to newer comers, the Mexican Americans. 18th is the neighborhood's main street.

Policeman Bellinger's Cottage
2121 Hudson. (William W. Boyington, pre-1871.) One of the few Lincoln Park-area structures to survive the Fire. The plaque reads: "This is Policeman Bellinger's Cottage, saved by heroic effort from Chicago Fire of October 1871."

Pontiac Building
542 South Dearborn. (Holabird & Roche, 1891.) Chicago's oldest surviving building by this famed pair of architects.

Prairie Avenue Historic District
South Prairie between 18th & 20th. The leading businessmen of the day—among them Pullman, Armour, Glessner, and Field—all dwelled here in houses designed by the leading architects of the day. Though much is gone, this, the city's most fashionable area ca. 1870s-90s, is being restored to its former 19th-century self as "a museum of urban change," with cobblestoned streets, period lampposts, and five restored period houses, including the city's oldest (*see* HISTORIC & NEW CHICAGO, Historic Buildings & Areas: Clarke House). A park will have architectural ornamentations from lost (to the wrecker's ball) Chicago buildings.

Printing House Row
South Dearborn between Polk & Congress Parkway. In the late 1880s the printing industry congregated in this area, nearest the railroad tracks. The commercial factories and warehouses are now being converted to residences, shops, and galleries while attempts are being made to maintain the buildings' external character. (*See also* HISTORIC & NEW CHICAGO, Historic Buildings & Areas: Transportation Building.)

Pullman Historic District
Boundaries: 103rd on the north, 115th on the south, Cottage Grove on the west & the Calumet Expressway on the east. (Solon S. Beman; land-

scape architect Nathan Barrett; 1880-94.) The far South Side town of Pullman, the country's first completely self-sufficient planned company town, was built in 1880 by George Pullman to provide housing for the 6,000 employees of the Pullman Palace Car Co., manufacturer of railway sleeping cars. In 1894 the experiment fell apart when a bitter strike resulted from wages being lowered while rents stayed the same (Jane Addams labeled Pullman "a modern King Lear"). Because the Illinois Central was disrupted, President Cleveland sent 14,000 federal troops to end the strike. The workers lost that round, but soon afterward a court ruling forced the town's sale to its people. More than 1,500 of the original 1,800 buildings remain. Almost 600 buildings, including brick row houses and manufacturing buildings, are being lovingly restored. *OPEN Tues-Fri 11am-2pm; Sun 10am-3pm.* Guided walking tours—first Sunday each month, from May to October, at 12:30 and 1:30pm—provide the only access to Greenstone Church. Start from Historic Pullman Center, 614 East 113th. 785-8181.

Hotel Florence
Pullman Historic District, 11111 South Forrestville. 785-8181. Contrary to the norm, George Pullman erected the best buildings *in front of* the Illinois Central railroad tracks. The centerpiece of his town was his four-story, 70-room hotel, which he named for his favorite daughter and where he maintained a suite for his own use. The ornate Queen Anne structure provided elaborately decorated accommodations for Pullman's wealthy friends; among its guests, Diamond Jim Brady and Lillian Russell. The hotel bar, the only one in Pullman, was for guests only. Being restored by the Historic Pullman Foundation, the restaurant and bar are now serving once again. Within several years the hotel will be in full operation offering 32 guest rooms with period furnishings and turn-of-the-century gracious service (*see* RESTAURANTS, Breakfast/Brunch: Hotel Florence).

Pullman Stables
East 112th & South Cottage Grove. These stables held the horses of all residents and

Hotel Florence

visitors. People could rent a horse and buggy here for $3 a day. Now a gas station/auto repair shop. Note the horse-head carvings above the entrance.

Greenstone Church (Pullman United Methodist Church)
Pullman Historic District, East 112th & South St. Lawrence. Dedicated in 1882. Its name derived from the green-colored New England crystalline-stone façade. The lovely stained-glass window has been restored, as have the steeple, the roof, and the organ. *OPEN to the public May-Oct only, first Sun of each month.*

Market Hall Colonnade
East 112th & South Champlain. These "circle buildings," which retain the original Romanesque façade, were built to house visiting European businessmen during the Chicago World's Columbian Exposition, 1893. Now an apartment building.

Reid, Murdoch & Company Building
320 North Clark. (George C. Nimmons, 1914.) This industrial building is an example of the early steel-frame construction characteristic of the Chicago School of architecture. Handsome clock tower and nice black-and-terra-cotta detail. Now the Central Office Building, City of Chicago. Houses the Traffic Court and the Commission on Chicago Landmarks.

Reliance Building
32 North State. (Charles Atwood, Daniel H. Burnham & Company, 1894-95.) A State Street jewel and landmark. Fifteen floors of white terra-cotta and lots of glass; forerunner of today's skyscrapers. Building of it began before the upper stories of the former structure on the site were completely vacated. Undaunted, the builders simply built a new ground level, and three years later the rest of the old building was demolished and replaced.

River Forest
(*See also* HISTORIC & NEW CHICAGO, Historic Buildings & Areas: Oak Park.)

River Forest Tennis Club
615 Lathrop Avenue, River Forest. (Frank Lloyd Wright, 1906.) Exterior: stained wood board and battened sheathing.

William H. Winslow House & Stable
515 Auvergne Place, River Forest. (Frank Lloyd Wright, 1893.) Roman brick and stone with terra-cotta trim. Wrightisms abound.

River North
La Salle Street (now La Salle Drive) from West Chicago Avenue to West Kinzie. Most often re-

Reliance Building

ferred to as Chicago's version of New York's SoHo—indicative of the number of artist-run or -owned galleries and collectives now occupying former warehouses and factory spaces. Boutiques and trendy exterior have followed. Go west and see for yourself.

Riverside Plaza Building
2 North Riverside Plaza. (Holabird & Root, 1928.) Early skyscraper, originally the *Chicago Daily News* Building.

Robie House
5757 South Woodlawn at 58th. (Frank Lloyd Wright, 1909.) In Hyde Park, this National Historic Landmark has been called "one of the most significant buildings in the history of architecture." It is Wright's renowned classic of the Prairie School, with its midwestern Prairie-inspired horizontal lines. Built for bicycle manufacturer

Market Hall Colonnade

Winslow House

Robie House

Robie, the master himself pronounced it his best residence. Restored in the 1960s, now part of the University of Chicago. Tours *Mon-Sat beinning at noon.* Groups by appointment only, call 753-4429. FREE. (*See also* HISTORIC & NEW CHICAGO, Historic Buildings & Areas: Oak Park.)

Robert W. Roloson Houses
3213-19 South Calumet. (Frank Lloyd Wright, 1894.) This early Wright commission pairs Tudor Revival-style houses around central courts; main stairwells capped by skylights.

The Rookery
209 South La Salle. (Burnham & Root, 1886.) Following the 1871 Fire, this was the site of a temporary city hall much favored by pigeons—hence the name Rookery, which was humorously adopted for this massive building, a distinguished progenitor of the modern skyscraper. The graceful lobby ornamentation and large (formerly) skylit central court, remodeled by Frank Lloyd Wright in 1905, are definitely worth a look. *OPEN Mon-Fri 8am-5:30pm.*

Rush Street
From Pearson north to Division. The former cow path, named for a signer of the Declaration of Independence (Dr. Benjamin Rush). Apt for a street where independence is pursued with a vengeance. Much Chicago nightlife is concentrated in this four-block strip: bars, movies, clubs, cabarets, and other diversions are available till the wee hours.

Carl Sandburg Mural
U.S. Post Office, 4850 North Broadway. 561-8916. (Henry Varnum Poor, 1943.) WPA ceramic tile mural, 10½ feet by 7½ feet. "From the sun and the fruits of the black soil poetry and song spring." *OPEN Mon-Fri 8:30am-5pm; Sat 8:30am-1pm.*

Soldier Field
425 East McFetridge. 294-2200. (Holabird & Root, 1924.) Designed to complement the nearby Field Museum, it was originally constructed as a war memorial with a capacity of 106,000. The north end permitted a view of the museum until closed up in 1935. Now home to the Chicago Bears football team.

South Chicago
Centered around Commercial (3000 East). A steel-mill workingmen's area, this strong, former Slavic enclave has given way to the Spanish accent of Mexican-American residents.

South Water Market
14th & Racine. Chicago's colorful produce market bustles early in the am.

Standard Club
321 South Dearborn. (Albert Kahn, 1926.) Italian Renaissance-style ten-story private club.

State Street
From Randolph to Congress Parkway. As the song says, "That Great Street," especially if you like to shop. It boasts the highest concentration of retail department stores in America. The recently created mall (when finished it will be the nation's largest) allows bus and pedestrian traffic only, plus entertainers and food vendors in summer.

Stock Exchange Archway
Rear of the Art Institute, Michigan, Monroe & Columbus Drive. Gone but not forgotten: Adler & Sullivan's Stock Exchange Building, erected in 1894 and demolished in 1972. The high-ceilinged trading room was reconstructed from salvage at the site and incorporated into the new (1978) east wing of the Art Institute of Chicago (*see* MUSEUMS & GALLERIES, Museums: General Art Museums.) The archway of the old building is the freestanding focal point in the garden in Grant Park at the rear of the museum. Recycling of sorts.

Streeterville
Includes the Magnificent Mile, Oak Street Beach, and East Lake Shore Drive. "Cap" George Wellington Street was a scoundrel and technically one of Chicago's first urban developers. On 180 acres of land, resulting from landfill surrounding his beached boat, and to which he claimed squatter's rights, he built a shantytown: Streeterville. Now probably the city's most valuable property, where Chicago's well-to-do live and romp.

The Rookery

Tin Pan Alley
64 West Randolph. At the turn of the century many of the top tunes, such as "My Blue Heaven" and "Let Me Call You Sweetheart," were from this Loop street.

Tower Building
6 North Michigan. (Richard E. Schmidt, 1899; addition Holabird & Roche, 1916.) Formerly the Montgomery Ward & Co. Building.

Transportation Building
600 South Dearborn. (Fred V. Prather, 1911; renovation Booth Hansen & Associates, 1981.) This large 22-story building, part of Printing House Row, formerly housed railroad offices. Now being turned into residential use in this up-and-coming South Loop area. (See also HISTORIC & NEW CHICAGO, Historic Buildings & Areas: Printing House Row.)

Tribune Tower
435 North Michigan. (Hood & Howells, 1925.) Trib owner Robert McCormick held an international competition in 1922 to select an architectural design for his building; Chicago's skyline was the winner. The Gothic edifice is impressive from any vantage point. John Ruskin quotation on lobby floor is apt.

Union League Club
65 West Jackson Boulevard. (Mundie & Jensen, 1926.) This 22-story private club still retains a separate ladies' entrance. (NOW, hear this!)

Union Station
210 South Canal. (Graham, Anderson, Probst & White, 1925.) Cavernous station recently renovated following a fire.

Union Stock Yard Gate
West Peoria & South Exchange. (Attributed to Burnham & Root, 1875.) Last remnant of the old (opened 1865, closed 1971) Chicago stockyards, the world's largest. "Sherman" the prizewinning steer gazes down on the ghost of an industry that once had 32,000 employees on 345 acres.

Unity Building
127 North Dearborn. (Clinton J. Warren, 1892.) Pisa has its tower, but Chicago has this 16-story building commissioned by Governor John Peter Altgeld. Famed for a tilt—2.82 feet—and a former tenant, Clarence Darrow. Listed in the National Register of Historic Places. Threatened with demolition.

Water Tower
800 North Michigan at Chicago Avenue. (W. W. Boyington, 1869.) Oscar Wilde notwithstanding (he called it a "monstrosity"), most people are charmed by this historic landmark built to camouflage a 138-foot standpipe. Across the street is the pump station, now headquarters for the Chicago Visitor Information Center. Though the tower's form is anachronistic in the city that gave birth to modern architecture, its spirit (the only public building to survive the Great Fire of 1871) is right on target. Symbolic of Chicago's motto, "I will."

Western Methodist Book Concern Building
12-14 West Washington. (Harry B. Whelock,

1899.) The first Chicago building to utilize a caisson system for support. The terra-cotta façade, though shabby, is still distinctive. Listed in the National Register of Historic Places. Now the Stop and Shop Warehouse, but not for long if developers have their way.

West Rogers Park
Devon from Western to Kedzie. Now the largest Jewish community within the city limits, claiming former residents of Albany Park, Humboldt Park, Lawndale, and, farther afield, the Soviet Union.

Wicker Park
Bounded by Augusta Boulevard and Armitage, Western & Ashland avenues. An inner-city neighborhood with a strong ethnic heritage and a fascinating architectural tradition. Following the Great Fire in 1871, German and Scandinavian immigrants—newly rich brewers, wine merchants, packers, and manufacturers—settled this area. The mid- to late-Victorian residence architecture, in a variety of styles—Queen Anne, Carpenter Gothic, Châteauesque—exhibits an exuberant bent toward the decorative, both internal and external: leaded, stained, and beveled glass; gazebos, gingerbread, and fretwork; turrets, bays, arches, and panels. At the turn of the century it became a Polish working-class area with Milwaukee its main street. Since the 1960s it's been drawing young professionals with an eye for bringing Chicago's past into the future.

Wrigley Building
400 North Michigan. (Graham, Anderson, Probst & White, 1921.) This white terra-cotta building with its graceful clock tower and Baroque ornamentation is a familiar Chicago landmark. The annex was built in 1924. Especially striking when floodlit at night.

Wrigley House
2466 Lake View. (Richard E. Schmidt, 1896.) Built for wealthy brewery president Joseph Theurer. Italian Renaissance style with Baroque-style terra-cotta ornamentation. The Wrigley chewing-gum family have owned it since 1919.

STATUES & MONUMENTS

The Alarm
Lincoln Park near 3000 North Lake Shore Drive. (John Boyle, 1884.) Dedicated by Chicago industrialist Martin Ryerson to the Ottawa Indians.

John Peter Altgeld
Lincoln Park near Lake Shore Drive. (Gutzon Borglum, 1915.) Bronze statue of the former governor of Illinois, here depicted as protector of the innocent.

Hans Christian Andersen
Lincoln Park near Armitage. (Johannes Gelert, 1896.) Famed Danish storyteller and his friend the former Ugly Duckling.

Arris
Amalgamated Trust Savings Bank, Congress &

Dearborn. (John Henry, 1975.) Elongated rectangular forms in bright-yellow-painted steel.

Balbo Column
Burnham Park, south of Soldier Field. An ancient marble column donated to the city of Chicago by the Italian government in 1933. Brought by air in sections in honor of the Century of Progress Exposition.

Brotherhood in Bronze
Amalgamated Meat Cutters and Butcher Workers Building, Diversey Parkway & Sheridan. (Egon Weiner, 1954.) Two groupings of kneeling figures, symbolic of unity among the peoples of Asia, Africa, Europe, and North America.

Robert Burns
Garfield Park near 3600 West Washington. (W. Grant Stevenson, 1906.) Famed Scottish poet in bronze.

Celebration of the 200th Anniversary of the Republic
In Grant Park at the Columbus Drive entrance to the School of the Art Institute. (Isamu Noguchi, 1976.) A water sculpture commemorating America's 200th birthday. "Water rises in the column and flows down its front, as water rises in trees and returns to earth again from the sky," is Noguchi's own description.

Ceres
Board of Trade Building, La Salle at Jackson Boulevard. (John Stoors, 1930.) Atop this 526-foot building, a 23-foot aluminum art deco Greek goddess of that all-important commodity—grain. At the time, Chicago's highest point.

Chicago
Façade of "Bird Cage" garage, 111 West Wacker. (Milton Horn, 1954.) The Mother of Chicago rising from Lake Michigan, with symbolic representations of the city as grain (the wheat sheafs), meat processing (the bull), and air (the eagle) center.

Chicago Fire Relic
Lincoln Park, entrance to the Chicago Historical Society. A piece of molten metal uncovered at State & Randolph following the Great Fire of 1871.

Christopher Columbus
Arrigo Park, Polk & Loomis. (Moses Ezekial, 1892.) Exhibited at the 1893 World's Columbian Exposition. It was cast in Rome, where it was blessed by the pope. Part of the façade of the Columbus Memorial Building at State and Washington until the building was demolished in 1959, it spent some years in storage until this home was found for the noble explorer.

Nicholas Copernicus
Adler Planetarium, west side. (Bertel Thorwaldsen and Bronislaw Koniuszy, 1973.) The noted Polish astronomer, erected to mark the 500th anniversary of his birth.

Defense & Regeneration
Michigan Avenue Bridge. Southwest corner: Defense, in memory of the Fort Dearborn Massacre. Southeast corner: Regeneration, to commemorate the Great Chicago Fire in 1871.

Diana & Statue of a Young Woman
Garfield Park Conservatory. These copies of sculptures from ancient Greece were unveiled in 1935.

The Discoverers & The Pioneers
Michigan Avenue Bridge. Limestone tributes. On the northeast pylon: to French explorers Jacques Marquette and Louis Joliet, whose expedition passed this spot in 1673, and to Sieur Robert Cavelier de La Salle, who in 1681 used the Chicago portage. On the northwest pylon: to first Chicago settler Jean-Baptiste Du Sable, a black Haitian trader.

Jean-Baptiste Pointe Du Sable
Entrance to Du Sable Museum, 740 East 56th Place. (Robert Jones, 1963.) Bronze tribute to Chicago's first permanent settler.

"Dream Lady"—The Eugene Field Memorial
Lincoln Park Zoo. (Edward McCarten, 1922.) Inspired by Eugene Field's *Fantasies of Childhood*. Children asleep in the land of Wynken, Blynken, and Nod, dreaming of the Sugar Plum Tree. With a caretaker of good dreams looking on.

Eagles
Grant Park on both sides of Congress. (Frederick C. Hibbard, 1931.) Former fountains seemingly poised for flight.

Leif Erikson
Humboldt Park, 1400 North block on Humboldt Drive. (Sigvald Asbjornsen, 1901.) The Viking explorer.

Father, Mother & Child
American Dental Association Building, 211 East Chicago Avenue. A simple yet striking freeze frame, in bronze.

Fountain of Time
Entrance to Washington Park. (Lorado Taft, 1922.) "Alas, time stays; we go." This poetic fountain depicts Time watching Man pass. (The sculptor included his own likeness in the processional.)

Benjamin Franklin
Lincoln Park, northeast of La Salle & Stockton. (Richard M. Parks, 1896.) American patriot and statesman.

Giuseppe Garibaldi
Lincoln Park, between Stockton & Lake Shore drives. (Victor Gherardi, 1901.) Atop a rugged boulder, the architect of Italy's unification.

Johann Wolfgang von Goethe
Lincoln Park at Diversey Parkway. (Herman Hahn, 1914.) Chicago's German community's unclad tribute to the "Genius" of famed poet, author, and countryman, Goethe.

Ulysses S. Grant
Lincoln Park near 1900 North Lake Shore Drive. (Louis T. Rebisso, 1891.) Grant on horseback. (In search of Grant Park?)

Alexander Hamilton
Lincoln Park near Diversey Parkway. (Samuel Marx, 1952.) Dramatic bronze-and-granite, limestone-and-slate tribute to the first U.S. secretary of the treasury.

Alexander Hamilton
Grant Park between Monroe & Madison. (Bela Lyons Pratt, 1918.) Cast bronze of the first U.S. secretary of the treasury.

Carter H. Harrison, Sr.
Union Park, 1501 West Randolph. (Frederick C. Hibbard, 1907.) Monument to the five-term mayor of Chicago—for stamina?

Heald Square Monument
East Wacker at Wabash. (Lorado Taft, dedicated 1941.) Bronze grouping of Washington with the principal financiers of the American Revolution. Completed after Taft's demise by his student Leonard Crunelle. Square named for ill-fated Fort Dearborn commander, Captain Nathan Heald.

Hebe
Grant Park near 1100 South Michigan. (Franz Machtl, 1893.) Chicago's "Fountain of Youth."

King & Queen
Lincoln Park, North Avenue Beach, Chess Pavilion. (Boris Gilbertson, 1957.) They stand in stony silence where the competition is at times keen.

Thaddeus Kosciuszko
West of Adler Planetarium, 1300 South Lake Shore Drive. (Alexander Chodinski, 1904.) Polish hero of the American Revolutionary War.

Robert Cavelier de La Salle
Lincoln Park near Clark & La Salle. (Count Jacques de La Laing, 1889.) Tribute to the famed explorer, who, as explorers are wont to do, gazes into the distance.

Abraham Lincoln
Grant Park, Congress Parkway between Michigan Avenue & Columbus Drive. (Augustus Saint-Gaudens, 1929.) Impressive seated Lincoln; the noted sculptor's last work.

Abraham Lincoln
Lincoln Park, North Avenue & Stockton. (Sculptor Augustus Saint-Gaudens; architect Stanford White; 1887.) Famed standing Lincoln. The face, done from a life mask, conveys dignity and grace.

Lincoln the Rail Splitter
Garfield Park, Washington & Central Park boulevards. (Charles J. Mulligan, 1911.) A young Lincoln in New Salem.

Lions
Entrance to the Art Institute of Chicago, Michigan & Adams. (Edward Kemeys, 1893.) These famed Chicagoans appeared first in plaster at the World's Columbian Exposition, 1893, then in bronze. One is defiant, the other on the prowl, so the tails tell.

General John A. Logan
Grant Park, 900 South Michigan. (Augustus Saint-Gaudens, 1897.) Noted sculptor's equestrian statue of Civil War general.

Logan Square
At 2600 North Milwaukee. Named for Civil War hero "Black Jack" Logan. The eagle-topped column by Evelyn Longman commemorates Illinois's 100th birthday.

William McKinley
McKinley Park, 38th & Western. (Charles J. Mulligan, 1905.) The 25th U.S. president.

Merchandise Mart Hall of Fame
Merchandise Mart, Wells & Orleans. Established in 1953. Bronze busts honor millionaire merchant princes: Marshall Field, Frank Woolworth, and Aaron Montgomery Ward.

Ludwig Mies van der Rohe
IBM Building lobby, between Wabash & State. (Marino Marin, 1972.) Bust of the director of architecture at the Illinois Institute of Technology from 1938 to 1968, during which time he left an indelible stamp on contemporary architecture. This was his final office-building design.

Richard J. Olgesby
Lincoln Park, south of Diversey Parkway. (Leonard Crunelle, 1919.) Former U.S. senator and three-time Illinois governor.

Putnam Chain
Chicago Historical Society, west entrance. American Revolutionary War artifact, 1773.

The Republic
Jackson Park, Richards Drive near 63rd. (Daniel Chester French, 1918.) Replica of monument from World's Columbian Exposition of 1893. Nicknamed "The Golden Lady."

Johann Christoph Friedrich Schiller
Lincoln Park Formal Garden, near Stockton & Webster. (Ernst Raus, 1886.) Famed German poet and dramatist.

Seated Woman
Belden Triangle Park, 401 West Belden. Limestone sculpture attributed to Lorado Taft and better known as "Lute Lady."

William Shakespeare
Lincoln Park near Belden. (William Ordway Partridge, 1894.) The desire to sit in the Bard's bronze lap is overwhelming.

General Philip Henry Sheridan
Lincoln Park, Sheridan near Belmont. (Gutzon Borglum, 1923.) Civil War general on horseback.

A Signal of Peace
Lincoln Park near Diversey Harbor. (Cyrus Dallin, 1894.) A handsome Indian equestrian statue.

The Spearman & the Bowman
Grant Park, Congress Plaza. (Ivan Mestrovic, 1928.) Seen by the sculptor as symbolic of the struggle to settle America. The bow and the spear are illusionary.

Spirit of Music
Grant Park, Columbus Drive at Congress Parkway. (Albin Polasek, 1924.) Dedicated to the Chicago Symphony Orchestra's first conductor, Theodore Thomas.

Spirit of the Great Lakes
Art Institute of Chicago, Michigan & Adams; south side. (Lorado Taft, 1913.) The fountain is a symbolic representation of the Great Lakes.

Storks at Play
Lincoln Park Formal Garden on Stockton Drive. (Augustus Saint-Gaudens and Frederick MacMonnies, 1887.) Also known as Bates Fountain.

It's lighthearted in a lovely setting.

Totem Pole (Kwa Ma Rolas)
Lincoln Park at Addison. (Haiden Indians, 1929.) Authentic totem pole depicts tribal history. From the Queen Charlotte Islands of British Columbia. (*See also* HISTORIC & NEW CHICAGO, Haunted Chicago.)

Viking Ship
Lincoln Park, south of the Children's Zoo. This copy of a 10th-century Viking ship sailed with a crew of 12 from Norway to Chicago for the World's Columbian Exposition of 1893. The elements have taken a toll.

George Washington
Art Institute of Chicago, entrance, Michigan & Adams. (1917.) Replica of famed sculptor Jean-Antoine Houdon's portrait bust of Washington, the original of which is at Virginia's State Capitol in Richmond.

CHURCHES & SYNAGOGUES

Chicago has approximately 2,000 houses of worship, including approximately 1,200 Protestant churches, 260 Catholic churches, and 60 synagogues.

Bahi'a House of Worship
See SIGHTSEEING, Day Trips: On Your Own.

Bond Chapel (Episcopal)
1025 East 58th near Ellis. 962-8200. On the campus of the University of Chicago, connected to Swift Hall by a lovely stone cloister, is this serene little jewel of a Gothic chapel. Picturesque stone carvings on the exterior and wood carvings in the interior depict scenes of the eternal struggle between good and evil. Mainly a sanctuary for student worship, the chapel seats approximately 250 people. Services Sunday am. *OPEN Mon-Fri 8:30am-5pm.*

Cathedral of the Holy Name (Roman Catholic)
751 North State at Wabash. 787-8040. This Neo-Gothic complex of church, parish houses, convent, and school buildings occupies an entire square block. Tours *Sun-Fri at 1pm or by appointment. Sun services 7, 8:15 (high mass), 9:30 & 11am, 12:15 & 5:15pm.*

Chicago Loop Synagogue (Orthodox)
16 South Clark. 346-7370. (Loebl, Schlossman & Bennett, 1957.) Above the entrance to this narrow edifice two metal outstretched "Hands of Peace" by Henri Azaz, surrounded by irregularly positioned letters in English and Hebrew: "The Lord bless thee and keep thee, the Lord make His face to shine upon thee and be gracious unto thee; the Lord lift up His countenance upon thee and give thee peace." *Office OPEN Mon-Fri 9am-4:30pm. Services Mon-Fri 8:05am, 1:05, 4:15 & 4:30 pm; Sat 9am, 3:30 & 4:30pm; Sun 9:30am, 4:15 & 4:30pm.*

Chicago Methodist Temple
77 West Washington at Clark. 236-4548. (Holabird & Roche, 1923.) This First United Methodist

Episcopal Cathedral of St. James

Church of Chicago is the city's oldest congregation, dating back to 1831. Since 1952, with the addition of the Chapel in the Sky above the 22nd floor, it's the world's tallest church building. Free tours begin at the second-floor reception desk *Mon-Sat at 2pm; Sun after the 8:30 & 11am (interpreted for the deaf) services.* Reserve for groups. Free parking. (*See also* SIGHTSEEING, On Your Own: Chapel in the Sky.)

Episcopal Cathedral of St. James
Huron & Wabash. 787-7360. (Burling & Bacchus, 1875.) Gothic Revival church built of local (Joliet) limestone. The headquarters and parish house, a contemporary glass design, was built in 1968. Tours by appointment only. *Sun services 8, 9 & 11am.*

Five Holy Martyrs Church (Roman Catholic)
4327 South Richmond. 254-3636. (Arthur Foster, 1919.) Visited by Poland's Cardinal Wojtla in 1969 and 1976, and again in 1979—but that time as Pope John Paul II. *Sun services in English 6, 8:30 & 9:45am & 12:15pm; in Polish 7:15 & 11am.*

Fourth Presbyterian Church
North Michigan & Chestnut. 787-4570. (Ralph Adams Cram, 1912; parish house Howard V. Shaw, 1925.) Gothic Revival church of carved Bedford stone provides interesting counterpoint to the modern architectural marvels nearby. Lovely stained-glass windows. *Sun services 11am; Vespers 5:30pm.*

Holy Name Cathedral (Roman Catholic)
751 North State at Superior. 787-8040. (Patrick Charles Keely, 1874; remodeled Henry J. Schlacks, 1915; renovated C. F. Murphy & Associates, 1969.) This limestone Victorian Gothic

cathedral has been the seat of the Roman Catholic Archdiocese of Chicago, the country's largest, since 1874. Tours by appointment. *Sun mass 7, 8:15, 9:30 & 11am, 12:15 & 5:15pm.*

Holy Trinity Orthodox Church
1121 North Leavitt. 486-6064. (Louis Sullivan, 1903.) Picturesque Russian Byzantine landmark church and parish hall funded in part by a $5,000 grant from Russia's Tsar Nicholas II. Lavish traditionally decorated interior, Sullivan touches in woodwork over the entrance and the chandelier. The icon screen is from Russia; the murals are copies of those in Kiev's Vladimir Cathedral. *Sun services 9:30am; Sat 4:30pm.*

Immanuel Presbyterian Church
1850 South Racine. 226-7550. (Loebl, Schlossman, Bennett & Dart, 1965.) The Mexican community's modern mission church. *Bilingual services Sun 11:15am.*

K.A.M. Isaiah Israel Temple (Reform Jewish)
1100 East Hyde Park Boulevard at 51st. 924-1234. (Alfred Alschuler, 1924.) In the Hyde Park-Kenwood area, this richly styled Byzantine structure (a Chicago landmark) houses the oldest Jewish congregation in the Midwest, Kehilath Anshe Maarav—Congregation of the Men of the West—founded 1847. In 1971 it merged with Temple Isaiah Israel, descended from the Beth Shalom Congregation organized in 1852. *OPEN Mon-Thurs 9am-5pm; Fri 9am-4pm; Sun 9am-1pm. Sat service 11:15am. Group tours by appointment.*

K.A.M./Pilgrim Missionary Baptist Church
3301 South Indiana. 842-5830. (Adler & Sullivan, 1890.) This ornate synagogue was built by Congregation Kehilath Anshe Maarav (the Midwest's oldest), whose first rabbi was designer Dankmar Adler's father. Bought in 1921 by the members of Pilgrim Missionary Baptist Church. *Sun services 10:45am* (coffee served after). Group tours available by appointment.

Midwest Buddhist Temple
435 West Menomonee at Ogden Mall. 943-7801. (Hideaki Arao, 1972.) Shin Buddhist temple also known as the Temple of Enlightenment. *Sun services in English 10 & 10:30am; in Japanese 11:45am.* Scene of a Ginza festival in August (*see* ANNUAL EVENTS, August).

Our Lady of Sorrows National Shrine (Roman Catholic)
3121 West Jackson Boulevard. 638-5800. Beautiful basilica in blighted area. Free tours by appointment. *Sun services 9am & noon.*

Quinn Chapel (African Methodist Episcopal)
2401 South Wabash. 791-1846. Built in 1892, it's home to Chicago's oldest Black congregation, formed in 1847. The original building, destroyed in the Great Fire, was a "stop" on the freedom-bound Underground Railroad. *Sun services 10:45am & 7pm.* Tours by appointment only.

Rockefeller Memorial Chapel (nondenominational)
5850 South Woodlawn at 59th. 962-7000. (Bertram W. Goodhue, 1928.) On the University of Chicago campus. Impressive Neo-Gothic chapel with 72-bell carillon that chimes on the quarter hour. The liturgical banners are from a collection of 44 created by Norman Laliberte for the New York World's Fair (1964) Vatican Pavilion. *Sun services 9 & 11am.* Tours *Wed noon; Sun 12:15pm.* No reservation necessary. Guided tours of chapel and carillon for groups by appointment only.

St. Chrysostom's Church (Episcopal)
1424 North Dearborn. 944-1083. Lovely stained-glass windows. *Sun services 8 & 11am.*

St. Clement Roman Catholic Church
642 West Deming Place at Orchard. 281-0371. French Romanesque style, built in 1905, with lovely rose window and an interior dome graced with mosaic figures. *Sun services 8, 9:30 & 11am & 12:30 pm; Sat 5pm.*

St. Gabriel's Church (Roman Catholic)
4500 South Lowe. 268-9595. (Burnham & Root, 1887.) The exterior has been considerably altered, but the original interior remains. *Sun services 8 & 10am & noon.*

St. Michael's Church (Roman Catholic)
Eugenie at St. Michael's Court. 642-2498. Original church building built in 1869 and partially destroyed by the Fire in 1871. Restored in 1872, it is now part of a huge complex of buildings. The congregation reflects a changing area. *Sun services in English 8 & 11am & 7pm; in Spanish 9 am.*

St. Nicholas (Roman Catholic)
838 North Oakley. 276-4537. (Ca. 1912-14.) Modeled after Kiev's Basilica of St. Sophia, albeit with 19 fewer onion domes. *Sun services in Ukrainian 7, 8:15, 9:30 & 11am; in English Sat 5pm.* Coffee and cake are sold after every mass on Sundays.

St. Patrick's Church (Roman Catholic)
718 West Adams. 782-6171. (Asher Carter and

St. Patrick's Church

Augustus Bauer, 1854.) Built to serve Chicago's large Irish population, this Romanesque Revival church building, dedicated in 1856, is the city's oldest. *Sun services 7, 8:30, 9:45 & 11am & 5pm.*

St. Paul's Cathedral (Roman Catholic)
2127 West 22 Place at Hoyne. 847-7622. (Henry J. Schlacks, 1900.) This Gothic terra-cotta and brick-masonry cathedral, which had the first brick vault in America, was built originally to serve a large German parish. Now it is predominantly Mexican. *Sun services in English 9 & 11am; in Spanish 1pm.*

St. Paul's Church & Parish House (Universal Church of Christ)
2335 North Orchard. 348-3829. Modified Spanish Romanesque. *Services 1st and 3rd Sun 9am in German, every Sun 11am in English.*

St. Paul's Evangelical Lutheran Church
2215 West North Avenue. 486-6244. (G. Isaacson, 1890-92.) The congregation dates from 1876 (when the Wicker Park area drew Scandinavian immigrants), the building itself from 1892. The interior woodcarvings project the illusion of an ark. *Sun service 10am.*

St. Peter's Church and Friary (Roman Catholic)
110 West Madison, 372-5111. (K. M. Vitzhum and J. J. Burns, 1953.) Five-story marble-clad Roman basilica in the Loop. The stirring "Christ of the Loop" crucifix (by Arvid Strauss), 18 feet high, weighing 26 tons, dominates the entranceway. *Sun mass 9 & 11am, 12:30 & 6pm.*

St. Stanislaus Kostka (Roman Catholic)
1351 West Evergreen. 278-2470. This church, dedicated to the patron saint of Chicago's Polish population, was the centerpiece of the largest Polish parish in the world. Now, a sign of the times, *separate services are celebrated in Polish Sun 9am, in Spanish Sun 11am & in English Sun 8am, Sat 5pm.*

St. Thomas the Apostle Church (Roman Catholic)
5472 South Kimbark. 324-2626. (Barry Byrne, 1922.) Designed by a former Frank Lloyd Wright apprentice, and happily it shows in the inviting church building. Inside, carvings of the Stations of the Cross by Italian A. Faggi. *Sun services 8 & 10am, 12:15 & 5:30pm; Sat 5:30pm.*

St. Vincent de Paul Church (Roman Catholic)
1010 West Webster at Sheffield. 327-1113. Large French Romanesque church. Particularly pretty stained-glass windows. *Sun services 9:30 & 11:30am, in Spanish; Sat 5pm.*

Sts. Volodymyr & Olha (Roman Catholic)
739 North Oakley. 276-3990. Golden-domed Byzantine edifice located in "Ukrainian Village." *High Ukrainian mass Sun 9 & 10:30am & noon.* Coffee and baked goods sold afterward.

Second Presbyterian Church
1936 South Michigan. 225-4951. (James Renwick, 1874; redecorated Howard Van Doren Shaw, Frederick Clay Bartlett, 1901.) This 60-foot-high sanctuary, part of the Prairie Historic

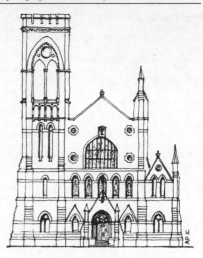
Second Presbyterian Church

District, was classic Gothic Revival until restored by congregant Shaw following a fire in 1900. Fourteen of its magnificent stained-glass windows are Tiffany designed; two others are by pre-Raphaelite designer Sir Edward Burne-Jones executed by William Morris; still another, by John La Farge, is from the World's Columbian Exposition, 1893. The wealthy society congregation, founded in 1842, counted among its members Mrs. Abraham Lincoln and son Todd, as well as Armours, Swifts, Pullmans, and Glessners. The organ was literally powered by horse, then by water. *OPEN Mon-Sat 9am-3:30pm or by appointment. Sun services 11am.*

Seventeenth Church of Christ Scientist
55 East Wacker. 236-4671. (Harry M. Weese & Associates, 1968.) Modern semicircular-designed, travertine-marble church.

GRAVEYARDS & TOMBS

Crouch Tomb
Lincoln Park, Stockton Drive near North Boulevard. Reminder of Lincoln Park's past as public cemetery. Ira Crouch was a pioneer hotel owner whose family successfully prevented movement of his tomb when the cemetery was discontinued.

Stephen A. Douglas Tomb
South 35th & Cottage Grove. 225-6353. (Leonard W. Volk, 1881.) The 96-foot-tall memorial stands on part of what was Douglas's 53-acre estate. Park *OPEN 7 days 9am-5pm.*

Getty Tomb
Graceland Cemetery, 4001 North Clark, north-

Getty Tomb

east section. (Louis Sullivan, 1890.) Built for Carrie Eliza Getty, wife of a prominent Chicago businessman. Sullivan's ornamentation on the bronze gates and upper half of the stone tomb is of unmatched delicacy and beauty. Now an Architectural Landmark, cited for being "a requiem for the dead, an inspiration for the living." (*See also* Graceland Cemetery.)

Graceland Cemetery
4001 North Clark at Irving Park Road. 525-1105. Founded August 30, 1860, on 119 serene acres, where the prominent among early Chicagoans came to rest: Potter Palmer, George Pullman, Marshall Field ("Equity—Integrity, Marshall Field"), and architects Louis Sullivan, John Root, and Daniel Burnham, as well as Mies van der Rohe. A tour map is available at the front gate. The monuments by sculptors Daniel Chester French and Lorado Taft are fascinating tributes to America's equivalent of royalty. A large granite baseball marks the grave of William A. Hulburt, founder of what would become the National Baseball League. *OPEN 7 days 8am-5pm. (See also* Getty Tomb.)

David Kennison Boulder
Lincoln Park, Clark & Wisconsin. Boulder placed by the Sons and Daughters of the American Revolution in 1920 to mark the grave of the last survivor of the Boston Tea Party, David Kennison, who died in Chicago in 1852 at age 115.

Oak Woods
1035 East 67th. 288-3800. Organized in 1853 on 183 acres. An obelisk marks the resting place, which came to be called Federal Mound, of 6,000 Confederate prisoners from Camp Douglas who died in 1867. (Twelve of their guards are interred there as well.) Among the famous from all areas of Chicago life buried here is Enrico Fermi, father of the A-bomb. Gates *OPEN 7 days 8:30am-4pm. Office OPEN Mon-Fri 8:30am-4:30pm. Sat 8:30am-2:45pm. CLOSED Sun.*

Rosehill Cemetery
5800 North Ravenswood. 561-5940. The site, Chicago's highest natural point, was consecrated in 1859, on 350 sylvan acres. If the castellated entranceway looks familiar it's because

it was done by W. W. Boyinton, the Water Tower's architect. There are 230 Union soldiers buried here, including casualties of General Grant's Mississippi River campaign. In 1864 a city ordinance prohibited further burial in Chicago City Cemetery and decreed that 3,000 tombs be moved to Rosehill, which, through its charter prohibiting either condemnation or appropriation of its land, could assure families of those displaced that it was indeed a *final* resting place. *OPEN 7 days 8am-5pm. Office OPEN Mon-Fri 8:30am-4:30pm; Sat 9am-3pm.*

MODERN ARCHITECTURE

Atrium Houses
1366-80 East Madison Park. (Y. C. Wong, 1961.) Eight town houses built around an interior open court that provides the only light to otherwise windowless buildings.

"The Bird Cage"
11 West Wacker. (Shaw, Metz & Dollo, 1954.) City parking facility better known by its nickname. On the façade, Milton Horn's metal sculpture "Chicago Rising from the Lake."

Burton Place
Between La Salle & Wells. Adjacent to Sandburg Village. Amateur architectural whimsy using recycled materials. Human.

Carbide & Carbon Building
230 North Michigan. (Burnham Brothers, 1929.) Entrance base and tower of this 40-story building are strikingly and colorfully art-deco detailed. By the sons of famed Chicago architect Daniel H. Burnham.

Chicago Mercantile Exchange
10-30 South Wacker Drive. 930-1000. (Fujikawa Johnson and Associates, 1983.) Two 40-story granite-clad towers; the top 38 floors are cantilevered over the trading floors. Fourth-floor Visitors Center *OPEN Mon-Fri 7:30am-3:15pm.*

Richard J. Daley Center Plaza (formerly Civic Center)
Washington & Randolph, Dearborn & Clark. (C. F. Murphy Associates and Skidmore, Owings & Merrill, 1964.) A 31-story powerhouse built of weathering Cor-Ten steel. The massive plaza proudly hosts the enigmatic Chicago Picasso, also of Cor-Ten steel (*see* HISTORIC & NEW CHICAGO, Outdoor Artwork & Sculpture). The plaza, a wonderful spot in which to sit and relax, is the site of daily entertainment events year-round at noon. Stop by the Fine Arts Information Booth in the lobby for a monthly calendar or call 346-3278, before noon, to find out that day's program.

Equitable Building
401 North Michigan. (Skidmore, Owings & Merrill and Alfred Shaw & Associates, 1965.) A 40-story steel-and-glass building on the Chicago River bank. Its plaza, dubbed Pioneer Court, is the site of Chicago's first house—that of Jean-Baptiste Du Sable. The fountain is inscribed with

names of the city fathers. The site of summer entertainment at noon.

Exchange Center
440 La Salle South. (Skidmore, Owings & Merrill, 1984.) Red polished-granite complex. Home of the seven-story Chicago Board of Options Exchange, the six-story Midwest Stock Exchange, and One Financial Plaza, a 40-story office tower.

Federal Center & Plaza
Jackson & Adams, Dearborn & Clark. (Mies van der Rohe; Schmidt, Garden & Erikson; C. F. Murphy Associates; A. Epstein & Sons; 1964, 1975.) The Everett Dirksen Building—27 steel-and-glass stories—and the John C. Kluczynski Building, plus a two-story post office, make up this fine urban complex. The large people-pleasing plaza is dominated by a Calder stabile, *Flamingo* (see HISTORIC & NEW CHICAGO, Outdoor Artwork & Sculpture).

First National Bank Building & Plaza
1 First National Plaza at Madison & Dearborn, (C. F. Murphy Associates and Perkins & Will Partnership, 1969.) This 60-story granite "A" is the world's tallest bank. Set in a lively, lovely bi-level outdoor plaza with Chicago's Chagall (see HISTORIC & NEW CHICAGO, Outdoor Artwork & Sculpture: The Four Seasons). Restaurants and an illuminated fountain. Nice spot to catch some sun on a summer day. Free tours available (see SIGHTSEEING, On Your Own: First National Bank).

Frank Fisher Apartments
1209 North State Parkway. (Andrew N. Rebori, 1936.) Small, distinctive apartment building with curved glass blocks and rounded corners typical of the art moderne style of architecture popular in the thirties.

John Hancock Center
875 North Michigan. (Skidmore, Owings & Merrill, 1969.) An *X* marks the spot for this 100-story (1,127 feet) modern office and residence (on floors 45 to 92) tower. The *X*'s are actually cross-bracings to deal with Chicago's winds, but they became unique decorative elements. The Ninety-Fifth restaurant and Images lounge (96th floor) (see RESTAURANTS, Room with a View *and* Bars & Burgers) and the Observation Deck (see SIGHTSEEING, Viewpoints) provide spectacular vantage points. Great views north and south.

Harris Trust & Savings Bank
Harris Bank Plaza, 111 West Monroe. (Shepley, Rutan & Coolidge, 1915; additions Skidmore, Owings & Merrill, 1957, 1975.) The original 20-story structure has been connected to the two additions. They all sit on a 5,000-square-foot public plaza graced by a lovely bronze fountain (Russel Secrest, 1975). In the lobby, a 7-foot loop-shaped structure, "City in Motion," revolves once every 2½ minutes.

IBM Regional Office Building
Wabash & State, north bank of the Chicago River. (Mies van der Rohe office and C. F. Murphy Associates, 1971.) Fifty-two stories in bronze-colored aluminum and tinted glass. Computer facilities on two floors entailed a highly sophis-

ticated temperature-and-humidity-control system. In the lobby, appropriately (in his last design), a bust of the master craftsman of modernity, Mies van der Rohe.

Illinois Bell Telephone Building
225 West Randolph. (Holabird & Root, 1967.) Modern white marble and smoke-gray glass. Dramatic in the pm. Telephony Museum in the lobby (see MUSEUMS & GALLERIES, Museums: Specialty Museums).

Inland Steel Building
30 West Monroe. (Skidmore, Owings & Merrill, 1957.) This 19-story structure was the first stainless-steel-and-glass building entirely supported by external steel columns. Lobby structure by Richard Lippold.

Lake Point Tower
505 North Lake Shore Drive. (Schipporeit-Heinrich Associates and Graham, Anderson, Probst & White, 1968.) A beautiful 70-story bronze-tinted-glass apartment building. Its cloverleaf design and mirrorlike effect make it an eye-catcher—especially at sunset.

Lake Shore Drive Apartments
860-880 and 900-910 North Lake Shore Drive. (Mies van der Rohe, with P.A.C.E. and Holsman, Holsman, Klekamp & Taylor, 1952; 900-910 completed in 1956.) No one throws stones at these "glass houses," acknowledged to be some of the master's best and certainly the most imitated.

Madison Plaza
Madison & Wells. (Skidmore, Owings & Merrill, 1982.) With its stepped roofline and its stunning lobby this 45-story reflective glass tower is considered a distinguished newcomer.

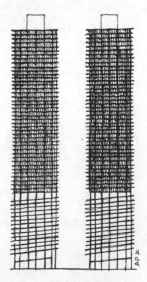

Marina City

Marina City
300 North State at the river. (Bertrand Goldberg Associates, 1964, 1967.) Chicago's tallest concrete building—60 stories. Unique, world-famed, multiuse complex: apartments (wedge-shaped!), offices, restaurants, 18 stories of garage, a theater, an ice rink, and, at ground level, a marina. Access with a view, via Dearborn Street drawbridge.

McClurg Court Center
Between Ohio & Ontario. (Solomon, Cordwell, Buenz & Associates, 1971.) A city within a city. The total. living environment includes 1,000 apartments, parking facilities, a 1,250-seat cinema, shops, tennis courts, health club, and swimming pool.

McCormick Place On-The-Lake
2300 South Lake Shore Drive. 791-6000. (Gene Summers for C. F. Murphy Associates, 1971.) Replacement for fire-damaged (1969) predecessor shows a marked Miesian bent. Contains 750,000 square feet of exhibition area (adding McCormick Place West for a total of 1 million). A 4,300-seat theater, 100,000 square feet of meeting rooms and suites, 42,000 square feet of food facilities comprise the world's busiest convention center.

Metropolitan Correctional Center (South Loop Federal Prison)
Van Buren at Clark. (Harry Weese & Associates, 1975.) Located near the Federal Center courts is this unique reinforced-concrete, 27-story tri-angular-shaped building. Unevenly spaced floor-to-ceiling slit windows five inches wide allow light and a view, albeit narrow, of the outside world while preventing escape. The innovative architecture allows inmates privacy and an uncrowded environment while maintaining the highest level of security.

Mid-Continental Plaza Building
55 East Monroe. (Alfred Shaw & Associates, 1972.) Fifty-story aluminum-and-gray-tinted-glass structure is a handsome newcomer to the Chicago skyline.

Museum of Contemporary Art
237 East Ontario. 280-2660. (Remodeled Brenner, Danforth & Rockwell, 1967.) Former home of *Playboy* magazine now serves another, many would say higher, art form. The museum has a permanent collection, and every seven weeks there is a new exciting avant-garde presentation. The exterior sculpture, "Interior Geography 2," by Zoltan Kemeny is a red copper bas-relief, 50 feet long and 80 feet high. (For hours *see* MUSEUMS & GALLERIES, Museums: General Art Museums.)

One & Two Illinois Center
111 East Wacker; 233 North Michigan (Mies van der Rohe, 1970, 1973); Hyatt Regency Chicago, 151 East Wacker (A. Epstein & Sons, Inc., 1974). Billed as the world's largest mixed-use urban development; being built over the Illinois Central Railroad tracks (aka the Illinois Central Air Rights Development). These two bronze-aluminum-and-glass towers, as well as the 1,000-room Hyatt Hotel, are just part of what will eventually cover 84 acres: office and residential high-rises, landscaped plazas, concourse-level shopping and dining facilities, covered pedestrian walkways, and ample parking facilities.

One Magnificent Mile
At Oak & North Michigan. (Skidmore, Owings & Merrill, 1980-83.) Three hexagonal pinkish granite towers on a shiny metallic base is a departure for the team that brought us the John Hancock and the Sears Tower. The first three floors are devoted to shops and restaurants, floors 4 to 19 house offices, and above that are the pricey condos.

190 La Salle South
(Philip Johnson & John Burgee, 1987.) Chicago's first by the famed New York duo. Forty-two stories of pink granite topped by a spired and gabled roofline. A triumphal arched entryway leads to a vast 55-foot-high lobby.

Piper's Alley
1608 North Wells. (Stanley Tigerman & Associates, 1976.) In Old Town, on the site of the Piper Bakery (1875) alley, an indoor restaurant, shopping, entertainment mall.

Plaza of the Americas
Between the Wrigley Building & the Uptown Savings & Loan (430 North Michigan). Where the flags of all North and South American nations fly. Entertainment in summer (*see* ANNUAL EVENTS, June: The Plaza Lunchtime Concerts, Plaza of the Americas).

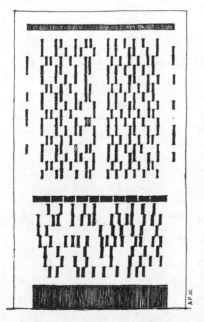

Metropolitan Correctional Center

Prairie Shores
2801-3001 Martin Luther King, Jr., Drive. (Loebl, Schlossman & Bennett, 1958-62.) Five glass high-rises, each with 1,700 apartment units, running parallel to one another—part of the South Side's urban renewal.

Promontory Apartments
5530 South Shore Drive. (Mies van der Rohe; Pace Associates; Holsman, Holsman & Klekamp; 1949.) Simple unfinished-concrete building, typical of its time.

Prudential Building
130 East Randolph (Naess & Murphy, 1955.) Chicago's "piece of the rock." A 41-story gray limestone monolith that, when built, was the city's tallest, most exciting skyscraper. A new plaza and complimentary 64-story tower are intended to bring back the thrill.

Quaker Tower
321 North Clark. (Skidmore, Owings & Merrill, 1987.) Green glass tower, the first of four buildings in a proposed complex called Riverfront Park.

River City
88 South Wells. (Bertrand Goldberg Associates, 1985.) Just south of the Loop, beside the Chicago River. Still to be expanded multilevel residential and commercial complex to include a private park and a 70-slip marina. The twin 17-story curved concrete residences are the work

of the architect who created Marina City; once again he is enticing people to reside downtown.

Sandburg Village
North Clark & La Salle. Slums were cleared for this urban-renewal project that consists of high-rise and town-house dwellings plus shops and landscaping.

Sears Tower
233 South Wacker at Jackson Boulevard. 875-9696. (Skidmore, Owings & Merrill, 1974.) The world's tallest building measures in at 1,454 feet! Its 110 stories occupy 129,000 square feet of a city block; construction took three years. From the observation tower you may not be able to see forever, but on a clear day you can see three other states (*see also* SIGHTSEEING, Viewpoints). A multimillion-dollar refurbishing added a 56-foot-tall glass atrium at the main entrance, a shopping mall, and seven restaurants. In the lobby, there is a Calder mobile universe, composed of five moving elements.

Sedgwick Street Houses
North Sedgwick between Wisconsin & Menomonee. In the Lincoln Park vicinity, an experiment in modern cityscaping. A row of ten single-family houses on the east side of the street, built ca. 1977 by some of Chicago's leading architects. Individually unique, collectively eccentric.

625 North Michigan Avenue
(Meister & Volpe Architects, 1971.) This 27-story

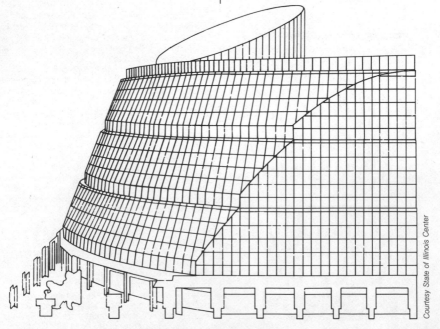

State of Illinois Center

office building has no structural corner columns, thus providing those corporate power points, corner offices, with unimpeded views of the top.

Standard Oil Building
200 East Randolph. (Edward D. Stone, 1974.) This trim 80-story tower (1,136 feet) is one of the world's tallest, narrowest, and boringest. In its plaza, Harry Bertoia's wonderful *Sounding Sculpture* (*see* HISTORIC & NEW CHICAGO, Outdoor Artwork & Sculpture).

State of Illinois Center
Randolph & Clark, La Salle & Lake. (C. F. Murphy/Jahn Associates and Lester B. Knight & Associates; completed 1983.) A striking and controversial North-Loop newcomer on the former site of the Sherman Hotel: Helmut Jahn's 17-story glass-sheathed steel Post-Modern interpretation of traditional Neoclassical government-building design. Fulfilling the aim of integrating both public and commercial functions, the building's concourse and first two floors house restaurants and shops, as well as a gallery and artisan's shop for the works of Illinois artists and craftspeople only. Floors 3 to 15 have balconied offices for state agency officials and the governor's office, and those of the state legislators are on the 16th floor. All this around a 332-foot central rotunda like no other—topped by a sloping glass ellipse 160 feet in diameter. Look up and see the sky, then take one of the glass elevators to the top floor and gaze down on one of the most invigorating interior spaces in this or any city. *See also* SIGHTSEEING, On Your Own: The Atrium *and* MUSEUMS & GALLERIES, Museums: State of Illinois Center Gallery.

30 North La Salle Building
(Thomas E. Stanley, 1975.) This 43-story building occupies the site of the 1894 Stock Exchange Building, designed by Adler & Sullivan, for which preservationists fought a valiant but vain battle, the salvaged entrance archway of which now stands behind the Art Institute in Grant Park.

303 West Madison
(Skidmore, Owings & Merrill, 1987.) Curtain wall of tinted glass, black painted spandrels, light gray and polished green granite, stainless steel window frames—an obvious salute to the Chicago School of Architecture.

333 North Michigan Avenue Building
(Holabird & Root, 1928.) Distinguished and distinctive early 24-story skyscraper with highly stylized art moderne details.

333 West Wacker Drive
(Kohn Pederson Fox Associates, 1983.) A prominent newcomer with a graceful sweeping reflective tower that follows the river's bend. It's one of Chicago's best new structures. On the Loop side, a more linear facade.

Time-Life Building
303 East Ohio at Grand. (H. Weese & Associates, 1971.) This 30-story concrete structure has curtain walls of weathering steel and gold-toned mirrored-glass windows. Built for efficiency during peak hours: the elevators have two-story cabs, entered from different lobby levels, depending on odd or even floor destination.

Tree Studios Building
North State between Ohio & Ontario. (Hill & Woltersdorf, 1894; Woltersdorf & Bernard, 1912, 1913.) Donated by Judge Lambert Tree for use as artists' studios. Through the Ohio entrance, enclosed by the building, is a lovely little park.

1212 Lake Shore Drive
(Barancik & Conte, 1970.) Handsome new addition to the fabled Gold Coast.

2400 Lake View Avenue Building
(Mies van der Rohe, 1963.) Luxurious apartment building with swimming pool adjoining the lobby.

200 South Wacker Drive
(Harry Weese and Associates, 1981.) Polygonal-configured office building at the edge of the Chicago River.

United Insurance Building
1 East Wacker. (Shaw, Metz & Associates, 1962.) This 41-story building is one of the tallest marble-faced buildings in the world.

University Apartments
1400-1450 East 55th. (I. M. Pei; Harry M. Weese & Associates; Loewenberg & Loewenberg; 1959-62.) Twin ten-story apartment buildings constitute a major urban-renewal project.

U.S. Gypsum Building
101 South Wacker. (Perkins & Will Partnership,

Xerox Center

1961.) Building design symbolic of gypsum crystals.

Water Tower Place
North Michigan between Chestnut & Seneca. 440-3165. (Loebl, Schlossman, Bennett & Dart, 1976.) A modern multiuse marble structure on the Magnificent Mile. Incorporates the Ritz-Carlton Hotel, condominium residences, offices, the Drury Lane Theater, and a seven-story luxury shopping complex housing 100 shops and built around a central atrium featuring glass elevators. A sybaritic shopper's dream come true albeit architecture critics find it out of size and place amid its human-scale neighbors. Mall *OPEN 7 days 9am-1am. Shops OPEN Mon & Thurs 10am-7pm; Tues, Wed, Fri & Sat 10am-6pm; Sun noon-5pm.*

Xerox Center
Monroe at Dearborn. (Helmut Jahn and C. F. Murphy Associates, 1980.) Forty stories of white aluminum and silver glass—the façade veritably shimmers. The soft curves, architectural echoes of 1930s deco styling.

OUTDOOR ARTWORK & SCULPTURE

There are more than 100 works of art in Chicago's parks and plazas.

Batcolumn
Social Security Administration Plaza, 600 West Madison. (Claes Oldenburg, 1977.) Dedicated April 14, 1977. Gray-painted-metal latticework baseball bat 101 feet tall, by hometown boy. The cost: $100,000. Many feel it strikes out.

Chicago Picasso (Untitled)
Richard J. Daley Plaza, Dearborn between Washington & Randolph. (Pablo Picasso, 1964-67.) Dedicated on August 15, 1967. Fifty feet tall and made of 162 tons of Cor-Ten weathering steel; Chicagoans first greeted it with puzzle-

Chicago Picasso

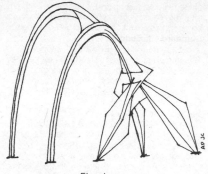

Flamingo

ınent, now shower it with pride. Your guess is as good as anyone else's, but there's no denying she/he/it works. Nearby a bronze plaque in braille with a small model, and a plan of the plaza. Picasso's original model is in the Art Institute.

Dawn Shadows
Madison Plaza, Madison & Wells. (Louise Nevelson, 1983.) No public art collection is ever complete without a Nevelson; forty-two feet, black painted steel.

Flamingo
Federal Center Plaza, Dearborn between Adams & Jackson. (Alexander Calder, 1973.) A graceful, red-painted Calder stabile, 53 feet high. It's said to be vandal-proof.

The Four Seasons (Les Quatre Saisons)
One First National Plaza, Dearborn & Monroe. (Marc Chagall, 1974.) Over 3,000 square feet of murals, containing over 300 shadings of glass, granite, and marble, make up this 70-foot-long, 14-foot-high, 10-foot-wide, 4-sided mosaic. On its top, seen only by workers in the world's tallest bank, a bouquet of mosaic flowers.

Goats
Deming Place at Clark. (John Kearney, 1975.) Thick steel car bumpers welded by an acetylene torch into a Noah's Ark full of animals, many of which dot the Chicago, not to mention national, landscape. My personal favorite by this "King of Bumper Sculptors" is of his favorite small animal—a pair of goats. Also check out the horse (*Horsepower,* 1971) at Arlington & Clark.

Goats

Ellsworth Kelly Sculpture
Lincoln Park, Cannon Drive & Fullerton Parkway. Erected by the Friends of the Parks with a little help from the National Endowment for the Arts. The 40-foot-tall, sleek stainless-steel sculpture is the first new artwork in a Chicago park in 30 years. Symbolic of Chicago's rise from the ashes of the Fire with an "I will" spirit.

La Salle Towers
1211 North La Salle. Richard Haas "fools the eye" once more with his painted tribute to architects Louis Sullivan and Daniel Burnham. Note their portraits as well as those of Frank Lloyd Wright and John Root.

Miró's Chicago
Brunswick Plaza, 59 West Washington. (Joan Miró, 1981.) This Chicago newcomer is a 37-foot bronze, concrete, and ceramic-inlaid lady with outstretched arms and generous proportions. It is said she will become more beautiful with age (how fortunate she is).

Monument to the Standing Beast
State of Illinois Center, 100 West Randolph. (Jean Dubuffet, 1985.) Sentinel at this fascinating structure's entrance. Huge—ten tons, 28 feet high—fiberglass abstract; a gift from the French artist.

Murals (Contemporary)
In the late 1960s-early 1970s city walls became canvases onto which energetic inner-city youth spilled out hope, fear, anger, dreams, frustrations, and aspirations—as well as the facts of daily life—in a creative and stirring burst of color. Public art in the truest sense: by the people, accessible to *all* the people. There are approximately 275 murals in Chicago, but, alas, much of it is here today, gone tomorrow, often because the wall, the building, the fence, the viaduct—the canvas—is destroyed in an effort

to "improve" the environment. Just, in fact, what the young muralists—Black, Chicano, Japanese, Puerto Rican, Polish, etc.—had in mind, and heart. A few are listed; the best attempt to catalog the genre is *Guide to Chicago Murals: Yesterday and Today*, edited by V. A. Sorel, available from the Chicago Council on Fine Art, 78 East Washington, Chicago, IL 60602.

For the People of the Future
Springfield & North. A cement-and-mosaic relief by the prolific Chicago Mural Group.

No Fads & Frills
50th & Lake Park. By artist Astrid Fuller. A rather bleak depiction of education in Chicago.

Reflections of Ravenswood
4662 North Lincoln, north wall. Sponsored in part by the Chicago Council on Fine Arts. A 25-by-96-foot mural depicts the area's history, executed by 27 volunteers.

Untitled
Lower level, North Michigan & Grand. (Sachio Yamashita, 1978.) A brilliant rainbow of color.

Nuclear Energy
University of Chicago Campus, South Ellis between 56th & 57th. (Henry Moore, 1967.) A 12-foot bronze sculpture commemorates the dawn of the Atomic Age: on December 2, 1942, at 3:25pm, the first self-sustained controlled nuclear reaction was achieved on this site. Mushroom cloud or death's head—or both?

Pillar of Fire
De Koven & Jefferson. (Egon Weiner, 1961.) Handsome bronze-flame sculpture at the point of origin of the Chicago Fire of 1871. Since 1961 the site of the Chicago Fire Academy (*see* SIGHTSEEING, On Your Own).

Sounding Sculpture
Standard Oil Building Plaza, 200 East Randolph. (Harry Bertoia, 1975.) Sculptor refers to it as "an offering to the wind." Eleven units of copper rods 4 to 16 feet high, set in the reflecting pool. Locust trees and 190-foot waterfall complete the lovely visual setting.

Universe
Sears Tower lobby, 233 South Wacker at Adams. (Alexander Calder, 1974.) Brightly painted slow-moving aluminum abstract, powered by seven motors placed behind the 55-by-33-foot wall. The simultaneous movements are reminiscent of a three-ring circus, a favorite theme of Calder.

Miró's Chicago

SCHOOLS

De Paul University
Lincoln Park Campus: 2323 North Seminary (1100 West). 341-8000. This campus's 28 acres, devoted mainly to music, drama, and housing, include three Holabird & Root buildings: the Stone Building (1968), McGaw Memorial Library and James McClure Memorial Chapel (both 1963). Also of note: the Arthur J. Schmidt Aca-

demic Center and the De Paul University Center, both C. F. Murphy Associates (1967 and 1971, respectively). Lewis Center Campus: 25 East Jackson Boulevard at Wabash. 341-8000.

Illinois Institute of Technology
3300 South Federal. 567-3000. (Mies van der Rohe & Ludwig Hilberseimer; Friedman, Alschuler & Sincere; PACE Associates; 1942–58. Skidmore, Owings & Merrill, 1963.) This 100-acre campus is the focal point of the South Side's urban-renewal efforts. Mies van der Rohe, who was the Institute's dean of the School of Architecture, Bauhaus-American Wing, designed much of the campus, including the Administration Building, the Commons Building, and the Chapel. Recent additions conform to his original plans for the campus. Tours, lasting approximately 45 minutes, *Mon, Wed & Fri 2pm; Tues & Sat 11am; Thurs 11am & 2pm.* Group tours by appointment only. Call 567-3025.

Loyola University
Lewis Towers Campus: 820 North Michigan; 670-3000. Lake Shore Campus: 6525 North Sheridan Road; 274-3000 (Schmidt, Garden & Erikson, 1925). Original building in downtown campus donated by Chicago philanthropist Frank Lewis. It's Chicago's oldest university and largest Jesuit institution in North America.

Northwestern University Chicago Campus
710 North Lake Shore Drive. 908-8649. (John Gamble Rogers, 1926-32; Holabird & Root, 1929-67; Schmidt, Garden & Erikson, 1966; Bertram Goldberg & Associates; 1974.) The complex includes the graduate schools of dentistry, medicine, business, and law as well as McGaw Medical Center, consisting of Northwestern Memorial Hospital, Prentice Women's Hospital and Maternity Center, the Passavant and Wesley pavilions, the Veterans Administration Research Hospital, and the Rehabilitation Institute of Chicago.

Francis W. Parker School
330 Webster (2200 North). (Holabird & Root, 1962.) Progressive private school housed in a three-story, red-brick structure. Courtyard wall contains remnants of the old Garrick Theater, torn down in 1961.

Quigley Preparatory Seminary
7740 South Western. Impressive French Gothic Revival complex attended by those in training for the priesthood.

Roosevelt University
430 South Michigan. 341-3623. An urban curiosity in location and philosophy. Since 1947 the university has been housed in the famed Auditorium Building (*see* HISTORIC & NEW CHICAGO, Historic Buildings & Areas). Classrooms, libraries, and laboratories now occupy the architectural masterpiece, testimony to the value of restoring and recycling landmark buildings. Work continues.

Carl Schurz High School
3601 North Milwaukee at Addison. (Dwight H. Perkins, 1910.) Named for the German-born political leader and poet. Perkins, the chief archi-

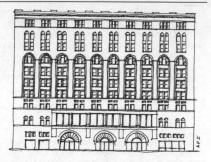

Roosevelt University (Auditorium Hall)

tect for the Chicago School Board, combined the rising verticals of the Chicago School of architecture with the high-pitched roofs and geometric details of the Prairie style.

James A. Sexton School
160 West Wendell. This landmark was opened in 1883 as North Division High. It's one of Chicago's oldest school buildings.

University of Chicago Campus
5801 South Ellis. 753-1234. (Henry Ives Cobb, 1897; Henry Hobson Richardson, Shepley, Rutan & Coolidge, 1903.) Founded in 1892, the original campus "Quadrangle" between Ellis and University, 57th to 59th streets, followed Cobb's original, mainly English Gothic, plan. Additions have respected the scale of existing buildings, and harmony results. Now the Midwest's largest and most prestigious private academic institution. Tours lasting 1½ hours every Saturday at 10am; tours of Robie House are Saturday at noon.

University of Illinois at Chicago
Halsted at Polk. (Walter A. Netsch of Skidmore, Owings & Merrill, 1965, 1968, 1971; Student Union building: C. F. Murphy Associates.) A vast, modern, urban university campus. Buildings are grouped around an open amphitheater. Built on the former immigrant-port-of-entry area, the campus fittingly incorporates the landmark Hull House (*see* HISTORIC & NEW CHICAGO, Historic Buildings & Areas), most of which the university displaced. Many architecturally exciting buildings. *OPEN Mon-Thurs 8am-7pm; Fri 8am-4pm.* One-hour guided tours by appointment; call 996-7000, Student Info Network Center, 750 South Halsted.

HAUNTED CHICAGO

(*See also* SIGHTSEEING, Chicago Tours: Specialized Tours: Chicago's Haunted City Tours *and* Chicago Supernatural Tours.)

Holy Family Church
1080 West Roosevelt. Records indicate that in 1890 church founder Reverend Arnold Damen was awakened by two young altar boys who led him to their seriously ill mother. The rub—the boys had died six years earlier. Today a statue of each boy, carved of wood, stands on either side of the altar.

Indian Boundary Division
8800 West Belmont. According to Indian folklore, the ghost of Potawatomi lays claim to the woods after dark.

Resurrection Cemetery
7200 South Archer. "Resurrection Mary" died in a car crash on her way home from a dance In 1931, only she is said to be "seen" hitchhiking along Archer Avenue—once more to the bal.

St. Valentine's Day Massacre Site
2122 North Clark. The S-M-C Cartage garage is gone, but on the spot where Bugs Moran's gang got Al Capone's message on February 14, 1929, grow five trees that allegedly not even neighborhood dogs go near.

Totem Pole
Lincoln Park at Addison. According to the late Chicago writer Norman Mark, the second-from-the-top man on the totem pole has changed the position of his hands—at least four times! The unromantic among us think it was done by terrestrials, during recent paint jobs.

Willow Brook
☎ 708 839 1000

8900 S. Archer Ave.
closed Wed + Thurs.
open Fri - singles
off. open 9 am

MUSEUMS
&
GALLERIES

Art Institute of Chicago

MUSEUMS

General Art Museums

Art Institute of Chicago
South Michigan & East Adams. 443-3500 (recording) or -3600. One of the nation's best art museums. Houses one of the world's largest and finest collections of French Impressionist and Post-Impressionist paintings. The galleries of European art have undergone a masterful refurbishing, a part of a $30 million building and renovation project. Works by El Greco, Rembrandt, Picasso, Dali, Renoir, Van Gogh, Seurat, and Monet are all beautifully displayed. Chagall's *American Windows,* Picasso's almost tiny manque of his sculpture in Daley Plaza. Fascinating are the Thorne miniature rooms, accurate, detailed replicas of rooms from palaces and mansions from the 16th century to modern times—scaled one inch to life!—and the reconstruction of Louis Sullivan's 19th-century Chicago Stock Exchange Trading Room. In McClintock Court, The Garden Restaurant, a lovely outdoor eatery with fountain (*see* RESTAURANTS, Garden/Outdoor Dining), a cafeteria, and the Members' Lounge & Dining Room. Gallery walk every Saturday at 1pm. Free lectures Monday through Friday at 12:15pm. For children's tours, call 443-3688 (*see* KIDS' CHICAGO, Museums for Children). Special: "A Touch of Art," Tactile Gallery, lower level—designed for the physically handicapped. *OPEN 7 days noon-4pm.* Group tours available, call 443-3688 or write to Museum Education Department. Gift shop features reproductions, art, books, and international gifts. Membership available. Museum *OPEN Mon, Wed-Fri 10:30am-4pm; Tues 10:30am-7:30pm; Sat 10am-4:30pm; Sun noon-5pm.* Suggested contribution; discount for senior citizens; FREE for all on Tuesday.

Martin D'Arcy Gallery of Art
Loyola University, Cudahy Library, 6525 North Sheridan Road. 508-2679 or -2677. Art, sculpture, textiles, and objects from medieval and Renaissance Europe (1100-1700) in a comfortable, contemplative setting, replete with Renaissance music. Lovely Christmas tree in December (*see* ANNUAL EVENTS). Group visits by appointment only; call for reservation. *OPEN Mon-Fri noon-4pm; Sun 1-4pm; in addition, Tues-*

Thurs 6:30-9:30 pm. CLOSED school holidays; call for summer schedule. FREE.

Museum of Contemporary Art
237 East Ontario. 280-2660. Sometimes controversial, almost always an adventure. A showcase for international avant-garde art—visual and performing. Permanent as well as changing exhibits. Contemporary artists in all media: installations, sculpture, video, crafts. Brief audiovisual orientation is presented. Museum Shop: contemporary and ethnic jewelry, ceramics, porcelain, books, and pamphlets. Group tours by appointment. Gallery talk every Saturday at 2pm. Membership available. *OPEN Tues-Sat 10am-5pm; Sun noon-5pm. CLOSED Mon. Thanksgiving, Christmas & New Year's Day.* Admission charge; discount for senior citizens, children under age 10, and students; children under age 6 FREE. FREE for all on Tuesday.

David & Alfred Smart Gallery
5550 South Greenwood. 753-2121. The University of Chicago's art museum. The permanent collection covers classical to modern art; four different special exhibits during the year, covering all aspects of not-living artists. This teaching gallery offers lectures, talks, films. Gift counter. Membership available. *OPEN Tues-Sat 10am-4pm; Sun noon-4pm. CLOSED Mon, holidays & month of Sept. FREE.*

State of Illinois Gallery
State of Illinois Center, 100 West Randolph, 2nd floor. 917-5322. Features changing exhibits of both historic and contemporary Illinois art. Wide range of media; painting, sculpture, drawing, prints, video, ceramics, photography, and textiles. Produced by the Illinois State Museum and the Illinois Arts Council. *OPEN Mon-Fri 10am-6pm.* FREE.

Terra Museum of American Art
664 North Michigan. 664-3939. Branch: 2600 Central Park Avenue, Evanston. 328-3402. A major new art institution on the Miracle Mile. One of only a few museums in the nation exclusively devoted to American art. The collection spans two centuries: Luminist and other 19th-century paintings, American Impressionist, 20th-century moderns and an outstanding collection of Maurice Prendergast oils, watercolors, and monotypes. Also, works by Copley, Morse, Bingham, Lane, Whistler, and Homer. Educational programs; museum store. *OPEN Mon-Sat*

10am-5pm; Sun noon-5pm. Admission, lower for students, seniors, and children age 12 to 18. Group tours and membership available. The original museum in Evanston will remain as a branch of the new Michigan Avenue Terra. *OPEN Tues-Sat 11am-5pm; Sun 1-5pm. CLOSED Mon.*

Ethnic Museums

Balzekas Museum of Lithuanian Culture
6500 South Pulaski. 582-6500. A permanent collection of cultural and historical art and objects (dating back to medieval times) as well as changing exhibits of contemporary art from Lithuania. Coins, stamps, folk art, antique weapons, native costumes, and an extensive amber collection. Research library and archives. Children's museum in which children can touch and feel in the rural Lithuanian exhibit. Gift shop (582-6500) features books, coins, dolls, maps, Christmas ornaments, ceramics, and textiles. Parking available. *OPEN Mon-Sat 10am-4pm; Sun 10am-8pm. CLOSED Christmas Day.* Admission charge; lower for children under age 12 and senior citizens.

Du Sable Museum of African-American History
740 East 56th Place. 947-0600. The historical and cultural contributions of Black Africans and Afro-Americans shown through paintings, sculpture, and artifacts. Lectures, classes, tours. Documents available for research. Parking facilities. *OPEN Mon-Fri 9am-5pm; Sat & Sun noon-5pm. CLOSED Christmas, New Year's Day & July 4.* Small suggested contribution; discount for children. FREE on Mondays. School classes, with teacher, FREE. A 45-minute tour available weekdays by appointment.

Mexican Fine Arts Center & Museum
1852 West 19th Street. 738-1503. Located in Pilsen's Harrison Park, the first Mexican cultural center and museum in the Midwest. Its goal is to stimulate the appreciation of the arts of Mexico through exhibitions of that culture's rich variety of visual and performing arts. Changing exhibitions. *OPEN Tues-Sun 10am-5pm. CLOSED Mon.* FREE.

Oriental Institute
University of Chicago, 1155 East 58th. 702-9521 (recording) or -9502. Egyptian and Near Eastern antiquities, art, archaeology, including sculpture, decorative arts, and monumental architectural remnants. Gift shop: jewelry and reproductions from the collection, books, posters, cards, and slides. Guided tours available for groups. *OPEN Tues-Sat 10am-4pm; Sun noon-4pm. CLOSED Mon & holidays.* FREE.

Polish National Museum
984 North Milwaukee. 384-3352. An ethnic museum depicting Polish history and culture. Folk art, traditional costumes and uniforms, religious art. Research center and library. Changing exhibits of Polish art. Gift shop features books, dolls, carvings, jewelry, leather goods. Tours available. Parking. *OPEN 7 days noon-5pm.* Library *OPEN Mon 12:15-8pm; Tues, Fri & Sat 10am-4pm; Wed 10am-6pm. CLOSED Christmas & Easter.* FREE.

Maurice Spertus Museum of Judaica
Spertus College of Judaica, 618 South Michigan. 922-9012. The most complete Jewish museum in the Midwest. Permanent collection of art and artifacts depicts Jewish life and culture through the centuries. Exhibits change several times a year. Zell Holocaust Memorial: a permanent visual record of the Holocaust 1933-45. Gift shop features jewelry, Israeli arts and crafts, books, Judaica. Museum *OPEN Mon, Wed & Thurs 10am-5pm; Tues 10am-8pm; Fri 10am-3pm; Sun 10am-5pm. CLOSED Sat & holidays.* Admission charge; lower for children, senior citizens, and students.

Swedish-American Museum of Chicago
5248 North Clark. 728-8111. Swedish ethnic museum and cultural center. *OPEN Mon-Fri 11am-2pm; Sat 11am-3pm. CLOSED Sun.* Suggested donation.

Ukrainian Institute of Modern Art
2230 West Chicago Avenue. 227-5522. Community cultural center and art gallery. Permanent collection of art and sculpture by contemporary Ukrainian artists. Changing exhibits six times a year devoted to contemporary art by artists of Ukrainian descent. Tours, seminars, lectures, concerts, performances, literary readings. Prints shop. *OPEN Tues-Sun 1-4pm. CLOSED Mon. Other times by appointment only.* Small donation suggested.

Ukrainian National Museum
2453 West Chicago Avenue. 276-6565. Ukrainian folk arts and cultural artifacts as well as modern Ukrainian art and sculpture. Research library and archives. *OPEN Mon-Fri 8am-1pm; Sun noon-3pm. CLOSED Sat.* Small contribution suggested.

Morton B. Weiss Museum of Judaica
K.A.M. Isaiah Israel Congregation, 1100 East Hyde Park Boulevard. 924-1234. Small museum of rare Judeo-Persian and Kurdish documents. *OPEN Mon-Fri 9am-4pm; Sun 9am-1pm. CLOSED Sat.* FREE.

Historical Museums

Chicago Historical Society
North Clark at North Avenue. 642-4600. Exhibits, ofttimes dramatic, depicting mainly Chicago and Illinois history, including an audiovisual presentation of the Great Chicago Fire of 1871. The Pioneer Gallery: full-sized replicas of rooms and a barn from the period. Good American folk-art collection. Interesting live demonstrations of frontier skills. Research library, lectures, films, seminars. The gift shop features reproductions of early historical documents and prints, good Lincoln, Fire, and Civil War book selection. (The museum is currently undergoing major renovation and expansion.) Membership available. *OPEN Mon-Sat 9:30am-4:30pm; Sun noon-5pm. CLOSED Thanksgiving, Christmas & New Year's*

Day. Admission charge; lower for children and senior citizens. FREE for all on Monday.

International Museum of Surgical Sciences
1524 North Lake Shore Drive. 642-3555; Saturday and Sunday 642-3632. A museum devoted to the healing arts. Depicts the history of surgical and medical science around the world from 2000 B.C. to the 19th century. Rare texts, historical displays, antique medical instruments, Napoleon's death mask, and a full-scale replica of an 1873 apothecary shop. Free lectures Wednesday at 8pm, from fall to spring. Parking; guided tours available; reserve for groups. *OPEN Tues-Sat 10am-4pm; Sun 11am-5pm. CLOSED Mon.* FREE.

The Peace Museum
430 West Erie. 440-1860. Opened in 1981 in the River North area, this unique museum is devoted to fostering public awareness of the causes and effects of war. Exhibits, lectures, concerts, and festivals all explore the issues of war and peace through visual, literary, and performing arts. Gift shop; membership available. *OPEN Tues, Wed & Fri-Sun noon-5pm; Thurs noon-8pm. CLOSED Mon.* Admission, lower for students.

Printers' Row Printing Museum
715 South Dearborn. 987-1059. In a fascinating area (*see also* HISTORIC & NEW CHICAGO, Historic Buildings & Areas: Printing House Row). A functioning replica of a 19th-century printing shop with original presses and type. Tended by men who know and care about a job well done. Displays; will sell print to order. *OPEN Sat & Sun only 9am-6pm.*

Science Museums

Adler Planetarium
1300 South Lake Shore Drive. 322-0300 (recording) or -0304. Three floors of exhibits about space exploration, navigation, and astronomy. Find out how much you would weigh on Mars, see a moon rock and a space suit, marvel at antique timekeeping and engineering instruments and navigational tools. There is a 13-minute introductory film in the Kroc Universe Theater. Snack bar set in futuristic moon-base environment with a good "view" of earth. The shop (322-0322) is great for astronomy buffs. Courses in astronomy and navigation are offered for adults. One-hour Sky Shows: *Sept 1-mid June, Mon-Thurs at 2pm; Fri at 2 & 8pm; Sat, Sun & holidays at 11am, 1, 2, 3, 4pm.*

June 16-Aug 30, 7 days 11am, 1, 2, 3, 4 & 8pm. The 8pm show concludes with a visit to Doane Observatory for a look into space at the planets and the stars. Exhibits *OPEN year-round Mon-Thurs 9:30am-4:30pm; Fri 9:30am-9pm; Sat & Sun 9:30am-5pm. CLOSED Thanksgiving & Christmas.* Admission charge to the Sky Shows, lower for children age 6-17; children under age 6 not admitted to the shows. Members and senior citizens FREE. Group shows are available by appointment. Exhibits FREE.

Chicago Academy of Sciences
Lincoln Park, 2001 North Clark. 549-0606. This museum, the city's oldest science museum founded in 1857—was originally devoted to the natural habitat of Chicago. Now a natural history museum using life-sized dioramas and exhibits, including canyons, caves, and forests. The Great Lakes exhibit (lobby and second floor) deals with the origin and development of the region. The Museum Shop features rock specimens, miniature wooden toys, nature books, jewelry, souvenirs, and postcards. A free science film of special interest to kids is presented every Sunday; at 2:30pm, there is a travel lecture (not during summer months). *OPEN 7 days a week 10am-5pm. CLOSED Christmas.* Admission charge; FREE for all on Mondays.

Chicago Museum of Holography
1134 West Washington Boulevard. 226-1007. Holography (three-dimensional laser-produced images) museum, school, library, and research institute. Permanent display of international holograms. Classes, workshops, lectures, films, and performances offered. Tours available by appointment. *OPEN Wed-Sun 12:30-5pm. CLOSED Mon & Tues.* Admission charge.

Field Museum of Natural History
1200 South Lake Shore Drive at Roosevelt Road. 922-9410. Devoted to anthropology, botany, geology, and zoology. One of the largest natural history museums in the world—over 13 million artifacts! Evolved from exhibits brought to the 1893 World's Columbian Exposition, it's a wonder-filled place with animal exhibits, dinosaurs, gems, and the world's largest collection of anthropological art from the Pacific Islands; excellent Egyptian, Tibetan, Philippine, American Indian, and Chinese collections. Special: "Place for Wonder": natural objects to be touched and held. (At museum entrance get a list of other touchables located throughout the museum. All are marked with braille explanation cards for the

Field Museum of Natural History

blind.) Pawnee Earth Lodge: full-scale replica of a 19th-century American Indian dwelling. "Man in His Environment": a multimedia ecology presentation that questions man's impact on nature. Group tours by appointment. Lectures, performances, weekend seminars, workshops and films, field trips, volunteer programs. McDonald's restaurant for breakfast and lunch is *OPEN 7 days 9am-5pm.* Gift shop: reproductions, international artifacts, postcards, books, and souvenirs. Limited free parking. Library of 200,000 volumes and journals *OPEN Mon-Fri 9am-4pm.* Obtain pass from main-floor desk. Membership available. Museum *OPEN Mon-Fri 9am-5pm. CLOSED Thanksgiving, Christmas, & New Year's Day* Admission charge; discount for senior citizens and students age 6-17; children under age 6 FREE. FREE for all on Thursday.

Lizzadro Museum of Lapidary Art
220 Cottage Hill Avenue, Elmhurst. 833-1616. A unique collection of 18th-, 19th-, and 20th-century lapidary art, as well as semiprecious stones, fossils, minerals, and petrified wood. Objects carved out of jet, jade, turquoise, and quartz. Gift shop. May to October picnic facilities in nearby Wilder Park, with lovely playground and conservatory. Special programs about gems every Saturday at 2pm, Sunday at 3pm: films, lectures. Reserve for large groups. *OPEN Tues-Sat 10am-5pm; Sun 1-5pm. CLOSED Mon.* Small admission charge, lower for teens; children under age 13 FREE. FREE for all on Friday.

Museum of Science and Industry
South Lake Shore Drive at East 57th, in Jackson Park. 684-1414. It's exciting and educational. An inquisitive person's dream museum. Designed to illustrate the impact of science and technology, the 2,000 displays in 75 exhibit halls are mostly participatory. The fascinating attractions include a full-scale coal mine (nominal admission fee), a 16-foot walk through a model of the human heart; a captured WWII German U-505 submarine (nominal admission fee); the Apollo-8 command module. Explore space while visiting the Henry Crown Space Center and Omnimax Theater. See yourself on videotape, see chicks hatching and an amoeba dividing. The building is a restored original (*see* HISTORIC & NEW CHICAGO, Historic Buildings & Areas) from the 1893 World's Columbian Exposition. It's *always* crowded, especially in summer. Lectures, performances, classes, seminars, films, and festivals. Reserve in advance for group visits. Parking; gift shop. *OPEN Memorial Day-Labor Day 7 days 9:30am-5:30pm; balance of the year Mon-Fri 9:30am-4pm; Sat, Sun & holidays 9:30am-5:30pm. CLOSED Christmas.* Museum FREE but certain exhibits have an admission fee.

Specialty Museums

Ripley's Believe It or Not Museum
1500 North Wells. 337-6077. Over 500 exhibits featuring the odd, odder, and oddest from around the world. *OPEN Sun-Thurs noon-9pm; Fri & Sat noon-midnight; in summer Sun-Thurs noon-11pm.* Admission charge; discount for children and senior citizens.

Telephony Museum
225 West Randolph. 727-2994. Illinois Bell's exhibition of the past, present, and future of telecommunications. Early to modern telephones; laser and satellite communications devices; picture phones. *OPEN Mon-Fri 8:30am-4pm. CLOSED Sat, Sun & holidays.* FREE.

Art Rental

Art Rental & Sales Gallery of the Art Institute
Art Institute of Chicago, Michigan & Adams, ground floor. 443-3503. Purchase or rental of paintings, watercolors, graphics, sculpture, by Chicago-area artists. Rental price may be applied to purchase price. *OPEN Sept-mid June, Mon-Fri 10:30am-4pm; Sat noon-4pm. Mid June-mid Aug, Mon-Fri 11am-3pm. CLOSED last two weeks in Aug.*

ART GALLERIES

Chicago's art scene is booming with galleries spreading from the Magnificent Mile to the newly gentrified River North area, with Superior and Huron streets at its heart (sometimes referred to as SuHu).

For current shows and gallery openings see the Chicago Tribune, Friday, Weekend section. Also obtain a copy of the monthly calendar, "Arts Chicago," available at the cultural information booth in the lobby of Daley Center, Dearborn & Randolph streets.

IMPORTANT NOTE: *The "art scene" slows during the summer months. Gallery hours and weeks may be shorter, and in many cases Never in August is the rule. In general, it is best to call for summer hours.*

Alice Adams, Ltd.
P.O. Box 11616, Chicago, IL 60611. 787-7295. Nineteenth- and 20th-century master prints and drawings. Beckmann, Nolde, Kirchner, Munch, Bonnard, Vuillard, Matisse, Picasso, Bellows, Marsh. *By appointment only.*

American West
2110 North Halsted. 871-0400. Contemporary southwestern art and Indian artifacts. David Bradley, Bruce Nowlin, R. C. Gorman, Amado Peña, Hal & Fran Larsen, Doug Coffin, Curtis Grubbs. *OPEN year-round Tues-Fri 1-6pm; Sat noon-6pm; Sun noon-5pm.*

ARC Gallery (Artists, Residents of Chicago)
356 West Huron. 266-7607. Co-operative of Chicago women artists. Contemporary art; exhibits change monthly. *OPEN Tues-Sat 11am-5pm.*

Artemisia Gallery
341 West Superior, 4th floor. 751-2016. Women's co-operative gallery. Exhibits member art-

ists as well as sponsors major outside shows.
Every year there is a performance series. *OPEN
Tues-Sat 11am-5pm.*

Arts Club of Chicago
109 East Ontario, 2nd floor. 787-3997. A private
club whose gallery is open to the public. Changing exhibits every six weeks, contemporary
American art and sculpture. *OPEN Mon-Sat
10am-5:30pm.*

Atlas Galleries
549 North Michigan. 329-9330. World's largest
collection of Dali lithos and etchings. Twentieth-
century masters, American artists Rockwell and
Neiman. Oil paintings by Raymond Page and
Ludwig Muninger. Nineteenth-century invest-
ment packages. *OPEN 7 days Mon-Sat 10am-
9pm; Sun 11am-6pm.*

Austin Galleries
677 North Michigan; 943-3730. And Woodfield
Mall, Schaumburg; 882-0030. Works by Chagall,
Miró, Calder, Dali, Vasarely. Contemporary
American and European artists. *OPEN Mon-Sat
10am-9pm; Sun noon-5pm.*

Balkin Fine Arts
120 South La Salle. 372-0160. Emerging artists,
particularly Chicago-area. Contemporary fine
prints, American and some European. *OPEN
Mon-Fri 9am-5pm; Sat noon-4pm.*

Jacques Baruch Gallery
40 East Delaware Place. 944-3377. Contemporary Slavic art including tapestries from Poland
and fine graphics from Czechoslovakia (featuring the work of Jiri Anderle), Yugoslavia, and
Hungary. *OPEN Tues-Sat 10am-5pm.*

Mary Bell
361 West Superior, 2nd floor. 642-0202. Contemporary abstract art; paintings, sculpture, tapestries, and prints. *OPEN Mon-Sat 9am-5pm.*

Benjamin-Beattie Galleries, Ltd.
1000 North Lake Shore Drive, Suite 1108. 337-
1343. Contemporary graphics: Gottlieb, Sam
Francis, Motherwell; regional American artists.
Sculpture—all media: Nevelson, Moore, Miró,
Jerome Kirk, Renzi, Vasa, James Myford. *By
appointment only.*

Roy Boyd Gallery
739 North Wells. 642-1606. Contemporary
American art and sculpture featuring, from the
Chicago area, Buzz Spector, Bruce White, Dan
Ziembo, Barry Tinsley, William Conger, Dan Ra-
miery, Vera Klement, Richard Loving, Frank Pia-
tek, Susan Sensemann, Sarah Krepp; from New
York, Joel Perlman, Jay Phillips, Tom Levine,
Mark Williams, Ford Crull, Frank Faulkner; from
the West Coast, Joe Fay, Liza Pang, Norman
Sunshine, Bob Nugent, David Bottini. *OPEN Mon-
Sat 10am-5:30pm.*

Campanile Galleries
200 South Michigan. 663-3885. American paintings of the late 19th and early 20th centuries:
The Ten, the Ashcan School, American landscape paintings, drawings, sculptures, and
bronzes. *OPEN Mon-Fri 9am-5:30pm; Sat 9:30-
4pm.*

Merill Chase
Water Tower Place, 835 Michigan, 2nd level;
337-6600. And Woodfield Mall, Schaumburg;
882-2822. Also Oakbrook Center, Oakbrook; 572-
0225. Paintings, prints, and sculpture of contemporary and historic artists such as Picasso, Miró,
Chagall, Dali, Erté, Hart, Kipniss, Addison, and
Altman. *OPEN Mon, Thurs-Fri 10am-8pm; Tues,
Wed & Sat 10am-6pm; Sun noon-5pm.*

Chicago Artists' Coalition
5 West Grand. 670-2060. Slide registry, 500
contemporary artists. *OPEN Mon-Fri 10am-5pm,
by appointment only.*

Chicago 200 Galerie
28 East Huron, 2nd floor. 787-6501. Contemporary Chicago artists: Bill Olendorf, Kay Sullivan, Gregory Palmer, Chuck Wood, Jackie
Sullivan, John Hooks, Jack Wright, Tom Hobbs,
Ed Rosen, Bruce Cascia. *OPEN Mon-Fri 9am-
5pm; weekends by appointment only.*

Jan Cicero Gallery
221 West Erie. 440-1904. Contemporary paintings, drawings, and prints. Joel Bass, James
Juszczqk, Susan Micod, Bill Kohn, Peter Marcus, among others. Some sculpture too. *OPEN
Tues-Sat 11am-5pm.*

Circle Gallery
Marriott Hotel, 540 North Michigan. 670-4304.
Circle Fine Art Corp., one of the largest-volume
publishers in the world. Contemporary Ameri-
can, European, and Asian graphics, jewelry,
paintings, and animation: Peter Max, Frank Gallo,
Jablonsky, Lebadang, Jamie Wyeth, Chuck
Jones, Montesino, Jan Balet, Leonor Fini, Erté,
Bledsoe, Will Barnet, Agam, Peter Hurd, Wayne
Cooper, Corning. *OPEN Mon-Wed & Fri 9:30am-
6pm; Thurs 9:30am-8pm; Sat 9:30am-6pm; Sun
noon-5pm.*

Contemporary Art Workshop
542 West Grant Place. 472-4004. Founded by
sculptor John Kearney, a nonprofit workshop
and exhibitions of new talent. *OPEN Mon-Fri
9:30am-5:30pm; Sat noon-5pm.*

Dart Gallery
212 West Superior, Suite 203. 787-6366. Contemporary American art including Chicago artists Robert Lostutter, Roland Ginzel, Jim Lutes,
Hollis Sigler, Nicholas Africano, Michael Hurson,
Phyllis Bramson, Donald McFadyen, David Snyder, Ken Warneke, Lynda Benglis, Paul Labus,
among others. *OPEN Tues-Sat 10am-5:30pm.*

Marianne Deson Gallery
340 West Huron. 787-0005. Promotes innovative
contemporary artists, many of whom are from
Chicago. Kass, Kowalski, Klamen, Brakke, Altman, Albuquerque, Justis, Davidson, Newman,
Nauman, Bertohot. *OPEN Tues-Fri 10:30am-
5:30pm; Sat 11am-5pm.*

Distelheim Galleries
1030 North State, Suite 38G. 642-5570. Contemporary American and School of Paris paintings,
graphics, and sculpture. *By appointment only.*

Fairweather Hardin Gallery
101 East Ontario. 642-0007. Twentieth-century

paintings, graphics, watercolors, drawings, and sculpture. Thirty years of experience in forming corporate collections. *OPEN Tues-Sat 10am-5:30pm.*

Feature
340 West Huron, 3rd floor. 751-1720. Postconceptual and Post-pop art. *OPEN Wed-Sat 11am-5pm.*

Wally Findlay Galleries
814 North Michigan. 649-1500. French Impressionist and Post-Impressionist masters: Monet, Renoir, Braque, Matisse. Contemporary Impressionists: Nessi, Fabien, Kluge, Gantner, Michel-Henry, Jean-Pierre Capron. *OPEN Mon-Fri 9:30am-5:30pm; Sat 9:30am-5pm.*

Gilman/Gruen Galleries
226 West Superior, 1st floor. 337-6262. Contemporary, often avant-garde, paintings and sculpture, mainly by midwestern artists. Frank Gallo, Roland Poska, Walter Fydryck, Bob Novak, Dennis Jones, Emily Kaufman, Stephen Hansen, Mildred Armato, Tom Balbo, Alba Corrado, Charles Herndon, Torn Parrish. Second floor offers jewelry. *OPEN Tues-Sat 10am-5:30pm; Sun & Mon closed.*

Goldman-Kraft
300 West Superior. 943-9088. Contemporary American as well as European and Israeli art. Arman Appel, Chagall, Henry Moore, Mark Tobey, Picasso. *OPEN Tues-Sat 10am-5pm; Mon by appointment.*

Richard Gray Gallery
620 North Michigan, 2nd floor. *301 West Superior, lower level. 642-8877. Modern European and American masters: Dubuffet, Avery, Léger, Anthony Caro, Hans Hofmann; contemporary prints; ancient and primitive art from Oceania, Africa, and the Americas. At the River North gallery more contemporary and emerging artists. *OPEN Tues-Sat 10am-5:30pm.* *Tues-Sat 11am-5pm.*

Grayson Gallery
356 West Huron, 2nd floor. 266-1336. Modern and contemporary paintings and sculpture; ancient and primitive art. *OPEN Tues-Sat 10am-5:30pm.*

Carl Hammer
200 West Superior. 266-8512. Specializes in the work of self-taught and outsider artists. Historical and contemporary. Includes contemporary furniture, quilts. *OPEN Tues-Sat 10am-5:30pm.*

Rhona Hoffman Gallery
215 West Superior. 951-8828. Major contemporary artists and photographers including Acconci, Haas, Judd, Lewitt, Golub. *OPEN Tues-Fri 10am-5:30pm; Sat 11am-5:30pm; Mon by appointment.*

Hokin/Kaufman Gallery, Inc.
210 West Superior. 266-1211. Contemporary, modern paintings, sculpture, and furniture. *OPEN Tues-Fri 10am-5pm; Sat 11am-4pm.*

B. C. Holland, Inc.
222 West Superior. 664-5000. Mainstream 20th-century drawings, paintings, and sculpture; antique objects including classical antiquities, textiles, and furniture. *By appointment only.*

Billy Hork Galleries, Ltd.
109 East Oak; 337-1199. And 3015 North Broadway; 528-7800. Also, 3033 North Clark, 935-9700; 1621 Chicago Avenue, Evanston, 492-1600. Contemporary European and American lithographs, serigraphs, and etchings. Charles Bragg, Calder, Miró, Dussau, Friedlander, Bruno Bruni, Will Barnet, Agam, Uzilevsky. *OPEN Mon-Sat 10am-6pm; Sun noon-5pm.*

Illinois Arts Council
100 West Randolph, Suite 10-500. 917-6750. Rotating exhibits of contemporary Illinois art. *OPEN Mon-Fri 9am-5pm.*

Illinois Bell Telephone Company
225 West Randolph. 727-2514. Lobby gallery: ten changing exhibits a year, of a varied nature. Ethnic, student, one-person, and group shows, in all media. *OPEN Mon-Fri 8:30am-5pm.*

Illinois Institute of Technology
Grover Hermann Hall, 3241 South Federal. 567-3075. Contemporary painting and photography exhibits. *OPEN Mon-Fri 8am-midnight; Sat 9am-midnight; Sun noon-midnight.*

R. S. Johnson International
645 North Michigan, Suite 234. 943-1661. Master graphics 15th to 20th centuries; 20th-century paintings, drawings, watercolors, and sculpture. *OPEN Mon-Sat 9am-5:30pm.*

Phyllis Kind
313 West Superior. 642-6302. Contemporary American artists, with an emphasis on Chicago painters and folk and native art. Jim Nutt, Gladys Nilsson, Ed Paschke, Ray Yoshida, Roger Brown, Christina Ramberg. *OPEN Tues-Sat 10am-5:30pm.*

Klein
356 West Huron, 2nd floor. 787-0400. Dimensional paintings and sculpture. *OPEN Tues-Sat 11am-5:30pm.*

R. H. Love Galleries
100 East Ohio. 664-9620. Nineteenth- and 20th-century paintings. Gilbert Stuart, Robert Goodnough, Ernest Lawson, Kenneth Noland, Louis Ritman, William Merritt Chase, Childe Hassam. *OPEN Mon-Fri 9am-5:30pm; Sat 9:30am-5pm.*

Peter Miller Gallery
356 West Huron. 951-0252. Contemporary art and sculpture: Chuck Walker, Maurice Wilson, Mark Kastabi, Mary Lou Zelazny, Daryl Trivieri. *OPEN Tues-Sat 11am-5:30pm.*

Mongerson Wunderlich
704 North Wells. 943-2354. Nineteenth- and 20th-century Western art, sculpture, and folk objects; Navajo weavings; American Impressionists. *OPEN Mon-Sat 10am-5pm.*

N.A.M.E.
361 West Superior. 642-2776. Artist-run alternative space: art, sculpture, music, performance. *OPEN Tues-Sat 11am-5pm.*

R. A. Nantus Gallery
2355 North Clark. 248-6660. European and American original prints from 17th century to

contemporary. Eighteenth- and 19th-century Japanese woodcuts. Botanical and genre European works. Paul Broom, George Rouault, Arthur Piza, Patrick Procktor. *OPEN Mon-Fri 1-7pm; Sat 10am-5:30pm.*

Isobel Neal Gallery
200 West Superior. 944-1570. Specializing exclusively in African American art. *OPEN Tues-Sat.*

Phyllis Needlman
642-7929. Contemporary art with an emphasis on Mexican and Latin-American artists. *By appointment only.*

Neville-Sargent Gallery
215 West Superior. 664-2707. Contemporary art, all media, prints and paintings. Glen Bradshaw, Melinda Stickney-Gibson, Daniel Joshua Goldstein, David Saber. *OPEN Mon-Sat 10am-5pm. Closed Sun.*

Jack O'Grady
333 North Michigan, Suite 2200. 726-9833. Nineteenth-century contemporary American art. Joe Sickbert, Mark English, Pegge Hopper, Fritz Scholder, Lu Bellmak, James Sessions, J. H. Sharp, Bernie Fuchs. *OPEN Mon-Fri 9:30am-4:30pm; Sat & Sun by appointment.*

Nina Owen, Ltd.
620 North Michigan, 5th floor. 664-0474. Contemporary sculpture, all mediums: enamel, glass, metal, wood, marble. *OPEN Tues-Sat 10am-5pm.*

The Perfect Touch
719 North State. 664-0130. Primarily 19th-century British and European oil paintings. *OPEN Mon-Fri 11am-6pm; Sat & Sun 11am-4pm.*

Prairie Lee Gallery
301 West Superior, lower level. 266-7113. Contemporary Southwest regional and American Indian art. *OPEN Tues-Sat 10am-5:30pm.*

Prestige
3909 West Howard Street, Skokie. 679-2555. Specialists in French, Dutch, and Italian paintings and bronzes of the 18th and 19th centuries. Also graphics by American Edna Hible and paintings by Italian Surrealist Tito Salomoni. Exclusive distributor of bronzes and graphics by Erté. *OPEN Mon-Wed 10am-9pm; Sat & Sun 11am-5pm; Thurs & Fri by appointment.*

Roger Ramsey
212 West Superior, Suite 503. 337-4678. Contemporary paintings, drawings, and prints. *OPEN Tues-Sat 10am-6pm.*

Randolph Street Gallery
756 North Milwaukee. 666-7737. Alternative space, on one floor. Installations, performance, exhibitions, on and off premises. *OPEN Tues-Sat noon-6pm.*

Betsy Rosenfield
212 West Superior. 787-8020. Contemporary American sculpture and painting. *OPEN Tues-Fri 10am-5:30pm; Sat 11am-4:30pm.*

J. Rosenthal Fine Arts
212 West Superior, 2nd floor. 642-2966. Contemporary American and European art, emerging and prominent artists. *OPEN Tues-Fri 11am-5pm; Sat noon-5pm.*

Esther Saks
311 West Superior, 3rd floor. 751-0911. Twentieth-century ceramic sculpture and paintings. *OPEN Tues-Sat 10am-5pm.*

Samuel Stein Fine Arts, Ltd.
620 North Michigan, Suite 340. 337-1782. Twentieth-century prints: Marc Chagall, Joan Miró, Paul Jenkins. Drawings, paintings, sculpture: Henry Moore, Picasso, Marini, Natkin, Mucha, Cheret. *OPEN Mon-Fri 10am-5:30pm; Sat 11am-5pm.*

Galleries Maurice Sternberg
Drake Hotel, West Michigan at Walton. 642-1700. Nineteenth- and 20th-century American and European paintings, drawings, and sculpture. *OPEN Mon-Fri 9am-5pm; Sat 10am-3pm.*

Struve Gallery
309 West Superior. 787-0563. Contemporary American paintings, sculpture, prints, and drawings. *OPEN Tues-Fri 10am-5:30pm; Sat 10am-5pm.*

Vanderpoel Gallery
2153 West 111th. 348-9616. Permanent collection: late 19th- and early 20th-century realism. Monthly changing exhibits as well. *OPEN Tues, Thurs & Sun 1-4pm.*

van Straaten Gallery
361 West Superior. 642-2900. Original prints, paintings, and works on paper. Dine, Motherwell, Oldenburg, Rauschenberg, Jasper Johns, Rosenquist, Helen Frankenthaler, David Hockney, Nevelson. *OPEN Mon-Sat 10am-5pm.*

Worthington
620 North Michigan, 2nd floor. 266-2424. Specializes in German Expressionism and contemporary American and European prints, drawings, sculpture, and paintings. *OPEN Tues-Sat 10am-5:30pm.*

Donald Young
325 West Huron. 664-2151. Well-known contemporary artists; Chicago artists as well. *OPEN Tues-Fri 10am-5:30pm; Sat 11am-5:30pm.*

Zaks Gallery
620 North Michigan, Suite 305. 943-8440. Contemporary paintings, drawings, sculpture. *OPEN Tues-Fri 11am-5:30pm; Sat noon-5pm.*

Zolla/Lieberman
356 West Huron, 1st floor. 944-1990. Located in a 100-year-old Adler & Sullivan building, it's one of Chicago's largest galleries. Contemporary artists: John Alexander, Deborah Butterfield, John Buck, Laddie John Dill, Suzanne Caporael, Terrence Laroue, Susanne Doremus, Dennis Nechvatal. Sculpture too. *OPEN Tues-Fri 10am-5:30pm; Sat 11am-5:30pm; Mon by appointment.*

Crafts

The Artisan Shop & Gallery
Plaza del Lago, 1515 Sheridan Road, Wilmette. 251-3775. Contemporary American handicrafts. *OPEN Mon-Sat 10am-5:30pm; Sun noon-5pm.*

Exhibit A
361 West Superior, 3rd floor. 944-1748. Fo-

cus is on contemporary ceramics and two-dimensional works of art. Peter Voulkos, Robert Turner, Thom Bohnert, Richard De Vore, Daniel Brush, George Timock, Dennis Mitchell, and others. *By appointment only.*

Joy Horwich Galleries
226 East Ontario, 3rd floor. 787-7486. Contemporary Chicago-area artists working in a variety of media. Porcelains, oils, woodcarvings, silk batiks, watercolors, bronzes, ceramics. *OPEN Tues-Sat 10am-5pm.*

The Indian Tree
642-1607. All American-Indian art, prehistoric, historic, and contemporary pottery; jewelry; Plains Indians material and weavings. *By appointment only.*

Lill Street Gallery
430 West Erie. 649-1777. An alternative space for ceramic and ceramic-related art, often large-scale. Children's classes given. *OPEN Tues-Sat 10am-5pm.*

Mindscape
1521 Sherman Street, Evanston. 864-2660. Contemporary American crafts in all media: fiber, metal, wood, ceramics, leather, glass; sculpture, jewelry, and wearable art. *OPEN Tues, Wed, Fri & Sat 10am-6pm; Thurs 10am-9pm; Sun 1-4pm.*

Objects
341 West Superior, 2nd floor. 664-6622. Primarily clay and artist-made furniture. Some American folk art. *OPEN Tues-Sat 10am-5pm.*

Eastern Art

Douglas Dawson
341 West Superior, 3rd floor. 751-1961. Ancient and historic textiles and related ethnographic art from Central Asia, Japan, Indonesia, Africa, and the Americas. Also Oceanic sculpture and historic ceramics. *OPEN Tues-Sat 10am-5:30pm.*

Linda Einfeld Primitive Arts
212 West Superior, Suite 503. 337-7894. Primitive art of Africa, Oceania, the Americas. *OPEN Tues-Sat 11am-5:30pm.*

Les Primitifs
2038 North Clark. 528-5200. Fine African and Oceanic (from New Guinea) ethnographic arts. Lots of jewelry. *OPEN Tues-Fri noon-7pm; Sat & Sun noon-6pm.*

Michael Wyman
300 West Superior. 787-3961. Traditional primitive art of Africa and Oceania. *OPEN Mon-Sat 12:30-5:30pm & by appointment.*

Photography, Prints, Posters

Balkin Fine Arts
120 South La Salle. 372-0160. Focus on emerging artists, particularly Chicago-area. Contemporary fine prints, American and some European. Photography too. *OPEN Mon-Fri 9am-5pm.*

Chicago Center for the Print, Ltd.
1509 West Fullerton. 477-1585. A fine graphics gallery and print atelier dedicated to the understanding and appreciation of the art of the print. Focus is on Chicago and midwestern printmakers. Rotating exhibits. Information and idea exchange. *OPEN Tues-Sun noon-8pm.*

Columbia Galleries & the Chicago Center for Contemporary Photography of Columbia College
600 South Michigan, lobby & 2nd floor. 663-1600. Gallery: all media with special emphasis on photography. Center: photo exhibits at all times. *OPEN Sept-June, Mon-Fri 10am-5pm, Sat noon-5pm; July & Aug, Mon-Sat 10am-4pm.*

Exchange National Bank Building
120 South La Salle. 781-8000. A 17-story Italian-Renaissance building. On display in the public areas of the bank since 1968: one of the nation's outstanding permanent photographic collections. Essentially presenting a history of photography from the first recorded photo, it includes most of the important photographers up to and including contemporary: Ansel Adams, Edward Weston, Julia Margaret Cameron, Paul Strand, Imogene Cunningham. *OPEN Mon-Fri 8am-4pm.*

Fly By Nite
714 North Wells. 664-8136; 337-0264. Leading Midwest dealer in art nouveau and art deco: graphics, paintings, ceramics, posters, jewelry, etc., 1890-1930. *OPEN Mon-Sat 10am-5pm & by appointment.*

Edwynn Houk Gallery
200 West Superior. 943-0698. Deals exclusively in major 20th-century photography. Eugene Atget, Diane Arbus, Irving Penn, Brassai, Weston. *OPEN Tues-Sat 10am-5pm.*

Kass/Meridian
215 West Superior, 2nd floor. 266-5999. Prints by Dine, Frankenthaler, Hockney, Katz, Lichtenstein, Motherwell, Paladino, Stella. *OPEN Mon-Sat 11am-5pm & by appointment.*

Douglas Kenyon, Inc.
1357 North Wells. 642-5300. Nineteenth- and 20th-century photography mainly. John James Audubon. Paper-conservation laboratory and archival framing. *OPEN Tues-Sat 9am-5pm.*

The Main Bank
1965 North Milwaukee. 278-6800. Chicago Imagists and other local artists. In the bank's public area. *OPEN Mon-Fri 9am-2pm; Fri 4-7pm as well.*

Mo Ming
1034 West Barry. 472-9894. Contemporary photography. Emphasis on work done by women. *OPEN Mon-Sat 10am-5pm.*

Poster Plus
2906 North Broadway. 549-2822. The city's largest poster source: art nouveau, deco, WWI, 20th-century greats. Chagall, Steinberg, Oldenburg, Miró. *OPEN Mon-Fri 11am-7pm; Sat 10am-6pm; Sun noon-5pm.*

Printworks
311 West Superior, Suite 105. 664-9407. Contemporary prints, drawings, photography, and artists' books. *OPEN Tues-Sat 11am-5pm.*

PARKS
&
GARDENS

Stock Exchange Archway in Grant Park

In this area, Chicago, with its lovingly created and tended formal and informal gardens, its conservatories and its vast parks system, is more reminiscent of London than is any other American city. (Its motto: Urbs in Horto, *City in a Garden.) The parks offer breathing space, a place in which to pause, to refresh, to rejoice. One cannot imagine a Chicago without them, and the way Chicagoans feel about them there is no need to say. Though nature, with a little help from man, makes the parks and gardens special all the time, each season has its own characteristic symbols and celebrations. See the* ANNUAL EVENTS *section for events in Chicago's parks and gardens throughout the year. For specific information on any city park call the Chicago Park District, 294-2200. Brochures on Chicago's parks and gardens are available from the Chicago Park District Public Information Office, 325 East McFetridge Drive, Chicago, IL 60605. 294-2493.*

NOTE: *Except for special events your park visits should be confined to daylight hours.*

GENERAL INFORMATION

Parks laws passed in 1869 established three Park Districts as municipal corporations—the West, South, and Lincoln Park systems. For the World's Columbian Exposition of 1893, the South Park Commission spent a whopping $24 million to develop a 2,000-acre system of parks and 35 miles of boulevards. By 1930 there was a total of 22 park districts. The Chicago Park District created in 1934 was a unification of these separate corporations. Today it has jurisdiction over 580 parks (156 major ones), which comprise a total of 6,748.68 acres.

Friends of the Parks
53 West Jackson Boulevard, Chicago, IL 60604. 922-3307. This nonprofit citywide citizens' organization is dedicated to improving Chicago's 580 parks. Some of its activities include musical happenings, art in the parks, and recreatioinal events.

PARKS

Burnham Park
(Includes East End & Promontory.) East Mc-Fetridge Drive to East 56th at Lake Michigan (1400 South). 294-2200. On 598 acres; in 1933, the site of "A Century of Progress," the celebration of Chicago's 100th birthday. At present, underutilized.

Outdoor facilities & programs: 1 senior baseball field; 2 softball fields; 2 football/soccer fields; 10 basketball standards; 2 volleyball courts; 8 tennis courts. Six playgrounds with spray pool, 3 sandboxes. Bridle path and bicycle path. Three beaches and a yacht-and-powerboat harbor with 3 launching ramps, 1,495 marine facilities; model-yacht basin. Soldier Field (*see also* HISTORIC & NEW CHICAGO, Historic Buildings & Areas).

Indoor facilities & programs: A field house with 4 club rooms, and a beach house.

Douglas Park
West 14th & South Albany (3100 West). 521-3244. On 174 acres. The site of Chicago's first outdoor gymnasium and public swimming pool, both built in 1896.

Outdoor facilities & programs: Swimming pool and swimming lagoon. Three senior and 2 junior baseball fields; 4 football/soccer fields; oval track; 15 basketball standards; 2 volleyball courts; 12 tennis courts. Five playgrounds with 2 spray pools, 2 sandboxes, and a day camp. Lagoon casting area. A bicycle path and cross-country skiing.

Indoor facilities & programs: A field house with gymnasium, gym/assembly hall, 8 club rooms and a kitchen.

Garfield Park

100 North Central Park Boulevard (3600 West). 826-3175. On 184 acres. Dedicated in 1869, and originally named Central Park. It contains the world's largest enclosed conservatory (see PARKS & GARDENS, Botanical Gardens & Conservatories: Garfield Park Conservatory).

Outdoor facilities & programs: Two swimming pools. Two senior and 1 junior baseball fields; 11 softball fields; 3 football/soccer fields; 10 basketball standards; 4 volleyball courts; 23 tennis courts; 6 horseshoe pitches. Four playgrounds with 3 spray pools, 2 sandboxes, and a day camp. Cross-country skiing. A bicycle path. Lagoon casting area. Model-yacht basin.

Indoor facilities & programs: A field house with gymnasium; assembly hall with stage; 7 clubrooms. Drama program: creative dramatics; improvisation, pantomime. Music program: piano, band, instrument, jazz.

Grant Park

East Randolph to East McFetridge Drive at Lake Michigan (150 Nortth). 294-4790. On 304 acres. The inspiration was Versailles, the plan was Daniel Burnham's, part of his famed Chicago Plan of 1909. Landfill created this green expanse where Lake Michigan once flowed. Attractions include formal gardens (see PARKS & GARDENS, Botanical Gardens & Conservatories: Grant Park Court of Presidents), Buckingham Fountain (see SIGHTSEEING, On Your Own), the Petrillo Music Shell (see ANNUAL EVENTS, June: Grant Park Concerts and July, Independence Day Weekend Celebrations: Concert & Fireworks), the Art Institute of Chicago (see MUSEUMS & GALLERIES, Museums: General Art Museums), Richard J. Daley Bicentennial Plaza (see SPORTS, Skating: Ice Skating). Chicagoans and visitors alike are indebted to Aaron Montgomery Ward, who is responsible for pursuing a cause to the Supreme Court of Illinois. The result: a decision barring any building (other than the Art Institute) from being built in Grant Park.

Outdoor facilities & programs: Two junior baseball fields; 6 softball fields; 3 football/soccer fields; 24 tennis courts; 8 volleyball courts (on tennis). Playground. Bicycle path. Yacht-and-powerboat harbor with 1,332 marine facilities. Ice rink.

Humboldt Park

West North & North Humboldt avenues (1600 North-3000 West). 276-0107. On 206.92 acres. Originally established as North Park in 1857.

Outdoor facilities & programs: Swimming pool and swimming lagoon. Three senior and 8 junior baseball fields; a softball field; 3 football/soccer fields; 8 basketball standards; 5 volleyball courts; 11 tennis courts. Five playgrounds with 2 spray pools, 3 sandboxes, and a day camp. Two ice-skating areas. Cross-country skiing. A bicycle path.

Indoor facilities & programs: A field house with 2 gym/assembly halls, 5 club rooms, and a kitchen. Boxing in a portable ring. Artcraft; craft shop—cabinetwork, woodturning; plastics.

Jackson Park East

East 63rd & South Stony Island (1600 East). 643-6363. On 542.89 acres. Created out of 700 acres of swamp as the site of the World's Columbian Exposition, 1893. Remaining are the Museum of Science and Industry (originally the Fine Arts Building) and the Convent of La Rabida, now a children's sanatorium. Lovely Japanese Garden on Wooded Island (see PARKS & GARDENS, Botanical Gardens & Conservatories).

Outdoor facilities & programs: Four senior baseball fields; 7 softball fields; 4 football/soccer fields; 13 basketball standards; 24 tennis courts; 2 bowling greens. Five playgrounds with sandbox and a day camp. Bicycle path; bridle path. Golf driving range; 18-hole golf course. Casting pool with pier. Three beaches; 3 yacht-and-powerboat harbors with 2 launching ramps, 738 marine facilities. Roller skating and cross country skiing.

Indoor facilities & programs: A field house with gymnasium, 2 club rooms, and a kitchen. Beach house. Drama—improvisation, creative dramatics, play reading, theater games for children, teens, and adults.

Kenwood Park

1330 East 50th. 924-9373. On 6.95 acres. Previously known as "Farmers' Field," a grazing area for cows.

Outdoor facilities & programs: Three junior baseball fields; a football/soccer field; 4 basketball standards; 4 volleyball courts; 2 tennis courts. Playground with spray pool and a sandbox. Ice skating.

Indoor facilities & programs: A gym-assembly hall; 6 club rooms and a kitchen. Recreation building with club room; music—piano, vocal, chorus, theory; drama—creative drama, improvision for children and teens.

Lincoln Park

West Armitage & North Clark & North Lake Shore Drive. West North Avenue to West Hollywood Avenue (2000 North to 231 West). 294-4750. Chicago's front yard. The city's largest park, encompassing 1,200 acres of land, much of which was formerly Lake Michigan. Part of a grant of 282,000 acres made by the federal government to the state of Illinois, it was acquired by the city in 1842 for the sum of $8,000. Once used as a cemetery (Chicago Cemetery, from North Avenue to Wisconsin Street to Asylum Place) to bury victims of an 1852 cholera epidemic as well as the remains of Confederate soldiers. In 1864 it was decided that the whole area be reserved as a park, necessitating transfer of the deceased to other cemeteries (see HISTORIC & NEW CHICAGO, Graveyards & Tombs: Crouch Tomb). By 1885 there was a zoo (see PARKS & GARDENS, Zoos & Aquariums) and a conservatory (see PARKS & GARDENS, Botanical Gardens & Conservatories), and Lake Shore Drive had already been built. The park's 250 acres were well on their way to becoming an urban Eden. Today there are four beaches, several yacht basins, a golf driving range, a 9-hole gold course (Waveland), an 18-hole miniature golf course, day/night tennis facilities, a fitness trail, a sledding hill, joggers in summer, cross-country skiers in winter, and unlimited opportunities for soaking up nature's bounty *without* ever leaving the city proper.

McKinley Park
2210 West Pershing Road (3900 South). 523-3811. On 69 acres, it contained the country's first field house, designed by Daniel Burnham and erected in 1905. A place "where physical and mental culture and wholesome recreation may be enjoyed by anyone who conducts himself properly," it housed a swimming pool, a gymnasium, and club rooms.

Outdoor facilities & programs: A swimming pool; 3 senior and 1 junior baseball fields; a softball field; a basketball/soccer field; 6 basketball standards; a volleyball court; 14 tennis courts; and 2 handball/racquetball courts. A playground with spray pool, sandbox, and a day camp. Bicycle path. Lagoon; casting area with pier and 2 ice-skating areas.

Indoor facilities & programs: A field house with 2 gymnasiums, 2 club rooms, and a kitchen. Artcraft—dressmaking, quilting; craft shop; music—piano, vocal, chorus, senior citizens' chorus. A senior-citizen center.

Midway Plaisance Park
West 59th & 60th & South Stony Island to South Cottage Grove (1600 East). This green lawn was the original formal entrance to the World's Columbian Exposition of 1893. Popular for sunbathing in summer (in official parlance "a passive recreation area") and ice skating in winter (two areas). A bicycle path too.

Olive Park
East Ohio & Lake Shore Drive. A lovely little pocket park.

Peterson Park
West Peterson & North Central Park (6000 North to 3600 West). 463-5839. The 23 acres comprising this park were acquired in 1977. It was previously occupied by the Municipal Tuberculosis Sanitarium.

Outdoor facilities & programs: Two junior baseball fields; 2 football/soccer fields; 8 basketball standards; 2 volleyball courts; 4 tennis courts. Two playgrounds. Cross-country skiing.

Union Park
1501 Randolph (150 North). 294-4736. Established in 1854 because residents petitioned the city in order to prevent developers from parceling out the land. The 13 acres were bought for $18,000.

Outdoor facilities & programs: A swimming pool with dressing rooms; a senior baseball field; 3 softball fields; a football/soccer field; straightaway track; 4 tennis courts; 4 shuffleboard facilities; 2 basketball standards. Playground with spray pool, sandbox, and a day camp. Two ice-skating areas. Cross-country skiing.

Indoor facilities & programs: A field house with

gymnasium, assembly hall with stage, 5 club rooms, and a kitchen. Artcraft—sewing, macramé, upholstery; drama—creative dramatics, pantomime, improvisation for children, teens, adults.

Washington Park
5531 South King Drive (400 East). 684-6530. On 366.84 acres. Site of the World's Columbian Exposition of 1893; laid out by Frederick Law Olmsted. Enhanced by a landscaped garden and the Du Sable Museum of African-American History (*see* MUSEUMS & GALLERIES, Museums: Ethnic Museums).

Outdoor facilities & programs: A swimming pool with dressing rooms. Six senior and 2 junior baseball fields; 6 softball fields; 4 football/soccer fields; 16 basketball standards; 18 tennis courts; 5 shuffleboard courts; 2 bowling greens. Five playgrounds with an adventure playland, a spray pool, 4 sandboxes, 2 day camps. Bicycle path; bridle path. Archery range. Lagoon; 2 casting areas, 1 with pier. Cross-country skiing.

Indoor facilities & programs: One field house with 2 gymnasiums, a gym/assembly hall, 6 club rooms, 1 kitchen, and a natatorium. Artcraft—dressmaking; disco dancing; yoga; craft shop—ceramics, lapidary, jewelry making, cabinetwork, plastics, woodturning; drama—creative dramatics, improvisation, theater games, acting technique for children, teens, adults; music—piano, vocal, chorus, theory. Camera club. Handball/racquetball. Senior-citizen center.

Wicker Park
North Damen & West Schiller (200 West to 1400 North). 276-1723. This triangular park, one of the city's smallest—4 acres—was donated by the brothers Wicker in 1870 for public use. Stiles at each end were to prevent cows from traversing. More recent lore has the late Mike Todd overseeing "crap games" here 40 years ago.

Outdoor facilities & programs: A softball field; 4 basketball standards; 1 volleyball court. Playground with spray pool and sandbox.

Indoor facilities & programs: A field house with 3 club rooms and a kitchen.

BOTANICAL GARDENS & CONSERVATORIES

Chicago Botanic Garden Horticulture Society
Lake Cook Road & Edens Expressway, Glencoe. 835-5440. The emphasis here is on learning. Three hundred acres of landscaped beauty: vegetable and flower gardens, 10 greenhouses, a prairie restoration, a nature trail through 15 acres of natural woodland, 110 varieties of native Illinois trees, and 3 Japanese islands. Their lagoons are a stopover point for migratory birds. There's an education center for classes and clinics, a floral-art museum, a horticultural library, exhibitions and demonstrations, an auditorium, a gift shop, and a restaurant. A 45-

minute narrated tram tour year-round; admission charge. Seasonal specialty shows. *OPEN 7 days 8am-dusk. CLOSED Christmas.* Education Center *OPEN Mon-Fri 9am-4pm; Sat & Sun 9am-6pm.* FREE.

Douglas Park Formal Garden
South of Ogden Avenue, east of Sacramento Boulevard. An exquisite formal garden with a natural lagoon, an open pergola, and a water-lily pool 160 feet long by 60 feet wide with a total of 40 day-blooming and 20 night-blooming lilies.

Daniel L. Flaherty Memorial Rose Garden
Near Congress Parkway, vicinity Buckingham Fountain. This garden contains 38 beds with approximately 8,000 plants of Hybrid Tea, Grandiflora, and Floribunda roses. Lovely day or night and a bonus for Buckingham Fountain viewers (*see* SIGHTSEEING, On Your Own).

Garfield Park Conservatory
300 North Central Park Boulevard. The world's largest enclosed horticultural conservatory (it covers 4½ acres). Over 5,000 varieties of plants, flowers, and trees. Eight halls include Palm House, Fernery, Cactus House, Warm House, Horticultural Hall, Aroid House, Economic House, and Show House. Four annual shoes (*see* ANNUAL EVENTS, February: Azalea Flower Show; March-April: Spring & Easter Flower Show; November: Chrysanthemum Show; *and* December: Christmas Flower Show). Guides are available for group tours, call 533-1281. *OPEN year-round, 7 days 9am-5pm; during major shows Sat-Thurs 10am-6pm; Fri 9am-9pm.* FREE.

Garfield Park Formal Garden
South of Madison between Central Park Boulevard & Hamlin. With an area of over 4 acres, this is one of Chicago's largest formal gardens. There are 56 geometrically laid-out beds with over 25,000 annual bedding plants. It also contains two huge lily pools (the north one being the largest tropical lily pool in the state) featuring 200 water lilies in 50 varieties.

Garfield Park Garden for the Blind
Just south of the Conservatory. Bounded by a 31-inch-high brick wall that meanders continuously for 360 feet. There are 59 4-by-5-foot planting areas identified in braille. Visitors are encouraged to touch and smell the 1,500 plants, and three fountains' jets produce a variety of sounds.

Grant Park Court of Presidents
North & south of Congress Parkway. A *very* formal garden originally conceived as a place to honor former U.S. chief executives with statuary, but to date Lincoln stands—no, he sits—alone (*see* HISTORIC & NEW CHICAGO, Statues & Monuments). Twenty thousand plants bloom here, and in summer Chicagoans and tourists alike are drawn to its beauty.

Humboldt Park Flower Garden
North of Division, west of Sacramento Boulevard. Two life-sized bison flank the entrance to this colorful circular formal garden on the west side. It blooms with 114,000 annuals.

Jackson Park Japanese Garden
On Wooded Island. A serene Oriental oasis, constructed by the government of Japan in 1893 as a place of rest for weary World's Columbian Exposition visitors. Destroyed by "patriotic" vandals in 1945, it was restored and rededicated in 1981. Japanese lanterns, thoughtfully placed rocks, a half-moon bridge, a waterfall, and water lilies create a romantic, as well as a tranquil, mood. Indeed, it has been a traditional university students' wooing spot. *OPEN 7 days 6 am-11 pm.*

Jackson Park Perennial Garden
The east end of Midway Plaisance, 59th & Stony Island Avenue. This outstanding public garden blooms with over 180 varieties of perennials and annuals. From April till the first frost, when hundreds of chrysanthemums bow out, elaborate floral displays are maintained.

Lincoln Park Conservatory
Stockton Drive at Fullerton. 294-4770. Covering an area of three acres, this conservatory, erected in 1891, is one of the nation's finest. There are four glassed buildings (Palm House, Fernery, Tropical House, and Grow House), 18 propagating houses, and several outdoor gardens (listed individually). Four annual shows concurrent with those at Garfield Park Conservatory (*see* ANNUAL EVENTS, February: Azalea Flower Show; March-April: Spring & Easter Flower Show; November: Chrysanthemum Show; *and* December: Christmas Flower Show). *OPEN year-round 7 days 9am-5pm; during major shows Sat-Thurs 10am-6pm, Fri 9am-9pm.* Group tours by reservation. FREE.

Lincoln Park Grandmother's Garden
Between Stockton Drive & Lincoln Park West. This old-fashioned garden, which covers an area of 130,000 square feet, has been in existence since 1893. Flowers that Granny loved predominate. There are 30,000 perennials, 10,000 annuals.

Lincoln Park Main Garden
South of the Conservatory. This dazzling garden is 800 feet long and 370 feet wide, covering an area of 296,000 square feet. Formal beds with 25,000 blooming plants. In the center, Bates Fountain, Storks at Play (*see* HISTORIC & NEW CHICAGO, Statues & Monuments).

Marquette Park Rose & Trial Garden
3540 West 71st (enter 67th & Kedzie and follow the signs). In the southern corner of this park is one of the Midwest's largest municipal rose gardens. It covers nearly one acre, in a contemporary free-form style. It contains approximately 4,000 roses in 80 varieties. The pool, fountains, and live swans add to the romance. To the west a trial ground for new annuals and perennials. Also, a cactus and succulent garden, a rock garden, herb and topiary gardens. There are approximately 17,000 plants, trees, and shrubs here.

Oak Park Conservatory
621 Garfield, Oak Park. 386-4700. Three showrooms: tropical rain forest, fernery, desert. Group

tours available, reserve in advance. Plant clinic Monday from 2 to 4pm. Seasonal floral displays; 500 species. *OPEN to the public Mon 2-4pm, Tues-Sun 10am-4pm.* FREE.

Rainbow Park Garden
Lakefront between 77th & 78th. 734-5976. Also known as the "Friendly Garden," this popular new perennial garden consists of eight rectangular beds, each 15 feet by 75 feet. The garden is enclosed by a privet hedge. Blooming bulbs in spring, mums in the fall.

Washington Park Formal Garden
Cottage Grove & 55th. This formal garden has one of Chicago's largest flower displays. The beds are arranged geometrically, with variously colored foliage plants arranged in formal designs; these are enhanced by flowering annuals in season.

BEACHES

There are 31 Lakefront beaches operated by the Chicago Park District. They are all OPEN to the public from June to mid September, 9am to 9:30pm, and they are all FREE. Call 294-2333 for information.

Major Beaches

Ardmore-Hollywood
5800 North.
Calumet (north)
9600 South.
Calumet (south)
9800 South. Lockers available.
Foster Street
5200 North. Lockers available.
Fullerton Avenue
2400 North.
Jackson (central)
57th-59th South.
Jackson (north)
51st, 49th, 47th South.
Jackson (south)
64th-67th South. Lockers available.
Loyola/Leone
7000 North.
Montrose Avenue
4400 North. Lockers available. Great views.
North Avenue
1600 North. Lockers available.
Oak Street
500-1000 North. The St.-Tropez of the Midwest just a credit card's throw away from the chic shops and boîtes. Lockers available.
Rainbow
7600 South. Lockers available.
31st Street
3100 South. Lockers available.
12th Street
900 East. Lockers available.

Minor Beaches

Chase
7300 North.
Columbia
6726 North.
Devon
6400 North.
Fargo
7432 North.
Granville
6200 North.
Hartigan (Albion)
6600 North.
Howard
7600 North.
Jarvis
7400 North.
Juneway Terrace
7800 North.
North Shore
6700 North.
Pratt
6800 North.
Rogers
7700 North.
Sherwin
7332 North.
Thorndale
5934 North.

ZOOS & AQUARIUMS

(For children's zoos, see KIDS' CHICAGO, Zoos & Animal Preserves.)

Brookfield Zoo
8400 West 31st Street at First Avenue, Brookfield. 242-2630; 485-0263 (suburbs). Eight miles from downtown Chicago. On over 200 acres: 24 exhibits with 2,000 animals (many in natural habitat settings) representing over 650 species, some of which are quite rare. How to see it? Motor Safari Coaches: a narrated zoo overview good for first-timer's orientation, mid April to October (nominal charge). In winter there is a free shuttle bus.

Highlights: *Predator Ecology,* a nocturnal addition to the Lion House, guided tours through five natural habitats of small carnivores, 11am to 3pm daily. *Seven Seas Panorama* for a daily dolphin show at 11:30am, 1, 2:30, and 3:45pm (admission charge). *Australia House,* a nocturnal walk-about mini tour in a cross section of Down Under. *Indian Lake Nature Trail* winds through a native mammal and bird sanctuary. *Tropic World,* the largest natural indoor exhibit in the U.S., presents rain forests of Asia, South America, and Africa.

The bookstore carries over 4,000 natural-history titles. Cafeteria or Nyani Lodge with a view of Baboon Island. Group tours reserve in advance for lunch and transport tour or free narrator guide. Be a Brookfield Parent, help feed an animal for a year (see SHOPPING, Specialty Shops & Services, Gifts: A.D.O.P.T. an Animal). OPEN year-round 7 days 10am-5pm; summer 10am-6pm. Admission charge, discount for children and senior citizens; children under age 6 FREE. FREE for all on Tuesday. Parking fee. (See also KIDS' CHICAGO, Zoos & Animal Preserves.)

Indian Boundary Park Zoo
2555 West Estes. 274-0644. This far North Side neighborhood zoo houses a small but representative collection of animals. OPEN year-round 7 days 8am-5pm. FREE.

Lincoln Park Zoo
Lincoln Park, 2200 North Cannon Drive. 294-4660. This wonderful home to many of God's great and little creatures (some endangered) is America's most-visited zoo (over 4 million people annually). It was begun in 1868 with a gift of two swans from New York's Central Park. With the $10 purchase of a bear cub in 1874 it was official—the Lincoln Park Zoological Garden. This fine city zoo (three miles from downtown) now houses over 2,000 animals on 35 Lakefront acres, many in natural habitat settings, more of which are being added with continuing modernization programs. Highlights: Great Ape House, the largest collection in captivity, in a rain-forest environment complete with waterfalls and thunderstorms. Feeding times are fun times: the apes eat at 10am and 3pm (Sinbad has no manners); at the Bird House chow time is 10am; Small Mammal House, 10:30am; Sea Lion Pool, 1:45pm; Lion House, 4pm. Rookery bird sanctuary provides serene environment for land and water fowl. Cafeteria. There are special programs, films, and lectures; Saturday and Sunday meetings and classes; call 294-4649 for information. OPEN year-round 7 days 9am-5pm. FREE. (See also KIDS' CHICAGO, Zoos & Animal Preserves: Children's Zoo and Farm-in-the-Zoo.)

John G. Shedd Aquarium
In Grant Park, at 1200 South Lake Shore Drive. 939-2426. Founded in 1929 to develop an understanding of man's relationship to and dependence upon the sea and its creatures. This is the world's largest indoor aquarium. A slide show in the auditorium every hour on the half hour orients the visitor. There are 4,500 underwater creatures, representing 500 species, housed in six fresh- and saltwater (made from Lake Michigan and their own recipe) tanks. The centerpiece is the 90,000-gallon Coral Reef exhibits featuring 350 of the Caribbean's most colorful swimmers. Watch and listen via microphone to a diver who enters the reef every day at 11am and 2pm (and again at 3pm in the summer) to hand feed the fish while describing their characteristics. The Sea Shop sells seashells, other aquatic artifacts, and books. The Aquatic Science Center offers educational opportunities and a library for use by school groups. Summer programs available for adults and kids. Groups must reserve 2 weeks in advance. Membership available. OPEN May-Aug, 7 days 9am-5pm;

Mar-Apr & Sept-Oct, 7 days 10am-5pm; Nov-Dec & Jan-Feb, 7 days 10am-5 pm. CLOSED Christmas & New Year's Day. Admission charge; lower for children age 6-17, students with ID, senior citizens. FREE for all on Thursday.

FOREST PRESERVES

Cook County

Chicago is once more blessed. No other American city has such a large area of publicly owned native land so readily accessible. There are nine major forest preserves in Cook County. They are sanctuaries of native landscapes with approximately 2,200 picnic areas along the borders. (Of these, 180 are designated for groups of 25 or more. A permit must be obtained for group sites at the Daley Civic Center, 50 West Washington, Room 4065, 443-6580. There is a small deposit required that is refunded after your picnic.) No cars are permitted within the preserves—only walking, hiking, bicycling, and horseback riding are allowed, and then only in the 150 miles of designated trails. There are ski trails and swimming pools also. There is no interference within these preserves—trees when they fall remain; there is no wildlife control or management (except for fish). Nature is simply allowed to do her thing and you can go and watch. Not even the picking of wildflowers is allowed—"love 'em and leave 'em," and have a nice picnic. (NOTE: Free Picnic Areas & Trail Maps are available for all nine preserves at each division headquarters and at the Cook County main headquarters at 536 North Harlem, River Forest, 261-8400 [city]; 366-9420 [suburbs]).

Calumet Division
Headquarters: 87th & Western, Chicago, IL 60620. 233-3766 or -3767. Located in the Chicago Plain (originally the bed of Lake Chicago), it consists of six small unconnected preserves. Near the far south and southwestern parts of the city of Chicago.

Beaubien Preserve
Calumet Expressway below 130th. Boating center on the Little Calumet River and Flatfoot Lake.

Burnham Woods
Between Burnham Avenue & the Indiana state line, south of 130th. Conservation center; Powder Horn Lake for good fishing; Burnham Woods Golf Course at Burnham & 142nd (862-9043).

Dixmoor & Kickapoo Playfields
South of 142nd and west of Halsted. Large wooded area on the Little Calumet River.

Dan Ryan Woods
East of Western between 83rd and 91st. Exceptional views of Chicago skyline.

Wolf Lake Preserve
South of 112th at the Indiana state line. Good fishing in Wolf Lake. Also contains Eggers

Grove with its native sassafras trees. Shore-birds nest in the marsh north of Wolf Lake; it's a migratory stop.

Des Plaines Division
Headquarters: River Road, Mount Prospect, IL 60056. 824-1900 or -1883. Follows the banks of the Des Plaines River for approximately 12 miles near northwestern suburbs. Heavily forested. Contains the remains of Indian charcoal pits, a former Indian village, and a pioneer cabin. Huge cottonwoods and—wonderful in fall—hard maples. Canoeing, rowing, and sailing on two lakes: Beck and Big Bend.

Indian Boundary Division
8800 West Belmont, Chicago, IL 60634. 625-0606 or -0607. Follows the Des Plaines River west of northern Chicago, contiguous with the city limits. Contains Evans Field—site of a former Indian village and chipping station, several burial sites and five mounds built by prehistoric Indians, as well as St. Joseph Cemetery; the Trailside Museum, at Chicago and Thatcher avenues, with exhibits of wildlife native to the area; model-airplane flying field off Irving Park Road near Cumberland Avenue; canoeing and rowing on Axehead Lake; Indian cemetery containing the remains of Chief Robinson and his family; wells referred to as the "Fountain of Youth."

North Branch Division
Headquarters: 6633 Harts Road, Niles, IL 60648. 775-4060 or -4194. Follow the banks of the Chicago River's North Branch from Beckwith Road south to Foster Avenue. Located in the former bed of glacial Lake Chicago. Contains two golf courses, swimming pool, bike path, walking trails, wooded trails. Carpenter and Gross Point roads are the northerly sections of former Indian trails.

Palos & Sag Valley Divisions
Palos Headquarters: 9900 South Willow Springs Road, Willow Springs, IL 60480; 839-5617 or -5618. Sag Valley Headquarters: 12201 West McCarthy Road, Palos Park, IL 60464; 448-8532 or -8533. Ten miles west of southern Chicago between 87th and 143rd streets. Thirty-two miles of hilly and scenic trails in 10,000 acres (the largest and most diversified) of woods, meadows, marshes, and lakes. Good wildlife area; raspberries, blackberries, and dewberries ripe for picking in July, mushrooms in autumn. Large concentration of shorebirds and waterfowl on Longjohn, Saganashkee, and McGinnis sloughs in spring and fall migration periods. Sledding, tobogganing; bicycling, horseback riding, hiking, model-airplane flying; cross-country skiing; fishing. The Little Red Schoolhouse (see PARKS & GARDENS, Nature Centers & Trails).

Salt Creek Division
Headquarters: 17th Avenue at Salt Creek, North Riverside, IL 60546. 485-8410 or -8411. West of Chicago between Roosevelt Road & 47th. This small preserve contains the Brookfield Zoo (see PARKS & GARDENS, Zoos & Aquariums) as well as the Chicago Portage off Harlem Avenue south of 47th—historically significant as the merging point of the most important Indian trails and as

the route between the St. Lawrence and Mississippi rivers. Also contains the Forest Preserve District Nursery, two nature trails, boat-launching site, toboggan slides and warming shelter, flying field for model airplanes.

Skokie Division
Headquarters: 1720 Cherry Street, Northfield, IL 60093. 446-5652 or -5676. Ten miles due north of Chicago, mainly along Edens Expressway. Contains the 190-acre Skokie Lagoon, developed for flood control but providing good picnic and fishing opportunities. Bicycle and foot paths, rowing, canoeing. Good wildflower areas.

Thorn Creek Division
Headquarters: Thornton-Lansing Road, Lansing, IL 60438. 474-1221 or -1227. Five to ten miles south of Chicago between the Indiana border and Halsted Street. Follows the banks of Thorn and North creeks. Hiking and bike trails. Pioneer-home site—the home of Revolutionary War soldier John McCoy and a station on the Underground Railroad for escaped slaves. Jurgensen Woods for blueberry patches. Sand Ridge Nature Center (see PARKS & GARDENS, Nature Centers & Trails). Green Lake region notable for sand dunes formed during last glacial period.

Tinley Creek Division
Headquarters: 13800 South Harlem Avenue, Orland Park, IL 60462. 385-7650 or -7654. Ten miles southwest of Chicago. Located on the "Tinley moraine," a ridge of glacial drift. Contains forested ravines, gullies; good fishing; nice vantage points; bird-watching during spring and fall migrations of waterfowl; Forest Preserve Tree Nursery; model-airplane flying field.

ARBORETUMS

Ladd Arboretum
2024 North McCormick Boulevard, Evanston. 864-5181. Twenty-two acres—hiking trails, prairie restorations, gardens, and a bird sanctuary. Run by the Evanston Environmental Association, call their Ecology Center for information, 864-5181. (They also run the Lighthouse Nature Center.)

Morton Arboretum
Route 53, Lisle. 969-5682. Founded in 1922. On 1,500 acres you will find every species of woody plant that this climate and soil can sustain. Start at the information building, where a slide presentation will orient you. Drive through on 16 miles of one-way roads or walk the systems of marked nature trails. Highlights include a Japanese collection; the May T. Watts Reading Garden, containing plants associated with botanical history; woodlands, wetlands, and prairie grasslands. Open-air guided bus tours are available during May and October, both colorful high times. Tearoom, bookstore, gift shop, and library. Good bird-watching area: migrating waterfowl around Arbor Lake. *OPEN year-round, weather permitting; Apr-Oct 9am-7pm; Nov-Mar 9am-5pm.* Ad-

mission charge (per car). Discount for senior citizens.

NATURE CENTERS & TRAILS

All maintained and operated by naturalists of the Conservation Department Forest Preserve District of Cook County. For information and group reservations, two weeks in advance, call 261-8400 (Chicago) or 366-9420 (suburbs). FREE.

Crabtree
Palatine Road, one mile west of Barrington Road. In the far-northwest corner of Cook County, on 1,100 acres set aside for educational purposes. Ecology is the theme, emphasizing relationships between plants, animals, and their environment. Native oak/hickory forests and prairies. At the center: a resident Canadian goose flock, wildlife observation blinds, wildflowers; prairie and aquatic exhibits. Several self-guiding nature trails ranging in length from 20 to 90 minutes. No pets, bicycles, or radios on trails. Exhibit building *OPEN 7 days 9am-5pm; Nov 1-Mar 1 9am-4pm. Trails & parking fields OPEN 7 days 8am-½ hour before sunset. CLOSED Christmas & New Year's Day.*

Illinois Prairie Path
616 Delles, Wheaton. 665-5310. A well-marked 40-mile trail for bikers and hikers traces the abandoned rail-bed of the old Chicago, Aurora & Elgin Railroad. It covers woodland, prairie, and marshland. Pack a picnic lunch. *Great* bird-watching—over 85 species have been sighted along this path.

Little Red Schoolhouse
West side of Willow Springs Road (104th Avenue), ½ mile south of 95th Street. Part of the Palos Preserve (*see* PARKS & GARDENS, Forest Preserves: Cook County). Located on Valparaiso terminal moraine (125 feet higher than downtown Chicago). On exhibit in this one-room 1886 schoolhouse are native mammals, reptiles, birds, fish, amphibians, and invertebrates; seasonal wildflowers; a farm garden and an orchard. Through a telescope, view wildlife on Longjohn Slough. There are three self-guiding nature trails: 15-, 30-, 60-minute walks. Parking facilities. No pets, bicycles, or radios on the trails. Building *OPEN Mon-Thurs 9am-4:30pm; Sat, Sun & holidays 9am-5pm; Nov-Mar 9am-4pm. CLOSED Fri. Trails OPEN 7 days 8am-½ hour before sunset. CLOSED Christmas & New Year's Day.*

River Trail
West side of Milwaukee Avenue (Route 21), ¾ mile southeast of River Road (Route 45), Northbrook. Located in the Des Plaines Valley, which was carved by meeting glaciers. The Nature Museum has seasonal exhibits on fish, insects, and plants; weather; geology; and animal life. There are outdoor exhibits reflecting the area's Indian history; there are also a bee colony, an orchard, an herb garden, and an organic garden, as well as self-guiding nature trails. Maple Syrup Festival every March and a Honey Festival every October. No pets, bicycles, or radios on trails. Exhibits *OPEN Mar-Sept, Mon-Thurs 8:30am-4:30pm; Sat, Sun & holidays 8:30am-5pm; Christmas & New Year's Day, Oct-Feb, Mon-Thurs, Sat & Sun 9am-3pm. CLOSED Fri. Trails & parking areas OPEN Mon-Fri till 5pm; Sat, Sun & holidays till 5:30pm.*

Sand Ridge
Paxton and 159th, 2 blocks north of South Holland. Located in the Calumet district, this center's emphasis is the area's geological and natural history. The Exhibit Room features special programs such as walks, films, and lectures year-round. Pioneer cabins have been reconstructed to portray the life of the area's 19th-century settlers. Spinning, weaving, and candlemaking are demonstrated on weekends. There are two self-guiding nature trails, and the Braille Trail— a 500-foot trail designed as self-guiding for the visually handicapped. No pets, bicycles, or radios on trails. Exhibit Room *OPEN Mon-Thurs 9am-4:30pm; Apr-Oct Sat, Sun & holidays 9am-5pm; Nov-Mar 9am-4pm. CLOSED Fri, Christmas & New Year's Day. Trails OPEN 7 days 8:30am-5pm.*

Trailside Museum
Thatcher & Chicago avenues, River Forest. On only 35 acres, good for short visits by families and small groups. No nature trails. *OPEN Sun-Wed & Fri 10am-5pm. CLOSED Thurs & holidays.*

BIRD-WATCHING

(*See also* PARKS & GARDENS, Forest Preserves *and* Nature Centers & Trails.)

Rare-Bird Alert
671-1522, *24 hours a day, 7 days a week*. Call to hear the Chicago Audubon Society's report of unusual sightings of birds in the area. To report unusual sightings of birds, call 673-4295.

**Bird-Watchers' Hotline
(Chicago Audubon Society)**
671-6446, *24 hours a day, 7 days a week*. Bird- and birding-related events. Seminars, field trips, bird walks during migration periods.

Chicago Audubon Society
4517 Wesley Terrace, Schiller Park. 671-6446. Bird walks, field trips, and workshops on bird-watching. Call for information.

Chicago Ornithological Society
241-6757. Since 1912 in Chicago, sponsors year-round bird-watching trips. One member has banded over 80,000 birds. Call between 5 and 10pm for information.

Jackson & Lincoln Park Bird Walks
Morning bird walks in Jackson (Wooded Island) and Lincoln parks, top city-bird stops. September to May, Monday, Wednesday, Friday, and

Saturday at 7am; from June to August, Wednesday at 7am and Saturday at 8am. Sponsored by the Chicago Ornithological Society; group meets at Darrow Bridge. Call the Academy of Science, 549-0606, for information.

Lincoln Park Bird Walks

Meet in front of the Bird House at Lincoln Park Zoo and go where the birds are. April to May, September to October, every Sunday, Tuesday, and Thursday at 8:30am. Call 294-4660 for information.

Morton Arboretum

Route 53 at east-west tollway, Lisle. 968-0074. Bird-watching on Arbor Lake. Great for winter birds. Special programs available. (*See also* PARKS & GARDENS, Arboretums.)

KIDS' CHICAGO

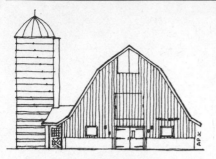

Farm-in-the-Zoo

SEEING CHICAGO: A KID'S-EYE VIEW

Here are some fun things to do with kids in the city. For more of the traditional attractions see SIGHTSEEING *and* HISTORIC & NEW CHICAGO. *Also see* ANNUAL EVENTS, *for parades, fairs, and festivals, many of which are kid-oriented and many are also* FREE.

Chicago Fire Academy
558 West De Koven. Where the Chicago Fire of 1871 started, they now train people to stop them. Thirty-minute tours include a visit to the Academy Fire Department Museum. Tours *Mon-Fri 10am & 1pm*. Reserve in advance, call 744-6691. FREE.

Chicago Police Department
1121 South State. 744-5570. Experience the excitement of a big-city police headquarters. Group tours of 15 to 30 kids, age 12 and over, of the world's most advanced law-enforcement headquarters—equipped with a sophisticated communications system. Reserve 2 weeks in advance. FREE.

Chicago *Sun Times*
401 North Wabash. 321-2032. The tour lasts 45 minutes and provides a fascinating glimpse of a big-city paper in action. Tours *Mon-Fri 10:30am*. Reserve in advance. FREE.

Cook County Criminal Courts Building
2600 South California. 443-7164. The court, a judge, jury. Visitors will be searched. Two-hour tours *Mon-Fri at 9:30am*. Reservations required. High-school age and over. FREE.

Glessner House
1800 South Prairie. 326-1393. A one-hour tour of the famed architectural landmark; designed for kids age 6 to 10. Nineteenth-century clothes, toys, and household objects depict life as it was for the Glessner family in the 1880s. Tours *Tues-Sun noon, 1, 2, & 3pm*. Reserve. CLOSED *Nov-Mar Mon, Wed & Fri*. Special group tours available by reservation only. Admission charge.

Thomas Hughes Children's Library
Chicago Public Library Cultural Center, 78 East Washington. 269-2835. Take a tour of the fabu-lous Cultural Center. For 8th graders and under. On a reservation basis. Call ahead. *OPEN Mon-Fri 9am-5:30pm; Sat 9am-5pm*. CLOSED *Sun*. FREE.

Jay's Potato Chips
825 East 99th. 731-8400. From spud to chip before your very eyes. Group tours only. *Mon-Thurs at 9:45am*. Reserve *very* well in advance. For age 7 to high school only. FREE.

O'Hare International Airport
Mannheim Road at Kennedy Expressway. 686-2300. The world's busiest airport. One- to 1½-hour tour of the facilities, usually including terminals, taxi ways, and a crash station. Individual tours are tailored to the age level and interests of each group. For 3rd graders/8-year-olds and up. If available, an airplane interior may be included in the tour. Reserve 2 to 6 months in advance. Tours for groups of 25 to 40 persons only. *Mon-Fri 10 & 11:30am*. FREE.

"Put Your Arms Around a Building"
ArchiCenter, 330 South Dearborn. 782-1776. A one-hour walking tour of the Loop for children age 6 to 12; serves as an introduction to the differences among styles of buildings—from historic to modern. Learn through touching and comparing. Children must be accompanied by an adult. Sponsored by the Chicago Architecture Foundation. *July & Aug only, Sat at 10:30am*. Reserve. Low admission charge.

Sears Tower Skydeck
233 South Wacker. 875-9696. Just try to find your house from the top of the world's tallest building, after riding in the world's fastest elevator. *OPEN 7 days 9am-midnight*. Admission charge, lower for children under age 16; children under age 5 FREE. Group rates available.

Wendella Sightseeing Boats
400 North Michigan, at the Wrigley Building. 337-1446. Combination Lake and river trips for groups of elementary-school children. From the Chicago River through the Locks onto Lake Michigan, north to Oak Street, and then south to the Planetarium, giving the kids a view of the famed Chicago skyline (one is never too young to start appreciating its beauty). The guided tour takes 1½ hours. Bring a picnic lunch. Call in advance for group reservations. (For individual passage *see* SIGHTSEEING, Lake & River Trips.)

MUSEUMS FOR CHILDREN

Also included are general museums with special attractions for kids.

Throughout the year the museums have special children's programs. Call the education department of the individual museum for details.

Adler Planetarium
1300 South Lake Shore Drive. 322-0304. See a moon rock, a NASA space suit, antique navigation and astronomy instruments. Explore the universe without leaving Chicago. *Special:* "Sky

Show"—five different shows each year (*see* AN-NUAL EVENTS, December). Saturday morning at 10am special sky show (½ hour) geared toward younger children. Admission charge. There are also astronomy courses Saturday mornings for kids age 3 to 12. Building *OPEN Mon-Thurs 9:30am-4:30pm, Fri 9am-9pm, Sat & Sun 9am-5pm. FREE. Sky Shows: Sept-mid June Mon-Thurs at 2pm; Fri at 2 & 8pm; Sat, Sun & holidays at 11am & 1, 2, 3 & 4pm. June 16-Aug 30 7 days 11am & 1, 2, 3, 4 & 8pm.* The 8pm show concludes with a visit to Doane Observatory for a look into space at the planets and the stars. Admission charge, lower for children age 6-17; children under age 6 not admitted.

American Police Center & Museum
1130 South Wabash, 2nd floor. 431-0005. Everything here is related to police matters. On display are uniforms, weapons, badges, etc. Films—with group tours only—on police in action, geared to the age level on crime prevention and security. Highly informative. Groups reserve 1 to 2 weeks in advance. *OPEN Mon-Fri 9am-4pm.* Donation.

Art Institute of Chicago: Junior Museum
Michigan & Adams. 443-3600. The galleries, auditorium, and library of this museum within a museum are designed to acquaint school-age youngsters with art through understanding and appreciation. Continuing exhibitions include photography, print-making, painting, and sculpture. *Special:* "Heritage Hikes," armed with clues in the free hike books (available in the Little Library, *OPEN Mon-Fri 10:30am-2pm, Sat 10:30am-4pm, Sun from noon; call* 443-3680), walk around the Loop discovering Chicago's architectural treasures. "I Spy," free games (from Little Library) provide clues to works of art in the Institute's permanent collection. "We Spy," for groups (call ahead). "Forms in Space I," a sculpture walk from the Art Institute to the Civic Center Picasso. The "Picnic Room"—which is open Monday to Friday from 11am to 2pm—is for groups of kids with bag lunches. Call for reservations, 443-3680. "Saturday Walks" are guided tours of the museum's collections. Meet in Blake Court of the Junior Museum. Family workshops on weekends. Each workshop includes a gallery walk and an art activity. Storytelling on Sundays at 1pm. Artist demonstrations on weekends. Drawing in the galleries on weekends. The gift shop has coloring books, miniatures, puzzles, wooden tops, and reproductions. Museum *OPEN Mon, Wed-Fri 10:30am-4pm; Tues 10:30am-7:30pm; Sat 10am-4:30pm; Sun and holidays noon-4:30pm.* Suggested contribution. FREE for all on Tuesday.

Chicago Academy of Sciences
2001 North Clark. 549-0606. This is Chicago's oldest science museum. Fascinating and educational natural history exhibits. Much information on how the Great Lakes were formed and on the animal and plant life associated with the area. Travel logs given Sundays at 2:30pm. For children's programs, call for information. *OPEN 7 days 10am-5pm. CLOSED Christmas.* Admission charge. FREE for all on Mondays.

Chicago Historical Society
1600 North Clark. 642-4600. Chicago history comes alive: a sizzling 11-minute panoramic slide show of the 1871 Great Fire; board Chicago's first steam locomotive (stationary, unfortunately); listen to snatches of music Chicago is famous for—blues, jazz. Fascinating, too, is the Pioneer Life Gallery where demonstrations are given in weaving, spinning, and candle dipping. *Special:* Alex Marx Educational Gallery where touch objects are on display: *Mon-Fri 10am-noon.* Museum *OPEN Mon-Sat 9:30am-4:30pm; Sun noon 5pm.* Admission charge, lower for children age 6-17. FREE for all on Monday.

Chicago Museum of Holography
1134 West Washington Boulevard. 226-1007. Focused laser beams become 3-D images that float in space. There are permanent and changing exhibits; a school and research facilities. The museum for the twenty-first century. Lectures and workshops too. *OPEN Wed-Sun 12:30-5pm. CLOSED Mon & Tues.* Admission charge.

Field Museum of Natural History
South Lake Shore Drive at Roosevelt Road. 922-9410. Discover Egyptian mummies, dinosaurs, Neanderthal man, wild animals from Africa, native American Indians—fascinating and exciting exhibits in this fine natural history museum. Available from the museum shop: "Journey," self-guided tours for families (nominally priced), help you wander through the exhibits with crossword puzzles and drawings. *Special:* "The Place of Wonder," a gallery where kids are encouraged to handle everything from shells to volcanic ash: *OPEN Mon-Fri 1-3pm; Sat & Sun 10am-noon & 1-3pm.* "Weekend Discovery Programs," free tours, demonstrations, and films that relate to the exhibits. There are Winter Fun workshops and Summer Fun workshops, which cover every aspect of natural history. Some include pottery, animal art, and Indian games. Free parking; McDonald's restaurant. Museum *OPEN year-round 7 days 9am-5pm. CLOSED Thanksgiving, Christmas & New Year's Day.* Admission charge, lower for children age 6-17; children under age 6 FREE. FREE for all on Thursday.

Museum of Science and Industry
57th & South Lake Shore Drive. 684-1414. Every one of the 4 million people who visit this museum yearly becomes a kid. There are so many things to see and do here—explore space while visiting the Henry Crown Space Center, and Omnimax Theater, walk through a 16-foot model of a human heart, play tic-tac-toe with a computer, or fly a plane (simulated flight, of course). For preschoolers, "The Curiosity Place" *(OPEN 7 days 10am-5pm.)*, with toddler-sized, activity-oriented "good stuff." Parents, wear comfortable shoes, it covers 4 acres! "3-2-1- Contact" guidebooks from the museum store (nominal price) guide a child through exhibits with questions, activities, and games. From October through November

there is the fine Children's Science Book Fair. In addition, during the school year, there are workshops, classes, and amusements designed for school-age youngsters, as well as a Science Summer Camp. Saturday Family Classes stress participation, and child must be accompanied by an adult. Reserve. Call 684-1414. Free parking; full-service Century Room Cafeteria; snack machines. Accessible to the handicapped. Museum *OPEN Sept-May Mon-Fri 9:30am-4pm; Sat, Sun & holidays 9:30am-5:30pm; Memorial Day-Labor Day 7 days 9:30am-5:30pm.* In addition, the Henry Crown Space Center and the Omnimax Theater are *OPEN Tues, Fri, Sat & Sun 6-9pm. FREE,* but special exhibits have a nominal charge.

Ripley's Believe It or Not Museum
1500 North Wells. 337-6077. The odd, odder, and oddest from around the world. *OPEN Sun-Thurs noon-9pm; Fri & Sat noon-midnight; in summer Sun-Thurs noon-11pm.* Admission charge, lower for children and senior citizens.

Telephony Museum
225 West Randolph. 727-2994. In the lobby of the Illinois Bell Building. The history of the telephone from Alexander Graham Bell's early models to picture phones. Some hands-on exhibits, telephone quiz games. Bell Theater for a film on communications. Group tours reserve 2 weeks in advance. *OPEN Mon-Fri 8:30am-4pm. FREE.*

ZOOS & ANIMAL PRESERVES

(See also PARKS & GARDENS, Zoos & Aquariums.)

Brookfield Children's Zoo
8400 West 31st Street, Brookfield. 242-2630; 485-0263 (suburbs). Domestic and selected wild animals provide a fun time. There's a milking parlor for cows and goats, a petting ring; chicks being hatched, bees in the hive; barnyard creatures such as snakes, rodents, owls. In spring and summer there are demonstrations of horsemanship and border collies herding sheep. Lassie the Pig, one of the Animals in Action, obeys commands in four languages, shakes hands, and curtsies. In winter on the second level of the Big Barn: "Touch Boxes," to identify objects by touch only. A new "Seven Seas Panorama" exhibit features the zoo's acrobatic dolphins. In all, six acres have been transformed into a marine showplace, with a 2,000-seat Dolphinarium and a naturalistic seascape with four exhibit pools. *OPEN year-round 7 days, June-Aug 10am-6pm; Sept-May 10am-6pm.* Admission charge, lower for children age 6-11 and senior citizens; children under age 6 FREE.

Children's Zoo
Lincoln Park, north end of the South Pond. 294-4660. Small animals can be petted. Outdoor summer garden. Chimpanzees' Tea Party daily at 1:30pm. *OPEN year-round 7 days 10:30am-5pm. FREE.*

Farm-in-the-Zoo
Lincoln Park, Lakefront at Fullerton, south of the Children's Zoo. 294-4678. A five-acre working Illinois farm provides a fun learning experience for city kids. Three barns for demonstrations, including cow-milking at 10am, noon, and 2 pm. Inhabitants include chickens, geese, ducks, sheep, pigs, horses, and cows. Tours available, reserve in advance, call 294-4649 between 9am and 5pm. *OPEN year-round 7 days 9:45am-4:45pm. FREE.*

Indian Boundary Park Zoo
2555 West Estes. 274-0644. A little North Side neighborhood zoo with a small but representative collection of animals. *OPEN year-round 7 days 8am-5pm. FREE.*

Willowbrook Wildlife Haven
525 South Park Boulevard, Glen Ellyn. 790-4900. A small preserve in the Du Page County system. Outstanding for its Willowbrook Wildlife Haven—where sick and injured birds and animals find refuge, among them turtles, coyotes, robins, hawks, and skunks. Easily combined with a trip to Morton Arboretum (*see PARKS & GARDENS, Arboretums*). *OPEN 7 days 9am-5pm; from 8:30am to bring in an animal. FREE.*

LIBRARIES

Neighborhood libraries present film programs, book sales, lectures, and children's story hours, call 269-3019 for the hours of one convenient to you.

Thomas Hughes Children's Library
Chicago Public Library Cultural Center, 78 East Washington. 269-2835. Year-round, every Saturday at 10:30am, a variety of entertainment programs for kids, including films, drama, puppetry, and magicians. In addition, there are the following special programs: "Summer Fun," films every Saturday in June, July, and August at 10:30am in the Theater. "Puppets in the Park," every Tuesday and Friday at 10:30am from the first week in July to the second week in August, in Grant Park, across from the Cultural Center. "Summer Reading Games," mid June to early August, an exciting six-week program of "Read on Down the Road," a citywide summer reading program; participatory in nature with games, reports, and certificates designed to make reading over the summer vacation attractive. *OPEN Mon-Thurs 9am-7pm; Fri 9am-6pm; Sat 9am-5pm. CLOSED Sun. FREE.*

NOTE: *All of the library branches have special summer programs; call the one in your neighborhood for a schedule.*

Libraries with Children's Rooms

Albany Park
5150 North Kimball. 588-3901. *OPEN Mon-Thurs 9am-9pm; Fri & Sat 9am-5pm.*

Public Library Cultural Center

Austin
5615 West Race. 287-0667. *OPEN Mon & Thurs 10am-6pm; Tues & Wed 11am-7pm; Fri & Sat 9am-5pm.*
Blackstone
4904 South Lake Park. 624-0511. *OPEN Mon-Thurs 9am-9pm; Fri & Sat 9am-5pm.*
Conrad Sulzer
4455 North Lincoln. 728-8652. *OPEN Mon-Thurs 9am-9pm; Fri & Sat 9am-5pm.*
Damen Avenue
2056 North Damen. 486-6022. *OPEN Mon & Thurs noon-8pm; Tues, Wed, Fri & Sat 9am-5pm.*
Douglass
3353 West 13th. 762-3725. *OPEN Mon-Wed, Fri & Sat 9am-5pm; Thurs noon-8pm.*
Eckhart Park
1371 West Chicago Avenue. 226-6069. *OPEN Mon & Thurs noon-8pm; Tues, Wed, Fri & Sat 9am-5pm.*
Edgewater
1210 West Elmdale. 262-3166. *OPEN Mon-Thurs 9am-9pm; Fri & Sat 9am-5pm.*
Hall
4801 South Michigan. 536-2275. *OPEN Mon-Thurs 9am-9pm; Fri & Sat 9am-5pm.*
Jefferson Park
5363 West Lawrence. 736-9075. *OPEN Mon-Thurs 9am-9pm; Fri & Sat 9am-5pm.*
Kelly
6151 South Normal Boulevard. 487-1545. *OPEN Mon-Thurs 9am-9pm; Fri & Sat 9am-5pm.*
Lake View
644 West Belmont. 281-7565. *OPEN Mon-Thurs 9am-9pm; Fri & Sat 9am-5pm.*
Legler
115 South Pulaski Road. 638-7730. *OPEN Mon & Thurs noon-8pm; Tues, Wed, Fri & Sat 9am-5pm.*
Lincoln Park
959 West Fullerton. 935-0286. *OPEN Mon-Thurs 9am-9pm; Fri & Sat 9am-5pm.*
Mayfair
4200 West Lawrence. 736-1254. *OPEN Mon & Thurs noon-8pm; Tues, Wed, Fri & Sat 9am-5pm.*
North Lake View
3754 North Southport. 525-2870. *OPEN Mon & Thurs noon–8pm; Tues, Wed, Fri & Sat 9am-5pm.*

Northtown
6435 North California. 465-2292. *OPEN Mon-Thurs 9am-9pm; Fri & Sat 9am-5pm.*
Northwest
4041 West North Avenue. 235-2727. *OPEN Mon-Thurs 9am-9pm; Fri & Sat 9am-5pm.*
Portage-Cragin
5110 West Belmont. 736-2577. *OPEN Mon-Thurs 9am-9pm; Fri & Sat 9am-5pm.*
Pullman
11001 South Indiana. 995-0110. *OPEN Mon-Thurs 9am-9pm; Fri & Sat 9am-5pm.*
Roden
6083 Northwest Highway. 631-4653. *OPEN Mon-Thurs 9am-9pm; Fri & Sat 9am-5pm.*
Scottsdale
4101 West 79th. 581-5545. *OPEN Mon-Thurs 9am-9pm; Fri & Sat 9am-5pm.*
South Chicago
9055 South Houston. 721-8065. *OPEN Mon-Thurs 9am-9pm; Fri & Sat 9am-5pm.*
South Shore
2555 East 73rd. 734-4780. *OPEN Mon-Thurs 9am-6pm; Fri & Sat 9am-5pm.*
Walker
11071 South Hoyne. 233-1920. *OPEN Mon-Thurs 9am-9pm; Fri & Sat 9am-5pm.*
Washington Park
448 East 61st. 363-1168. *OPEN Mon-Fri 10am-6pm; Sat 9am-5pm.*
Woodlawn
6247 South Kimbark. 752-3761. *OPEN Mon & Thurs noon-8pm; Tues, Wed, Fri & Sat 9am-5pm.*

LEARNING

Arts & Crafts

Albany Park Community Center
3401 West Ainslie. 539-5907. From June to August for boys and girls age 6 to 12. Crafts, dance, drama, storytelling, puppetry, music, sports, and nature studies.
Beverly Art Center
2153 West 111th. 445-3838. School of art: young people's program for age 5 and up. Drawing, painting, ceramics, photography, dance, and dramatics.

Chicago Park District
Department of Arts & Crafts. 294-2320. Art, dressmaking, macramé, quilting, stained glass, silversmithing, lapidary, furniture repair and upholstery, boat building. Call the Park District number above or your neighborhood park or playground for information.

Children's Art Exhibit
Lincoln Park Zoo, 294-4633. Artwork submitted by Chicago schoolchildren is exhibited in the Lion House during the month of June, daily from 9am to 5pm. (Deadline for entries: May 1.)

Horwich/Kaplan JCC
3003 West Touhy. 761-9100. Crafts, cooking, magic, self-defense. Dance: jazz, ballet, tap. All afterschool programs. For age 6 to 13.

Hyde Park Art Center
1701 East 53rd. 324-5520. Classes for kids age 6 to 14 and adults in photography, cartooning, printing, and ceramics. Family membership required.

Lill Street Studios
1021 West Lill. 477-6185. Beginning ceramic classes for kids age 10 and up. Also, school tours of the 100-year-old horse barn that houses seven co-operative potters. Call for information.

Logan Square Boys' Club
3228 West Palmer. 342-8800. After-school arts and crafts year-round, including ceramics, painting, sculpture, and photography. Age 6 to 12.

Old Town Triangle Art Center
1763 North North Park. 337-1938. Reasonably priced classes in drawing and painting for age 6 to 12. Weekday afternoons.

School of the Art Institute of Chicago
Columbus Drive & Jackson Boulevard. 443-3777. For age 5 to 7, one special class for drawing, painting, ceramics, sculpture, dance, writing.

South Side Community Arts Center
3831 South Michigan. 373-1026. Developed in the 1930s to encourage Black art and literature. Six eight-week courses year-round. For age 6 to 13. FREE.

YWCA
Harris, 6200 South Drexel; 955-3100. And West Side, 5080 West Harris; 379-8332. A variety of arts-and-crafts classes for kids age 4 to 16 are offered. Call for information.

Dance

Accounters Community Center
1155 West 81st. 994-5514. Preschool, day-care, and after-school programs and activities, including ballet, Afro-Cuban dance, music, and a theater program. For age 5 to 14.

Boitsov Classical Ballet
Fine Arts Building, 410 South Michigan, Suite 733. 663-0844. Pre-ballet starting at four years of age. Many graded levels for different age groups.

City Ballet School
223 West Erie. 988-4233. Training ground for the Chicago City Ballet. Affiliated with the School of American Ballet in New York. For age 3½ to 17.

Hyde Park Jewish Community Center
Temple K.A.M. Isaiah Israel, 1100 East Hyde Park Boulevard at 51st. 268-4600. Dance, drama, cooking, music, and more for kids of all ages.

Mayfair Academy of Fine Arts, Inc., Dance School
1025 East 79th. 846-8180. Tap, ballet, modern jazz, and acrobatics for kids age 3 and up. Offered September to June.

Moming Dance & Arts Center
1034 West Barry. 472-9894. Creative movement for age 4 to 13; jazz, ballet, and performance workshops.

Ruth Page Foundation School of Dance
1016 North Dearborn. 337-6543. Pre-ballet starting at age 6.

Drama

Chicago Park District Drama Section
Children age 8 to 8th grade are instructed in creative dramatics, improvisations, pantomime, and play production. Workshops are usually after school, three days a week till 5:30pm. Following instruction sessions, auditions are held for a show to be presented at their local park. Theater workshops for high schoolers emphasize the development of acting skills. Semester ends in the spring with the presentation of a three-act play. Call 294-2320 for information. FREE.

School for the Creative Arts
Bernard Horwich Center, 3003 West Touhy. 761-9100. Piano for age 6 to 12; drawing, painting, and printmaking for age 10 to 13.

Music

The Chicago Park District, Music Section
The Department of Recreation sponsors a cultural division that brings music instruction into neighborhoods. All musical instruments are taught. They have an annual talent search, four salsa bands, three mariachi bands, and a city-wide concert band. Opportunities include beginning and intermediate jazz workshops. Open to kids, teens, and adults. Call 294-2320 for information and the location of the park closest to you.

Old Town School of Folk Music
909 West Armitage. 525-7793. Learn piano, fiddle, mandolin, guitar, dulcimer, harmonica, or voice. Group learning for all ages. Private lessons for age 4 and up.

SPORTS

Jane Addams Center
3212 North Broadway. 549-1631. Comprehensive after-school programs for kids age 6 to 13. Swimming, athletics, some crafts.

Catholic Youth Organization
1637 South Allport. Boxing instruction for half pints, 8 years and up. Call 421-8046 for information, FREE.

McFetridge Sports Center
3845 North California. 478-0210. Boys hockey for age 4 to 18: four ten-week sessions year-round; call for cost and information. Figure-skating program for age 3½ and up: four ten-week sessions year-round. Indoor tennis lessons for age 6 and up: five eight-week sessions year-round. Call for fee and information.

Mid-Town Tennis Club
2020 West Fullerton. 235-2300. Classes for kids age 4 to 18. Members and nonmembers.

Park District Junior Football Program
294-2363. Mid August for kids age 12 to 14. Learn punting, passing, rushing. In mid September play begins on six Saturday mornings and culminates in the Mum Bowl in early November. In conjunction with the Wilson Sporting Goods Co. FREE.

Park District Moms or Dads & Tots Program
294-2333. Develop motor skills; games, some swimming. Age 1½ to 3. Ten-week sessions, one hour weekly; classes start in October and end April 30.

Park District Public Pools
294-2333. From October to April, competitive swim teams at 33 indoor pools. Age-grouped: 8 and under, 9 and 10, 11 and 12, 13 and 14. Championships in March, April, and May at Whitney Young High School, 211 South Laflin.

Park District Tiny Tots Program
294-2333. Swim program for kids age 18 months to 5 years. Parent must accompany the child into the pool. Two sessions: mid October to January and January to April. Water acclimation. One-hour classes at 12 locations throughout the city. Call for the one nearest you.

Park District Youth Tennis Program
294-4790. Beginning in mid June for seven weeks. Two age levels: 8 to 12 and 13 to 16. Culminates in a tournament. Call for information. FREE.

Rainbow Fleet
Learn sailboating: 2-hour lesson per week for age 14 and older; call 294-2399. Meets daily at Burnham Harbor, mid June to Labor Day at 9am. Junior Rainbow Fleet also, age 11 to 13.

Tiny Tots Gym & Swim
Lawson YMCA, 30 West Chicago Avenue. 944-6211. Done with the parents. For kids 3 months to 2 years. Arm and leg stretches; eye and hand coordination and water acclimation.

KIDS' DINING

Choo Choo Restaurant (Hamburger on Wheels)
600 Lee Street, Des Plaines. 298-5949. It's a natural for kids. An electric train brings the food from the kitchen to the counter. The kids' menu features their-sized burgers. No credit cards. *OPEN Mon-Sat 6am-8pm (call first).*

Ed Debevic's
See RESTAURANTS, American.

Marshal Field's Narcissus Room
111 North State, 7th floor. 781-1000. Kids' menu with checkoff list for speed. *Good* fast-food. No-smoking section. AE, MC, V, Marshall Field's charge. *OPEN 11am-3pm.*

Flukey's
6821 North Western. 274-3652. Great hot dogs, but who ever heard of hot-dog-shaped bubble gum? Outdoor patio in summer. No reservations. No credit cards. *OPEN Mon-Thurs 7am-10:30pm; Fri & Sat 7am-midnight; Sun 8am-10:30pm.*

Gertie's Own Ice Cream
5858 South Kedzie. 737-7634. The hot fudge sundaes get A+ from the pint-sized set at this, Chicago's oldest ice-cream parlor. *OPEN 7 days 10:30am-11pm.*

Halsted Street Fish Market
2048 North Halsted. 525-6228. Fish and chips and a paper tablecloth kids are encouraged to draw on. No reservations. AE, MC, V. *OPEN Mon-Thurs 11am-10:30pm; Fri & Sat 11am-11:30pm; Sun noon-10:30pm.*

D. B. Kaplan's
Water Tower Place, 835 North Michigan, 7th floor. 280-2700. The place is infectious; the menu will make them giggle. But their eyes may be bigger than their stomachs; order judiciously. No-smoking section. No reservations taken. No credit cards. *OPEN Mon-Thurs 10am-11pm; Fri & Sat 10am-1am; Sun 11am-11pm.*

Redamak's New Buffalo Chicago
2263 North Lincoln. 787-4522. Great burgers! Special kids menu. Reservations for 8 or more only. AE only. *OPEN Mon-Thurs 11:30am-midnight; Fri & Sat 11:30am-1:30am; Sun noon-11pm.*

CHILDREN'S CLOTHES

All of the major department stores in Chicago have large departments for children's clothing. See SHOPPING, Large Stores.

All Our Children
2217 North Halsted. 327-1868. Clothes, infant to size 14, including a large selection of Esprit. Also, Absorba, Osh Kosh, Dijon, Choozie, Ozona. Some stuffed animals, too. AE, MC, V. *OPEN 7 days.*

Banana Moon
554 West Diversey Parkway. 525-8080. Moderately priced children's clothing boutique: sweaters, overalls, outerwear. Much that is unusual. Infant to size 7. Also toys, dolls, and accessories. AE, MC, V. *OPEN Mon-Fri 11am-7pm; Sat 10am-5pm; Sun noon-4pm.*

Benetton 012
121 East Oak. 944-0434. Scaled-down, albeit relatively expensive, versions of the Benetton

sweaters, tees, pants for children age 1 to 12. AE, MC, V. *OPEN 7 days.*

Born Beautiful
3206 North Broadway. 549-6770. The best of everything little: Ton Sur Ton, Petit Beteau, Absorba, Ozona, Dan Jean. Layettes to size 14. Educational toys and games; accessories too. Moderate to expensive. AE, MC, V. *OPEN Mon-Wed & Fri 9:30am-6pm; Thurs 9:30am-8pm; Sat 10am-5:30pm; Sun noon-5pm.*

My Own Two Feet
2148 North Halsted. 935-3338. A boutique specializing in upscale children's shoes. AE, MC, V. *OPEN Tues-Sun.*

Rubens Baby Factory
2340 North Racine. 348-6200. Factory outlet for no-frills infants' (birth to 3 years) diapers, undies, and waterproof pants. No credit cards. *OPEN Mon-Fri 9am-3:30pm.*

Resale Clothes

An idea that makes sense.

Hand-Me-Downs
2609 Broadway, Evanston. 475-0803. Nice selection of resale clothes for boys and girls, infant to size 14. Also toys, high chairs, and car seats. Fast turnover. No credit cards. *OPEN Tues-Sat 10am-4pm.*

Mother's Clearing House
1141 West Belmont. 929-4878. Newborn to size 12, previously used clothes. Also maternity clothes, toys, books, and baby equipment. No credit cards. *OPEN Tues-Fri 11am-5pm; Sat 10am-5pm. CLOSED Sun & Mon.*

Twice Upon a Time
103 North Seymour, Mundelein. 949-0999. Recycled baby clothes and accessories. Up to size 14. Maternity wear as well. MC, V. *OPEN Mon-Wed 10am-4pm; Fri & Sat noon-5pm. CLOSED Thurs & Sun.*

CHILDREN'S SPECIALTY SHOPPING

Bikes

Beverly Schwinn Cyclery
9121 South Western. 238-5704. Ross, Panasonic, Schwinn. Emphasis on service. AE, DC, MC, V. *OPEN Mon, Thurs, Fri 9:30am-8pm; Tues & Wed 9:30am-6pm; Sat 9am-5:30pm. CLOSED Sun.*

Buckingham Bike Shop
3332 North Broadway. 975-0050. Small neighborhood shop will get any bike not stocked as soon as possible. Service with a smile. AE, CB, DC, MC, V. *OPEN Apr-Sept, Mon-Fri noon-7pm; Sat 10am-5pm; Sun 10am-5pm. Sept-Apr call ahead for hours.*

Cycle Smithy
2468½ North Clark. Fuji, Panasonic, Raleigh,

Trek; some well-priced used bikes. Expert repair. MC, V. *OPEN 7 days.*

Kozy's Bicycle Shop
1610 West 35th; 523-8576. And 3712 North Halsted; 281-2263.* Bikes for the whole family. Well-stocked and service-oriented. Lifetime parts guarantee. MC, V. *OPEN Mon & Thurs 10am-9pm; Tues, Wed & Fri 10am-7pm; Sat 10am-5pm. CLOSED Sun. *OPEN Mon & Thurs 11am-9pm; Tues, Wed & Fri 11am-7pm; Sat 11am-5pm. CLOSED Sun. AE accepted at this store only.*

Morrie Mages
620 North La Salle. 337-6151. Over 1,200 bikes stocked, including many Japanese and European models. Custom-built too. Eight floors of athletic equipment in this sporting-goods mecca. AE, CB, DC, MC, V. *OPEN Mon, Tues, Thurs & Fri 9am-9pm; Wed & Sat 9am-6pm; Sun 10am-5pm.*

Sportiff Importer Ltd.
525 West Lawrence. 685-0240. Large shop offers a choice of over 50 imported brands. AE, MC, V. *OPEN Mon-Fri 10am-7pm.*

Books

Barbara's Bookstore
1434 North Wells; 642-5044. And 2907 North Broadway; 477-0411. Also 121 North Marion, Oak Park; 848-9140.* Good kids' section, plus a wide variety of activity books. AE, MC, V, Barbara's charge. Wells: *OPEN Mon-Sat 10:15am-9:45pm; Sun 11am-8pm.* Broadway: *OPEN Mon-Fri 10am-9:45pm; Sat 10am-8:45pm; Sun 11am-9:45pm.* Oak Park: *OPEN Mon-Fri 10am-9:45pm; Sat 10am-5:45pm; Sun 11am-5:45pm. *Story Hour, Sat at 10:30am with milk & cookies.*

Stuart Brent Books
670 North Michigan. 337-6357. Very extensive collection of hardcover and paperback books for kids, among them unique and beautiful one-of-a kinds. Special orders taken. Children's Book Club. Also, preschool educational toys. This is a very special place. MC, V. *OPEN Mon-Fri 9am-8pm; Sat 9am-6pm; Sun noon-5pm.*

The Children's Bookstore
2465 North Lincoln. 248-2665. The Midwest's largest selection of children's books; also, children's cassettes and toys geared to age 1 to 8. Very special about the store are the theme programs every Saturday at 10:30am; also, story hours year-round Monday and Friday at 10:30am for age 2 to 4. Program details are available at the store or get on their mailing list. AE, MC, V. *OPEN 7 days.*

Women & Children First
1967 North Halsted. 440-8824. Terrific well-stocked bookstore for kids and women. Nonracist; nonsexist too (though the name of the shop smacks of the opposite). Playroom for kids. AE, MC, V. Tuesday afternoon readings and special programs. Call for schedule. *OPEN Mon-Fri 11am-*

7pm; Thurs 11am-8pm; Sat 10am-6pm; Sun noon-5pm.

—Comics

Larry's Comic Book Store
1219-A West Devon. 274-1832. New comics hot off the press weekly. Oldies too. *OPEN Mon-Sat noon-6pm (sometimes Sun).*

Variety Book Store
4602 North Western. 334-2550. New and used comics. *OPEN Mon-Sat noon-6pm; Sun noon-5pm.*

Dolls & Dollhouses

Antique Doll Hospital
3110 West Irving Park Road. 478-7554. Expert, albeit expensive, "surgical" repair of mainly antique and collectible dolls. No credit cards. *OPEN Tues-Sat 11am-5pm.*

Beauty and the Beast
Water Tower Place, 835 North Michigan, 7th level. 944-7570. A treasure house of beautiful imported and limited-edition dolls and stuffed beasts, including handmades to tempt the child in us all. AE, MC, V. *OPEN Tues, Wed, Fri 10am-6pm; Mon & Thurs 10am-7pm; Sun noon-5pm.*

Fran's Miniatures
3831 North Lincoln. 525-1770. The specialty is dollhouses and miniature custom-made furnishings and fittings, including electric-light fixtures. *OPEN Tues-Fri 10:30am-5:30pm; Sat 10am-5pm; Sun noon-5pm. CLOSED Mon and Sun in July and Aug.*

Hobbies

(See also KIDS' CHICAGO, Children's Specialty Shopping: Trains.)

American Science Center
5696 Northwest Highway. 763-0313. Science supplies, including telescopes, microscopes, and chemistry kits. MC, V. *OPEN Mon-Wed, Fri 10am-6pm; Thurs 10am-9pm; Sat 9am-5pm. CLOSED Sun.*

Brighton Park Art & Hobby Center
4238 South Archer. 523-3334. Craft and model-train supplies; art supplies; other hobbies too. Senior-citizen discount. AE, MC, V. *OPEN Tues, Wed & Fri 10am-7pm; Mon & Thurs 10am-8pm; Sat 10am-6pm; Sun (Oct-May) 11am-4pm.*

Magic, Inc.
5082 North Lincoln. 334-2855. A source for magic supplies as well as for puppeteers and magicians for your party. MC, V. *OPEN Mon-Sat 10:30am-5:30pm.*

Puppets

Clothworks
110 Oakbrook Center, Oakbrook. 571-6062. Whimsical string puppets, all handmade from natural wood. Scandinavian fabric and colorful yarn. Mobiles and stuffed animals too. MC, V.

OPEN Mon-Fri 10am-9pm; Sat 10am-5:30pm; Sun noon-5pm.

Lincoln Park Zoo Gift Shop
2200 North Cannon Drive. 294-4660. Puppets, coloring books, hats, tees, and stuffed animals. All inexpensive and for a good cause. AE, MC, V. *OPEN 7 days 10am-5pm.*

Toy Gallery
1640 North Wells. 944-4323. Hand puppets, stuffed animals, and party favors. Lots of games. AE, CB, DC, MC, V. *OPEN Mon-Sat 10am-6pm; Sun (Sept-June) 11am-4pm.*

Stuffed Animals

Ace Novelty Company
221 East Cullerton. 225-6311. A place to buy Christmas presents, since this wholesaler requires a $50-minimum purchase. Small novelty items but mostly a wonderful collection of stuffed animals. No credit cards. *OPEN Mon-Fri 9am-5pm, CLOSED Sat & Sun.*

Aged Experience
2034 North Halsted. 975-9790. This antique shop has lovely handmade patchwork dolls and stuffed animals supplied from all over the U.S. No credit cards. *OPEN Tues-Sun 11am-6pm.*

Friends of the Public Library Store
Cultural Center, 78 East Washington. 269-2922. Inexpensive gift items, stuffed animals, T-shirts. No credit cards. *OPEN Mon-Sat 10am-4pm, but it is suggested you call first.*

Ada Michaels
743-6219. This craftswoman creates a beautiful, albeit expensive, selection of stuffed animals. Some are of real fur, others have wardrobes, still others talk. *By appointment only.*

Toys

Bellini
2201 North Halsted. 943-6696. Stylish and practical European furniture that grows with your child—cribs become youth beds, changing tables convert to bookcases. Bedding, toys, books, and accessories. MC, V. *OPEN 7 days.*

Circus World Toy Stores
7601 South Cicero. 767-6606. From preschool to electronic toys. Also sports equipment. AE, MC, V. *OPEN Mon-Fri 10am-9pm; Sat 10am-5:30pm; Sun noon-5pm.*

Ed's Toys & Hobbies
10101 South Western Avenue. 238-1482. Over 10,000 toys in stock. All hobbies catered to. Discount prices. MC, V. *OPEN Mon-Sat 9am-6pm; Sun 10am-4pm.*

F.A.O. Schwarz
Water Tower Place, 835 North Michigan, 4th level. 787-8894. Branch of the famed New York toy emporium, it's a treat for the eye and heart but ofttimes hard on the pocket. Known for carrying the *very* best—though there are less expensive items, too. AE, CB, DC, MC, V. *OPEN*

Tues, Wed, Fri & Sat 10am-6pm; Mon & Thurs 10am-7pm; Sun noon-5pm.

Saturday's Child
2146 North Halsted; 525-8697. *And Garland Court, 50 East Washington, second level; 372-8697. *Classic* toys, dolls, and books—the better to engage a child's imagination. A large selection of stuffed animals as well as puzzles, art supplies, and much more. AE, MC. V. *OPEN 7 days. *CLOSED Sun.*

Toys 'Я' Us
3350 North Western; 525-1690. And 9200 West North Avenue, 343-9000. Also 8900 South Lafayette, 846-2600; plus eight suburban stores. Very well-stocked supermarket of toys. AE, MC, V. *OPEN Mon-Sat 9:30am-9:30pm; Sun 11am-6pm.*

Toys Et Cetera
5206 South Harper; 324-6039. And 711 Main Street, Evanston; 475-7172. Also Arlington Heights. Well-priced imported and domestic toys and games. Kites too. MC, V. *OPEN Mon-Sat 9:30am-5:30pm; Sun noon-5pm.*

Trains

Downtown Hobby
6017 North Northwest Highway. 775-4848. Everything you ever wanted to know about model railroading in this haven for railroad buffs. Every size and model, accessories, books, magazines. MC, V. *OPEN Mon-Thurs 11am-7pm; Fri 11am-9pm; Sat 10am-5pm; Sun 11am-3pm. CLOSED Sun June, July & Aug.*

Golden Spike Train Shop
6357 West 79th. 598-3114. Complete supply of trains and supplies. Specializes in H.O. gauge, also Lionel and American Flyer, new and used. MC, V. *OPEN Mon, Tues, Thurs & Fri 1-9pm; Sat 10am-6pm; Sun (Oct-May) 1-5pm. CLOSED Wed.*

Lake Shore Model Railroad Association
Calumet Park Field House, 98th & Lake Michigan. 721-3925. Meets year-round every Monday, Wednesday, and Friday from 7:30 to 9:30pm. Just drop in.

Trost Hobby Shop
3111 West 63rd. 925-1000. *The* shop for Lionel, among others. Also model cars, planes, and boats. MC, V. *OPEN Tues, Wed & Fri 9:30am-6pm; Mon & Thurs 9:30am-8:30pm; Sat 9am-5pm. CLOSED Sun.*

ENTERTAINMENT

(*See also* KIDS' CHICAGO, Libraries.)
On Friday both the Chicago Tribune *and the* Chicago Sun Times *have features devoted to weekend fun and learning opportunities for kids of all ages. Also check* Chicago *magazine's "Kid Stuff" listings.*

Beverly Arts Center
2153 West 111th. 445-3838. From October to March, for one Saturday afternoon a month at 2pm, live or puppet shows, musical and nonmusical. Preschool to grade school. Admission charge.

Damen Avenue Puppeteers
2825 West Leland. 478-6272; 348-6149. Shows for kids age 2 to 6. Special shows for the handicapped. Storytelling, workshops, and puppet shows.

Dancing Wheels
4150 West 55th. 767-1800. From September to May, every Sunday from 10:30am to 1pm. Teenyboppers' sessions, age 10 and younger. Music and games. Admission charge; accompanying parent free.

Drury Lane Children's Theatre
2500 West 95th Street, Evergreen Park. 422-8000. Professional children's theater company. Plays geared toward kids from preschool to 5th grade. Performances school days at 10:30am and Sunday at 12:30pm. Reservations necessary. Admission charge.

Facets Multimedia
1517 West Fullerton. 281-9075. From mid September to mid June, every Saturday and Sunday at 2pm. Showings of children's films. Call 929-KIDS for information. Admission charge.

Free Street Theater
441 West North Avenue. 642-1234. Weekends and some weekdays. Touring company with outdoor showmobile sponsored by block associations, the parks, companies, etc. Aimed at the entire family. FREE.

Rogers Park Branch of the Chicago Public Library
6907 North Clark. 764-0156. Preschool storyhour on Wednesday at 10:30am, along with film and finger plays. Films for school-age children in fall, spring, and summer. Call for information.

Second City Children's Theater
1616 North Wells. 929-6288. Year-round, every Sunday at 2:30pm. Geared to kids age 4 and up and their families. Audience participation for approximately 20 minutes after the 45-minute show. Must reserve. Admission charge.

Six Flags Over Great America
Gurnee, Illinois. 249-1776. On 200 acres, a fun-for-the-whole-family amusement park. Includes the roller coaster with the world's longest drop, 15 gut-wrenching stories! In all, 37 rides, 5 shows, numerous shops. AE, MC, V. *OPEN May 2-17, Sat & Sun only 10am-8pm; May 18-June 12, Mon-Fri 10am-8pm, Sat & Sun 10am-10pm; June 13-Aug 23, 7 days 10am-10pm; Aug 24-Sept 7, Mon-Fri 10am-8pm, Sat & Sun 10am-10pm; Sept 12-Sept 27 Sat & Sun only 10am-8pm.*

U.S.A. Rainbow
4836 North Clark. 271-5668. From 9am to 11am every Saturday and Sunday. Funskate for kids age 12 and younger. Group skate dances, DJ, kid-oriented music. Admission charge; accompanying parent free.

PARTIES

Party Entertainers

A-1 Entertainment and Concession
880-8000. A 45-minute comedy/magic show with rabbits and doves. Ventriloquism, puppetry, balloon sculpture. Children's and adult parties; audience participation. Age 2 and up.
Kin Ki the Clown
848-2329. Balloon animals, stories, mime. Audience participation. Tailored to age level of group.

Party Places

Second City Children's Theater
1616 North Wells. 929-6288. A preshow birthday party can be arranged at no extra charge. You must bring all the fixings and clean up after yourself. Reserve in advance.
U.S.A. Rainbow
4836 North Clark. 271-5668. A "Funskate" birthday package for kids age 12 and under. Includes admission, skate rental, popcorn, hot dogs or pizza, and a soft drink. Free gift for the birthday child. Reserve in advance.

PLAYGROUNDS

(*See also* PARKS & GARDENS, Parks.)
Chicago Park District
516 playgrounds, 355 sandboxes, 211 spray pools. Call 294-2200 for information.

FOR PARENTS

Dial-a-Story
366-3533. Three-minute recorded children's stories, folk tales, fables. For kids age 3 to 10. Changes six times a week.

Illinois Department of Children & Family Services
For referrals to day-care centers, call 793-8600. For referrals to family-care homes, call 793-8846.
Midwest Association of Private Camps
36 South State, Chicago, IL 60603. 332-0833. Free annual directory that lists camps and their programs, directors, costs, etc.
Park District Summer Day Camps
Approximately 175 summer day camps for kids age 7 to 12. Sports, camping, swimming, field trips, arts and crafts, cookouts. Begins early July, from Monday to Friday, 10am to 4pm, for six weeks. Call the information office, 294-2492.
Student Camp & Trip Advisors
1845 Mission Hills Lane, Northbrook. 564-1845. A free guidance and counseling service pairs kids age 8 to 18 with suitable summer vacations, in the U.S. and overseas, following interviews focusing on budget and interests.
YMCA Day Care
1500 North Halsted. 266-5400. They can help you find someone to take care of your child. Serves metropolitan Chicago.

Baby-sitters

Also check with day-care centers.
American Registry for Nurses & Trained Sitters
3921 North Lincoln. 248-8100. North Side sitting only, by sitters age 22 to 72. *OPEN Mon-Fri.*
Dial A Babysitter Inc.
207 South Wabash. 939-5626.

SCOUTS

Boy Scouts of America
730 West Lake. 559-0990. Cub Scouts age 8 to 10; Boy Scouts age 11 to 16; Explorers age 14 to 20.
Girl Scouts of Chicago
55 East Jackson, 14th floor. 435-5500. Girls age 6 to 17.

SPORTS

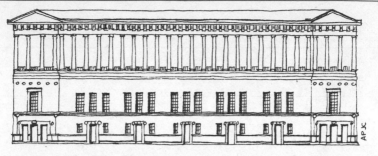

Soldier Field

STADIUMS

Chicago Avenue Armory
234 East Chicago Avenue. 753-5210.
Chicago Stadium
1800 West Madison. 733-5300.
Comiskey Park
324 West 35th. 924-1000.
De Paul University
1011 West Belden. 341-8010.
Dyche Stadium (Northwestern University)
1501 Central Street, Evanston. 491-7070.
Eckersall
2433 East 82nd. 721-4697.
Hanson Park
5411 West Fullerton. 637-5511.
Lane
2501 West Addison. 880-8100.
Loyola University
6525 North Sheridan. 274-3000, ext 381.
McGaw Hall
1501 Central Street, Evanston. 491-7070.
Rockne
1117 South Central. 261-4900.
Soldier Field
425 East McFetridge Drive. 294-2200.
Stagg
1035 West 74th. 483-6623.
Thillens
Devon & Kedzie. 743-5140. For rain and games information call 866-7044.
Winnemac
5101 North Leavitt. 989-3793.
Wrigley Field
1060 West Addison. 281-5050.

TICKET AGENTS

Barnes Ticket Service
Palmer House, 17 East Monroe. 726-3486. *OPEN Mon-Fri 10am-5pm; Sat 10:30am-4pm.*
Chicago Athletic Club, 12 South Michigan. 726-0544. *OPEN Mon-Fri 10:30am-2pm. CLOSED Sat & Sun.*

Carey Theater Ticket Service
225 North Wabash. 332-3122. *OPEN Mon-Fri 11am-7pm; Sat 11am-4pm.*
Ticketron
Attraction information, 842-5389. Ticket information available 9am-4:30pm; 842-5389. Charge by phone 853-3636.
Union Tysen Theater Ticket Service
32 West Randolph. 372-7344. *OPEN Mon-Sat 8am-7:30pm.*

GENERAL INFORMATION

Board of Education
1819 West Pershing. 890-8000. Recreational services.
Chicago Park District
425 East McFetridge Drive. 294-2200.
Cook County Forest Preserve
536 North Harlem Avenue, River Forest. 261-8400 (city); 366-9420 (suburbs).
Department of Human Services: District Operations
744-4040. Youth clubs or programs.
Illinois Department of Conservation:
917-2070.
Sportsphone
976-1313.

SPORTS

Archery

Archery Sales & Service
3542 West Lawrence. 588-2077. Twenty-yard indoor range. Lessons by appointment. Equipment sales, service, and rental. *OPEN Mon-Fri 11am-9pm; Sat 11am-6pm; Sun 2-5pm.*
East Side Archery
3711 East 106th. 721-0115. Bow hunters' workshops and lessons. Sells and services bow-hunting equipment and accessories. *OPEN Mon-Fri 10am-9pm; Sat & Sun 10am-6pm.*

Badminton

Evanston Badminton Club
Beardsley Gym, Evanston Township High School, 1600 Dodge Avenue, Evanston. 492-3877. Sponsored by the Evanston High School Adult Education Department. Instruction, open play, and tournaments *Mon & Wed 7-9:30pm*. Session fee.

McKinley Park Badminton Club
39th & Western. 523-1534. Harold Deeman, teaching coach, has all the information on Chicago-area badminton and clubs. *Call Mon-Fri 2-5pm*.

Ballooning

Illinois Balloons
Clow Airport, Naperville. 739-0400. Balloon rides April through November. Ballooning instructions year-round. Sunrise and two hours before sunset, weather permitting. Call for information.

Windy City Balloonport
Fox River Grove. 639-0550. Balloon flights at dawn and two hours before sunset. One-hour flight wherever the winds carry you. Ballooning lessons also. *May 1-Oct 31, 7 days.*

Baseball

Chicago has two professional baseball teams; the Chicago Cubs (National League), who play at Wrigley Field, 1060 West Addison (878-CUBS), and the Chicago White Sox (American League) at Comiskey Park (the oldest baseball park in the major leagues), 324 West 35th (924-1000). The baseball season begins around the first week in April and continues through mid October. Call the ball parks for specific game or ticket information or check the local papers. NOTE: The Cubs play day games only; Wrigley is not equipped with lights.

The Chicago Park District has 172 senior diamonds and 321 junior diamonds. Call the local park supervisor for available playing times, as there are many leagues.

The Park District also has a summer baseball league for children age 9 and up. The season runs from May till August. For information call 294-2325 or 294-2341.

Basketball

Chicago has one professional basketball team, the Chicago Bulls, who play their season from October to March at the Chicago Stadium, 1800 West Madison (943-5800).

Chicago also has several college teams. The De Paul Blue Demons play at De Paul University, 1011 West Belden (341-8010). The Loyola Ramblers play at Loyola University, 6525 North Sheridan Road (274-3000, ext 381). The Northwestern Wildcats play at McGaw Hall, 1501 Central Avenue, Evanston (491-7070). College basketball

starts in late November and continues through March. Call for ticket prices and times.

—Municipal Basketball Courts

The Chicago Park District has approximately 1,254 outdoor basketball backboards. Call 294-2352 or the local park supervisor for locations and availability.

Bicycling

The Chicago Park District has 21 bicycle paths. They are OPEN 7 days 6am-11pm, weather permitting. The most spectacular is the Lakefront path from 5700 North to 7700 South past museums, parks, harbors, and city skyscrapers. The paths are marked by signs. Call 294-2200 for more information and other locations.

The Department of Streets and Sanitation, 121 North La Salle, Room 700 (744-7386), will send you a pamphlet on bicycle paths in the city.

Cook County Forest Preserve has nearly 50 miles of trails (some still under construction). Call 261-8400 for maps and information.

Village Cycle Center
1337 North Wells. 751-2488. Three-speed bicycle rental. Deposit plus ID required. Two-hour minimum. Year-round, weather permitting. *OPEN Apr-Aug, 7 days 10am-7pm; Sept-Mar, Wed-Mon noon-6pm. CLOSED Tues.*

Billiards

Chris's Billiards
4637 North Milwaukee. 286-4714. Seven billiard, 10 pool, and 1 snooker tables. Women's 9-ball tournament every Tuesday. Pool lessons and billiard tournament every Monday and Thursday night. Food available. *OPEN Mon-Sat 10-1am; Sun 11-1am.*

Illinois Billiard Club
2435 West 71st. 737-6655. Private billiards club for serious players and those who want to be. Call for information after 12:30pm. Eight-ball tournaments that are held on Friday nights are open to amatuer players.

Boating

The most popular inland yacht race is held in July. The Chicago-to-Mackinac race leaves from Monroe Harbor near the lighthouse. Sponsored by the Chicago Yacht Club; call 861-7777 for more information. (See also ANNUAL EVENTS, July.)

—Nonpower Boating

American Youth Hostels
3712 North Clark. 327-8114. Organized activities in canoeing, backpacking, bicycling, skiing, hiking, and sailing. Call for information between 12:30 and 5pm.

Chicagoland Canoe Base, Inc.
4019 North Narragansett. 777-1489. THE canoe source in Chicago. Over 150 models of canoes

and kayaks, even antique and custom-built ones. Accessories, supplies, and over 200 canoeing titles. They will rent you a canoe and steer you to some of the hundreds of miles of out-of-the-way canoe trails to explore, all within one day of Chicago. They also sponsor an annual 19-mile canoe race in May, the Sunday before Memorial Day, to celebrate Clean Streams Month. Call for information. *OPEN Mon-Sat 9am-5pm. Thurs 9am-9pm.*

City Sailors
703 West Wellington. 975-0044. In-boat sailing instruction for the beginner through advanced. Classes run from mid May to mid October. Sailboat rental, supplies, and accessories. *OPEN Mon-Fri 9am-5pm; Sat & Sun 9am-noon; later hours during the summer.*

Fairwind Sail Charter
Burnham Park Harbor. 427-1525. Learn to sail on a 33-foot Pearson on Lake Michigan from May through October. In the winter learn to sail on a cruise to the Caribbean. *OPEN 7 days 8am-5pm.*

The Offshore Marine
901 West Irving Park Road. 549-4446. Indoor sailing instruction during the winter. Mid April to mid October sailing instructions on the Lake. Individual or small group, weekdays, weekends, evenings too. Marine supplies, boat rentals, service, and sales. MC,V. *OPEN Mon-Fri 9:30am-6pm; Sat 9am-5pm; Sun 10am-4pm. CLOSED Sun in winter.*

Cook County
The Cook County Forest Preserve allows canoes, rowboats, and/or sailboats on the following lakes:

Beck Lake
Central & East River roads. Sailboats, rowboats, and canoes. Launching ramp.

Big Bend Lake
Golf & East River roads. Sailboats, canoes, and rowboats.

Maple Lake
95th west of Willow Springs Road. Rowboat rentals only.

Powderhorn Lake
Brainard & Burnham. Sailboats, rowboats, and canoes. Launching ramp.

Saganashkee Slough
107th between Route 83 & Willow Springs Road. No rentals and only private rowboats allowed, May 15 to September 30.

Skokie Lagoons (Erickson Preserve)
East of Edens Expressway, west of Winnetka between Willow & Dundee roads. Sailboats, rowboats, and canoes. Launching ramp at Tower Road parking area.

Tampier Lake
Wolf Road & 131st. Rowboats and rowboat rentals. Launch south of 131st Street off Will-Cook Road *only.*

—Power Boating

The Chicago Park District, Harbor Division (294-2270), will give information about boating on Lake Michigan. A permit is needed to use the CPD harbor facilities in Lake Michigan. Diversey Harbor, Jackson Inner, and Jackson 59th Street harbors are for power boats only. Call the CPD Harbor Division for information and permits. Harbor season is from May 15 to October 15.

The Cook County Forest Preserve allows power boating on the Des Plaines and Calumet rivers only. Call 443-6580 for the location of free launching ramps.

Boccie

The Chicago Park District has 14 outdoor boccie courts. Call the local park supervisor for playing times.

Blackhawk
2318 North Lavergne. 237-3877. Two courts.

McGuane
2901 South Poplar. 294-4692. Three courts.

Riis
6100 West Fullerton. 637-8952. Two courts.

Shabbona
6935 West Addison. 283-6787. Two courts.

Smith
2526 West Grand. 227-0020. Two courts.

Bowling

Diversey River Bowl
2211 West Diversey Parkway. 227-5800. Thirty-six lanes. Call for open bowling times. *OPEN Sun-Fri 9-2am, Sat 9-3am.*

Ford City Bowl
7601 South Cicero. 585-2900. Forty-eight lanes; also pool tables. Call for open bowling times. Private lessons available by appointment, from 9am to 5pm. *OPEN Sun-Thurs 9am-midnight; Fri & Sat 9-2am.*

Howard Bowl
1777 West Howard. 274-5200. Thirty lanes. Pool tables. No instruction. *OPEN 7 days 9-1am.*

Marigold Arcade
828 West Grace. 935-8183. Thirty-two lanes. Private instruction available through the pro shop. Vending machines. *OPEN Mon-Thurs 9-1am; Fri-Sat 24 hours; Sun closes at midnight.*

Oak Forest Bowl
15240 South Cicero Avenue, Oak Forest. 687-2000. Thirty-two alleys. Free instruction on Wednesday from 1 to 5pm. Snack bar. Call for open bowling times. *OPEN Mon-Thurs 9am-midnight; Fri 9am-6pm; Sat & Sun 9-2am.*

Southport Lanes
3325 North Southport. 472-1601. Nonmechanical pin-setters and a nice bar. Only four alleys, so call ahead. *OPEN Sept-June 7 days 3pm-2am.*

Spencer's Marina City Bowling
300 North State. 527-0747. Thirty-eight lanes. No instruction. Snack bar. *OPEN Sun-Thurs 9-2am; Fri & Sat 9-3am.*

Waveland Bowl
3700 North Western Avenue. 472-5900. *OPEN 7 days, 24 hours.*

Boxing

Catholic Youth Organization (CYO)
1637 South Allport. 421-8046. Boxing instruction for boys over age 15. Must bring your own personal equipment and a medical certificate from a doctor. Gymnasium, regulation-size ring, and an interested staff. *OPEN Mon-Fri 1-6pm.*

Degerberg Martial Arts & Fitness Academy
4717 North Lincoln. 728-5300. Men's and women's boxing instruction. Regulation-size ring, speed bags and heavy bags, mirrored walls in this new facility. Fitness and martial arts also. *OPEN Mon-Thurs 2-10pm; Fri 2-8:30pm; Sat 10am-6pm; Sun 10am-1pm.*

Broomball

Similar to hockey except that shoes, brooms, and a soccer ball are used instead of skates, sticks, and a puck. You do need ice. A fun, coeducational winter sport.

U.S. Broomball Hockey Association
274-1800. Irv Finston, good source who wrote the rule book for broomball. Has information on where it's played in the city and the suburbs.

Cricket

Evanston-Skokie Area Cricket Club
7358 North Clark. 761-6668. There are about 15 teams in the Chicago area. The season runs from early June through late October. Call the club after 7pm for game or practice times and locations.

Diving

The Chicago Park District teaches a 13-week basic scuba-diving course in the evenings at several locations starting in February. Registration fee. Call 294-2200 for information.

Aqua Center
43 East Downer, Aurora. 896-3596. Local reps of the National Association of Scuba Diving Schools. They teach scuba, snorkeling, and underwater photography. They also rent, sell, and service equipment and organize diving trips. *OPEN Mon-Sat; call for hours.*

Illinois Institute of Diving
P.O. Box 2638, Glen Ellyn, IL 60138. 858-8884. All-level scuba and snorkeling courses year-round, evenings and weekends, at many different city and suburban locations. Also underwater photography, specialty and leadership courses. NAUI, PADI, YMCA, and SSI approved. Diving trips to local, midwestern, Caribbean, and South Pacific areas. Call for information.

Fencing

Illinois Fencers' Club
411 Maple, Mt. Prospect. 835-1888. Excellent source for fencing in the Chicago area. Will direct you to teachers, tournaments, and other fencers. Good beginners' course is taught at Lions Park in Mt. Prospect; call for information and class times. The Chicagoland Open is held at the end of March and is open to anyone who fences; call the club for information.

Fishing

To fish in Illinois you must have a license if you are between the ages of 16 and 65. Residents must purchase a season license; nonresidents may purchase a one- or ten-day license. Licenses may be obtained at the City Clerk's office, 121 North La Salle, Room 107, or at any major sporting-goods store. Call 917-2070 for information.

For specific information on fishing locations call the Illinois Department of Conservation at 917-2020. Also, see Tom McNally's column on Thursday in the Chicago Tribune.

Chicago Sportfishing Association
25 East Washington. 922-1100. A nonprofit organization to promote sportfishing on Lake Michigan. Will give information on charter boats and sportfishing. Has a booking service to arrange charter fishing trips. *OPEN Mon-Sat 9am-5pm.*

International Sport Fishing Museum
2625 Clearbrook Drive, Arlington Heights. 364-4666. Run by the American Fishing Tackle Manufacturers Association, this museum has everything on sportfishing. Fishing equipment and instructions, tackle records, history of tackles and casting, learning aids, and a reference library. Seminars in the summer. *OPEN Mon-Fri 9am-4:45pm; Sat 10am-5pm.* Tours available by reservation. Admission charge; children under age 16 FREE.

Salmon Unlimited
4608 North Elston. 736-5757. Information on how to fish Lake Michigan and catch salmon and trout. Nonprofit group keeps the Lake in shape and stocked. Membership club. Call the Hotline, 736-8900, spring and fall for sportfishing information.

—Fishing: Chicago Park District
Lake Michigan has coho and chinook salmon; brown, rainbow, and lake trout; and yellow perch. Fishing is done from piers, seawalls, and jetties, in lakefront lagoons and harbors. Call the Chicago Park District at 294-2493 for specifics on fishing in Lake Michigan or in any of the 17 park lagoons or 9 casting ponds. Below is a partial list.

Harbors: North
Belmont Harbor
3200 North. 281-8587.
Diversey Harbor
2400 North. 327-4430.
Montrose Harbor
4400 North on the Lake. 878-3710.

Harbors: South
Burnham Harbor
1500 South Linn White Drive on the Lake. 294-4614.

59th Street
5900 South on the Lake. 493-8704.
Jackson Park
2200 East 65th on the Lake. 363-6942.
Monroe Street Harbor
100 South on the Lake. 294-4612.

Lagoons: North
Lincoln Park
2400 North Fullerton on the park, and 2200 North Cannon Drive behind the zoo. The latter contains some salmon and is great for kids and nonexperts. The park also offers many other activities for the nonfishers in the family *(see* PARKS & GARDENS, Parks).

Lagoons: South
Jackson Park
6401 South Stony Island Avenue.
Marquette Park
6700 South Kedzie.
McKinley Park
2210 West Pershing.
Washington Park
5531 South Martin Luther King, Jr., Drive.

Lagoons: West
Columbus Park
500 South Central.
Douglas Park
14th & South Albany.
Garfield Park
1400 North Sacramento.

The Chicago Park District also sponsors free fishing clinics, especially on how to catch the coho salmon, at various parks. Tips are also given on competing in the Coho Fishing Derby held in May. For specifics call 294-2493.

Smelt fishing starts in early April and runs for about six weeks. Smelts run in a water temperature of 38-45°F. They try to spawn on the smooth bottom in and near the harbors. Nets go in by sunset and are hauled up periodically until 3am. Lanterns are lighted to attract the fish. A fishing license is needed, and only one net per person is allowed.

—Fishing: Cook County Forest Preserve

Cook County has over 28 lakes, ponds, and sloughs for hook-and-line fishing. A guide and depth maps are available; call the Cook County Forest Preserve at 261-8400 (city) or 366-9420 (suburbs). There are no seasons or limits on most fish, with the exception of largemouth and smallmouth bass, northern pike, and rainbow trout. Call for specific regulations. Some locations are listed below.
Belleau Lake
West of the Tri-State Tollway off Busse Highway. Twelve acres. Largemouth bass, bluegill, yellow perch, bullhead. Trout are stocked twice each spring and late fall.
Busse Lake
South of Higgins Road, between Interstate 90 & Arlington Heights Road. Three separate bodies of water: North Pool (25 acres), South Pool (146 acres), Main Pool (419 acres). Stocked fish:

largemouth bass, bluegill, bullhead, northern pike, carp, sunfish, crappie, and channel catfish. Boat rental available.
Des Plaines River
Between the towns of Wheeling and Lemont, 50 miles long. Large natural stream; the best fishing area is between Wheeling and Rosemont. Fish available include northern pike, largemouth bass, bluegill, sunfish, bullhead, crappie, channel catfish, yellow bass, carp, goldfish, and suckers. Boating, power and nonpower, is permitted. Launching ramps in Lyons and Willow Springs.
McGinnes Slough
Off Mannheim Road, approximately ½ mile north of Orland Park; 303 acres. Only the east end is open to fishing. Bullhead, goldfish. The remainder of the area is a waterfowl refuge.
Powderhorn Lake
Two miles north of Calumet City, ½ mile east of Burnham Avenue on the north side of Brainard Avenue; 35 acres. Northern pike, largemouth bass, bluegill, crappie, yellow perch, bullhead, sunfish, channel catfish, and carp. The marsh to the north is a wildlife refuge—no fishing allowed. Private nonpower boats are permitted.
Skokie Lagoons
Between Willow & Dundee roads, east of Edens Expressway. Seven interconnected lagoons, 190 acres. Some bass, sunfish, bullhead, carp, bluegill, and crappie. Private nonpower boats only. Launching ramp by Tower Road parking area.

Ice fishing is permitted on certain lakes only if the ice is at least 4 inches thick. Call the Cook County Forest Preserve for conditions and locations. A license is required.

—Fishing: Du Page County
For information on fishing locations, call the Du Page County Forest Preserve, 790-4900.

Flying
Aviation Professionals, Inc.
5320 West 63rd. 284-1220. Graded instruction for those seeking a private license up through airline pilots. Single- and multiengine planes, flight school, and instrument rating school. Also airplane rentals, fuel sales, and pilot supply shop. *OPEN 24 hours a day, 7 days a week.*
Chicago Beechcraft Aero Club
Du Page Airport, West Chicago. 584-6700. Private lessons, from private-pilot level up through commercial-airline training and instrument instruction. Sales, service, plane rentals, and fueling. Lessons *7 days 7:30am-10pm.*
Chicago Skyline Limited.
5245 West 55th. 585-1382. Instruction for private, commercial, multiengine, and ground school. Also group course to prepare for private pilot's license. Airplane rentals. *OPEN 7 days 8am-7pm.*
Hinkley Soaring
Hinkley Airport, Hinkley. (1-815) 286-7200. Glider planes, demonstration rides, instruction, rentals,

CHICAGO
HOUSE NUMBER MAP

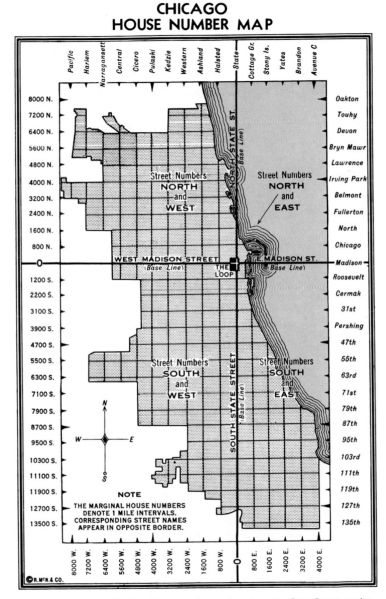

Chicago is divided by Madison Street running east-west, and by State Street running north-south. These two streets form the base lines from which all house numbers and street names are designated.

DOWNTOWN CHICAGO
INDEX TO STREETS

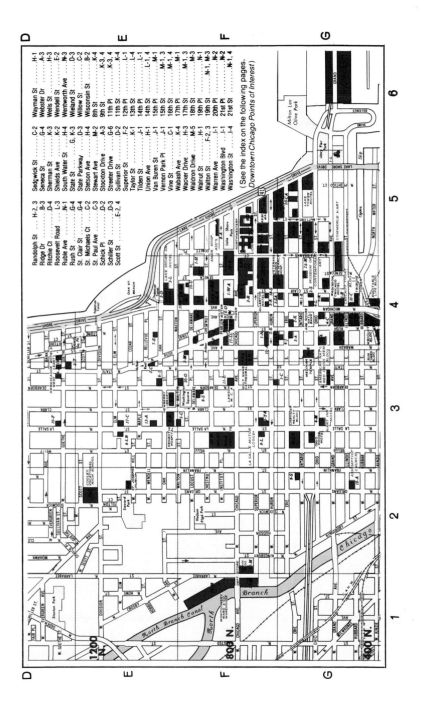

(See the index on the following pages.
Downtown Chicago Points of Interest)

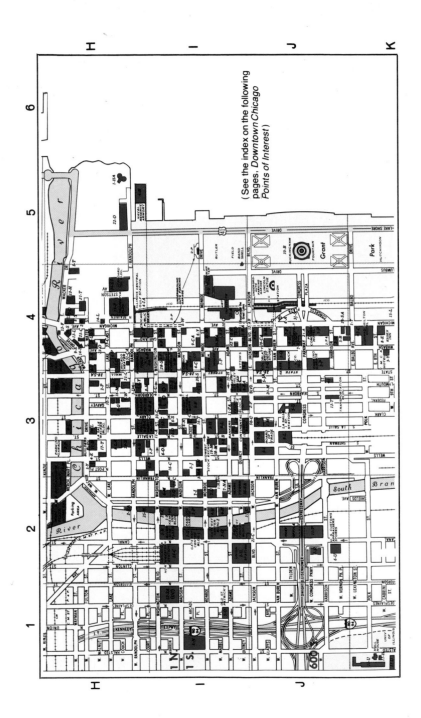

(See the index on the following pages, *Downtown Chicago Points of Interest*)

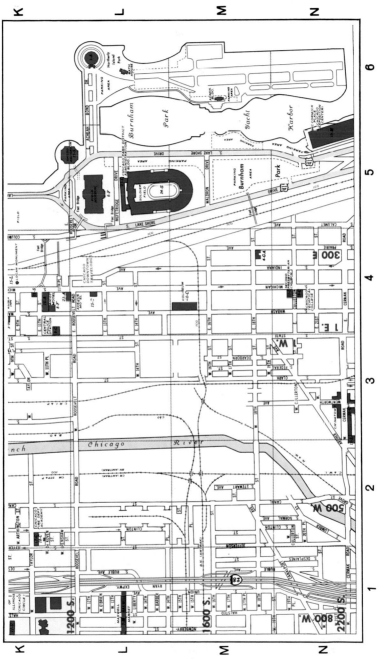

Downtown Chicago Points of Interest

(This index refers to the Chicago Street Plan on the previous four pages.)

and supplies. *OPEN Apr-late Nov. Tues-Sun 10am-dusk.*

Windy City Soaring
Naperville & Boughton roads, Bolingbrook. 759-2046. Glider flight school, instruction, rentals, demonstration rides, and sales. Flights out of Clow Airport, 4 miles south of Naperville. *OPEN Apr-Nov, 7 days 10am-dusk.*

Football

The Chicago Bears, the city's championship pro football team (NFL), usually plays from early August (preseason) to mid December at Soldier Field, 425 East McFetridge Drive. Call the box office, 663-5100, for game times and ticket information. Tickets are also available through Ticketron outlets, and by calling Teletron at 853-3636. Outside Chicago call (1-800) 382-8080.
College team: The Northwestern Wildcats play at Northwestern University's Dyche Stadium, 1501 Central Avenue, Evanston. For information call 491-7070.
The Chicago Park District has 217 football fields. Schedules and availability are determined by the local park supervisor. Call 294-2200 for locations.
The Park District also runs football leagues and clinics. Call 294-2357 for information. Football season runs from October through November.

Golf

—Municipal Golf Courses

The Chicago Park District has six golf courses. They are open from mid April to November, weather permitting. Hours are sunrise to sunset. These are daily-fee courses. A discount is available at certain times for those under age 16 and over 65, if they have a Chicago Park District ID card. Call 294-2200 for information on how to obtain one.

Columbus Park
5200 West Jackson Boulevard. 294-2274. Nine holes; 2,832 yards.
Jackson Park
63rd & Stony Island Avenue. 294-2274. Eighteen holes; 5,538 yards.
Marquette Park
67th & Kedzie. 294-2274. Nine holes; 3,300 yards.
Robert A. Black
2045 West Pratt. 294-2274. Nine holes; 3,200 yards.
South Shore Country Club
7059 South Lake Shore Drive. 294-2274. Nine holes; 2,903 yards.
Waveland
3600 North at the Lakefront in Lincoln Park. 294-2274. Nine holes; 3,290 yards.

—Municipal Golf Driving Ranges

Diversey Driving Range
141 Diversey (2800 North). 294-2274.

Jackson Park
6401 South Stony Island Avenue. 294-2274.
Robert A. Black
2045 West Pratt. 294-2274. Bucket charge. *OPEN mid Apr-mid Nov, 7 days 8am-10:45pm.*

—Municipal Miniature Golf

Lincoln Park
141 Diversey. 294-2274. Eighteen holes. Admission charge. *OPEN Apr-mid Nov, 7 days 8am-10:30pm.*

—Cook County Golf Courses

Cook County Forest Preserve has eight golf courses throughout the county. The courses are open from mid April through November, weather permitting. They are daily-fee courses. Senior citizens (over 65) and juniors (age 17 and under) can play at a discount during certain times if they have a Cook County Forest Preserve ID card. Call 261-8400 (city) or 366-9420 (suburbs) for information on how to obtain one.

Burnham Woods
142nd Street & Burnham Avenue, Burnham. 862-9043. Eighteen holes; 6,480 yards.
Billy Caldwell
6200 North Caldwell. 792-1930. Nine holes; 3,029 yards.
Edgebrook
5900 North Central. 763-8320. Eighteen holes; 4,626 yards.
Chick Evans
6145 Golf Road, Morton Grove. 965-5353. Eighteen holes; 5,691 yards.
Highland Woods
Ela Road near Route 62, Hoffman Estates. 359-5850. Eighteen-hole championship course; 6,995 yards. Lighted driving range also.
Indian Boundary
8600 West Forest Preserve Drive. 625-9630. Eighteen holes; 6,003 yards.
Meadowlark
11599 West 31st Street, Hinsdale. 562-2977. Nine holes; 3,333 yards.
Pipe O'Peace
131st & Halsted streets, Riverdale. 849-1731. Eighteen holes; 6,429 yards. Also, lighted driving range at 138th.

—Other Suburban Golf Courses

Cog Hill Golf & Country Club
119th Street & Archer Avenue, Lemont. 242-1717 (Chicago); 257-5872 (suburbs). Four complete 18-hole courses measuring 6,199, 6,103, 6,298, and 6,619 yards, respectively. Great respect is due #4, "Dub's Dread," the world-famous course pitted with 120 sand traps. There is a daily fee from early April to mid November. *OPEN 7 days, courses #1 & #3 6am-6:30pm, #2 6am-7pm, #4 6am-7:30pm.*
Glenview Park Golf Course
800 Shermer Road, Glenview. 724-0250. Eighteen holes; 6,080 yards. Daily fee. *OPEN Apr-Nov, 7 days dawn to dusk.*

Golden Acres Country Club
Roselle Road, Schaumburg. 885-9000. Three 9-hole courses; 9,660 total yards. Daily fee. *OPEN Mar-Nov, 7 days 5am-9pm.*

Hickory Hills Country Club
8201 West 95th Street, Hickory Hills. 598-6460. One 18-hole course and one executive 9-hole course. Championship course 6,018 yards; other course 1,630 yards. Daily fee. *OPEN year-round, 7 days sunrise-sunset.*

Old Orchard Country Club
700 West Rand Road, Mt. Prospect. 255-2025. Two courses: 18-hole, 6,110 yards; 9-hole, 2,700 yards. Daily fee. *OPEN Apr-Nov, 7 days 5am-6pm.*

Woodridge Golf Club
6300 South Route 53, Lisle. 971-3000. Two 18-hole courses: one 6,035 yards, the other 6,387. Daily fee. *OPEN Mar-Nov, 7 days sunrise-sunset.*

—Golf Instruction

The Chicago Park District begins golf instruction in early January, running through March. Call 294-2274 for locations and times.

Annex-Pro Shop
8130 Lincoln Avenue, Skokie. 267-5717. Private indoor lessons with a pro. By appointment only. Largest selection of golf supplies in the U.S. *OPEN Mon-Fri 10am-9pm; Sat 10am-6pm; Sun 11am-5pm.*

Cog Hill
119th Street & Archer Avenue, Lemont. 242-1717. Outdoor lessons from early April through early November. Group or private instruction with at least three pros. Golf supplies and accessories. *OPEN 7 days 6am-dusk.*

Gillespie Golf School
Golfland Golf Range, 1701 North River Road, Melrose Park. 345-6320. Group or private instruction by appointment. Indoor instruction and outdoor driving range. Range open to the public. *OPEN 7 days Nov-mid Mar 8:30am-6pm; mid Mar-Oct 8:30am-11:30pm.*

Pheasant Run Golf
Pheasant Run Lodge, St. Charles. 584-6300. Private lessons by appointment, seven days a week from 8am to 5pm. Outdoor driving range *OPEN May-Oct, 7 days 7am-7pm.* Indoor driving range *OPEN Nov-Apr, 7 days 8am-10pm.*

Gymnastics & Fitness

The Chicago Park District offers fitness courses and gymnastics for men and women at many parks in the city. Call for class times and locations: male, 294-2340; female, 294-2363.

Degerberg Martial Arts & Fitness Academy
4717 North Lincoln. 728-5300. Exceptional fitness facility. Weight room, bar bells, balance log, ropes, rings, and much more. Instruction for men and women, children and teens. *OPEN Mon-Thurs 2-10pm; Fri 2-8:30pm; Sat 10am-6pm; Sun 10am-1pm.*

Lake Shore Academy of Artistic Gymnastics
1650 West Foster. 878-1110. Gymnastic instruction for the whole family. *OPEN Mon-Thurs 9:30am-8:30pm; Fri 3-10pm. Sat morning.*

Lincoln Turners
1019 West Diversey. 248-1682. A nonprofit, self-supporting organization in operation for 100 years, they teach gymnastics and swimming. Call for class times.

Handball

—Municipal Courts

The Chicago Park District has 23 outdoor handball/racquetball courts (see SPORTS, Racquetball) and 5 indoor courts, Check with the local park supervisor for times that the following indoor courts are available. You need your own equipment.

Pottawattomie
7340 North Rogers. 743-4313. Two indoor courts.

Washington
5531 South Martin Luther King, Jr., Drive. 684-6530. One indoor court.

West Lawn
4233 West 65th. 582-6850. Two indoor courts.

Hiking

The Cook County Forest Preserve has nearly 200 miles of hiking trails. Maps and information can be obtained by calling them.

Forest Trails Hiking Club
475-4223. Knowledgeable guides lead 8- to 12-mile hikes through various Chicago-area forest preserves every Sunday year-round. Hikes usually begin around 9am and return sometime after 3pm. Call evenings for more information.

Prairie Club
6 East Monroe. 236-3342. One-day group walks in and around Chicago. Mostly nature hiking, sometimes city streets. Call Monday to Friday from 9am to 3pm.

Hockey

The Chicago Black Hawks (NHL) play their professional hockey season from mid October to mid April at the Chicago Stadium, 1800 West Madison. Call 733-5300 for game times and ticket information.

Hockey is played at many of the 194 outdoor park ice-skating rinks. Check with the local park supervisor as to times and regulations. The Park District also sponsors a hockey league. For information call 294-2493.

Northbrook Sports Complex
1710 Pfingston Road, Northbrook. 498-0685. Over-30, no-check league, 10:30pm-midnight Wednesday and Sunday. On Friday (same times) the over-30 rule is relaxed and beginners are invited.

Robert Crown Center
1701 Main, Evanston. 328-0040. Adult no-check games; Saturday at 9pm. Admission charge.

Horseracing

Illinois Racing Board
100 West Randolph. 917-2600. Information on Illinois racetracks and racing schedules. *OPEN Mon-Fri 8:30am-4:30pm.*
Arlington Park Race Track
Euclid Avenue & Wilke, Arlington Heights. 255-4300. Thoroughbred racing late May till late September. (*See also* ANNUAL EVENTS, August: Arlington Million Week.)
Balmoral Park
Between Route 394 & Route 1, Crete. 568-5700. From late February to mid April: harness racing. From mid May to late August: thoroughbred racing. From mid September to late December: harness racing. Post time Wednesday to Saturday is 8pm; Sun 2pm. Results Hotline: 672-4550.
Hawthorne Park Race Course
3501 South Laramie Avenue, Cicero. 780-3700. Thoroughbred racing from mid September through mid December. Harness racing in January and February. Post time is 1:30pm.
Maywood Park Race Track
8600 West North Avenue, Maywood. 343-4800. Harness racing from late September through late December; late February through early May also. Post time Monday to Saturday is 8pm.
Sportsman's Park Race Track
3301 South Laramie Avenue, Cicero. 242-1121. Thoroughbred racing from late February through late May. Harness racing early May through late September. Post time Monday to Saturday is 1:30pm for thoroughbreds, 8pm for harness

Horseshoe Pitching

The Chicago Park District has 291 horseshoe pitches. Check with the park supervisor as to availability. You will need your own equipment.
Lincoln Park
2045 North Lincoln Park West. 294-4750. Twenty-eight courts.
Marquette
6700 South Kedzie. 776-9879. Five courts.
Portage
4100 North Long. 545-4337. Five courts.
Trumbull
2400 East 105th. 768-1434. Eight courts.
Welles
2333 West Sunnyside. 561-1184. Ten courts.

Lawn Bowling

The Chicago Park District has four lawn-bowling greens. Call the local park supervisors for information on leagues and playing times.
Columbus
500 South Central. 378-0643. Two greens.
Jackson
6401 South Stony Island Avenue. 643-6363. Two greens.

Martial Arts

Chicago Center for Tai Chi and Chi Kung
907 West Belmont. 472-2220. Tai Chi Chuan lessons. Forms, pushing hands, self-defense, and energy cultivation exercises. Free trial class. Classes at various times. Call for information, 7 days from 9am to 10pm.
Chicago Ki-Aikido Society, Inc.
1016 West Belmont. 525-3141. Group instruction for men, women, and children, beginner or advanced, in the philosophy and technique of martial arts. *OPEN 7 days.* Call for class times.
Degerberg Martial Arts & Fitness Academy
4717 North Lincoln. 728-5300. Realistic approach to self-defense combines American style and kick boxing, karate, kung-fu, and "kili"—Filipino stick fighting. *OPEN Mon-Thurs 2-10pm; Fri 2-8:30pm; Sat 10am-6pm; Sun 10am-1pm.*
Jiu-Jitsu Institute, Inc.
20 East Jackson Boulevard. 922-8322. Classes for anyone in jiu-jitsu, karate, or judo in this long-established city school. Private or group instruction. *OPEN Mon-Fri noon-8:30pm; Sat 10am-2pm.*

Polo

From December till March the winter polo games are played indoors at the Chicago Avenue Armory, 234 East Chicago Avenue. There is an admission charge for the games, usually played on Saturday at 7pm. Practice sessions are free. Call 793-5210 for times.
Oakbrook Polo Club
2700 South York Road, Oakbrook. 571-7656. Summer games from Memorial Day Weekend through mid October are played here. Admission charge; children under age 12 FREE. There is no charge for the practice games; call to find out when.
U.S. Polo Association
(1-606) 255-0593. Information on the Governor's Cup, Butler Handicap, and Continental Cup played from July to September. Also other USPA-sponsored events. Call for schedule.

Racquetball

—Municipal Racquetball Courts

The Chicago Park District has 18 outdoor racquetball/handball courts. Check with the local park supervisor for times. (See SPORTS, Handball for indoor courts.)
Armour Square
3309 South Shields. 294-4732. Two courts.
Bessemer
8931 South Muskegan. 768-1079. Two courts.
Gage
2411 West 55th. 434-6393. Two courts.
Loyola
1230 West Greenleaf. 262-0690. Two courts.
McKinley
2210 West Pershing Road. 523-3811. Two courts.

Palmer
East 111th & South Indiana. 785-4277. One court.
Rainbow
75th & the Lake. 734-5976. Three courts.
Sheridan
910 South Aberdeen. 294-4717. Two courts.
Sherman
1301 West 52nd. 268-8436. Two courts.

—Racquetball Clubs

Downtown Sport Club
441 North Wabash. 644-4880. Membership club with many other locations. Facilities for racquetball, tennis, handball, swimming, track, and exercise. *OPEN Mon-Fri 6am-11:30pm; Sat & Sun 7am-11pm.*
Hyde Park Athletic Club
1301 East 47th. 548-1300. Ten indoor tennis courts, 12 racquetball courts, 1/10-mile running track, exercise room, sauna, whirlpool. Members only. *OPEN Mon-Thurs 6:30am-11pm; Fri 6am-10pm; Sat & Sun 7am-8pm.*
McClurg Court Sports Center
333 East Ontario. 944-4546. Racquetball, tennis, handball, pool, and exercise at this membership club. *OPEN Mon-Fri 7am-10pm; Sat & Sun 7am-9pm.*
Riviera 400 Club
400 East Randolph. 527-2525. Complete health and racquetball club with overnight laundry facilities and free bus service to the Loop. Membership. *OPEN Mon-Fri 7am-9pm; Sat & Sun 9am-7pm.*

Riding

There are four bridle paths in the Chicago parks. However, there are no facilities for horses in the city; bring your own! Call 294-2200 for information. To ride on the Cook County Forest Preserve's trails you must have a rider's permit. It is available at any stable where you rent a horse. Call the Forest Preserve at 261-8400 for other locations.
Circle H Ranch
9400 South Kean, Hickory Hills. 598-2900. English or Western. Lessons in outdoor or indoor rings. Trail rides. Also sell, train, and board horses. *OPEN 7 days 9am-10pm.*
Forest View Farms
16717 South Lockwood, Tinley Park. 560-0306. English riding lessons. Western trail rides. Indoor and outdoor rings. *OPEN year-round 7 days 8am-8pm.*
North Shore Stable
9453 Harms Road (between Dempster Street & Edens Expressway), Morton Grove. 967-5060. Indoor and outdoor riding instruction, year-round. Trail rides on Forest Preserve trails. *CLOSED Mon.*
Palos Hills Riding Stables, Inc.
10100 South Kean Avenue, Palos Hills. 598-7718. Group or private riding lessons, mostly

English. *OPEN Mon-Fri 7am-10pm; Sat & Sun 7am-6pm.*
Riteway Farms
4475 Lake Cook Road, Northbrook. 272-0450. Riding lessons, group or individual, English. Tuesday, Thursday & Saturday indoor polo from 5pm to 8pm. *OPEN Mon, Wed, Fri 9am-9pm; Tues, Thurs, Sat & Sun 9am-5pm.*

Rugby

Chicago Lions
621-1137. Call for information on men's rugby in Chicago. Two seasons: Labor Day to early November and late March to late May. Practice Tuesday and Thursday at 6:30pm in Lincoln Park near North and Lakeshore Drive. Games most Saturdays at 1pm in Lincoln Park near Foster and Lakeshore Drive.

Running

The Chicago Park District has 25 oval tracks and 7 straightaways. They also have a track-and-field program. Call 294-2493 for information.
"Parcour"
Lincoln Park at Fullerton Parkway. There are 20 stations designed for joggers or walkers to exercise their muscles along the way.
Chicago Area Runners Association
708 North Dearborn. 664-0823. Membership organization for many of Chicago's runners. They organize and host races, work with the Park District on running programs, arrange travel to out-of-town races, and much more. Information on both local and individual running activities and clubs.

The America's Marathon is held one Sunday in early May. It starts 8:45a.m. at Daley Plaza, Dearborn & Washington streets, runs through many of Chicago's ethnic neighborhoods and the Lakefront and finishes in Lincoln Park on Cannon Drive between Fullerton & Diversey. Spectators are more than welcome along the route to cheer on the nearly 20,000 runners from all over the world. Call 951-0660 for information.
Lakewood Forest Preserve
Route 176 & Fairfield Road, Wauconda. 526-5290. Walk or run between the 20 stations in this 3/4-mile physical-fitness trail. Each station has illustrated exercises for the athlete or non-athlete to perform. *OPEN year-round 8am-sunset.*

Shuffleboard

The Chicago Park District has 109 shuffleboard courts. You need your own equipment. Check with local park supervisors for schedules.
Foster
1440 West 84th. 723-7215. Five courts.

Galewood
1714 North Mango. 622-3877. Six courts with a sun canopy.
Rosenblum
1936 East 76th. 375-3468. Six courts with a sun canopy.

Skating

—Ice Skating

Chicago Park District

Outdoor
The Chicago Park District has 178 outdoor skating areas. Certain weather conditions are necessary to maintain the ice, so call the local park supervisor for information. For the locations of the rinks call the Park District, 294-2493.
Daley Bicentennial Plaza
337 East Randolph. 294-4790. Outdoor 80-by-135-foot rink with stunning views of the Lake and the Loop. Admission charge; discount for children under age 14 and senior citizens. Skate rentals available. *OPEN (weather permitting) Dec-Mar Mon-Fri 9am-10pm; Sat & Sun 9am-6:30pm. Two-hour sessions 9-11am, 11:30am-1:30pm, 2-4pm, 4:30-6:30pm.*
Indoor
McFetridge Sports Center
3843 North California. 478-0210. Newly renovated center with indoor ice rink. Skate rentals. Special times for hockey leagues, ice dancers, and adults. Hours for open skating vary daily, be sure to call ahead. Group lessons available. Admission charge; discount for children under age 17 and senior citizens. *OPEN year-round 7 days. CLOSED August.*
Park Ridge Speed Skating Club
Oakton Ice Arena, 2800 Oakton, Park Ridge. 255-7527. Indoor instruction in speed skating by appointment. Also information about suburban speed-skating meets and other clubs.
Cook County Forest Preserve
The Cook County Preserve District has many areas for ice skating out of doors. Call 261-8400 for information and locations.
Schiller Woods
Irving Park & River roads, Schiller Park. 261-8400. Charming forest setting when the pond freezes for ice skating. (Must have 4 inches of ice before skating is permitted; call first.) *OPEN Dec-Mar 7 days 6am-dusk, weather permitting.*

—Roller Skating

The Chicago Park District has 320 multiuse paved areas. Check with local parks for any special activities or restrictions.
United Skates of America Rainbow
4836 North Clark. 271-6200 (recording); 271-5668. Indoor skating rink and skate rentals. Call for skating times and activities.
Westchester Wheels & Sports
10411 Cermak Road, Westchester. 562-0330.

Skate rentals plus 6 miles of paved outdoor trails. Hourly rates. *CLOSED Wed.*

Skiing

—Cross-Country Skiing

Municipal Parks
The Chicago Park District has 48 cross-country ski areas. They are OPEN Mon-Fri 2-9pm, Sat & Sun noon-5pm, weather permitting. There is equipment rental available at some of the parks. Call 294-2493 for conditions. Skiing is free.
The CPD also teaches a four-week course in cross-country skiing. It starts in early January. Call 294-4792 for information. Registration fee.
Some of the parks are listed below.

Central

Columbus
500 South Central. 378-0643.
Douglas
1401 South Albany Boulevard. 521-3244.
Garfield
100 North Central Park. 826-3175.
Harrison
1824 South Wood. 294-4714.
Humboldt
1400 North Sacramento Avenue. 276-0107.

North

Eugene Field
5100 North Ridgeway. 478-1210.
Horner
2741 West Montrose. 267-2444.
Lincoln
2045 North Lincoln Park West. 294-4750.
Loyola
1230 West Greenleaf. 743-8282.
Peterson
5601 North Pulaski Road. 463-5839.
Portage
4100 North Long. 545-4337.
Riis
6100 West Fullerton. 637-8952.
River
5100 North Francisco. 561-2145.

South

Marquette
6700 South Kedzie. 776-9879.
Ridge
9625 South Longwood Drive. 238-1655.
Washington
5531 South King Drive. 684-6530.
West Lawn Park
4232 West 65th. 582-6850.
West Pullman
123rd & South Stewart. 785-6963.

Cook County Forest Preserve

The Cook County Forest Preserve permits cross-country skiing on most of its trails and open

areas. Call 261-8400 for information, conditions, and maps. There is equipment rental at some of the areas. Areas OPEN sunrise to sunset, 7 days.
Arie Crown Forest
Mannheim Road north of 67th, use the Sundown Meadow parking lot. Lake Ida, located north of the parking lot, is used for ice skating, weather permitting.
(*See also* SPORTS, Tobogganing, Sledding & Coasting.)

—Downhill Skiing

Chestnut Mountain
Chestnut Mountain Lodge, Galena. (1-815) 777-1320.
Four Lakes Ski Area
5750 Lakeside Drive, Lisle. 964-2550.
Villa Olivia
Villa Olivia Ski Area, Bartlett. 289-5200.

Soccer

The Chicago Sting plays indoor soccer at Rosemont Horizon from November through May. Call 245-5425 for ticket information and game times.
The Chicago Park District has 217 soccer/football fields. They also run soccer clinics and leagues. Call the Park District at 294-2493 for information. The soccer season runs concurrently with the football season, so check with local park supervisors on the availability of the fields.
Illinois Soccer Association
2903 West Irving Park. 463-0653. Member of Federation of International Football Associations. Has information on the 60-odd soccer clubs in Illinois. Call Monday to Friday, noon to 10pm.
National Soccer League of Chicago
275-2850. A league of 60 clubs, some with several teams, in and around Chicago. For adults age 19 and up; the youth division groups kids age 8 to 19 by level. Three seasons: indoor, January to March; outdoor, April to May and late August to late October.

Softball

The Chicago Park District has 333 softball diamonds. Check with the local park supervisor for playing times, as they are shared by many leagues. The Park District also runs many softball leagues. Call 294-2308 for information. Softball season starts in April and runs through the summer.

Swimming

The shore of Lake Michigan is lined with sand beaches for sunning and swimming. The ones closest to downtown, especially the Oak Street, are the most popular and the most crowded. Farther north the crowds lessen. See PARKS & GARDENS, Beaches.

—Chicago Park District
The District has 2 swimming lagoons, 72 outdoor pools, and 30 natatoriums (indoor pools). They also have swimming classes and special activities. Call 294-2333 for information.
  Lagoons
Douglas
1401 South Albany. 521-3244. *OPEN mid June-Labor Day, 7 days 9am-9:30pm.*
Humboldt
1400 North Sacramento Avenue. 276-0107. *OPEN late June-end of Aug, 7 days 9am-9:30pm.*
  Natatoriums (Indoor Pools)
Austin Town Hall
5610 West Lake Street. 378-0126.
Beilfuss
1725 North Springfield. 235-0282.
Blackhawk
2318 North Lavergne. 237-3877.
Bogan School
3939 West 81st. 582-4464. *OPEN Oct 1-May 31 only.*
Carver
939 East 132nd. 928-6555.
Roberto Clemente
2334 West Division. 227-8565.
Curie School
4949 South Archer. 581-3230.
Dyett School
525 East 51st. 548-1816.
Eckhart
1330 West Chicago Avenue. 294-4710.
Foster
1440 West 84th. 723-7215.
Gill
833 West Sheridan Road. 525-7238.
Griffith
346 West 104th. 785-0794.
Harrison
1824 South Wood. 294-4714.
Independence
3945 North Springfield. 478-1039.
Jackson
3506 West Filmore. 638-1310.
Kelly School
4150 South California. 927-1663. *OPEN Oct 1-May 31 only.*
Kosciuszko
2732 North Avers. 252-2596.
La Follette
1333 North Laramie. 378-0124.
Mann
East 130th & Carondolet. 646-2633.
Mather School
5835 North Lincoln. 561-1460. *OPEN Oct 1-May 31 only.*
McGuane
2901 South Poplar. 294-4692.
Orr School
730 North Pulaski. 826-3713.
Portage
4101 North Long. 777-3660.
Ridge
96th & South Longwood Drive. 238-1655.

Shabbona
6935 West Addison. 283-6787.
Sheridan
910 South Aberdeen. 294-4717.
Stanton School
650 West Scott. 294-4733.
Welles
2333 West Sunnyside. 561-1184.
Wentworth-Kennedy
5625 South Mobile. 585-1881. *OPEN Oct 1-May 31 only.*
West Pullman
123rd & South Stewart. 785-6963.

Outdoor Pools
The Park District outdoor pools are OPEN end of June-Labor Day. For locations and schedules call 294-2333.

—Cook County Forest Preserve

Outdoor Pools
The Cook County Forest Preserve has three outdoor pools. Admission charge; children under age 12 FREE on Wednesday. Children under age 6 are not allowed. Call 261-8400 for information. OPEN Memorial Day-Labor Day, 7 days noon-9pm.
Cermak Pool
Ogden, west of Harlem, at the Des Plaines River, Lyons.
Green Lakes
Torrence & 159th, Calumet City.
Whealen
Devon & Milwaukee.

—Swimming Instruction

American Red Cross Water Safety
440-2009. Water safety and lifeguard courses. Age requirements; swimming skills necessary. Call for details.

Tennis

—Municipal Tennis Courts
The Chicago Park District has approximately 688 outdoor tennis courts. The nets go up in mid-April, weather permitting. Reservations are not necessary for most courts; just put your racquet by the net, and the players currently using the court understand you want it when their game is over. It's called the honor system. Do check with the local park supervisors, though, for court hours and any special programs they may have scheduled. The Park District also has tennis lessons; for information call 294-4790.
Some FREE outdoor Park District tennis courts:
Garfield
100 North Central Park Avenue. 826-3175. Fourteen courts, 8 lighted; tennis practice board.
Jackson
6401 South Stony Island. 643-6363. Twenty-four courts, 12 lighted.
Lake Shore
808 North Lake Shore Drive. 294-4720. Two lighted courts.

Lincoln Park
294-4750. Near Wilson: 5 courts.
McKinley
2210 West Pershing Road. 523-3811. Fourteen courts, 8 lighted.
Rainbow
75th and the Lake. 734-5976. Sixteen courts, 8 lighted; tennis practice board.
Rils
6100 West Fullerton. 637-8952. Ten lighted courts; tennis practice board.
Tuley
501 East 90th Place. 723-0150. Thirteen courts, 10 lighted.

The following park tennis courts charge a fee, and you must call to reserve a court.
Daley Bicentennial Plaza
337 East Randolph. 294-4790.
Grant Park
9th & Columbus.
McFetridge Sports Center
3845 North California. 478-0210. Six indoor courts.
Waveland
In Lincoln Park (3700 North). 281-8987.

—Other Tennis Courts

Chicago Indoor Tennis Association
337-0145. For information on where to play in the city. Call Monday to Friday 9am-5pm.
Lake Shore Athletic Club
1320 West Fullerton. 477-9888. Indoor and outdoor tennis courts, pool, and running track. Other health-club amenities. Members only. *OPEN Mon-Fri 5am-midnight; Sat & Sun 6am-11pm.*
Mid-Town Tennis Club
2020 West Fullerton. 235-2300. Seventeen metropolitan club locations in the city and suburbs. Individual or group instruction. Private lessons in foreign languages. Other health and fitness facilities available. *OPEN Mon-Fri 7am-midnight; Sat & Sun 8am-midnight.*
Oak Lawn Racquet Club
10444 South Central Avenue, Oak Lawn. 857-2215. Eight indoor tennis courts and 5 racquetball courts with glass-wall observation decks. Weight room, sauna, whirlpool, and bar. Members only. *OPEN 7 days 6:00am-midnight.*
Oak Park/River Forest Racquet Club
301 Lake Street, Oak Park. 386-2175. Members-only club with 8 tennis and 6 racquetball courts, workout room, and sauna. *OPEN Mon-Fri 6am-midnight; Sat 7am-6pm; Sun 7am-11pm.*
Tam Tennis & Fitness Complex
7686 North Caldwell, Niles. 967-1400. Indoor tennis and racquetball courts. Pro-rated club. Complete fitness center. Membership club, but does rent courts on an hourly basis. *OPEN Mon-Fri 6 am-11:30pm; Sat & Sun 6am-10pm*

Tobogganing, Sledding & Coasting
The Cook County Forest Preserve has 16 toboggan slides in 5 areas. The slides are OPEN Dec 1-Mar 1, 7 days 10am-10pm, weather and conditions permitting. Toboggan rentals are

available for a fee. Personal toboggans are permitted following inspection. Call 261-8400 for information.

Bemis Woods
Ogden Avenue west of Wolf Road, Western Springs. 485-8410. Tobogganing, sledding and coasting; a shelter and cross-country ski trails. No toboggan rentals.

Deer Grove
Quinten & Dundee roads, northwest of Palatine. 437-8330. Tobogganing, sledding and coasting, ice skating, cross-country skiing; shelter. No toboggan rentals.

Jensen Slides in Caldwell Woods
Milwaukee Road & Devon. 775-4060. Tobogganing, sledding and coasting; shelter. Rentals available.

Dan Ryan Woods
87th & Western. 233-3766. Tobogganing, sledding and coasting; shelter. No toboggan rentals.

Swallow Cliff (Palos Park)
Route 83 west of Mannheim Road, near Palos Park. 448-8532. Tobogganing and cross-country skiing. Rentals available.

Volleyball

The Chicago Park District has 412 indoor and outdoor volleyball courts. They also have organized leagues and activities. Call 294-2493 for information and the courts nearest you.

Volleyball Clinic (V. B. C. Inc.)
472-4286. Clinic every Monday at the Latin School, 59 West North Boulevard. Admission. Information on other programs, classes, tournaments, and leagues. Try the Volleyball Hotline, 472-4286 (Monday through Friday, 6 to 10pm), for current activities.

Wrestling

The Chicago Park District teaches wrestling at various parks. Call 294-2493 for times and locations.

Three citywide championships are held at McKinley Park (523-3811), 2210 West Pershing Road, in January, February, and March.

Yoga

The Chicago Park District has morning, afternoon, and evening classes in yoga at various parks throughout the city. Call 294-2317 for locations. Registration fee.

Yoga Sri Nerode of India
5442 South Dorchester. 493-7454. Over 55 years of classic yoga instructions. Individual lessons in exercises, breathing, meditation, and philosophy. Call Monday through Sunday between 9am and 9pm.

ENTERTAINMENT

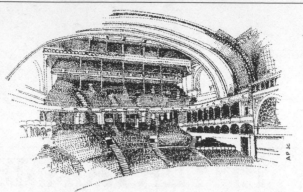

Auditorium Theatre

TICKETS

Tickets may be bought in advance by mail or in person at the box office (call for hours). Some theaters will take telephone orders and charge to major credit cards. Curtain Call, 977-1755, is a 24-hour theater information line to let you know what's playing on any given night and what tickets are available. Updated at 10am, 1, 3, and 5pm. Below is a discount ticket source set up by the League of Chicago Theaters, 977-1730; half-price tickets are available, same day only. Be prepared to line up and have alternate selections, as shows may be sold out while the line progresses.

Hot Tix Booth
24 South State. And, 1616 Sherman, Evanston.* Also Park Square, Lake & Marion, Oak Park Mall.* Offers half-price tickets (plus a service charge) on day of performance to downtown and off-Loop theaters, music, and dance throughout the city. Availability listed on booth. Tickets sold on a first come, first serve basis. Cash only. Also advance full-price tickets. *OPEN Mon noon-6pm; Tues-Fri 10am-6pm; Sat 10am-5pm. CLOSED Sun. *OPEN Tues-Sat 10am-3pm; CLOSED Sun & Mon. (Purchase Sunday and Monday tix on Saturday.)*

Ticket Brokers

Barnes Ticket Service, Inc.
Palmer House main lobby, 17 East Monroe; 726-3486 *(OPEN Mon-Fri 10am-5pm; Sat 10:30am-4pm; CLOSED Sun).* And Chicago Athletic Club, 12 South Michigan; 726-0544 *(OPEN Mon-Fri 10:30am-2pm. CLOSED Sat & Sun).* Theater, concert, dance, opera, and sporting events tickets.

Carey Theatre Ticket Service
225 North Wabash. 332-3122. Theater, opera, ballet, concerts, sports. *OPEN Mon-Fri 11am-7pm; Sat 11am-4pm.*

Union Tysen Theatre Ticket Service
32 West Randolph. 372-7344; 726-0021. Sports, theater, concerts. *OPEN Mon-Sat 9am-7:30pm.*

Theater Tix
853-0505. The centralized box office number for tickets to more than 50 Chicago theaters. AE, MC, V. *OPEN 7 days 10am-8pm.*

Ticketron
Attraction information: 842-5389. To charge tickets by phone call 853-3636.

NOTE: *"Tickets Please," $5, contains the seating plans for Chicago-area theaters, stadiums, and playhouses.*

THEATERS

Major theaters mainly offer road companies of Broadway musicals, as well as some Broadway-bound shows. But in recent years the local theater scene has witnessed the development of "off-Loop" theater. Mainly on the North Side, these nonprofit companies tend to produce what is innovative and freewheeling in nature, contemporary in theme.

For current theater and movie information see the Chicago Tribune, *the* Chicago Sun-Times, *and* Chicago *magazine. For information on the more avant-garde see the* Reader.

Absolute Theater Company
1225 West Belmont. 327-5252.

Albright Theatre Co./Kid's Co.
413 North Main, Glen Ellyn. 858-7256.

Apollo Theater Center
2540 North Lincoln. 935-6100.

Arie Crown
McCormick Place, East 23rd & Lake Shore Drive. 791-6000.

Auditorium Theatre
70 East Congress Parkway. 922-2110.

Black Ensemble Theater Corporation
4520 North Beacon. 281-9329; 769-3159.
Blackstone Theatre
60 East Balbo. 977-1700.
Body Politic Theater
2261 North Lincoln. 871-3000.
Briar Street Theater
3133 North Halsted. 348-4000.
Candlelight Dinner Playhouse
5620 South Harlem Avenue, Summit. 496-3000.
Center Theater
1346 West Devon. 508-5422.
Chicago City Theatre Company
3340 North Clark. 880-1002.
Chicago Comedy Showcase
1013 West Webster. 348-1101
Chicago Theatre
175 North State. 236-4300.
Civic Center for the Performing Arts
20 North Wacker. 332-2244.
Court Theatre
5535 South Ellis. 753-4472.
Drama Group
10th & Dixie Highway, Chicago Heights, 755-3444.
Drury Lane South
2500 West 95th Street, Evergreen Park. 422-8000.
Facets Performance Ensemble
1517 West Fullerton. 281-9075.
First Chicago Center
Dearborn & Madison. 732-4470.
Forum
5620 South Harlem Avenue, Summit. 496-3000.
Generic Theatre Company
4921 West Irving Park Road. 337-5131.
Goodman Studio
220 South Columbus. 443-3800.
Goodman Theatre Main Stage
200 South Columbus. 443-3800.
Illinois Theatre Center
400 Lakewood Boulevard, Park Forest. 481-3510.
Imagination Theater
5875 North Lincoln Avenue. 989-5300.
Jane Addams
3212 North Broadway. 549-1631.
Kuumba Theatre
218 South Wabash. 461-9000.
La Mont Zeno
1512 South Pulaski. 277-9582.
Marriott's Lincolnshire
Route 21 (Milwaukee Avenue), Lincolnshire. 634-0200.
Mayfair Theatre
Blackstone Hotel, 636 South Michigan Avenue. 786-9120.
North Light Repertory
2300 Green Bay Road, Evanston. 869-7278.
North Shore Theater Company
Highcrest Center, Hunter & Illinois roads, Wilmette. 256-6100, ext 309.
Oak Park Festival Theater Company
Austin Gardens, Forest Avenue at Lake Street. 524-2050.

Organic Theatre Company
3319 North Clark. 327-5588.
Palmer House Gaslight Club
17 East Monroe. 782-8326.
Pegasus Player House
1145 West Wilson/Truman College. 271-2638.
Performance Community
Theatre Building, 1225 West Belmont. 327-5252.
Pheasant Run Playhouse
Route 64, St. Charles. 261-7943.
Playwrights Center
3716 North Clark. 975-7711.
Puppet Place
1915 West School. 525-5944.
Remains Theatre
3319 North Clark. 327-5588.
Roosevelt University Theater
430 South Michigan. 341-3719.
Second City
1616 North Wells. 337-3992.
Shubert Theater
22 West Monroe. 977-1700.
Steppenwolf Theatre Company
2851 North Halsted. 472-4141.
Theatre of Western Springs
Hillgrove & Hampton avenues, Western Springs. 246-3380.
Victory Gardens Theatre
2257 North Lincoln. 871-3000.
Village Players
1010 Madison, Oak Park. 383-9829.
Wisdom Bridge Theatre
1559 West Howard. 743-6442.

DANCE

In addition to the following resident companies, national and international companies visit Chicago annually.
Chicago City Ballet
223 West Erie. 943-1315.
Columbia College Dance Center
4730 North Sheridan Road. 271-7804. Resident: Mordine & Company.
Fine Arts Building
410 South Michigan. 939-0181. Resident: Chicago Dance Medium.
Hubbard Street Dance Company
218 South Wabash. 663-0853.
Moming Dance & Arts Center
1034 West Barry. 472-9894.

OPERA

American Conservatory
116 South Michigan. 263-4161. Variety of performances year-round.
Chicago Opera Repertory Theater
P.O. Box 921 60690. 338-3096.

Chicago Opera Theater
410 South Michigan Avenue. 663-0555. Season:
Feb-June.
Lyric Opera of Chicago
Civic Opera House, 20 North Wacker. 332-2244.
Season: *late Sept-late Jan.*

CONCERT HALLS

Aragon
1106 West Lawrence. 561-9500.
Atheneum Theater
2936 North Southport. 935-6860.
Auditorium Theatre
70 East Congress Parkway. 922-2110.
Chicago Public Library Cultural Center
78 East Washington. 269-2837.
Circle Theatre
University of Illinois Campus, 1040 West Harrison. 996-2939.
Civic Opera House
20 North Wacker. 346-0270.
Civic Theatre
20 North Wacker. 346-0270.
Fullerton Hall
Art Institute, Adams & Michigan. 443-3794.
Ganz Hall
Roosevelt University, 430 South Michigan. 341-3787.
Holiday Star Theater
Interstate Highway 65 & U.S. Highway 30, Merrillville, Indiana. 734-7266.
Horwich Jewish Community Center
3003 West Touhy. 761-9100.
Lecture Hall Auditorium
Foster & Kedzie. 583-2700, ext 4300.
Mandel Hall
University of Chicago, 5706 South University Avenue. 962-8511.
Medinah Temple
600 North Wabash. 266-5000.
Murray Theater
Ravinia Park; 433-8800. And Highland Park, 432-1236.
Northeastern University: Stage Center
5500 North St. Louis. 583-4050, ext 535.
Old Town School of Folk Music
909 West Armitage. 525-7793.
Orchestra Hall
220 South Michigan. 435-8111. Houses the fabulous Chicago Symphony Orchestra. Season: *Sept-May.* You can charge tickets by phone to AE, MC, V: 435-6666.
Paramount Arts Center
23 East Galena Boulevard, Aurora. 896-7676.
Park West
322 West Armitage. 929-5959.
James C. Petrillo Music Shell
Grant Park, Columbus Drive & Jackson Boulevard. 819-0614.
Pick-Staiger Concert Hall
1977 Sheridan Road, Evanston. 491-7303.

Orchestra Hall

Poplar Creek Music Theater
4777 West Higgins Road, Hoffman Estates. 559-1212.
Rosemont Horizon Arena
6920 North Mannheim Road, Rosemont. 635-6601.
St. James Cathedral
Huron & Wabash. 787-7360.
Soldier Field
425 East McFetridge Drive. 294-2200.
Theatre-on-the-Lake
Lincoln Park, Fullerton Parkway & Lake Shore Drive. 294-2320.
Woodstock Opera House
121 Van Buren, Woodstock. (1-815) 338-5300.

MOVIE THEATERS: FIRST RUN

Downtown

Fine Arts
180 North Dearborn. 263-5005.
United Artists
45 West Randolph. 782-6919.
Woods
54 West Randolph. 332-3752.

Near North

Bijou
1349 North Wells. 943-5397.
Biograph
2433 North Lincoln. 348-4123.
Chestnut Station
830 North Clark. 337-7301.

Esquire
58 East Oak. 337-1117.
400 Theater
6746 North Sheridan. 761-1700.
McClurg Court
330 East Ohio. 642-0723.
Three Penny
2424 North Lincoln. 281-7200.
Village
1548 North Clark. 642-2403.
Water Tower
835 North Michigan. 649-5790.

North Shore

Bryn Mawr
1125 West Bryn Mawr. 728-0881.
Davis
4614 North Lincoln. 784-0894.
Lake Shore
3175 North Broadway. 327-4114.
Lincoln Village
6101 North Lincoln. 539-9214.
North Shore
7074 North Clark. 764-3656.
Nortown
6320 North Western. 764-4224.
Plaza
3343 West Devon. 539-3100.

Northwest

Logan
2646 North Milwaukee. 252-0627.
Luna
4743 West Belmont. 283-6660.
Milford
3317 North Pulaski. 545-5922.
Portage
4050 North Milwaukee. 685-5597.
Will Rogers
5635 West Belmont. 237-8340.

South

Colony
3208 West 59th. 476-0800.
Double Drive-In
2800 West Columbus. 925-9600.
Ford City
7601 South Cicero. 582-1838.
Hyde Park
5238 South Harper. 288-4900.
Ramova
3518 South Halsted. 927-5957.

Evanston

Evanston
1702-16 Central. 864-4900 or -1545.

Suburban

Bel-Air Drive-In
3101 South Cicero, Cicero. 656-3800.

Bolingbrook
I-55 & Route 53, Bolingbrook. 739-3901.
Deerpath
272 East Deerpath Road, Lake Forest. 234-4700.
Edens
303 Skokie Highway, Northbrook. 272-4473.
Evergreen
98th & Western, Evergreen Park. 636-8800.
Golf Mill
9200 North Milwaukee, Niles. 296-4500.
Highland Park
445 Central, Highland Park. 432-3300.
Hillside Mall
Wolf & Harrison, Hillside. 449-8230.
Hillside Square
4200 Frontage Road, Hillside. 547-6001.
La Grange
80 South La Grange, La Grange. 354-0460.
Mercury
7230 West North, Elmwood Park. 453-4515.
Norridge
4520 North Harlem, Norridge. 452-9000.
Oakbrook
2020 Spring, Oakbrook. 654-1160.
Old Orchard
9400 Skokie Boulevard, Skokie. 674-5300.
Olympic
6134 West Cermak, Cicero. 652-5919.
Orland Square
151st at Route 45, Orland Park. 349-6000.
Pickwick
5 South Prospect, Park Ridge. 825-5800.
River Oaks 1, 2, 3 & 4
300 River Oaks Drive, Calumet City. 868-3400.
Skokie
7924 Lincoln, Skokie. 673-4214.
Tivoli
5021 Highland, Downers Grove. 968-0219.
Wilmette
1122 Central, Wilmette. 251-7411.
Woodfield
700 Woodfield Mall, Schaumburg. 882-1620.
Yorktown
Butterfield Road at Highland, Lombard. 495-0010.

MOVIE THEATERS: REVIVAL (CLASSICS)

Chicago Filmmakers
6 West Hubbard. 329-0854.
Facets Multi-Media
1517 West Fullerton. 281-4114.
Film Center of the School of the Art Institute of Chicago
Columbus & Jackson. 443-3737.

FREE ENTERTAINMENT

Call the Visitor Event Line, 225-2323, daily for current events in the Chicago area, some of which will be free. Also dial F-I-N-E-A-R-T (346-3278), Mon-Fri 9am-5pm, *for specific information on cultural events in the city.*

A monthly calendar of events is available at the Daley Center lobby information booth, the Cultural Center, or the Water Tower Information Center.

In addition, check the ANNUAL EVENTS *chapter of this book for listings of many very special happenings, downtown and in the neighborhoods, especially during the summer months, many of them are FREE.*

Below are two places that offer free entertainment on a regular basis year-round.

Richard J. Daley Plaza
Randolph & Dearborn. Free performances daily at noon on the plaza, weather permitting, or in the east lobby if not. Call 346-3278 before noon for specifics.

Chicago Public Library Cultural Center
78 East Washington. Each month there are 50 or 60 free cultural events—music, dance, concerts, etc. Call 346-3278 for information. *OPEN Mon-Thurs 9am-7pm; Fri 9am-6pm; Sat 9am-5pm. CLOSED Sun.*

TELEVISION STATIONS

WBBM (Channel 2), CBS
630 North McClurg Court, Chicago, IL 60611. 944-6000.
WCFC (Channel 38)
1 North Wacker, Chicago, IL 60606. 977-3838.
WCIU (Channel 26)
141 West Jackson Boulevard, Chicago, IL 60604. 663-0260.
WFLD (Channel 32), Fox Network
300 North State, Chicago IL 60610. 645-0300.
WGN-TV (Channel 9)
2501 West Bradley Place, Chicago, IL 60618. 528-2311.
WLS (Channel 7), ABC
190 North State, Chicago, IL 60601. 750-7777.
WMAQ (Channel 5), NBC
Merchandise Mart Plaza, Chicago, IL 60654. 591-4000.

WSNS (Channel 44)
430 West Grant Place, Chicago, IL 60614. 929-1200.
WTTW (Channel 11), PBS
5400 North St. Louis Avenue, Chicago, IL 60625. 583-5000.

RADIO STATIONS

AM Radio

WBBM-AM: 780. News/talk.
WBEE-AM: 1570. Jazz.
WCEV-AM: 1450. Ethnic/international.
WCFL-AM: 1000. Pop adult/news.
WCRW-AM: 1240. Spanish.
WEDC-AM: 1240. Ethnic/international.
WGN-AM: 720. Contemporary/talk.
WIND-AM: 560 News/talk.
WJJD-AM: 1160. Country.
WLS-AM: 890: Rock.
WMAQ-AM: 670. Country.
WMBI-AM: 1110. Educational/religious.
WSBC-AM: 1260. Ethnic.
WVON-AM: 1390. Black contemporary.

FM Radio

WBBM-FM: 96.3. Pop adult.
WBEZ-FM: 91.5. Public service.
WBMX-FM: 102.7. Black contemporary.
WCYC-FM: 88.7. Spanish.
WFMT-FM: 98.7. Classical. (Chicago's premier fine-arts station broadcasts *24 hours a day, 7 days a week.*)
WFYR-FM: 103.5. Pop adult.
WGCI-FM: 107.5. Black contemporary.
WKQX-FM: 101.1. Adult pop.
WLAK-FM: 93.9. Beautiful music.
WLS-FM: 95. Rock.
WLUP-FM: 97.9. Rock.
WMBI-FM: 90.1. Educational/religious.
WMET-FM: 95.5. Rock.
WNIB-FM: 97.1. Classical/jazz.
WOJO-FM: 105.1. Spanish/24-hour.
WXRT-FM: 93.1. Rock.
WYEN-FM: 106.7. Pop adult.

NIGHTLIFE

Second City

NIGHTSPOTS INDEX

The following is an index of the clubs described in this section. The categories are: Blues; Cabaret; Comedy; Country/Western & Bluegrass; Dance Bars & Clubs; Dinner/Dancing; Ethnic; Folk; Jazz; Piano Bars; Rock/Reggae. A club's category appears in parenthesis following its name. Full descriptions of the nightspots follow this index.

Wise Fools Pub (Blues)
Zanie's (Comedy)

BLUES

Biddy Mulligan's
7644 North Sheridan Road. 761-6532. The main
thrust of this low-frills Rogers Park club (named,
ironically, for a rabid Irish prohibitionist) is great
live blues. But on Mondays reggae is featured,
Wednesdays there's rock, sometimes jazz or
rockabilly. Music starts at 10pm. Dancing on a
stamp-sized floor, reasonably priced drinks,
snack food, and darts too. Cover; no minimum.
Cash only. *OPEN Wed-Mon 8pm-2am. CLOSED
Tues.*
Blue Chicago
937 North State at Walton. 642-6261. Come and
dance the blues away on the spacious dance
floor of this comfortable, close-to-Gold-Coast
blues club. Good sounds and vibes in a nattier
than usual setting. Music from 8pm Monday to
Saturday. Cover varies; two-drink minimum as
well on Friday and Saturday. Cash only. *OPEN
Mon-Fri 7pm-2am; Sat 7pm-3am. CLOSED Sun.*
B.L.U.E.S.
2519 North Halsted. 528-1012. Your basic colorful, smoke-filled, intimate—make that crowded—
Chicago blues bar where you can hear *great
live music every night of the year* from 9pm till
1:30am, on Saturday till 2:30am. Monday night
jam. No food, reasonably priced drinks. Minimal
cover charge. Cash only. *OPEN Sun-Fri 8pm-
2am; Sat 8pm-3am.*
Kingston Mines
2548 North Halsted. 477-4646. Popular late-night
blues stop where topflight music people often
jam after their own gigs. Two rooms for music.
In the front bar on weekends; the house band;
the back room for name acts Monday jam;
music Tuesday to Sunday from 9:30pm to 4am.
In summer, a food tent in the backyard. Cover
varies; one-drink minimum. AE, MC, V.
Lilly's
2513 North Lincoln. 525-2422. Intimate Lincoln
Park blues café with small stage for the smooth
sounds of some good local talent. Music Thursday to Saturday from 9:30pm. Light menu. Jukebox. Cover Friday and Saturday only. AE, MC,
V. *OPEN Sun-Fri 8pm-2am; Sat 8pm-3am.*
New Checkerboard Lounge
423 East 43rd. 624-3240. This joint is jumpin'!
Top South Side survivor blues bar where top
Chicago blues performers make music. Blues
jam Monday at 8pm; Tuesday and Thursday to
Sunday from 9:30pm; no live music Wednesday.
(Food on Saturday and Sunday only.) Cover
charge, higher on weekends. Cash only. *OPEN
Mon-Fri 9am-2am; Sat 9am-3am; Sun noon-2am.*
Rosa's
3420 West Armitage. 342-0452. In the Logan
Square area, a friendly family-owned and -run
spot for live blues seven nights a week. Home

base for guitarist Melvin Taylor. Music Sunday
to Friday 9pm to 2am; Saturday 9:30pm to 3am.
Drinks $1 every Wednesday 7pm to 11pm. Cover
varies, none before 9pm. Cash only. Free parking.
Wise Fools Pub
2270 North Lincoln. 929-1510. Crowds beat a
path to the door of this rustic Lincoln Park club
for live Black blues. Cozy, barely lit music room
usually filled to capacity for sets at 9:30pm nightly.
Big-band jazz Monday night. Comfortable bar
has pool table, good jukebox. Snack food. Admission charge and two-drink minimum on Saturday. Cash only. *OPEN Sun-Fri 4pm-2am; Sat
4pm-3am.*

CABARET

Baton Show Lounge
436 North Clark. 644-5269. Boys will be girls in
the glitzy, Las Vegas-style revues at this 200-
seat cabaret. Shows Wednesday to Thursday
and Sunday at 10pm, midnight, and 2am; Friday
at 10pm, 12:30am, and 3am; Saturday at 10pm,
12:30am, and 3:30am. Cover charge; two-drink
minimum. AE, MC, V. Reserve.
Byfield's
Omni Ambassador East, 1301 North State Parkway. 787-6433. Cozy front bar, but in the elegant
art deco-nightclub shows feature comedy and
musical newcomers. Shows Wednesday and
Thursday at 8pm; Friday and Saturday at 8pm
and 10:30pm. Entertaining and fun. No food.
Cover; two-drink minimum. AE, MC, V. *OPEN
Mon-Thurs 5-11pm; Fri & Sat 5pm-midnight.
CLOSED Sun.*
Cross Currents
3206 North Wilton. 472-7884. Mini-progressive
arts center. A small bar and two venues for
improv comedy and diverse theater and musical
events: one is a 175-seat theater, the other a
subterranean cabaret. Cover and minimum varies. Call for current programs. Bar *OPEN 7 days
5pm-2am.*
Gaslight Club
Palmer House, 17 East Monroe; 440-7070. And
O'Hare Hilton at O'Hare International Airport;
686-0200. Primarily businessmen. Opulent settings, scantily clad waitresses who take part in
the Gaslight Revue. Steaks, rack of lamb, duck.
Hotel guest gets a complimentary key. Entertainment in several different rooms, but usually
a piano with jazz, show tunes, and pop tunes
plus the Gaslight girl revue. Cover for nonmembers. Gaslight Key, AE, CB, DC, MC, V. Hours
vary at the different clubs.
King Richard's Manor
2122 West Lawrence. 275-8400. Unsophisti-
cated fun in the medieval manor: wenches,
minstrels, jesters (no jousts). Evening includes
six-course medieval banquet (no silverware
supplied), unlimited wine and ale, and the "ri-
bald" show. Shows Wednesday and Thursday

at 7:30pm; Friday at 8pm; Saturday at 6pm and 10pm; Sunday at 6pm. Reserve well in advance for weekends. Cover charge. DC, MC, V. *CLOSED Mon & Tues.*

The Raccoon Club
812 North Franklin. 943-1928. Cozy and romantic art deco ambiance for jazz, pop, and cabaret. Every Saturday night, owner Jan Hobson and her Bad Review. Shows at 9pm and 11pm. Elegant crowd. Light supper menu, wines, cognacs, coffees. Food and drink can add up. Cover charge. AE, DC, MC, V. *OPEN Mon-Thurs 5pm-1am; Fri & Sat 5pm-2am. CLOSED Sun.*

The Roxy
1505 West Fullerton. 472-8100. Lively neighborhood spot with one room for talking and another for music. Local talent most nights. Thursday is comedy/talent showcase night; Wednesday there's a 16-piece big band 9pm to midnight. Shows Friday and Saturday at 8pm and 10:30pm. The decor is movie memorabilia—the seats are from the old Biograph. Food available (teriffic burgers). Cover Friday and Saturday only. Cash only. *OPEN Tues-Fri 11am-2am; Sat 12:30pm-3am. CLOSED Sun-Mon.*

COMEDY

Chicago Hysterical Society
3136 West Montrose. 583-5651. "Lost in Chicago" comedy revue followed by improvisation. Shows Thursday and Sunday at 8:30pm; Friday and Saturday at 8:30pm and 11pm. Admission charge.

Comedy Cottage
9751 West Higgins, Rosemont. 696-4077. Longtime comedy showcase club for reliably funny regulars and "names" who often drop in. Shows Wednesday and Thursday (new talent night) at 8:30pm; Friday at 8:30pm and 10:30pm; Saturday at 8:30pm, 10:30pm, and 12:30am. Doors open one hour before showtime. Munchie food. Two-drink minimum. Cover charge Friday and Saturday. Free parking. AE, MC, V.

ComedySportz
Frankie's Sports and Grill, 6215 North Broadway. 274-8059. Located in a popular sports bar. Teams of improvisational whizes go head to head to the audience's delight. Outdoor beer garden for al fresco performances in good weather. Comedy Friday and Saturday at 7:30pm. Cover charge.

Comedy Womb
8030 Ogden Avenue, Lyons. 442-5755. Longtime successful comedy club features those who have made it and those still trying. New talent and free pizza slices every Thursday night. Shows Thursday, Friday, and Saturday at 9pm and 11pm. Doors open a half hour before showtime. Cover; minimum. Reserve two days in advance. Parking.

Second City
1616 North Wells. 337-3992. This "bastion of improvisation" is in its 26th year and still going strong. Famed alumni include John Belushi, Joan Rivers, and Alan Arkin. Shows Tuesday, Wednesday, Thursday, and Sunday at 9pm; Friday and Saturday at 8:30pm and 11pm. Free improvisation bonus Tuesday, Wednesday, Thursday, and Sunday at 11pm; Saturday at 1am. Sandwiches, ice cream, and liquor available. Cover charge; no minimum. AE, CB, DC for food and drink only. Reservations required (for weekends call *very* well in advance).

Zanie's
1548 North Wells. 337-4027. Good Old Town comedy club, crowded on weekends. Up-and-coming Chicago and national stand-up comics: shows Wednesday, Thursday, and Sunday at 8:30pm; Friday and Saturday at 7pm, 9pm, and 11:15pm. Cover; two-drink minimum. MC, V. Reservations are a must.

COUNTRY/WESTERN & BLUEGRASS

Buffoons III
1934 West Irving Park Road. 871-3757. Country & western and oldies Friday 9pm to 2am; Saturday 10pm to 3am. Food available Monday to Friday only, 11am to 7pm. Cover charge Friday and Saturday only. AE, MC, V. *OPEN Mon-Sat 9am-2am; Sun noon-2am.*

Carol's Inn
4659 North Clark. 334-2402. Country bar with live country & western music Thursday to Sunday 9pm to 4am. Sandwiches available from 7am to 9pm. *OPEN Mon-Sat 7am-4am; Sun noon-4am.*

Deadwood Dave's Wildwest Saloon
1132 West Granville. 274-1853. The Old West in Rogers Park. Neighborhood crowd comes to listen to the country & western bands on Friday at 9:30pm and Saturday at 10pm. Biker's hangout. Homemade chili, sandwiches, and pizza available. No cover or minimum. *OPEN Mon-Sat 11am-2am; Sun noon-2am.*

Iron Rail
5843 West Irving Road. 736-4670. Go West to this honky-tonk to dance or just listen to some good bluegrass, folk, country rock, rock, and blues. Local and national entertainers. Music Wednesday to Saturday from 9:30pm to 1:30am. Cover charge; no minimum. No reservations. Cash only. *OPEN Mon-Fri 6pm-2am; Sat 6pm-2:30am.*

Nashville North
101 East Irving Park Road, Bensenville. 595-0170. Country club has western duds for sale up front, dance floor for C & W discoers. Free country & western dance lessons Tuesday, Wednesday, and Sunday. Good house band; Nashville guest stars. Live music Wednesday to Sunday from 8:30pm to 1:45am. Pizza, barbecue, sandwiches, and dinners available till 1am. Shirts must have collars. Cover; minimum

Wednesday to Sunday. AE, CB, DC, MC, V. *OPEN Tues-Sun 11am-2am. CLOSED Mon.*

Remington's
1007 North Rush. 951-6522. Near North singles' bar with a dash of Southwest flavor. Good jukebox and even better food, including Buffalo Burgers. Kitchen closes at 6pm. No cover. AE. *OPEN 7 days 11am-4am.*

RR Ranch
56 West Randolph. 263-8207. For over 35 years urban cowboys and cowgirls have come for the country music by the Sundowners, the home cookin' (28 kinds of chili), and the dancin'. Music Wednesday to Friday from 8:30pm to 3:30am; Saturday 8:30pm to 4:30am. Food available from 10:30am to 2am; Sat till 3am. Jukebox. No cover or minimum. AE, MC, V. *OPEN Mon & Tues 10am-2am; Wed-Fri 10am-3:30am; Sat 10am-4:30am; Sun noon-2am.*

DANCE BARS & CLUBS

(*See also* NIGHTLIFE, Rock/Reggae.)

Beaumont
2020 North Halsted. 281-0177. Drink and dance in a romantic turn-of-the-century ambiance. D.J. from Tuesday to Saturday. Bowling available for nondancers. Limited menu; lovely candlelit outdoor garden café in the summer; tent used in winter. No cover. Cash only. No reservations. *OPEN 7 days 11am-4am.*

Berlin
954 West Belmont. 348-4975. Creative video bar dance. New Wave music, tiny, crowded dance floor. Theme nights; some evenings feature male strippers and other nights, female wrestlers. Mixed gay and straight crowd. Cover Friday and Saturday. No credit cards. *OPEN Sun-Fri 4pm-4am; Sat 4pm-5am.*

Clubland
3145 North Sheffield. 248-7277. Huge club at the Vic, a century-old theater favored by Chicago's dancing fools. *Great* sound system, 75 TV monitors and five large video screens. Young crowd and always a wait to get in. Thursday is Ladies night. Cover charge. *OPEN Wed-Sat 9pm-2am.*

Culpeppers
6600 West Gunnison. 867-6681. Pleasant wood- and plant-filled Northwest Side bar/restaurant. Music starts on Friday and Saturday at 11pm. No cover or minimum. Food served till midnight. AE, MC, V. *OPEN Mon-Thurs 11am-11:30pm; Fri & Sat 11am-midnight; Sun 10am-11pm.*

Erik's North
6255 North McCormick. 267-0090. Cavernous bi-level club with sports on the TV screens, video, and neon. A DJ spins tunes for a young singles' crowd. Porch greenhouse and beer garden. No credit cards. *OPEN Tues-Thurs & Sun 8pm-2am; Fri 8pm-3am; Sat 8pm-4am.*

Faces
940 North Rush Street. 943-0940. Beautiful-

people members-only club. No cover or minimum. No blue jeans. AE, CB, DC, MC, V. *OPEN Tues-Fri 9pm-4am; Sat 9pm-5am. CLOSED Sun & Mon.*

Gaffer's
2873 North Broadway. 525-2560. Staple New Town young-singles' bar. Casual. Large dance floor. DJ from Wednesday to Saturday 9pm to 2am. *OPEN Sun-Fri 4pm-2am; Sat 4pm-3am.*

Gaslight
1547 West Howard. 262-3309. Local jazz, rock, and disco bands in this Rogers Park club. Nicely dressed good dancing crowd. Music starts at 9pm and goes till 3am on Friday; till 4am on Saturday. Cover Friday and Saturday. *OPEN Mon-Fri 12:30pm-3am; Sat noon-4am; Sun 4pm-4am.*

Jukebox Saturday Night
2251 North Lincoln. 525-5000. Formerly the Rodeo, *Newsweek* has called this the nation's "ultimate nostalgia club." The 1957 Chevy marks the spot where you can dance to the pop sounds of the 50s and 60s till the dawn's early light. Neon, balloons, arcade games, jukeboxes, pinball machines. Hula hoop and twist contests. Moderately priced drinks and "junk" foods. Classic 50s fare on the TVs. Live music Friday and Saturday. Cover charge. AE, DC. *OPEN Mon-Fri 7pm-4am; Sat 7pm-5am. CLOSED Sun.*

Limelight
632 North Dearborn. 337-2985. In River North, the old Chicago Historical Society castle takes on new life as the Limelight, via New York and London, takes on Chicago. VIP room, 2,800-foot dance floor, plenty of BPs, and dancing till dawn. The whole is less than the sum of its parts. Expensive drinks. Cover charge varies. AE ($15 minimum). *OPEN Mon-Fri & Sun 9pm-4am; Sat 9pm-5am.*

Medusa's
3257 North Sheffield. 549-9212. No-alcohol juice bar on three floors. A mostly young crowd flocks here to dance till dawn to New Wave rock. Live performances on occasion. Special session Saturday 6:30pm to 11pm for under 18. No credit cards. *OPEN Fri midnight-6am; Sat 6:30-11pm; midnight-6am (closes 11pm to midnight to clear out the youngsters).*

Mother's
26 West Division Street. 642-7251. The largest dance floor on Division Street makes this a popular singles' destination. A DJ plays top 40 tunes and oldies; music videos too. The café for pizza by the slice and deli sandwiches. AE, DC, MC, V. No cover. *OPEN Sun-Fri 8pm-4am; Sat 8pm-5am.*

NEO
2350 North Clark. 528-2622. Large, dimly lit New Town progressive dance and music club. Large, albeit packed dance floor; loads of energy, especially after midnight. New Wave videos and a DJ does the spinning. Great sound system. Cover Friday and Saturday only. Cash only. Must be 21 or over. *OPEN Sun-Thurs 8pm-4am; Fri 6pm-4am; Sat 6pm-5am.*

950-Lucky Number
950 West Wrightwood. 929-8955. Popular New Wave dance club. The latest in progressive music and people. Innovative yet inviting. Frequent theme nights. No food. Cover Friday and Saturday. Cash only. *OPEN 7 nights 9pm-2am.*

P.S. Chicago
8 West Division. 649-9093. Casual plant and singles-filled bar. A DJ spinning top 40 dance music starts at 8pm. Large dance floor. Frivolity like "the best-fitting jeans" contest for men and women. Complimentary buffet during the daily 4pm to 8pm "attitude adjustment hour." AE, MC, V. *OPEN 7 days 11am-2am.*

Riviera Nightclub
4746 North Racine. 769-6300. In a renovated uptown theater, a loud, lively club where a mixed crowd dances till the wee hours. Lots of laser, neon, smoke, and glitter. Valet parking (note: the neighborhood encourages care). Cover varies. *OPEN Wed-Thurs 9pm-2am; Fri 9pm-4am; Sat 9pm-5am. CLOSED Sun-Tues.*

DINNER/DANCING

Empire Room
Palmer House, 17 East Monroe. 726-7500. Extremely elegant cosmopolitan setting in which to dine and dance. Orchestra for dancing Tuesday to Thursday from 7pm to midnight; Friday and Saturday 7:30pm to 12:30am. Dinner Tuesday to Thursday 5:30pm to midnight, Friday till 1am, Saturday 6pm to 1am. No cover or minimum. Jacket required for men. Reserve. AE, CB, DC, MC, V.

Fitzgerald's
6615 West Roosevelt Road, Berwyn. 788-2118. A vintage 40s nightspot called the Hunt Club redone with cypress paneling and skylights. The modern incarnation features a blend of jazz, blues, rock, and folk Sunday and Tuesday to Thursday from 9pm to 1am; Friday and Saturday 10pm to 2am. Dancing Tuesday to Sunday. Complete dinner menu. Cover charge. AE, MC, V. *OPEN Sun & Tues-Thurs 7pm-1am; Fri & Sat 7pm-3am. CLOSED Mon.*

Pheasant Run
I-11 Highway 64, west of I-11 Highway 59 in St. Charles. 261-7366. Dining and dancing Friday and Saturday from 7pm. For dancing only: admission but no minimum from 10pm till 1am. Nostalgic and contemporary music. Garden terrace setting. Jacket required. AE, CB, DC, MC, V.

The Pump Room
1301 North State Parkway. 266-0360. For a sophisticated evening go to this restored 1938 café society watering hole where the chic of Chicago still meet and eat and dance cheek to cheek. Small orchestra with vocalist Friday and Saturday from 8:30pm to 1am; Sunday to Thursday piano music 5pm to midnight and Friday and Saturday 5pm to 8:30pm. Reserve. No cover

or minimum. AE, MC, V. Jackets for men; no denim, please. (*See also* RESTAURANTS, Continental.)

Willowbrook Ballroom & Restaurant
8900 South Archer Avenue, Willow Springs. 839-1000. Dining and dancing, or just dancing, in this very romantic big-band palace. Dinner Saturday from 6pm, Sunday from 4:30pm. Buffet or menu. Dancing Thursday 8pm to 11:30pm; 50s & 60s rock on Friday 7pm to 1am; Saturday till 1am; Sunday tea dance 2:30pm to 6pm and 6:30pm to 10:30pm. Free dance instruction Thursday only from 7:30pm to 8:30pm. Reserve for dinner. Admission charge if only dancing. AE, MC, V.

ETHNIC

Abbey Pub
3420 West Grace. 478-4408. Guinness and Harp on tap in this fun neighborhood Irish pub. Irish bands perform on weekends beginning at 9pm, sometimes during the week too. No food. No cover or minimum. Cash only. *OPEN Tues-Fri 6pm-2am; Sat 6pm-3am; Sun noon-2am. CLOSED Mon.*

Asi Es Colombia
3910 North Lincoln. 348-7444. Large Latin nightspot for *salsa* bands, hot dancing, and Latino snacks. Jackets required for men. Cover charge. Cash only. *OPEN Wed & Fri-Sun 9pm-2am. CLOSED Mon. Tues & Thurs.*

Baby Doll Polka Club
6102 South Central. 582-9706. The polka lives! Bands on hand Friday and Saturday from 9:30am to 2am; Sunday 5pm to 11pm. Free Polish food the third Sunday of every month. Jukebox; sandwiches and snack food. No cover or minimum. AE, MC, V. *OPEN Sun-Fri 6pm-2am; Sat 6pm-3am.*

Deni's Den
2941 North Clark. 348-8888. Go late for lively Greek music (a six-piece band and three singers) and delicious homemade Greek food. Seafood specialties. Food served 5pm to 4am. Music from 8:30pm to 4am; Saturday 8:30pm to 5am. Much of the clientele is Greek and they love to dance till dawn. No cover or minimum. Reserve Friday and Saturday only. AE, MC, V. *OPEN Wed-Sun 5pm-4am. CLOSED Mon & Tues.*

Erin's Glen Pub
2434 West Montrose. 478-3714. Enormous Irish pub with two stone fireplaces and a giant 10-foot TV screen for sports fans. Dancing to a jukebox. Pizza and sandwiches and lots of fun folks. DJ on weekends. *OPEN 7 days 9am-2am.*

Glenshesk Public House
4102 North Kedzie. 267-1755. Authentic Irish bar. Guinness stout on tap. Sandwiches available. *OPEN Mon-Fri 11am-2am; Sat noon-3am; Sun noon-2am.*

Golden Shell
10063 South Avenue N. 221-9876. Spacious

Yugoslavian club with ethnic entertainment and an international menu to match. Inexpensive daily specials. Music Friday and Saturday 7:30pm to 11:30pm. Food till closing. No cover or minimum. MC, V. *OPEN 7 days 6am-midnight.*

Irish Village
6215 West Diversey. 237-7555. Irish folk artists from the U.S., Canada, and Ireland play Friday and Saturday at 9pm; Tuesday to Thursday and Sun at 8pm. Extensive American menu in a country-style setting. Guinness stout and Harp lager on tap. Reserve on weekends. Cover Friday and Saturday after 8:30pm. AE, MC, V. *OPEN Tues-Fri 11am-2am; Sat 4pm-4am; Sun 4pm-2am.*

Kitty O'Shea's
Chicago Hilton, 720 South Michigan. 922-4400. An authentically re-created Irish pub with Guinness on tap and Irish music and dance. Music Monday to Friday from 5pm to 7pm and 9pm to 1am; Saturday 8pm to 1am. Note the "Snug." No cover. AE, CB, MC, V.

Latin Village
2528 North Lincoln. 472-6166. Popular *salsa* club draws a dressy crowd for dancing. Music 10pm to 4am. No food. No jeans, sneakers, or T-shirts. Cover charge, two-drink minimum at the tables. Cash only. *OPEN Mon, Wed, Fri & Sun 7pm-4am; Sat 7pm-5am. CLOSED Tues & Thurs.*

Matt Igler's Casino
1627 West Melrose. 935-2000. Shows feature waiters who sing after they've served you German schnitzel and sauerbraten. Shows at 8:30pm; Friday and Saturday there is an additional show at 11pm. Reserve. *OPEN Wed-Thurs & Sun till 1am; Fri & Sat till 2am. CLOSED Mon & Tues.*

Miomir's Serbian Club
2255 West Lawrence. 784-2111. Home-style Eastern European food and exotic drinks. Gypsy music with a gypsy orchestra, songs sung in many languages. Ballroom dancing. Music starts at 7:30pm. Food served 5:30pm to 1am. Reserve. No cover. MC, V. *OPEN Sun-Fri 5:30pm-2am; Sat 5:30pm-3am.*

Tania's
2659 North Milwaukee. 235-7120. Cuban club for Latin music in a knockout setting. *Salsa,* food, and an elegant crowd. Music weekdays 10pm to 2am, on the weekend till 3am. Kitchen open till 2am. No cover or minimum. No jeans. AE, MC, V. Reserve Friday and Saturday only. *OPEN Mon-Sat 10:30am-4am; Sun 1pm-2am.*

FOLK

Earl's Pub
2470 North Lincoln. 929-0660. Welcoming inexpensive spot for folk, country, blues, and more. Good chili and burgers. Open stage Wednesday and Sunday nights. Music Wednesday to Sunday from 9pm. No cover; one-drink mini-

mum. *OPEN Mon-Fri 3pm-2am; Sat & Sun noon-2am.*

Holstein's!
2464 North Lincoln. 327-3331. Owned by the Holstein brothers of folk-music fame. A bar and separate concert room for some of the best folk acts on the national and international scene, nightly at 8:30pm and 10pm. Cover; two-drink minimum. *OPEN 7 days 6pm-2am.*

No Exit Café & Gallery
6970 North Glenwood. 743-3355. Good, authentic Rogers Park coffeehouse complete with folk music Wednesday and Thursday at 9pm; Friday and Saturday at 9:30pm. Saturday and Sunday afternoons feature jazz and Monday is open-mike night. Relaxed atmosphere. Nice assortment of coffees, teas, pastries, and sandwiches. No alcohol. Cover charge. Cash only. *OPEN Mon-Thurs 4pm-midnight; Fri 4pm-1am; Sat-Sun noon-1am.*

JAZZ

Jazz Hotline: 666-1881.

Andy's
11 East Hubbard. 642-6805. Large friendly place with *terrific* hot home-grown jazz. Downtown crowds flock to the extremely popular "Jazz at Five," Monday and Thursday 5pm to 8pm, Wednesday to Friday 5pm to 8:30pm. Also popular, "Jazz at Noon," Wednesday to Friday noon to 2:30pm. Friday Late-Night Blues 8:30pm to 12:30am; Saturday music 9pm to 1am. Food available from an eclectic menu. No reservations. Cover charge Monday to Friday evenings. AE, CB, DC, MC, V. *OPEN Mon-Fri 11am-11pm; Sat 7pm-1am. CLOSED Sun.*

The Backroom
1007 North Rush. 751-2433. Chicago's oldest jazz club (since 1939) located in a former horse barn. Traditional jazz in a smoky, small club—just as it should be. Music from 8:30pm till closing. Cover varies; two-drink minimum Friday and Saturday only. No food. No reservations. AE, DC. *OPEN Sun-Fri 8pm-2am; Sat 8pm-3am.*

Bulls
1916 North Lincoln Park West. 337-3000. An extremely popular late-night stop. Casual, youth-filled basement club for interesting progressive jazz and good eclectic eats (terrific pizzas and burgers). Music every night of the year 9:30pm to 2:30am. Kitchen till 3am. Cover charge. MC, V. *OPEN 365 days a year: Sun-Fri 8pm-4am; Sat 8pm-5am.*

Deja Vu
2624 North Lincoln. 871-0205. Neighborhood club and bar. Very popular jazz program on Sunday nights; Tuesday night it's the sounds of the big bands. The eclectic jukebox fills in the rest of the time. Good chili; food served 5pm to midnight. Video games; young crowd. No cover or minimum. Cash only. *OPEN 7 days 11am-4am.*

Fireside
8740 South Ashland. 238-8740. Jazz on Friday at 9:30pm and Saturday at 10:30pm. Chinese-American menu. Cover on Friday and Saturday. AE, CB, DC. *OPEN Sun-Fri 11am-2am; Sat 11am-3am.*

George's
230 West Kinzie. 644-2290. An elegant venue for good jazz and fine Northern Italian cuisine and wine. Live performances by the likes of Ahmed Jamal, Ray Brown, Herb Ellis. Music starts Monday at 9pm, Tuesday to Thursday at 10pm, Friday and Saturday at 10pm and 11:45pm. Dressy crowd. Cover charge; two-drink minimum. AE, MC, V. Valet parking. *OPEN Mon-Thurs 5:30pm-1am; Fri & Sat 5:30pm-2am. CLOSED Sun.* (See also RESTAURANTS, Italian.)

Get Me High Lounge
1758 North Honore. 278-8154. A low-frills, smoky spot for easy jazz and ambiance. Popular with musicians and artists. Good jammin'. Tuesday to Sunday at 6pm. Poetry on Monday night at 8pm. Outdoor garden. No food. Minimal cover charge. Cash only. Bar *OPEN Sun-Fri 3pm-2am; Saturday 3pm-3am.*

The Green Mill
4802 North Broadway. 878-5552. A restored uptown club (it once belonged to Al Capone) with a good sound system and an atmospheric 40s feel. Local jazz men swing Monday to Thursday from 9pm to 1:30am; Friday 9pm to 4am, Saturday 8pm to 5am; Sunday 7 to 10pm. (Friday and Saturday feature late-night jams.) Nice-sized dance floor for those who can't just listen. No food. Cover varies.

Joe Segal's Jazz Showcase
Blackstone Hotel, 636 South Michigan. 427-4300. Joe Segal's is a Chicago institution to jazz buffs, booking the best for over 40 years. At this highly rated jazz café off the hotel lobby, huge photos of Ellington and Charlie Parker dominate the decor. Shows are Friday and Saturday at 9pm, 11pm, and 1am; Sunday 8:30pm and 10:30pm. No food. Call for current roster. Classy club and crowd. Cover charge. AE, CB, MC, V. Student and musician discounts on Sunday.

Milt Trenier's Show Lounge
610 North Fairbanks Court. 266-6226. Small cozy showroom owned by a former member of the group The Treniers. Top names have been known to drop in. Shows Tuesday to Friday at 10:30pm, 12:30am, and 2:30am; Saturday at 11pm, 1am, and 3am. Dancing starts around 8pm or 9pm on Saturday. Minimum at shows. Reserve. No denim. AE, MC, V. *OPEN Mon-Fri 5pm-2am; Sat 5pm-3am. CLOSED Sun.*

Moosehead Bar & Grill
163 West Harrison. 922-3640. In the South Loop, a large inviting room for afterwork jazz by seasoned musicians. Monday to Friday music starts at 5:30pm; Saturday at 9pm; Sunday at 6pm. Good burgers. No cover Tuesday and Thursday. AE, DC, MC, V. *OPEN Mon-Thurs 11am-mid-night; Fri 11am-2am; Sat noon-3am; Sun noon-7pm.*

Orphans
2462 North Lincoln. 929-2677. Top showcase club where newcomers, regulars, local favorites, and out of towners offer an eclectic range of music, including jazz, blues, and rock. Sets at 9:30pm, 11:30pm, and 12:45am. The need for reservations depends on the group. Cover and two-drink minimum (except Sunday). *OPEN Mon-Fri 3pm-2am; Sat 2pm-3am; Sun 2pm-2am.*

Oz
2917 North Sheffield. 975-8100. Sleek modern environment for contemporary jazz fusion. Serious jazz devotees come here *to listen.* Nice selection of brandies. Outside garden in summer. Music Thursday and Friday 9:30pm, 11pm, and 12:30am; Saturday 10pm, 11:45pm, and 1:30am. No credit cards. Cover Friday and Saturday.

Pops for Champagne
2934 North Sheffield. 472-1000. Classy jazz club/champagne bar. Champagnes, wines, cognacs; appetizers and desserts till 2am. Patio noon to dusk for dancing. Music Thursday to Saturday 9pm to 1am; Sunday 8pm to midnight. Minimum; cover varies.

PIANO BARS

Acorn on Oak
See RESTAURANTS, Bars & Burgers.

Ambassador Bar
Ambassador East Hotel, 1301 North State Parkway. 787-7200. Elegant yet comfortable setting for easy listening. Sit near the fireplace or around the padded piano. Ike Cole, brother of Nat "King," also a fine singer-pianist, occasionally performs here. Music Monday to Friday 7pm to 11pm; Saturday 8pm to midnight. No food. No cover or minimum. Men must wear jackets; no denim. AE, CB, DC, MC, V. *OPEN Mon-Sat 4pm-1am.*

Cricket's Hearth
Tremont Hotel, 100 East Chestnut. 280-2100. Jacket and tie required in this oh-so-civilized little bar of this oh-so-wonderful little hotel. Sophisticated piano music Monday from 9pm to 1:30am; Tuesday to Friday from 9pm to 1am; Saturday from 8pm. AE, CB, DC, MC, V.

Gold Star Sardine Bar
666 North Lake Shore Drive. 664-4215. A compact little jewel of a bar where romance, style, and jazz piano (every night from 7pm to 1am) are the constants. On "Big-Name Nights" the tiny stage just may be graced by Bobby Short or—can it be—Tony Bennett. The dark walls are lined with photos of glamorous film sirens and the ice cubes are Perrier! Alas, the "in" nosh are "sliders," reheated White Castle burgers. (The club's guiding light is Treasure Island's Bill Allen.) No cover; one-drink minimum. AE, MC, V. *OPEN Mon-Fri noon-2am; Sat 7pm-3am.*

Oak Terrace
Drake Hotel, 140 East Walton. 787-2200. Old-fashioned hotel elegance, romantic candlelit ambiance. Singer Tuesday to Saturday 5:30pm to 10:30pm; Sunday and Monday 5:30pm to 10pm. Jackets for men; no denim. No cover or minimum. Reserve. AE, CB, DC, MC, V.

Ritz Carlton Bar
Ritz Carlton Hotel, 160 East Pearson. 266-1000. Sophisticated spot for dancing to a trio; recorded music between sets. Music Tuesday to Thursday 8:30pm to 1am; Friday and Saturday 9pm to 2am. No cover or minimum. AE, DC, MC, V.

Tiff's
Sheraton-Plaza Hotel, 160 East Huron. 787-2900. Small, comfortable drinking place with a limited menu. Piano music Tuesday to Saturday 8:30pm to 1am. AE, CB, DC, MC, V. *OPEN 7 days 11am-2am.*

ROCK/REGGAE

(See also NIGHTLIFE, Dance Bars & Clubs.)
Cabaret Metro/Smart Bar
3730 North Clark. 549-3604. Adventurous club in the Wrigley Field area showcases punk and New Wave bands. On the first two floors there are Video Metro concerts, on Friday and Saturday there is video after the concerts. Wednesday night: "Rock Against Depression" features a low-priced, high-value evening of live music. Downstairs, the low-ceilinged Smart Bar for dancing in a constantly changing art fully decorated environment. Extremely popular with a young and funky ethnically mixed crowd. No credit cards. On Friday there is an all inclusive admission to the three floors. *OPEN Sun-Fri*

9:30pm-4am; Sat 9:30pm-5am. Smart Bar *OPEN Sun-Thurs (except concert nights).*
Exit
1653 North Wells. 944-9495. Dark multimedia punk club for late-night progressive music and video shows, live and DJ rock and dancing (some slamming). It's quite a place! Borders on the bizarre. Cover Friday and Saturday only. Tickets in advance depending on the event. Cash only. Call to see what's happening. *OPEN Sun-Fri 8pm-4am; Sat 8pm-5am.*

Gaspar's
1359 West Belmont. 871-6680. Chicago and national New Wave rock groups perform on the small stage in this comfortable old beerhall-like club. Lots of dancing. Shows are at 10pm and midnight. Good jukebox in spacious front bar. Cover and minimum. *OPEN Sun-Fri 4pm-2am; Sat 4pm-3am.*

Negril Cafe & Nightclub
6232 North Broadway. 761-4133. Dark and crowded late-night reggae club. Jamaican island sounds; Caribbean, African, and Cajun food. Music nightly 11pm to 2am. Cover charge.

Park West
322 West Armitage. 929-5959. Swank, sleek, high-tech interior seats 750. Best listening room in town for big names on tour: rock, country, pop, blues, and New Wave. Dancing too. Schedule depends on the act appearing, usually two shows nightly. Try their A.I.R. (Anti-Inflation Rock budget nights: two sets by two local bands and no drink-minimum). Cover and minimum. Call for schedule.

The Wild Hare & Singing Armadillo Frog Sanctuary *4273*
3530 North Clark. 327-~~0000~~. Authentic live reggae and Caribbean rum from 10:30pm in this roomy Northside tavern. Crowded dance floor. No food. Cover charge. *OPEN Sun-Fri 8pm-2am; Sat 8pm-3am.* *#7*

RESTAURANTS

Cricket's

RESERVATIONS

Telephone to make a reservation, since this will determine that the particular restaurant is still in business and that a table will be available. If reservations are not accepted you can determine whether to expect a long wait prior to being seated.

TIPPING

The rule of thumb is approximately 15% of the total (exclusive of tax).

Generally, Chicago restaurants do not add a service charge; when they do it is noted.

KEY

The price of dinner at these restaurants has been classified on the basis of dinner for two, excluding wine, tax, and tip, as follows:

$	$19 or less
$$	$20-35
$$$	$36-45
$$$$	more than $46
$$$$+	more than $100

The key used for meals served is:

B	Breakfast
L	Lunch
D	Dinner

The key used for credit cards is:

AE	American Express
CB	Carte Blanche
DC	Diners' Club
MC	MasterCard
V	Visa

RESTAURANT INDEX

The following represent a good cross section of every type of food and price range. The restaurant may be found in the category listed in parentheses.

The Abacus (Chinese)
Abril (Mexican)
Acorn on Oak (Bars & Burgers)
Alouette (French)
Ambria (French)
Ananda (Thai)
Ann Sather (Swedish)
Arcadia (Polish)
Army & Lou Restaurant & Lounge (Soul)
Arnie's Cafe (Continental)
Ashkenaz Old World Deli (Jewish)
Atlantic Restaurant (British Isles)
Avanzare (Italian)
Bacino's (Pizza)
The Bagel (Jewish)
Bagel Nosh (Jewish)
The Bakery (Continental)
Bangkok House (Thai)
The B.A.R. Association (Middle Eastern)
The Bar at the Whitehall (Bars & Burgers)
Barney's Market Club (American)
Belden Corned Beef Center (Delicatessen)
Benchers Club Room & Grille (American)
Benihana of Tokyo (Japanese)
Beppino's (Italian)
The Berghoff (German)
Biggs (Continental)
Big John's (Soups, Salads & Sandwiches)
Billy Goat (Bars & Burgers)
Binyon's (German)
Blackhawk on Pearson (American)
Blue Mesa (American)
Bob Elfman's (Delicatessen)
Boca del Rio (Mexican)
Bombay Palace (Indian)
Boudin Bakery (Soups, Salads & Sandwiches)
Bratislava (Czechoslovakian)
Bread Shop Kitchen (Vegetarian)
Bruna's Ristorante (Italian)
Butch McGuire's (Bars & Burgers)
Café Angelo (Italian)
Café Azteca II (Mexican)
Cafe Ba-Ba-Reeba! (Spanish)
Café Bernard (French)
Café du Parc/La Fontaine (French)
Café Provençal (French)
Cafe Royal (British Isles)
Caffè Pergolesi (Cappuccino & Espresso)
Cape Cod Room (Fish & Seafood)
Capt'n Nemo's (Soups, Salads & Sandwiches)
Carlos' (French)
Carlyn Berghoff (Soups, Salads & Sandwiches)
Carson's—The Place for Ribs (American)
The Casbah (Middle Eastern)
Chapman Sisters Calorie Counter (Soups, Salads & Sandwiches)

RESTAURANTS

Afternoon Tea

*Perhaps part of the Europeanization of America,
afternoon tea is catching on, and it's oh-so-
civilized.*

Drake Hotel
140 East Walton. 787-2200. Served in the comfy,
inviting Palm Court. Tea, sandwiches, scones,
and pastries. Piano music. No reservations. AE,
CB, DC, MC, V. Prix-fixe tea *served 7 days*
3pm-5:30 pm. $

The Mayfair Regent
181 East Lake Shore Drive. 787-8500. A romantic, flower-filled setting. In the lobby lounge;
fireplace ablaze in winter. Tea served in a china
pot, finger sandwiches and cakes; piano accompaniment. A standout. Saks Fashion Show
first Tuesday of every month. No reservations.
AE, CB, DC, MC, V. Prix-fixe tea *served 7 days*
3 pm-5:30 pm. $

Park Hyatt Hotel
800 North Michigan. 280-2222. *Haute* tea (espresso, cafe au lait, and cappuccino too) served by butlers in black tie and tails in the serene Lobby Salon. Assorted savories, sandwiches and scones, sweets and teas (from a choice of 14) accompanied by harpsichord (8pm to 2am) or piano music (3 to 8pm). Business attire. No reservations. AE, CB, DC, MC, V. A la carte tea *served 7 days 2:30pm-5pm.* $

Ritz-Carlton Greenhouse
Water Tower Place, 160 East Pearson, 12th floor. 266-1000. A panoramic view for tea (north up Michigan Avenue). Skylit, green, and soothing. Finger sandwiches, tea cakes, scones, and Cornwall banana bread. No reservations. No denim. AE, CB, DC, MC, V. Prix-fixe tea *served Sun-Fri 3pm-5pm.* $

The Walnut Room
Marshall Field's, 111 North State, 7th floor. 781-3693. Club-style dining setting (with no-smoking section) for afternoon tea. Assorted pastries, fruits, and cheese available. AE, MC, V, Field's charge. A la carte tea *served Tues, Wed, Fri & Sat. 3pm-5pm.* $

Whitehall Hotel
105 East Delaware Place. 944-6300. Sit on a sofa in the lobby and have a lavish formal tea in the *proper* English tradition. Consists of three courses: light finger sandwiches; warmed scones, with thick Devonshire cream and strawberry preserves; followed, if you have room, by assorted pastries. A selection of teas, brewed in a china pot. All beautifully served with Laura Ashley appointments completing the picture. All for a reasonable fixed price. No reservations. AE, CB, DC, MC, V. Prix-fixe tea *served Tues-Sat 3pm-5pm.* $

American

This list includes the traditional as well as the latest food rage, "new" American or "regional" American cooking. (See also RESTAURANTS, Bars & Burgers and Cajun/Creole and Steak.)

Barney's Market Club
741 West Randolph. 372-6466. Located in the Randolph Street produce-market area since 1919. A colorful, old-fashioned spot where politicians come for steak and ribs (on the sweet side), accompanied by shoestrings or onion rings, and everyone's called "senator." Another specialty: 2½-pound Maine lobsters. Cheesecake for dessert. Reserve. AE, DC. MC, V. *L, Mon-Fri 11am-3pm. D, Mon-Sat 4pm-11pm; Sun 5pm-10pm.* $$

Benchers Club Room & Grille
Sears Tower, 233 South Wacker. 993-0096. The more formal of this two-faced restaurant is the refined Club Room where the emphasis is on seafood: Cajun shrimp, lobster and avocado salad, grilled fish with a selection of sauces. Grilled meat and poultry entrées as well. Wines

by the glass. Next door, the more casual less costly Grille, a noisy drinking and meeting spot. Burgers, etc.
The Club Room: Reserve. AE, CB, DC, MC, V. *L, Mon-Fri 11:30am-3pm. D, Mon-Sat 5pm-7:45pm. CLOSED Sun.* $$$
The Grille: No reservations. AE, CB, DC, MC, V. *OPEN Mon-Fri 11am-8pm. CLOSED Sat & Sun.* $

Blackhawk on Pearson
110 East Pearson. 943-3300. Don Roth's attractive newer, smaller, more casual Blackhawk features a salad bar (that doesn't spin) and fresh catch *du jour.* Reserve. AE, DC, MC, V. *L, Mon-Sat 11:30am-2:30pm. D, Mon-Thurs 5pm-9pm; Fri 5pm-10:30pm; Sat 5pm-10:30pm; Sun 5pm-9pm.* $$$

Blue Mesa
1729 North Halsted. 944-5990. The American Southwest is saluted in this popular, inviting white-adobe rustic-style restaurant with fire place ablaze in winter and outdoor dining patio in summer. Aim for one of the cozy booths and chow down on blue corn enchiladas, grilled carnitas, skirt steak with sautéed cactus, or Santa Fe pizza. Colorful drinks, Mexican beers, wines by the glass. Reservations taken for eight or more on weekdays only, so expect a wait. AE, MC, V. *L, Mon-Fri 11:30am-2:30pm; Sat 11am-2:30pm. D, Mon-Thurs 5pm-10pm; Fri & Sat 5pm-midnight; Sun 4pm-10pm.* $$

Carson's—The Place for Ribs
612 North Wells; 280-9200. And 5970 North Ridge; 271-4000. Also 8617 Niles Center, Skokie; 675-6800. The Lake is always east, and Carson's is *the* place in Chicago for meaty baby back ribs. Homey and unpretentious, great for kids (low-priced menu). Expect a wait or take out. Free dinnertime parking. AE, DC, MC, V. Reservations taken for large parties only. *OPEN Mon-Thurs 11am-midnight; Fri 11am-1am; Sat noon-1am; Sun noon-11pm.* $$

Cricket's
Tremont Hotel, 100 East Chestnut. 280-2100. High marks for its "clubby" (à la New York's "21" Club) atmosphere, good people-watching, impeccable service, extensive and consistently good food, and first-rate wine selections. Jacket and tie are required. Interesting and popular New Orleans-style brunch. Reserve! AE, CB, DC, MC, V. *L, Mon-Fri noon-2:30pm. D, Sun-Thurs 6pm-10:30pm; Fri & Sat 6pm-11:30pm. Brunch, Sat noon-2:30pm; Sun 11am-2:30pm. (See also NIGHTLIFE, Piano Bars: Cricket's Hearth.)* $$$$

Don Roth's River Plaza
405 North Wabash. 527-3100. Attractive multi-level restaurant on riverfront plaza. Downstairs, a pleasant, airy, casual bar/dining area for house specialties: prime rib, Boston scrod, barbecued spare ribs, and burgers on croissant. Service outdoors in fine weather. Upstairs, Cajun/Creole specialties and lovely salads enhanced by a river and skyline view. Hot fudge sundae for

dessert; wines by the glass. Reserve for lunch if later than 1:15pm and for dinner. AE, DC, MC, V. *L, Mon-Sat 11:30am-2:30pm. D, Mon-Thurs 5pm-9pm; Fri & Sat 5pm-10:30pm; Sun 5pm-9pm.* $$$

Ed Debevic's
640 North Wells. 664-1707. If you entered a time capsule and emerged in 1952, Ed's is probably how it would look and sound. This giggle of a re-created period piece is another from Richard Melman. The food is American—before regional, before nouvelle, it's original. Meat loaf with gravy; chili dogs; three-, four-, or five-way chili; burgers; fries; macaroni and cheese; black cows; malts; Jell-O; and cream pies. Served by gum-chewing, polyester-clad waitresses (who have to audition for the job). Though it seats 300 in four separate dining areas, the wait can be long. Obviously, a lot of people want to go home again, even if they've never been there. (P.S. There is no Ed.) As one of the signs says, "If you think you have reservations, you're in the wrong place." No credit cards. Valet parking. *OPEN Mon-Thurs 11am-midnight; Fri & Sat 11am-1am; Sun 11am-10pm.* $

Eugene's
1255 North State Parkway. 944-1445. Da menu appears ta have been penned by Nathan Detroit. The decor is elegant turn-of-the-century, the crowd is well-heeled Gold Coast. Satisfying grilled steaks and ribs as well as fish entrées. Fire ablaze in winter and, to accompany it, a fine cognac selection. Extensive wine list. Jacket required. Reserve. AE, DC, MC, V. *OPEN Mon-Thurs 4:30pm-midnight; Fri & Sat 4:30pm-1am; Sun 4:30pm-11pm.* Bar with entertainment till 1am weekdays, Friday and Saturday till 2am. $$

Fireplace Inn
1448 North Wells. 664-5264. Old Town standby for good barbecued ribs as well as other American staples like potato skins and steaks. A two-story-high wood-beamed and brick-walled dining room with large wood-burning fireplace ablaze in winter. Reserve. AE, CB, DC, MC, V. *OPEN Mon-Thurs 4:30pm-midnight; Fri-Sat 4:30pm-1:30am; Sun 3pm-midnight* $$

Foley's
211 East Ohio. 645-1261. A celebration of American foodstuffs prepared to dazzle the eye and the palate by super-Chef Michael Foley. Grilled duck foie gras, veal medallions in puff pastry, turkey breast with arugula and lime, fillet of broiled salmon with crème fraîche. There are lovely pasta choices and the fresh seafood dishes are standouts. Desserts change daily. Wines by the glass. Outdoor café in season. Reserve. AE, CB, DC, MC, V. *L, Mon-Fri 11:30am-2:30pm. D, Mon-Thurs 5:30pm-10pm, Fri & Sat 5:30pm-11pm. CLOSED Sun.* $$$$

Fritz, That's It!
1615 Chicago Avenue, Evanston. 866-8506. A funky, youthful place for chicken and beef dishes and an astounding salad bar! Unusual milk shakes too. No reservations. AE, DC, MC, V. *OPEN Mon-Thurs 11:30am-9:30pm; Fri & Sat 11:30am-11pm; Sun 10:30am-9pm. Brunch, Sun 10:30-3pm.* $

Genesee Depot
3736 North Broadway. 528-6990. Friendly, charming, and small (17 tables) storefront draws crowds with its inexpensive complete dinners. Tasty choice of entrées; homemade bread and outstanding desserts. Bring your own wine. No reservations are taken, so expect a wait. AE, MC, V. *OPEN Tues-Thurs 5pm-10pm; Fri & Sat 5pm-10:30pm; Sun 5pm-9pm CLOSED Mon.* $$

Hard Rock Cafe
63 West Ontario. 943-2252. High-energy tribute to rock music—memorabilia-bedecked walls reverberate from the beat. Good burgers, chili, and thick shakes. Successful formula that draws hordes in London, New York, and LA. Minimum after 6pm. No reservations, expect to wait. AE, CB, DC, MC, V. *OPEN Mon-Thurs 11am-midnight; Fri & Sat 11am-1am. CLOSED Sun.* $

Lawry's The Prime Rib
100 East Ontario. 787-5000. Beautiful setting in former McCormick mansion for the best prime rib in town. Your dinner decisions are kept to a minimum: How do you like your roast prime rib of beef done? Carved tableside and served with mashed potatoes and gravy, horseradish, Yorkshire pudding, and salad. A wider choice at lunch with excellent salads and a fresh seafood special daily. Trifle is *the* dessert if you have room. Free hors d'oeuvres in the bar from 4pm to 7pm. Reserve (though you may still have a wait). AE, MC, V. *L, Mon-Fri 11:30am-2pm. D, Mon-Thurs 5pm-11pm; Fri & Sat 5pm-midnight; Sun 3pm-10pm.* $$$

Miller's Pub & Restaurant
23 East Adams. 922-7446. Stained-glass-enhanced; busy and nostalgic pub atmosphere. Famous for its Canadian baby back hickory-grilled ribs. Steaks too. AE, DC, MC, V. *OPEN 7 days 10:30am-4am.* $$

Printer's Row
550 South Dearborn. 461-0780. A former printing building, in the newly fashionable South Loop area, provides a comfortable inviting setting for imaginative and beautiful new American cooking. Menu reflects seasonal offerings; emphasis on grilled and roasted dishes. Wines by the glass feature many Americans. In all, memorable. Jacket and tie required. Reserve! AE, CB, DC, MC, V. *L, Mon-Fri 11:30am-2:30pm. D, Mon-Thurs 5:30pm-10pm; Fri & Sat 5:30pm-11pm. CLOSED Sun.* $$$

Randall's
11 East Superior. 280-2790. Ribs go upmarket—applewood smoked, no less. In addition, fried catfish Cajun-style, grilled seafood, steak too. For dessert, whiskey-soaked bread pudding or homemade ice cream. Over 40 beers and a good selection of American wines. Outdoors in season. Reserve. AE, CB, DC, MC, V. *OPEN Mon-Thurs 11:30am-10pm; Fri & Sat 5pm-11pm; Sun 4pm-9pm.* $$$

R. D. Clucker's
2350 North Clark. 929-5200. Attractive casual place for chicken lovers. The variety of preparations include whole or half grilled on an in-view wood fire served with a choice of sauces; skewered with a Thai peanut sauce; in a casserole; baked, batter-fried, blackened, or smoked in a salad; and, of course, in soup complete with matzoh ball. In addition, some meat and seafood including a distinguished blackened redfish. Reserve for six or more. AE, CB, DC, MC, V. *L, Mon-Fri 11:30am-2:30pm. D, Mon-Thurs 5pm-10:30pm; Fri & Sat 5pm-11:30pm. Sun 4pm-10pm. B, Sat & Sun 10am-2:30pm.* $$

R. J. Grunts
2056 North Lincoln Park West; 929-5363. And 1615 North Milwaukee Avenue, Glenview; 635-7707. First of Richard Melman's Lettuce Entertain You eateries with menus to tickle your funny bone as well as fill your belly. Though the effect has been dulled by time, it still serves a very good half-pound burger. Generous salad bar and imaginative drink choices including a peanut butter shake. Great value-for-volume brunch on Sunday: steak and eggs or omelette; caviar, chopped liver, juice, bagels, and pastries. Be prepared for a wait. Reserve for six or more only. AE, DC, MC, V. *OPEN Mon-Thurs 11:30am-11pm; Fri & Sat 11:30am-midnight; Sun 10am-10pm. Brunch, Sun 10am-3pm.* $

Sage's on State
1255 North State. 944-1557. Inviting spot, plush setting for consistently good basics, mainly the steak, the lamb chops, and the lobster tails. Extensive wine list. Excellent cheesecake. Fireplace in winter. Jacket required; no denim, please. Reserve. AE, CB, DC, MC, V. *OPEN Sun-Thurs 4:30pm-midnight; Fri & Sat 4pm-1am.* $$$

Sauer's
311 East 23rd. 225-6171. Near McCormick Place. Huge skylit former German restaurant now for hearty burgers on rye, steaks, sandwiches, and daily specials. No credit cards. Free parking. *OPEN Mon-Sat 11am-8pm. CLOSED Sun.* $

Sessions Pullman
605 East 111th. 785-7578. Located in a charming turn-of-the-century town house in the fascinating historic Pullman section. Limited menu features *great* ribs, lamb chops, steak *au pouvre*, fresh seafood. Included in the price of the entrée, homemade soup or salad. Nice prix-fixe Sunday brunch. Tempting desserts; small, select wine list. Commendable service. Reserve. MC, V. *L, Mon-Fri 11am-2pm. D, Wed-Sat 5pm-10pm; Sun 3pm-7pm. Brunch, Sun 11am-3pm.* $$

Sweetwater
1028 North Rush. 787-5552. On the former site of famed Mr. Kelly's, an attractive, sleek setting with a busy central-skylight bar—serves free hors d'oeuvres at cocktail time. Sports ticker and Bears star-owner Doug Buffone provide the sports connection. Eclectic menu; stay simple. No jeans, shorts, sandals, or sneakers in the

more formal Gourmet Room; enclosed sidewalk café is more casual for burgers and omelettes. Reservations for five or more only. AE, MC, V. *L, 7 days 11:30am-4pm. D, Sun-Thurs 5pm-11:30pm; Fri & Sat 5pm-12:30am. Champagne brunch, Sun 11:30am-3:30pm.* $$$

Tamborine
200 East Chestnut. 944-4000. Attractive casual cabaret/restaurant for all-American basic foods. Steaks, ribs, duck, seafood, soft-shelled crabs in season. Piano music nightly. Reserve. AE, CB, DC, MC, V. *L, Mon-Sat 11:30am-4pm. D, Mon 5pm-10pm; Tues-Thurs 5pm-11pm; Fri & Sat 5pm-12:30am. CLOSED Sun.* $$

Two Doors South
3220 North Clark. 935-0133. Attractive combination gift shop/storefront restaurant. All-American basics; the specialty: roast duck. No reservations. AE, MC, V. *OPEN Sun-Thurs 5pm-10pm; Fri & Sat 5pm-11pm.* $

Wrigley Building Restaurant
410 North Michigan. 944-7600. Long-established restaurant in revered Chicago landmark building. Steaks, chops, fresh fish, and highly touted steak tartare. Crowds at noon and cocktail time at the rear bar for the oh-so-dry 4-ounce martini. Jacket required; no denim, please. Reserve. Free parking. AE, CB, DC, MC, V. *L, Mon-Fri 11:30am-2:30pm. D, 5pm-8:30pm (last seating). CLOSED Sat. Sun & holidays.* $$$

Bars & Burgers

(See also NIGHTLIFE, Dance Bars & Clubs.)

Acorn on Oak
116 East Oak. 944-6835. Inviting pub atmosphere for what many Chicagoans call the best—a "gourmet" burger: ¾ pound of beef with chopped green onions and peppers cooked in the burger. Good large steak and fries. Full lunch and dinner menu available. Congenial torchy-tunes piano bar, Monday to Saturday from 10:30pm to 4am (minimum). Reserve for dinner. AE only. Kitchen *OPEN Mon-Sat 11:30am-10:15pm; Sun 11:30am-9pm. Bar OPEN Mon-Sat till 4am.* $

The Bar at the Whitehall
105 East Delaware. 944-6300. This elegant little bar just off the lobby claims to serve the largest drinks in Chicago—11 ounces! Brace—and pace—yourself. AE, CB, DC, MC, V. *OPEN Mon-Fri 4pm-2am; Sat & Sun 11am-2am.* $

Billy Goat
430 North Michigan, lower level (entrance on Hubbard Street). 222-1525. Do as the newspaper folk do at this basement bar: have the "doubla cheeze bugger" made (in)famous by the late John Belushi on "Saturday Night Live." Or perhaps a grilled salami and cheese washed down with a couple of beers. A real taste of old Chicago. Can you spot the real Mike Royko? Reservations? You must be kidding. Credit cards? Ditto. *OPEN Mon-Fri 7am-2am; Sat 7am-3am; Sun noon-2:30am.* $

Butch McGuire's
20 West Division. 337-9080. This, "the first singles' bar in America," is a still-popular holdover from the 60s single-scene heyday. Good afterwork watering hole with jukebox, backgammon. AE, CB, DC, MC, V. Food *Mon-Fri 8am-3pm; brunch, Sat & Sun 9:30am-3pm. Bar OPEN Sun-Thurs 11am-2am; Fri 11am-4am; Sat 8am-5am.* $

Chicago Claim Company
2314 North Clark. 871-1770. A casual young crowd is drawn to this original home of the huge charbroiled "Motherlode" burger: topped with American, blue, cheddar, or Swiss cheese, sautéed mushrooms, fried onions, and barbecue or teriyaki sauce—on black bread, onion roll, or traditional sesame bun; accompanied by cottage fries. Good unlimited salad bar. Dim, candlelit gold-mining motif; working fireplace in winter. Reservations taken for more than six only. Expect a wait. Burgers available for takeout. AE, MC, V. *OPEN Mon-Thurs 5pm-10pm; Fri & Sat 5pm-midnight; Sun 3:30pm-9:30pm.* $

Clark Street Café
2260 North Clark. 549-4037. Lively Tiffany-glass-bedecked bar with music blasting. Good snacking on onion soup. Flute and guitar music during Sunday brunch. Reserve for six to eight people only. AE, MC, V. *L, Mon-Fri 11:30am-3pm. D, Sun-Thurs 5pm-10pm, Fri & Sat 5pm-11pm. Brunch, Sat 11:30am-3pm; Sun from 11am.* $

Eliot's Nesst
20 East Bellevue. 664-7010. Fun party-bar filled with advertising people. Two fireplaces in winter, an outdoor café in summer. DJ spins a mix of top 40, Motown, and oldies. Dancing when there's room. No food. Proper dress. AE. *OPEN Mon-Thurs 4pm-4am; Fri 2pm-4am; Sat noon-5am; Sun noon-2am.* $

Hamburger Hamlet
44 East Walton. 649-6601. Very popular home of the *haute* burger, well, "meejum," or rare, with crispy french fries, in a pretty turn-of-the-century setting. Free tostado bar during cocktail time Monday to Thursday. Classical harp music with New Orleans-style Sunday brunch, noon to 3 pm. (NOTE: Service charge of 15% added to bill for parties of six or more.) No reservations. AE, CB, DC, MC, V. *OPEN Mon-Thurs 11:30am-11pm; Fri & Sat 11:30am-midnight; Sun 11:30am-11pm.* $

Harry's Café
1035 North Rush. 266-0167. This bar and restaurant caters to the lively young single habitués of the Near North. Fresh fish entrées, sandwiches, salads till 10:45pm weekdays, till midnight on Saturday. Attractive atrium dining rooms; outdoor sidewalk café and rooftop dining May 1 to October 15, weather permitting. AE, DC, MC, V. *OPEN Mon-Fri 11:30am-2am; Sat 11am-3am; Sun 11am-2am. Brunch, Sun 11am-3:30pm.* $$

Hillary's
Water Tower Place, 845 North Michigan, mezzanine level. 280-2710. A chic, well-appointed Near North draw for singles; popular with fashion plates and ad people at 5pm. Half-pound burgers, salads, soups, and fried chicken till 10:30pm. *Great* Bloody Marys! AE, DC, MC, V. *OPEN Mon-Thurs 11am-midnight; Fri & Sat 11am-1am; Sun noon-midnight.* $

Images
John Hancock Center, 172 East Chestnut. 787-7230. On the 96th floor, sky-high sips. Absolutely dazzling at sunset. Happy hour 4pm to 7pm, with complimentary hors d'oeuvres. A wine bar features specialty California wines. Minimum, no cover. No denim, please. AE, CB, DC, MC, V. *OPEN Mon-Fri 4pm-1:30am; Sat, Sun & holidays 11:30am-1:30am.* $

Marina City Bar
300 North State. 321-0786. It overlooks the Chicago River. Sip and watch the boats go by. Steak and seafood Monday to Thursday 11am to 10pm; Friday and Saturday 11am to 11pm; Sunday 11am to 8pm. AE, MC, V. Bar *OPEN 7 days 11am-2am.* $

Moody's Pub
5910 North Broadway. 275-2696. Sans frills, but colorful. Great winter spot for hot cider in front of two roaring fires. In summer a spacious beer garden for charcoal-broiled burgers; Löwenbräu (dark too), Michelob, and Miller on tap. Reserve for large groups. No credit cards. *OPEN Mon-Fri 11:30am-2am; Sat 11:30am-3am; Sun noon-2am.* $

Nick's
1973 North Halsted. 664-7383. Good neighborhood bar with great jukebox and room to dance. Booze only, no food (except the peanuts on the bar). *Very* crowded on weekends. AE only. *OPEN Mon-Fri 3pm-2am; Sat 1am-3am; Sun 1pm-2am.* $

Old Town Ale House
219 West North Avenue. 944-7020. Neighborhood bar frequented by the eclectic residents of Old Town: artists, writers, Second City folks. The bar, with a huge mural and a free library but no food, can get wild and crazy as dawn approaches. Jukebox has jazz, classical, opera, and r 'n r. Dancing permitted. *OPEN 7 days noon-4am.* $

O'Rourke's Pub
319 West North Avenue. 944-1030. Yellowing pix of Joyce, Behan, Shaw, and O'Casey grade this colorful old watering hole where literary folk have been known to do serious drinking. Darts, pinball machine, and jukebox. Thursday and Friday late nights are most colorful times. No food. No credit cards. *OPEN Sun-Fri 3:30pm-2am; Sat 3:30pm-3am.* $

Redamak's New Buffalo Chicago
2263 North Lincoln. 787-4522. From New Buffalo, Michigan, this burger arrives with its reputation intact. Pan-fried juicy, served on dark or light rye, or on a bun; waxed paper-wrapped in a basket. Homemade fries. Art deco decor makes this a good far-from-roadside burger outpost. Casual crowd sips specialty drinks. Special kids'

menu. AE only. Reservations for eight or more. OPEN Mon-Thurs 11:30am-midnight; Fri & Sat 11:30am-1:30am; Sun noon-11pm. $

Red's Place
2200 West Cermak Road. 847-8874. Established in 1905, this friendly neighborhood tavern serves great burgers on onion rolls or fresh rye. Accoutrements: fries and slaw, horseradish, mustard, and dill pickles. Breakfast and sandwiches too. OPEN Mon-Fri 7am-6pm. Sat 7am-4pm. Kitchen closes at 2:30pm. $

The Sign of the Trader
Board of Trade, 141 West Jackson, lobby level. 427-3443. Where the commodity traders wet their well-used whistles while several well-placed quote machines keep them in touch. Reserve. AE, CB, DC, MC, V. OPEN Mon-Fri 11am-8:30pm. Kitchen closes at 7:30pm. $

Breakfast/Brunch

Hotel Florence
11111 South Forrestville. 785-8181. Historians note: The elaborate old Queen Anne-style Florence Hotel, showpiece of George Pullman's Pullman District, provides a handsome setting for a bargain-value-for-volume prix-fixe brunch; the food is basic: eggs, French toast, muffins, Stroganoff, and quiche. Trips unlimited, so is the coffee, and the cause is a good one: profits go toward the restoration of the hotel. Brunch, Sun 10am-3pm. Before noon, a complimentary glass of wine. Reserve for very large groups only. P.S.: Take a peek upstairs on a guided tour. Lunch served Mon-Fri 11am-2pm; breakfast and lunch served Sat 9am-1pm. (See also HISTORIC & NEW CHICAGO, Historic Buildings & Areas: Pullman Historic District.) $

Jerome's
2450 North Clark. 327-2207. This attractive spot excels with Sunday brunch, one of this town's best. A choice of entrées plus a complete cold buffet featuring smoked trout, tame guacamole, curried chicken, fruit, and all accompanied by baked on premises whole-wheat bread and tempting pastries. Outdoor umbrella-shaded patio in summer for salads, sandwiches, and an à la carte brunch. Reserve. AE, CB, DC, MC, V. Brunch, Sun 10am-3pm. $$

La Tour
Park Hyatt Hotel, 800 North Michigan. 280-2230. A luxurious prix-fixe brunch beautifully served in a setting to match. With a view of Water Tower Square and the castellated Tower, dine on stuffed avocado or scrambled eggs in pastry and fresh fruit out of season. Champagne bar—classical pianist. (See also RESTAURANTS, Rooms with a View.) Reserve! AE, CB, DC, MC, V. Brunch, Sun & holidays 11am-2:30pm. $$$

Lou Mitchell's
565 West Jackson Boulevard. 939-3111. Before brunch there was breakfast, and this is the place to have it in Chicago. The ham and eggs and the fluffy omelettes come to the table in a skillet; the Greek-bread French toast is deep fried; the double-yolk fried eggs are farm fresh; the orange juice is hand-squeezed; indeed, everything is natural, homemade, and wonderful. Lou Mitchell himself greets diners with free boxes of Milk Duds; he's his own best ad. Note the waiters' T-shirts; they refer to the penchant patrons have for lingering over the great coffee. No reservations; no credit cards. OPEN Mon-Fri 5:45am-4pm; Sat 5:45am-2:30pm. CLOSED Sun & holidays $

Normandie Lounge
Chicago Hilton and Towers, 720 South Michigan. 922-4400, ext 4376. Lavish and grand venue for a sumptuous Sunday buffet brunch. Choices range from pâtés to pastas; salads, eggs, and Belgian waffles to ambitious entrées. Dessert, too, and unlimited sparkling wine. Children under age 5 eat free. All for a reasonable fixed price. Reserve. AE, CB, DC, MC, V. Brunch, Sun 10:30am-2:30pm. $

The Original Pancake House
2020 North Lincoln Park West; 929-8130. And 22 East Bellevue; 642-7917. Also 1517 East Hyde Park Boulevard, 288-2322; 10437 South Western, 445-6100.* Everyone craves pancakes for breakfast at some time. Well, this is where to have them when you do. In addition to buttermilk and wheat there are cherry, strawberry, and mandarin-orange crêpes. No credit cards. OPEN Mon-Fri 7am-3pm; Sat & Sun 7am-5pm. *7 days 7am-3pm. $

Ted's Snack Shop
930 West Diversey. 348-8533. Breakfast at the counter with an eclectic mix of Chicagoans. No credit cards. OPEN Mon-Sat 5am-1pm. CLOSED Sun. $

*The following also offer breakfast and/or Saturday or Sunday brunch; an * indicates a standout:*

The Abacus (Chinese)
Abril (Mexican)
Arnie's Cafe (Continental)
The B.A.R. Association (Middle Eastern)
Butch McGuire's (Bars & Burgers)
Café Angelo (Italian)
Cape Cod Room (Fish & Seafood)
Chestnut Street Grill (Fish & Seafood)
Clark Street Café (Bars & Burgers)
Cricket's (American)
Dixie Bar & Grill (Cajun/Creole)
Fritz, That's It! (American)
Frontera Grill (Mexican)
Hamburger Hamlet (Bars & Burgers)
Harry's Café (Bars & Burgers)
Hong Min (Chinese)
***La Creperie** (Crêpes)
***Le Ciel Bleu** (Rooms with a View)
L'Escargot (French)
The Magic Pan Creperie (Crêpes)
The Ninety-Fifth (Rooms with a View)
Pinnacle Restaurant & Lounge (Rooms with a View)
The Pump Room (Continental)
R. D. Clucker's (American)

Ritz-Carlton Dining Room (French)
R. J. Grunts (American)
Sessions Pullman (American)
Sweetwater (American)
Szechuan House (Chinese)
Three Happiness (Chinese)
Villa Sweden (Swedish)
The Waterfront (Fish & Seafood)

British Isles

(See also NIGHTLIFE, Ethnic, for Irish pubs.)
Atlantic Restaurant
7115 West Grand. 622-3259. A warm and welcoming pub and restaurant featuring the cooking of the British Isles with emphasis on pasties, filling pies, and stews. Beef and Yorkshire pudding, Irish soda bread. Unlimited fish, chips (alas, not wrapped in newsprint); folk singing on Friday and Saturday night. A lively game of darts is usually in progress. Guinness, Bass, and Harp on tap. Reserve. MC, V. No cover or minimum. Free parking, *OPEN Mon-Fri 3pm-2am; Sat noon-3am; Sun 10am-10:30pm.* $
Cafe Royal
1633 North Halsted. 266-3394. A former candle factory transformed into a restaurant with stunning decor. Several dining spaces on several levels—including some romantic private areas. English and Scottish specialties: shepherd's pie, jugged hare, Cornish hen, crab cakes, Stilton cheese; à la carte or fixed-price dinners. Spacious wine bar with a fine selection of wines by the glass. British and Irish beers. Reserve. AE, CB, DC, MC, V. *OPEN Tues-Sun 5pm-11pm. CLOSED Mon.* $$$

Cajun/Creole

(See also RESTAURANTS, Soul.)
Cricket's
See RESTAURANTS, American.
Dixie Bar & Grill
225 West Chicago. 642-3336. This cavernous former warehouse with its vaulted skylit ceiling and Bayou decor is a place to see and make the scene. Hordes of Yuppies feast on food with its roots in the South and the Caribbean. Blackened fish of the day, pan-fried rabbit, chicken Montego Bay, coco beer shrimp, and, to wash it all down, Jamaica Red Stripe or Dixie beer. Adding to the clamor in the first-level lounge is live jazz, Monday to Thursday from 7:30pm to midnight; Friday and Saturday 8pm to 12:30am (cover). Reservations for lunch only. AE, CB, DC, MC, V. *L, Mon-Sat 11:30am-2:30pm. D, Mon-Thurs 5:30pm-10:30pm; Fri & Sat 5:30pm-11:30pm; Sun 5pm-9pm. Brunch, Sun 11:30am-2:30pm.* $$
Don Roth's River Plaza
See RESTAURANTS, American.
Maple Tree Inn
10730 South Western. 239-3688. This unpreten-

tious outpost of authentic Louisiana cooking, housed in several rooms of a Victorian house, predates the present Cajun/Creole food craze. Aficionados of the genre still think it the best. New Orleans oyster loafs, lightly battered deep-fried soft-shelled crabs or catfish nuggets, andouille sausage, jambalaya with tasso ham, carpetbagger steak, and such. Start with a lethal Cajun martini to put you in the mood, then wash it all down with Dixie beer. In summer, the delightful garden with its maples is an added treat. Upstairs, live jazz on Friday and Saturday from 8:30pm to 12:30am (no food). Reserve, but expect a wait. MC, V. Restaurant *OPEN Tues-Thurs 5pm-9:30pm; Fri & Sat 5pm-10:30pm. CLOSED Sun & Mon.* $$

Cappuccino & Espresso

(See also RESTAURANTS, Afternoon Tea.)
Caffè Pergolesi
3404 North Halsted, 472-8602. The owner, a refugee from Greenwich Village's beatnik generation, ca. 1950; the atmosphere, *very* relaxed and quiet. Cappuccino, espresso, Turkish coffee, homemade cheesecake; soups and omelettes too. No credit cards. *OPEN Mon-Thurs 11am-1am; Sat 9pm-2am; Sun 10am-1am. CLOSED Fri.* (Call first in any case.) $
Il Giardino
2859 Harlem. 889-2388. Espresso Italian-style accompanied by *dolce:* cannoli or cassata. No credit cards. *OPEN 7 days 9am-9pm.*
Kennessey Wine Cellar
Hotel Belmont, 403 West Belmont. 929-7500. Upstairs, or downstairs in the wine-cellar atmosphere, for ground-to-order espresso and delectable homemade pastries. AE, MC, V. *OPEN Mon-Thurs 11am-11pm; Fri & Sat 11am-midnight; Sun noon-9pm. (See also RESTAURANTS, Hungarian.)* $
Lutz
2456-8 Montrose. 478-7785. In summer sit in the high-walled little garden with its pond and sip Viennese coffee, tea, or chocolate and savor the richest pastries this side of Vienna: tortes, coffee and cream cakes, petits fours. Light meals too. Reserve for eight or more only. No credit cards. Bakeshop *OPEN Tues-Sat 7am-10pm.* Café *OPEN Sun & Tues-Thurs 11am-10pm; Fri & Sat 11am-11pm. CLOSED Mon.* $
No Exit Café
7001 North Glenwood. 743-3355. Entering this Rogers Park coffeehouse is like walking back into the 60s, perhaps even 50s, which isn't surprising, since it's a survivor of those eras (opened 1958; at this location since 1967). Coffees, teas, hot chocolate; pastries, yogurt, sandwiches too. Entertainment ranges from folk music Thursday to Saturday at 9:30pm to jazz. Sunday from 3:30pm to 7pm. Jazz or classical Sunday from 8:30pm to 11pm. Monday at 8:30pm: open mike. No reservations. No credit cards. *OPEN Mon-Fri 4pm-midnight, Sat & Sun noon-1am.* $

Something's Brewing
The Century, 2828 North Clark, top level. 871-7475. Sit-down or stand-up espresso bar. Tea too. No smoking permitted. MC, V. OPEN Mon-Fri 10am-7pm; Sat 10am-6pm; Sun noon-5pm. $

Theater Café
Water Tower Place, 835 North Michigan, 2nd level. 943-8443. Pass the food and go directly to the cappuccino, Irish coffee, espresso, caffè amaretto, or Viennese coffee. No-smoking section. AE, CB, DC. OPEN Mon-Thurs 8am-9:30pm; Fri & Sat 8:30am-11pm; Sun 9am-9pm. $

Chinese

The Abacus
2619 North Clark. 477-5251. Lively, well-respected Chinese restaurant in New Town serves Mandarin-, Cantonese-, Szechuan-, and Shanghai-style specialties. Steamed whole fish, hot green-pepper beef, lemon chicken, lobster Shanghai, Peking duck. Reserve. Valet parking. AE, CB, DC, MC, V. OPEN 7 days 5pm-midnight. Dim Sum brunch, Sun 11am-2:30pm. $$

Charlie Lui's
2741 West Howard. 465-5252. Near Evanston, very large, very good Chinese restaurant features Szechuan/Mandarin cooking. Fireplace. Reserve. AE, MC, V. OPEN Sun-Thurs 11:30am-10pm; Fri & Sat 11:30am-11pm. $

Formosa
7108 West Higgins. 763-3652. Unassuming treat for the taste buds. Mandarin, Cantonese, and some unusual Taiwanese dishes. Wonderful steamed dumplings, hot and sour soup, Formosa sizzling shrimp or chicken. Taiwan-style noodles. Mongolian hot pot available daily, order one day in advance. Pleasant service. Carryout too. Reserve. No credit cards. OPEN Tues-Fri 11:30am-10:30pm; Sat & Sun 3pm-11pm. CLOSED Mon. $

Hong Min
221 West Cermak. 842-5026. No frills Chinatown storefront where standout Dim Sum is served weekdays from 10am to 3pm; 10am to 4pm on weekends. A good, albeit usually crowded, alternative to Sunday brunch American style. Reserve. MC, V. OPEN 7 days 10am-2am. $

House of Hunan
535 North Michigan. 329-9494. Comfortable reliable choice with an interesting, extensive (over 100 dishes), and tempting variety of regional Chinese dishes (Hunan, Szechuan, Shanghai, Mandarin). The specialty, hung yan niu li'o—willow beef with watercress—is fiery hot. Among the seafood dishes, sung tzu hsia jen—shrimp with pine nuts—is less so. Mild seasoning for timid palates. Full service bar. Reserve. AE, CB, DC, MC, V. OPEN 7 days 11:30am-10:30pm. $$

Hunan Palace
1050 North State. 642-1800. George Kuan and Austin Koo's lavish Near North outpost features Mandarin cooking in an elegant setting with an atrium garden. Emphasis is on seafood preparations; Peking duck without 24 hours' notice. Jacket requested. Reserve. AE, DC, MC, V. OPEN Sun-Thurs 11:30am-11pm; Fri & Sat 11:30am-midnight. $$

Lee's Canton Café
2300 South Wentworth. 225-4838. Popular Chinatown spot for consistently good authentic Cantonese cuisine. Bring your own beer or wine. They cater too. Reserve. AE, DC, MC, V. OPEN 7 days 11am-midnight. $

Moon Palace
2206 South Wentworth, 2nd floor. 225-4081. Foods of Canton, Hunan, and Szechuan provinces are served in this Chinatown find. Go with a hungry group and sample them all. Popular with Chinese families. Reserve for five or more. AE, MC, V. OPEN Sun-Thurs 11am-10pm; Fri & Sat 11am-11pm. $

On the Tao
1218 West Morse. 743-5955. In a choice of several stylish dining rooms, feast on classic Cantonese cuisine. From the limited menu choose crackling skin hen, crispy boneless duck in an apricot ginger sauce, pike fillets in a black bean sauce, quail in a bean-thread "nest." Fruit sorbets for dessert. Full service bar. No MSG; low-salt and low-cholesterol selections are noted. Reserve for four or more. No-smoking area. MC, V. OPEN Tues-Sun 5pm-11pm. CLOSED Mon. $

Restaurant Chang
1525 West Howard. 973-3412. Consistently good hot and spicy Szechuan and Mandarin dishes. Spun-glazed bananas for dessert, yum. Reserve for four or more only. MC, V. OPEN Tues-Sun 11:30am-10pm. CLOSED Mon. $

Szechuan House
600 North Michigan. 642-3900. Another George Kuan/Austin Koo eatery. Features Chinese country cooking with the emphasis on spicy Szechuan specialties. Some Taiwanese dishes. Peking duck without advance notice. Weekday lunch buffet and the Sunday brunch buffet are good-value affairs. Reserve. AE, DC, MC, V. OPEN Mon-Thurs 11:30am-10:30pm; Fri & Sat 11:30am-11pm; Sun noon-10:30pm. $$

Three Happiness
209 West Cermak; 842-1964. And 2130 South Wentworth; 791-1228.* Touted as Chinatown's best, it's certainly one of the most popular. The original location sans ambiance. A large selection of savory Dim Sum served at both locations daily from 10am to 2pm. Bring your own wine or try their Chinese beer. No reservations, expect a wait. AE, CB, DC, MC, V. OPEN Mon-Wed & Fri-Sun 9am-4pm; Thurs 9am-8pm. *Full service bar. OPEN 7 days 10am-midnight. $

Wing Yee's
2556 North Clark. 935-7380. Recommended as a pleasant New Town spot for always-well-prepared Cantonese food: sweet-and-sour pork and shrimp, great vegetable dishes. Bring your own wine or beer. No reservations. No credit cards. OPEN 7 days 3pm-10:30pm. $

Continental

Arnie's Cafe
1030 North State. 266-4800. Stylish art deco decor; central atrium filled with plants; continental menu. Glass-enclosed café (outdoors in summer) for more casual dining—good burgers and people watching. Copious well-priced Sunday brunch buffet. Reserve (except for brunch). Jacket not required but preferred (not for brunch). AE, DC, MC, V. Restaurant *L, Mon-Fri 11:30am-2:30pm. D, Mon-Thurs 5:30pm-11pm; Fri & Sat 5:30pm-midnight; Sun 5:30pm-10pm. Café OPEN 7 days: food 11:30am-midnight; drinks 11:30am-2am; Sun 11:30am-midnight. Bar Mon-Fri 11:30am-2am; Sat 11:30am-2am; Sun noon-11pm.* $$

The Bakery
2218 North Lincoln. 472-6942. Humble beginnings as a bakeshop, since 1962 several storefronts comprise this well-known little restaurant. Lovely seasonal prix-fixe five-course dinners consist of pâté maison, freshly made soup, salad, entrée—among them duck with cherries, stuffed Cornish game hen, beef Wellington—and dessert. Bouillabaisse Friday and Saturday. Limited wine list. Jackets requested for men. Reserve! AE, CB, DC, MC, V. *OPEN Tues-Thurs 5pm-11pm; Fri & Sat 5pm-midnight. CLOSED Sun & Mon.* $$$$

Biggs
1150 North Dearborn. 787-0900. Good food and wine in the former John De Kovan mansion, built in 1874. The setting is romantic with a fireplace in every room and some seating in the wine cellar. Prix-fixe or à la carte dinner menu. Choices include roast quail, poached salmon, beef Wellington, roast duckling. No-smoking area. Reserve. AE, CB, DC, MC, V. *OPEN 7 days 5pm-10:30pm.* $$$

Gordon
500 North Clark. 467-9780. A standout for well-prepared, imaginative food, especially the seafood choices, in a fascinating fantasy setting. The must-have starter: batter-dipped deep-fried artichoke fritters with Béarnaise sauce. The menu changes daily; seasonal specials. Desserts include a flourless chocolate cake and a sinful chocolate mousse. Wines by the glass; a good list. Singer in the lounge Friday and Saturday from 7pm till closing. Jacket and tie suggested. Reserve. No kids! AE, CB, DC, MC, V. *L, Tues-Fri 11:30am-2pm. D, Tues-Thurs 5:30pm-10:30pm; Fri & Sat 5:30pm-11pm; Sun 5pm-9:30pm. CLOSED Mon.* $$$$

The Pump Room
Ambassador East Hotel, 1301 North State. 266-0360. October 10, 1938, Gertrude Lawrence sat in Booth One for the first of 90 straight nights; her record stands. But others to sit in *the* famed booth (to the right of the bar and to the left of the steps) have included Frank Sinatra, David Bowie, Lauren Bacall, and finicky Morris the Cat. The continental food's good too. Now run by Lettuce Entertain You Enterprises. Sunday from 6pm to 10pm, Monday till midnight, live harp music. Cocktails Monday to Friday from 5pm to 7:30pm with lavish complimentary hors d'oeuvres buffet. Jackets requested; no denim, please. Reserve. AE, MC, V. *B, 7 days 7am-10am. L, Mon-Sat 11am-2:30pm. D, Mon-Thurs 6pm-midnight; Fri & Sat 6pm-1am; Sun 6pm-10pm. Late-supper menu after 10:30pm. Brunch, Sun 10:30am-2:30pm. (See also NIGHTLIFE, Dinner/Dancing.)* $$$$

Crêpes

La Creperie
2845 North Clark. 528-9050. Highly recommended for the authentic wheat and buckwheat Brittany crêpes and the casual Brittany ambiance. Three separate dining rooms, small bar at the entrance. Expect a wait both before and after being seated, but it's well worth it. In addition, onion soup, escargot. The dinner special is a consistently delicious steal. Garden with fountain. You may bring your own wine. No reservations. AE, MC, V. *OPEN Mon-Sat 5pm-11pm; Sun 4:30pm-10pm. Brunch, Sun 11:30am-4:30pm.* $

The Magic Pan Creperie
Oakbrook Shopping Center, Oakbrook. 571-7620. Very pleasant French country-inn setting for a wide variety of delicious crêpe entrées; choose from over 20 fillings. Dessert crêpes too. Weekend champagne brunch. No-smoking section. Special children's menu. Reserve. AE, DC, MC, V. *OPEN Mon-Thurs 11am-9:30pm; Fri & Sat 11am-10pm; Sun 11am-5:30pm. Brunch, Sun 10:30am-2:30pm.* $$

Czechoslovakian

Bratislava
2525 North Clark. 348-6938. Unpretentious New Town storefront restaurant features Czech and Hungarian specialties: duck and dumplings, goulash, stuffed cabbage. Reserve on weekends. AE, MC, V. *OPEN Tues-Sat 5pm-10:30pm; Sun 4pm-9pm. CLOSED Mon.* $

Pilsner
6725 West Cermak Road, Berwyn. 484-2294. Reasonably priced Czech home cooking. Reliably good roast goose or duck, bread dumplings, and sauerkraut. A specialty: svickova—pickled beef tenderloin with sour-cream gravy. On Friday fruit dumplings. Go hungry. Reserve for five or more only. No credit cards. *OPEN Tues-Sun 11am-9pm. CLOSED Mon.* $

Delicatessen

(See also RESTAURANTS, Jewish.)
Belden Corned Beef Center
2315 North Clark. 935-2752. Six-page menu features corned beef and other kosher-style deli delights. Monday to Friday between 3pm and 5pm, mix and match menu specials at a special price. *Never closes!* $

Bob Elfman's
308 West Randolph. 236-0170. Corned beef and pastrami on onion rolls or rye. Hot dogs, bratwurst, reubens. Beer. No credit cards. *OPEN Mon-Fri 7:30am-7pm; Sat 10am-1:45pm. CLOSED Sun.*　　$

D. B. Kaplan
Water Tower Place, 845 North Michigan, 7th level. 280-2700. A C. B. De Mille extravaganza of a deli. Chicago's best. If you have trouble making decisions this is not the place for you—approximately 150 delicious choices, each with a "punny" name that's worth a giggle at least. No-smoking section. No reservations taken. No credit cards. *OPEN Mon-Thurs 10am-11pm; Fri & Sat 10am-1am; Sun 11am-11pm.*　　$

Ricky's East
3181 North Broadway. 549-3136. Long-established kosher-style delicatessen. Takeout too. No credit cards. *OPEN Mon-Thurs 5:30am-1am; Fri & Sat 5:30am-2am; Sun 5am-1am.*　　$

Ethiopian

Mama Desta's Red Sea Restaurant
3216 North Clark. 935-7561. This homey storefront is Chicago's first Ethiopian restaurant. Mama Desta, who came here via Washington, DC, where Ethiopian restaurants abound and hers was one of the best, is in the kitchen. The basis of this cuisine is stews: *wats* are highly spiced with berbere sauce, *alitchas* are mild. They are eaten *sans* silverware. A spongy pancakelike bread, *injera*, is used to wrap the food and get it without mishap into your mouth. The food and the customs are interesting, and extremely inexpensive. Reserve. AE, CB, DC, MV, V. *OPEN Mon 4:30pm-11pm; Tues-Sun 11:30am-11:30pm.*　　$

Fireplaces

The following have working fireplaces:
The B.A.R. Association (Middle Eastern)
Biggs (Continental)
Blue Mesa (American)
Charlie Lui's (Chinese)
Chez Paul (French)
Chicago Claim Company (Bars & Burgers)
Eliot's Nesst (Bars & Burgers)
Eugene's (American)
Fireplace Inn (American)
Golden Bull (Hungarian)
Half Shell (Fish & Seafood)
Café du Parc/La Fontaine (French)
The Mayfair Regent (Afternoon Tea)
Moody's Pub (Bars & Burgers)
Sage's on State (American)
Tap Root Pub (Fish & Seafood)

Fish & Seafood

Cape Cod Room
Drake Hotel, 140 East Walton. 787-2200. Unanimously well recommended for the New England ambiance, the wide selection of fresh seafood, and the service (except during big conventions). Specialty: pompano and lobster cooked in paper. Soft-shell and stone crabs in season. Small attractive oyster bar. Good wine list. Jacket and tie required. Reserve! AE, CB, DC, MC, V. *OPEN 7 days noon-11pm.*　　$$$$

Chestnut Street Grill
Water Tower Place, 835 North Michigan, mezzanine. 280-2720. Handsome in a turn-of-the-century way. Popular partly because of location, but mainly due to perfectly grilled (in view, over wood) fresh fish and seafood specialties, the fried calamari appetizer, and the spicy San Francisco cioppino. Nice selection of Californias in wine bar; sourdough bread and a don't-miss cappuccino ice-cream finale. Steaks and chops for carnivores. No reservations for dinner. AE, MC, V. *OPEN Mon-Thurs 11:30am-10:30pm; Fri & Sat 11:30am-11:30pm; Sun 4:30pm-9:30pm. Brunch, Sun 11am-2:30pm.*　　$$$

Half Shell
676 West Diversey. 549-1773. Hard-to-find, *very* casual basement seafood eatery well known to fish lovers on a budget. The combination platter presents a good mix. Two working fireplaces. No reservations. No credit cards. *OPEN Mon-Fri 11:30am-12:30am; Sat 11:30am-1am; Sun noon-12:30am.*　　$$

Ireland's
500 North La Salle. 337-2020. Reliable casual seafood restaurant. Features well-prepared catch of the day; good salad bar. The Clambake: a bucket of lobster, crab, shrimp, mussels, and corn on the cob for two. Reserve. Free parking. AE, CB, DC, MC, V. *L, Mon-Fri 11am-4pm. D, Mon-Thurs 4pm-11pm; Fri 4pm-11:30pm; Sat 5pm-11:30pm; Sun 5pm-10pm.*　　$

Nantucket Cove
1000 North Lake Shore Drive. 943-1600. Attractive New England setting for good seafood. Maine lobster, lobster Savannah, bouillabaisse, scallops in yogurt-and-mustard sauce. No denim. Reserve. AE, CB, DC, MC, V *OPEN Sun-Thurs 5:30pm-10pm; Fri & Sat 5:30pm-11pm.*　　$$

Nick's Fishmarket
1 First National Plaza, Monroe at Dearborn, plaza level. 621-0200. Much recommended, always with the admonition "very expensive." But fish lovers bravo the selection and the preparation, mainly Hawaiian and West Coast seafood, with many unusual dishes (mahi mahi; opakapaka). Also recommended: the oysters Rockefeller and the clams casino. Service excels. Booths for privacy. Jacket preferred. Braille menu. Reserve. AE, CB, DC, MC, V. *L, Mon-Fri 11:30am-3pm. D, Mon-Thurs 5:30pm-11:30pm; Fri & Sat 5:30pm-midnight. CLOSED Sun.*　　$$$$

Philander's Oak Park
1120 Pleasant, Oak Park. 848-4250. This smashing-looking restaurant features excellent fresh seafood. Bouillabaisse is a flavorful Marseilles-style house specialty. In season, oyster lovers are rewarded with more than 2 dozen varieties. Noisy central bar. Live music in the evening.

Reserve. AE, CB, DC, MC, V. *OPEN Mon-Thurs 5pm-11pm; Fri & Sat 5pm-midnight.* $$$$

Shaw's Crab House and Blue Crab Lounge
21 East Hubbard. 527-2722. Cavernous, crowded yet comfortable destination for good value seafood. Seafood stews, grilled fish, sautéed frog legs with garlic, stone and soft-shell crabs in season, fried crab cakes, blue-point oysters; daily specials. Great hash browns accompany dishes; award-winning pecan pie. Next door, the less comfortable, albeit less expensive, lounge/raw bar; gumbo, jambalaya, seafood salads, too.
Shaws Crab House: Reservations for lunch only. AE, CB, DC, MC, V. *L, Mon-Fri 11:30am-2pm. D, Mon-Thurs 5:30pm-10pm; Fri 5:30pm-11pm; Sat 5pm-11pm; Sun 4pm-9:30pm.* $$
Blue Crab Lounge: No reservations. AE, CB, DC, MC, V. *OPEN Mon-Thurs 11:30am-11pm; Fri & Sat 11:30am-11pm. CLOSED Sun.* $

Tap Root Pub
636 West Willow. 642-5235. Established in 1862, and very "in" with the casual "in crowd." Good seafood; their lobsters are a bargain even by non-Palm standards. Also a bargain: all-you-can-eat fish fries on Friday; Sunday all-you-can-eat clambake (be sure to reserve). Two summer beer gardens, open fireplaces. AE, CB, DC, MC, V. *OPEN Sun-Fri 11am-2am, Sat 11am-3am.* $$

The Waterfront
16 West Maple. 943-7494. Newly ensconced in a renovated brownstone, a Cape Cod atmosphere—friendly and casual. *Very* wide selection of fresh fish; good choices include cioppino—spicy seafood in a skillet—and a carpetbagger-broiled steak stuffed with seasoned oysters. Nonfish snacks. After-theater menu nightly (except Sunday) after 10pm. Reserve. AE, DC, MC, V. *L, Mon-Fri 11:30am-4pm. D, Mon-Thurs 4pm-midnight; Fri & Sat 4pm-1am. Brunch, Sat & Sun 11:30am-3pm.* $$

Fondue

Geja's Café
340 West Armitage. 281-9101. Dimly lit and intimate below-street-level fondue "den." Cheese, beef, chicken, seafood, or vegetable and, for dessert, what else but chocolate fondue. Nice wine list with many available by the glass. Flamenco guitarist every night. A romantic throwback but not as inexpensive as you'd think. Reserve Sunday to Thursday only, Friday and Saturday expect a *long* wait. AE, MC, V. *OPEN Mon-Thurs 5pm-10:30pm; Fri 5pm-midnight; Sat 5pm-12:30pm; Sun 4:30pm-10pm.* $$$

French

Alouette
440 Green Bay Road, Highwood. 433-5600. Creative nouvelle cuisine in a calm, comfortable, charming *auberge* ambiance. Four-course prix-fixe dinner Sunday to Thursday. Jacket and tie

required for men. Free parking. Reserve! AE, CB, DC, MC, V. *OPEN Mon-Thurs 5pm-10:30pm; Sat 5pm-12:30am; Sun 5pm-10pm.* $$$$

Ambria
Belden-Stratford Hotel, 2300 North Lincoln Park West. 472-5959. A *must* for the elegant, sophisticated ambiance and the innovative cuisine beautifully prepared and served with a flourish. The attention to detail is impressive. Recommended: any of the appetizers; any of the gorgeous fresh-fish preparations; the filet of veal with goose-liver pâté; and for dessert, the light-as-air dessert soufflé or a white chocolate mousse. One day's notice is needed for the *dégustation* dinner, a seven-course no-choice prix-fixe meal for four or more—it's a special treat. Jacket required for men; no denim. Reserve *well* in advance. No kids! AE, MC, V. *OPEN Mon-Thurs 6pm-9:30pm; Fri & Sat 6pm-10:30pm. CLOSED Sun.* $$$$+

Café Bernard
2100 North Halsted. 871-2100. French country food and ambiance. Bouillabaisse every day. Reserve. DC, MC, V. *L, Mon-Fri 11:30am-2pm. D, Sun-Thurs 5pm-11pm; Fri & Sat 5pm-11:30pm.* $$$$

Café du Parc/La Fontaine
2442 North Clark. 525-1800. Classic French cuisine in a romantic elegant town house setting. Leisurely fine dining; fireplaces ablaze in season. Hearty onion soup, veal Normande, chestnut mousse for dessert. Reserve. AE, CB, DC, MC, V. *OPEN Sun-Thurs 5pm-10pm; Fri & Sat 5pm-midnight.* $$$$

Café Provençal
1625 Hinman Avenue, Evanston. 475-2233. French provincial fare in a romantic, flower-filled, wood-paneled country ambiance. Limited though very fine menu. Seasonal specials; menu changes daily. Suffer the service. Valet parking. No pipes or cigars. Reserve. AE, CB, DC, MC, V. *OPEN Mon-Thurs 6pm-9pm; Fri & Sat 6pm-9:30pm. CLOSED Sun.* $$$$

Carlos'
429 Temple Avenue, Highland Park. 432-0770. One of the best anywhere. In the art deco-accented dining room the finest seasonal offerings are beautifully presented. Start with the fresh fole gras, follow with any of the inspired nouvelle creations. The crème brûlée with fresh fruit chunks should not be missed. Complimentary hors d'oeuvres and between-course sorbets. Tiny (50 seats) and can be cramped; opt for a booth when you reserve—*very* well in advance. jacket and tie required. AE, DC, MC, V. *Two seatings for dinner: Mon, Wed-Sun 5:30pm & 6:30pm; Sun, Mon, Wed, Thurs 8:30pm & 9pm; Fri & Sat 9:15pm & 9:45pm. CLOSED Tues.* $$$$+

Chez Paul
660 North Rush. 944-6680. Dine on simple French fare in a lovely 1875 Victorian Chicago mansion. Veal Normande, brochette of beef, and for wine connoisseurs, a superior list. For romantics, a fireplace. Jacket required for men. Reserve. AE,

CB, DC, MC, V. *L, Mon-Fri noon-2:30pm. D, 7 days 6pm-10:30pm.* $$$

The French Baker
26 West Madison. 346-3532. Patisserie, boulangerie, and a French restaurant for light supper and snacks. Breads and pastries baked on premises. Monday to Friday, from 4:30pm to 7pm, complimentary hors d'oeuvres. Reserve for dinner; AE, CB, MC, V. *OPEN Tues-Sun 11am-8pm; Mon L only, 11am-3pm.* $

Froggy's
306 North Green Bay Road, Highwood. 433-7080. An opportunity to savor fine French preparations—albeit in plain surroundings—without mortgaging your house. Menu changes monthly, several specials daily. Small, reasonably priced wine list. Private party rooms available by reservation. DC, MC, V. *L, Mon-Fri 11:30am-2pm. D, Mon-Thurs 5pm-10pm; Fri & Sat 5pm-11pm. CLOSED Sun.* $$

Gare St. Lazare
858 West Armitage. 871-0062. French countryside ambiance. Onion soup stands out. Sidewalk café in summer. Reserve. MC, V. *L Sat 11:30am-2:30pm. D, Tues-Sun 5:30pm-11pm. CLOSED Mon.* $$$

Jackie's
2478 North Lincoln. 880-0003. Modest yet inviting storefront for superb, beautifully prepared nouvelle cuisine. The emphasis is on seafood. Good selection of wines by the glass. Reserve! *L, Tues-Sat 11:30am-2pm. D, Tues-Thurs 5:30pm-8:30pm; Fri & Sat 5:30pm-9:30pm. CLOSED Sun & Mon.* $$$

Jimmy's Place
3420 North Elston. 539-2999. Main dining room and greenhouse seating with opera theme decor. From the quality and preparation of the food served, it's obvious there's an expert in the kitchen. Menu changes monthly. Mainstays are the goose-liver pâté with chicken-liver mousse, sautéed veal medallions, and exceptional daily fresh-fish specials. Reserve. Free parking. CB, DC, MC, V. *L, Mon-Fri 11:30am-2pm. D, Mon-Sat 5pm-9pm. CLOSED Sun.* $$$$

La Tour
See RESTAURANTS, Rooms with a View.

Le Bordeaux
3 West Madison. 372-2027. Small basement bar/restaurant. Commendable onion soup. Reserve. AE, CB, DC, MC, V. *L, Mon-Fri 11:30am-4:30pm. D, Mon-Fri 5pm-9pm. CLOSED Sat & Sun.* $

Le Ciel Bleu
See RESTAURANTS, Rooms with a View.

Le Français
269 South Milwaukee Avenue, Wheeling. 541-7470. The French food is, in a word, superb. Just 30 miles northwest of the Loop, one of the area's, some say the country's, others say the world's, best restaurants. Chef Banchet, a Bocuse disciple, is a master *saucier*. Every dish is a masterpiece. The pâtés and terrine, exquisite. The Grand Marnier dessert soufflé, nirvana. Impressive wine list, knowledgeable sommelier. Jacket and tie required. Reserve *very* well in advance, especially for weekends. AE, MC, V. *Two seatings only, Tues-Sun 6pm-6:30pm & 9:15pm-9:45pm. CLOSED Mon.* $$$$+

Le Perroquet
70 East Walton. 944-7990. Despite the departure of its creator, Jovan Trboyevic (who now reigns over the private dining club Les Nomades), still perfectly wonderful and consistent. The ambiance, the service, and, most importantly, the food—finely prepared and presented nouvelle cuisine—always add up to a stylish evening. Prix-fixe lunch and dinner. Jacket and tie required. Reserve! No children! AE, CB, DC. *L, Mon-Fri noon-3pm. D, Mon-Sat 6pm-10pm. CLOSED Sun.* $$$$+

L'Escargot
701 North Michigan, 2nd floor. 337-1717. Old favorite for very good country-style French cooking. The onion soup and the duckling are excellent. Seasonal specialties. Cassoulet every day. Don't miss dessert. Good-value early-bird (before 6pm) dinners. Reserve. Free parking. AE, CB, DC, MC, V. *B, Mon-Sat 7am-10am. L, Mon-Sat 11:30am-2:30pm. D, Mon-Thurs & Sun 5pm-10pm; Fri & Sat 5pm-10:30pm. Brunch, Sun 11:30am-2:30pm.* $$$

Les Plumes
2044 North Halsted. 525-0121. Tops for delectable French food from two Blanchet (Le Français) alumni. Tiny, handsome (but noisy) setting. Outdoor patio in season. Four-course prix-fixe pre-theater dinner Monday to Saturday 5:30 to 6:30pm. Reserve! AE, MC, V. *OPEN Mon-Thurs 5:30pm-9:30pm; Fri & Sat 5:30pm-10pm.* $$$$

Le Titi de Paris
2275 Rand Road, Palatine. 359-4434. Small, well-known suburban restaurant and well worth a trip for lovely nouvelle cuisine in a pleasant setting. Special requests are accommodated with notice. Creative, congenial, and considered by those who know as one of the very best. Jacket required. Reserve! AE, CB, DC, MC, V. Free parking. *L, Tues-Fri 11:30am-2pm. D, Tues-Thurs 5:30pm-10pm; Fri & Sat 5:30pm-11pm.* $$$$

Le Vichyssoise
220 West Route 120, Lakemoor. (1-815) 385-8221. The chef-owner of this unpretentious country-French charmer is a former Troisgros apprentice. Best: the skillfully prepared fish entrées and fresh vegetables. Good choice of seductive sweets. Moderately priced wine list. Jacket required. Reserve. MC, V. *D, OPEN, Wed & Thurs 5pm-9pm; Fri & Sat 5pm-10pm; Sun 4:30pm-9pm. CLOSED Mon & Tues & month of Jan.* $$$$

Ritz-Carlton Dining Room
Water Tower Place, 160 East Pearson, 12th floor. 266-1000. A luxurious prix-fixe dining experience. Seasonal menu may include rack of lamb, fresh fish flown in from France, breast of duck; whiskey mousse or apricot cake for dessert. Extensive wine list. Wonderful buffet brunch. Piano music Monday to Friday from 6pm to 11pm. Jacket and tie required for dinner. Re-

serve. AE, CB, DC, MC, V. *L, Mon-Sat 11:30am-2:30pm. D, Mon-Sat 6pm-11pm; Sun 6pm-10pm. Brunch, Sun 10:30am-2pm.* $$$$

Rue St. Clair
640 North St. Clair. 787-6974. Very good French bistro-Parisienne. Pâté, steak, and pommes frites, escargots, veal Calvados. Wines by the glass. Dinning outdoors in fine weather. Reserve. AE, CB, DC, MC, V. *L, Mon-Sat 11:30am-2:30pm. D, Sun-Thurs 6pm-10pm; Fri & Sat 6pm-11pm. Brunch, Sun 11am-2pm.* $$$$

Toulouse
51 West Division. 944-2606. This cozy, elegant spot is renowned as one of Chicago's most romantic restaurants. A la carte menu changes nightly. Fresh fish and Wisconsin veal are the specialties; also game in season. *Terrific piano bar Monday to Saturday from 8pm to 4am. Reserve. AE, CB, DC, MC, V. OPEN Mon-Sat 5:30pm-11pm. CLOSED Sun.* $$$

Un Grand Café
Belden Stratford Hotel, 2300 North Lincoln Park West. 348-8886. Sophisticated yet casual bistro-like light dining in a pleasant, lively setting. Pâtés, grilled seafood, terrific steak, and sinful selection of chocolate desserts; cappuccino. Wines by the glass. Pricey. AE, MC, V. *OPEN Mon-Thurs 6pm-11pm; Fri & Sat 6pm-midnight. CLOSED Sun.* $$$

Yoshi's Café
3257 Halsted. 248-6160. Yoshi Katsumura's small popular café for imaginative nouvelle cuisine. Salads are often fascinating; fresh seafood stands out. Green tea ice cream for dessert. Limited reasonably priced wine list. Reserve and expect a wait. AE, MC, V. *D, Tues-Thurs 5:30pm-10pm; Fri & Sat 5:30pm-10:30pm; Sun 5pm-9pm. CLOSED Mon.*

Garden/Outdoor Dining

Dearborn Café
First National Plaza, Monroe & Dearborn. Wonderful Loop people-watching spot for breakfast, lunch, desserts, and cocktails. All tables are outdoors and there's entertainment daily at noon in the plaza. No reservations. AE, MC, V. *OPEN day after Memorial Day through Labor Day weekend ONLY, Mon-Fri: B, 7:30am-9am; L, 11am-2:30pm; desserts, coffee & cocktails, 2:30pm-4pm; cocktail hour, 4pm-6:30pm. Call for evening hours. CLOSED Sat & Sun.* $

The Garden Restaurant
McKinlock Court, Art Institute, Michigan & Adams. 443-3530. A charming setting for *al fresco* dining, weather permitting. No credit cards. *OPEN June 1-Sept 2, Mon-Sat 11am-3:30pm; Sun 11am-noon.* $

Melvin's Café
1116 North State. 664-0356. Best when you can sit in the Parisian-like open-to-the-sky outdoor café (there's a minimum), sip a fresh daiquiri, and watch the passing parade. Burgers, sandwiches, etc. No reservations. No credit cards.

Beginning of May-end of Sept, OPEN 7 days, 11am-2am. $

The following have outdoor dining facilities in season:
Arnie's Cafe (Continental)
Avanzare (Italian)
The B.A.R. Association (Middle Eastern)
Beppino's (Italian)
Big John's (Soups, Salads & Sandwiches)
Blue Mesa (American)
Café Azteca II (Mexican)
Cafe-Ba-Ba-Reeba! (Spanish)
Chicago Pizza & Oven Grinder Company (Pizza)
Como Inn (Italian)
Don Roth's River Plaza (American)
Eliot's Nesst (Bars & Burgers)
El Jardin (Mexican)
Foley's (American)
Gare St. Lazare (French)
Golden Bull (Hungarian)
Harry's Café (Bars & Burgers)
Hashikin (Japanese)
Heartland Café (Vegetarian)
Hemingways's Movable Feast (Soups, Salads & Sandwiches)
Hillary's (Bars & Burgers)
Jerome's (Breakfast/Brunch)
La Choza (Mexican)
La Creperie (Crêpes)
Les Plumes (French)
Lutz (Cappuccino & Espresso)
Maple Tree Inn (Cajun/Creole)
The Mirabell Restaurant (German)
Moody's Pub (Bars & Burgers)
Randall's (American)
Resi's Bierstube (German)
Riccardo's (Italian)
Rue St. Clair (French)
71-Club (Rooms with a View)
Stefani's (Italian)
Sweetwater (American)
Tap Root Pub (Fish & Seafood)

German

The Berghoff
17 West Adams. 427-3170. Since 1898, a bustling Chicago institution in the Loop. Hand-painted murals, stained glass, and a no-longer-segregated Men's Bar. German-style specialties include red cabbage, hasenpfeffer (seasonal), Wiener schnitzel, and Kassler rippchen (smoked pork loin), and their own all-malt light or dark beer; private stock bourbon too. Daily specials, all moderately priced. Strawberry whipped-cream cake for dessert. The café, with its standup bar, is popular for hand-carved corned beef sandwiches and the oyster bar. There's probably a wait, but do. Lots of judges eat here, perhaps a few felons, it's next to the Federal Building. No-smoking section. Reserve for five or more only. AE, MC, V. Reduced-rate

parking after 5pm. *OPEN Mon-Thurs 11am-9:30pm; Fri & Sat 11am-10pm. CLOSED Sun.* $

Binyon's
327 South Plymouth Court. 341-1155. This German-style Loop restaurant serves large portions of always-good, fresh, unadorned basics: corned beef and cabbage, pork shanks, steaks, and schnitzel. Popular and crowded. Reserve. AE, MC, V. *OPEN Mon-Sat 11:30am-10pm (CLOSED Sat in summer). CLOSED Sun.* $$

The Golden Ox
1578 North Clybourn. 664-0780. Established in 1921 when this area was solidly Germantown. An authentic German rathskeller with mural-covered walls and ceilings. The food is good, traditional, and traditionally filling: liver dumpling soup, Wienerbraten, hassenpfeffer, Bavarian veal, Wiener schnitzel. Six German beers on tap. Friday and Saturday 6pm-10:30pm live zither music. Buffet lunch Monday to Saturday from 11am to 3pm. Buffet dinner Friday and Saturday 5pm to 11pm. Reserve. Free parking. AE, CB, DC, MC, V. *OPEN Mon-Sat 11am-11pm; Sun 3:30pm-9:30pm.* $$

Heidelberger Fass
4300 North Lincoln. 478-2486. Charming old-fashioned German atmosphere complete with costumed waitresses. Well-priced, stick-to-your-ribs meals. Standouts: liver dumpling soup, roast goose (in season), crispy roast duck, the combination platter, the potato dumplings, the cream of cabbage soup. Strudel or Black Forest cake for dessert. Draft beer in ¼, ½, or full liter gulps. Reserve. Free parking. AE, CB, DC, MC, V. *OPEN Mon, Wed, Thurs 11:30am-10pm; Fri & Sat 11:30am-11pm; Sun noon-10pm. CLOSED Tues.* $$

The Mirabell Restaurant
3454 West Addison. 463-1962. German-American fare. Beck's Dark, Gösser, B.B.K on tap as well as bottled German and Austrian beers. Also "Weissbeer," a wheat-based German beer, served with lemon slice. Indoor gardenlike dining room. Outdoor beer garden in summer. Reserve. AE, CB, DC. *L, Mon-Sat 11:30am-2:30pm. D, Mon-Thurs 5pm-10pm; Fri & Sat 5pm-11pm. CLOSED Sun.* $

Resi's Bierstube
2034 West Irving Park Road. 472-1749. The best of wursts: bratwurst, knockwurst. Stocks 50 different beers, many German; Beck's dark on tap. A friendly, informal beer garden—draws crowds on weekends in summer. No reservations after 8pm on weekends. No credit cards. *OPEN Mon-Fri 2pm-2am; Sat 2pm-3am; kitchen open 5pm-11pm.* $

Schullen's Restaurant & Saloon
2100 West Irving Park. 478-2100. A tradition for more than 100 years. Hearty German food and a family magic show. Crisp duck, pork chops, schnitzel, baked ribs. Reservations taken (except Friday and Saturday nights). AE, CB, DC, MC, V. Parking. *OPEN Mon-Thurs 11:30am-midnight; Fri 11:30am-1am; Sat 4pm-1am.* $

Zum Deutschen Eck Restaurant
2924 North Southport. 525-8389 or -8122. Huge popular German restaurant for home-style cooking and *Gemütlichkeit*. Friday and Saturday (7pm to 1am) and Sunday (6pm to 10pm) the entertainment is provided by *you* accompanied by an oom-pah band. Sheet music is distributed. Good for groups. Nightly specials. Fresh seafood, steaks, and ribs. Homemade desserts too! Reserve. AE, DC, MC, V. *L. Mon-Fri 11:30am-3pm; Sat noon-3pm. D, Mon-Thurs 3pm-10:30pm; Fri 3pm-12:30am; Sat 3pm-1am; Sun noon-10pm.* $$

Greek

Courtyards of Plaka
340 South Halsted. 263-0767. A cut above the rest in terms of ambiance and service. Outstanding moussaka, roast leg of lamb, fried squid. Special: a 12-item Athenian feast. Mainly Greek wines. Live music, good fun. Free parking. Reserve. AE, CB, DC, MC, V. *OPEN Sun-Thurs 11am-midnight; Fri & Sat 11am-1am.* $

Dianna's Oppa
212 South Halsted. 332-1225. Authentic, lively, spontaneous Greek Town staple where every night's an occasion. When owner Petros is not dancing in the aisles he's welcoming women patrons with a kiss. Daily specials. Free parking. Reserve. AE, CB. *OPEN 7 days 11am-2am.* $

Greek Islands
200 South Halsted. 782-9855. Newer, larger quarters with five separate dining areas. Still one of Chicago's best for authentic Greek food, wines, and atmosphere. Good value family-style dinners. Reserve before 6pm only. AE, CB, DC, MC, V. *OPEN Sun-Thurs 11am-midnight; Fri & Sat 11am-1am.* $

My Place For
7545 North Clark. 262-5767. An enjoyable casual Greek-style tavern. Well-prepared fresh-fish dishes among a wide variety of other choices. No-smoking section. Reservations taken till 6:30pm only. AE, CB, DC, MC, V. *OPEN Mon-Fri 11:30am-11pm; Sat 3pm-11:30pm; Sun 3pm-9:30pm.* $$

Parthenon
314 South Halsted. 726-2407. Another lively Greek Town favorite, featuring many unusual dishes like tigania—marinated, then sautéed pork tenderloin. Flaming cheese saganaki is *the* specialty. Family dinners are excellent value. Crowded on weekends. You *will* definitely leave smiling, and possibly not sober. Reserve except for Saturday evening. Free parking. AE, CB, MC, V. *OPEN Sun-Fri 11am-1:30am; Sat 11am-2:30am.* $

Roditys
222 South Halsted. 454-0800. Well-respected Greek Town restaurant for always-well-prepared seafood and lamb dishes; ambiance and service to match. Reserve. Free parking. AE only. *OPEN Sun-Thurs 11am-1am; Fri & Sat 11am-2am.* $

The Taberna
303 East Ohio. 329-0262. If you like your Greek food without all the *opaa*, this is an attractive place to try. Wide variety of Greek and seafood specials daily in addition to steaks, chops, and other standard American dishes. The combination dinner for four is a good choice. Reserve. AE, MC, V. *OPEN Mon-Fri 7am-9:30pm. CLOSED Sat & Sun.* $

Hungarian

Golden Bull
7308 North Rogers. 764-1436. A Hungarian restaurant offering such old-world dishes as stuffed cabbage and chicken paprikash. For dessert, palascinta—an apricot-jam-filled crêpe. Game dishes in season; advance order is necessary. Hungarian wines. Fireplace in lounge area. Beer garden in summer. Reserve. AE, CB, DC, MC, V. *OPEN Tues-Sun 5pm-10pm; in summer Sat & Sun from 1pm. CLOSED Mon.* $$

Kennessey Wine Cellar
Hotel Belmont, 403 West Belmont, downstairs. 929-7500. A cozy wine cellar provides the setting for Hungarian specialties: Weiner schnitzel, Hungarian beef goulash. Interesting crêpe choices. Save space for the strudel. Wine selection of over 2,000 bottles. Music Wednesday to Friday. Reserve. AE, MC, V. *L, Mon-Sat 11am-4pm. D, Mon-Thurs 6pm-11pm; Fri & Sat 6pm-midnight; Sun noon-9pm.* $

Ice Cream

Five Faces Ice Cream Parlor
10 West Division. 642-7837. Ice cream for sweet-freaking insomniacs. Gyro sandwiches, popcorn, and cookies too. OPEN 7 days, 24 hours. $

Gertie's Own Ice Cream
5858 South Kedzie. 737-7634. Chicago's oldest ice-cream parlor—and still going strong. Made daily at this traditionally decorated location since 1901. *OPEN 7 days 10:30am-11pm.* $

Zephyr Ice Cream Restaurant
1777 West Wilson. 728-6070. A deco diner for delicious delights named for vintage Hollywood flicks and chicks. Casablanca: a blueberry dessert oasis; Rainbow sherbet: as in somewhere over the. . . ; or the Titanic: a colossal "unsinkable" soda. Café serves "real" food. AE, MC, V. *OPEN Sun-Thurs 10:30am-midnight; Fri & Sat 10:30am-1am. Dec-Apr 1 ice-cream parlor is CLOSED Mon-Wed.* $

Indian

Bombay Palace
50 East Walton. 664-9323. Sophisticated contemporary setting for some of the best Indian dishes to be found, especially the tandoor choices prepared in clay ovens. Complex seasoning, searingly hot if you desire it so, milder if not.

Afterward, lassi—a yogurt-based drink—or rice pudding made with rosewater, soothes. NOTE: Vegetarians will find much to their liking. Reserve. AE, CB, DC, MC, V. Dinner parking available. *L, Mon-Fri 11:30am-2:30pm; Sat & Sun 11:30am-3pm. D, Sun-Thurs 5:30pm-10:30pm; Fri & Sat 5:30pm-11pm.* $$

Gaylord India Restaurant
678 North Clark. 664-1700. Internationally known Indian restaurant, specializing in classic northern tandoori (clay-oven) cooking—chicken, lamb, shrimp, and vegetables. Good Mulligatawny soup. NOTE: Service charge of 15% included in bill. Free parking. Reserve. AE, DC, MC, V. *L, Mon-Fri 11:30am-2:30pm; Sat & Sun noon-3pm. D, Sun-Thurs 5:30pm-10:30pm; Fri & Sat 5:30pm-11pm.* $$

Italian

(*See also* RESTAURANTS, Pizza.)

Avanzare
161 East Huron. 337-8056. Another from Richard Melman, this one slick and sophisiticated (yet casual) like the crowd it draws. "Modern" Italian cooking: wonderful pastas, perfectly prepared and available in half portions; grilled seafood; vitello tonnato; carpaccio; veal chop; sautéed duck breast; ricotta cheesecake or gelato for dessert. A few wines by the glass. The large bar is popular with media and advertising types, and others making the scene. Reserve! AE, CB, DC, MC, V. *L, Mon-Fri 11:30am-2pm. D, Sun-Thurs 5:30pm-9:30pm; Fri & Sat 5:30pm-10:30pm.* $$$$

Beppino's
845 West Ohio. 421-5222. Have a drink and a snack, Italian style, in this swell café/bar section of the long-established Como Inn. Piano music from 7pm till closing. Outdoors in summer. Jacket requested. Free parking. AE, CB, DC, MC, V. *OPEN Mon-Thurs & Sun 11:30am-11:30pm; Fri & Sat 11:30am-12:30am.* $

Bruna's Ristorante
2424 South Oakley. 847-8875. For close to 55 years large portions of homemade pasta have been the reliable treats at this homey, small, old-fashioned Little Italy bar and restaurant. High-quality veal dishes and interesting specials as well. Modest wine selection. Reserve. AE, MC, V. *L, Mon-Sat 11am-3pm. D, Mon-Thurs 4pm-10pm; Fri & Sat 4pm-11pm; Sun 2:30pm-10pm.* $$

Café Angelo
Quality Inn, 225 North Wabash. 332-3370. A popular place for lunch. Home-style Italian cooking using all fresh ingredients. Large selection of regional pasta dishes, cooked perfectly. Good seafood preparations too. Special inexpensive prix-fixe pre-theater dinners from 5pm to 6:30pm. Lovely service. Reserve. AE, CB, DC, MC, V. *B, Mon-Fri 7am-10:30am. L, Mon-Fri 11:30am-4:30pm. D, 7 days 5pm-11pm.* $$

Chef Eduardo's
1640 North Wells. 266-2021. Lovely setting in

Old Town. Choices are limited, and the emphasis is on fish and veal. Well-prepared, large portions of pasta: tortellini alla panna; linguini with fresh clam sauce; fettuccine with pesto. Plan to relax, service is laid-back Italian style. Reserve. AE, MC, V. OPEN Mon-Thurs 5:30pm-10:30pm; Fri & Sat 6pm-11pm; Sun 5pm-10pm. $$$

Como Inn
546 North Milwaukee. 421-5222. Long-established, well-respected spot to wine and dine Italian, in style. Good-weather sidewalk café for drinks and hors d'oeuvres. Piano and singer during the dinner hour. Reserve. Jacket and tie preferred. No denim. Free parking. AE, CB, DC, MC, V. L, Mon-Fri 11:30am-4pm; Sat & Sun noon-4pm. D, Sun-Thurs 4pm-11:30pm; Fri & Sat 4pm-12:30am. $$

Danilo's
1235 West Grand. 421-0218. Consistently outstanding home-cooked Italian food now on the North Side. Delicious homemade pastas, beautifully prepared veal dishes, good steaks. Cappuccino cheesecake for dessert. Reserve for five or more. AE, DC, MC, V. L, Tues-Fri 11am-3:30pm. D, Tues-Sat 3:30pm-10:45pm. CLOSED Sun & Mon. $$

Febo Restaurant
2501 South Western. 523-0839. Good neighborhood Italian restaurant features home cooking in an atmosphere (casual, friendly) to match. The family-style dinner is a buy for four or more. Mange! Reserve. Free parking. AE, MC, V. OPEN Mon-Thurs 11am-11pm; Fri & Sat 11am-midnight. CLOSED Sun. $

Florence Restaurant
1030 West Taylor. 829-1857. Small relative newcomer to this Italian neighborhood. Serves satisfying, albeit limited number of Northern Italian specialties in a charming old-world ambiance. Reserve. No credit cards. L, Tues-Fri 11:30am-2pm. D, Tues-Fri 5:30pm-9pm. CLOSED Sun & Mon. $

Gene & Georgetti, Ltd.
See RESTAURANTS, Steak.

Gennaro's
1352 West Taylor. 243-1035; 733-8790. A remnant of the once-thriving Italian area. Behind the locked door you'll find satisfying pasta, homemade from scratch daily by Mama Gennaro (27 years in the kitchen). Standouts: gnocchi, cheese ravioli, and manicotti. Calamari and linguini with clam sauce on Friday. Expect a wait. Reserve. No credit cards. OPEN Thurs 5pm-9pm; Fri & Sat 5pm-10pm; Sun 4pm-9pm. CLOSED Mon-Wed. $

George's
230 West Kinzie. 644-2290. Spacious attractive bar and restaurant, lovingly restored following a fire. Extremely good Northern Italian-style pastas. Specialties: shrimp diavolo, stuffed veal chop, fresh fish, and pasta specials daily. Great mousse-topped chocolate cake. Complimentary cold pasta from 5pm to 7pm. Well-priced wine list. Will accommodate nonsmoking customers.

Presents jazz as good as the food (see also NIGHTLIFE, Jazz). Reserve. AE, MC, V. L, Mon-Fri 11:30am-3pm. D, Mon-Thurs 5:30pm-10pm; Fri & Sat 5:30pm-11pm. CLOSED Sun. $$

House of Bertini
See RESTAURANTS, Steak.

La Fontanella
2414 South Oakley. 927-5249. A favorite of many Chicagoans. In the old ethnic Italian area a small storefront family-run restaurant serves wonderful cooked-to-order Italian specialties. The appetizers and pastas are good value. Reserve. AE only. L, Tues-Fri 11:30am-3pm. D, Tues, Wed & Sun 4:30pm-9:30pm; Thurs 4:30pm-10:30pm; Fri & Sat 4:30pm-11:30pm. CLOSED Mon. $

Mategrano's
1321 West Taylor. 243-8441. Longtime family-run homespun establishment in old Italian area. Thursday and Saturday are the nights to go for the excellent all-you-can-eat Neapolitan buffet. The vegetables are standouts, especially the fried zucchini. Reserve for the buffet. Free parking. AE, MC, V. L, Tues-Fri 11:15am-3pm. D, Tues-Fri 3pm-9pm; Sat 4pm-10pm; Sun 1pm-8pm. CLOSED Mon. $

Pronto
200 East Chestnut. 664-6181. Very attractive restaurant where there is much ado about making fresh pasta (in view) but seemingly less ado about cooking it. Room for improvement at these prices. Reserve. AE, DC, MC, V. OPEN Mon-Thurs 11:30am-11:30pm; Fri & Sat 11:30am-midnight; Sun 4pm-10:30pm. $$$

Riccardo's
437 North Rush. 944-8815; 787-2874. Favored watering hole of reporters and editors from nearby Chicago Sun-Times and Tribune, who make the crowded scene at the bar from 5pm to 9pm nightly and most especially on Friday. Palette bar and murals reflect a former era, and the late artist-owner Rick Riccardo. The mainly Italian menu offers few surprises, albeit good spaghetti carbonara. Great pecan pie. Thursday and Friday pm strolling musicians. Outdoor café (Chicago's first) in summer. Reserve if you plan to do more than drink. AE, CB, DC, MC V. L, Mon-Fri 11:30am-3pm. D, Mon-Fri 5pm-10pm. $$

Ristorante Italia
2631 North Harlem. 889-5008. Expanded to accommodate the crowds who heard about the high-quality, nicely prepared food. Mussels redolent with garlic, a wide selection of homemade pastas; wonderful homemade bread. Affordable wine list. Reserve, especially on weekends. No credit cards. OPEN Sun, Tues-Thurs 4pm-midnight; Fri & Sat 4pm-1am. CLOSED Mon. $$

The Rosebud
1500 West Taylor. 942-1117. Popular spot on the West Side. Turn-of-the-century Victorian charm, family-style Italian cooking. Steak the "Italian way" is a good choice, so too the chicken Vesuvio with roasted potatoes. Suffer the service. Extensive wine list. Parking. Reserve. OPEN Mon-Thurs 11am-11pm; Fri 11am-midnight; Sat 5pm-midnight. $$

Salvatore's
525 West Arlington Place (through the building lobby). 528-1200. Sophisticated and attractive setting and crowd enhance the dining experience. Well-prepared Northern Italian cuisine. The pastas are wonderful. Attentive service. Reserve. AE, MC, V. *OPEN Sun-Thurs 5:30pm-10:30pm; Fri & Sat 5:30pm-11:30pm.* $$$

Scoozi!
410 West Huron. 943-5900. At this noisy River North destination that seats over 300, you'll find better food than you would guess. Meats are roasted on a wood-fired grill; mozzarella is made on premises; fine risotto, fried zucchini, and carpaccio. The large menu encourages sharing. Try a Bellini to start, a Venetian invention, blending fresh peach nectar and champagne. For dessert, profiteroles or espresso ice. No reservations, expect a wait. AE, MC, V. *L, Mon-Fri 11:30am-2pm. D, Mon-Thurs 5pm-10:30pm; Fri & Sat 5pm-11:30pm; Sat 4pm-9pm.* $$

Sogni Dorati
660 North Wells. 337-6500. A delightfully refreshing spot (the in-town outpost of Mama di Pinto) for innovative regional Italian specialties. There's a special prix-fixe piatti della casa in the pm. Jacket required. Reserve. AE, CB, DC, MC V. *L, Mon-Fri 11:30am-2pm. D, Mon-Sat 5:30pm-9:30pm. CLOSED Sun.* $$$

Spiaggia
One Magnificent Mile, 980 North Michigan. 280-2750. Excellent modern Northern Italian cooking in a sophisticated post-modern setting. Overlooking Oak Street Beach, the clientele is as sophisticated as the decor. Glass-enclosed in-view kitchen. Menu changes daily, utilizing the freshest ingredients. Grilled veal chop, fettucini with tuna; grilled fish; salads shine. Wonderful sweets. Modestly priced Italian-only wine list. Service is up to the food. Jacket required; no denim. Reserve! AE, CB, DC, MC, V. *OPEN Mon-Thurs 11:30am-11pm; Fri & Sat 11:30am-11:30pm; Sun 11am-8pm.* $$$$

Stefani's
1418 West Fullerton. 348-0111. Traditional trattoria setting and food: spaghetti alla carbonara, fried calamari, tortellini alla panna. Amaretto mousse pie for dessert. Outdoor garden in summer. Reserve for dinner. AE, CB, MC, V. *L, Mon-Fri 11am-4pm. D, Mon-Fri 5pm-11pm; Sat 5pm-midnight. CLOSED Sun.* $$

Toscano's
2439 South Oakley Boulevard. 376-4841. Friendly family-run archetypal Italian restaurant featuring the cooking of the Tuscany region of Italy. Free parking. AE, CB, DC. *L, Tues-Sat 11am-3pm. D, Tues-Thurs 5pm-10pm; Fri & Sat 5pm-midnight, Sun 2pm-10pm. CLOSED Mon.* $

Trattoria Pizzeria Roma
1557 North Wells. 664-7907. This small, noisy, and tightly packed Roman delight serves pastas cooked to perfection; individual pizzas, a few daily entrées. No alcohol served, bring your own wine. Reserve. *OPEN Tues-Fri noon-11pm;*

Sat 5pm-11pm; Sun 4pm-10pm. CLOSED Mon. $

Vernon Park Tap
1073 West Vernon Park Place. 226-9878. Thriving homey, budget-priced spot for hearty Sicilian fare. Features ten tables and a wait. Full service bar. No reservations. No credit cards. *OPEN Tues-Sat 5pm-9:30pm; Sun 4pm-9pm. CLOSED Mon.* $

Japanese

Benihana of Tokyo
166 East Superior. 664-9643. The ubiquitous hibachi-style steak, chicken, shrimp, in a pleasant setting. Each table of six has its own "show man" chef. Fun for large parties. No denim. Reserve. AE, CB, DC, MC, V. *L, Mon-Sat 11:30am-2pm. D, Mon-Thurs 5:30pm-10:30pm; Fri & Sat 5:30pm-11:30pm; Sun 4pm-10pm.* $$$

Happi Sushi
3346 North Clark. 528-1225. Aptly named sushi bar. Outstanding fresh sashimi and sushi prepared before your eyes at the bar; teriyaki and tempura too. No reservations. AE, MC, V. *L, Tues-Sun noon-2:30pm. D, Tues-Thurs 5pm-10:30pm; Fri & Sat 5pm-midnight. CLOSED Mon.* $

Hashikin
2338 North Clark. 935-6474. Lovely service, very good food, some sushi. Private tatami tearooms available. Outdoor teahouse in summer. Reserve. Free parking. AE, CB, DC, MC, V. *L, Mon-Fri noon-3pm. D, Sun-Thurs 5pm-11:30pm; Fri & Sat 5pm-12:30am.* $$

Hatsuhana
160 East Ontario. 280-8287. Sushi connoisseurs agree this is the best sushi bar in town. Over 35 varieties of raw seafood, fresh daily, served in a beautiful setting (opt for downstairs). Fresh fruit for dessert. Reserve. AE, DC, MC, V. *L, Mon-Fri noon-2pm (except on holidays). D, Mon-Sat 5:45pm-10pm. CLOSED Sun.* $$$

Kamehachi of Tokyo
1617 North Wells. 664-3663. Well-regarded sushi bar; one of the first in Chicago. Watching the chef is always fascinating. Also, tempura, yakitori, teriyaki, and sukiyaki. Reserve. AE, MC, V. *L, Wed-Sat noon-2pm. D, Tues-Thurs & Sun 5pm-9:30pm; Fri & Sat 5pm-11:30pm. CLOSED Mon.* $

Kotobuki
5547 North Clark. 275-6588. Fine welcoming ethnic choice. Unusual fare, interesting presentation. Warm sake or Japanese beers. *L, Mon, Tues, Thurs & Fri 11:30am-2pm. D, Mon, Tues, & Thurs 5pm-10pm; Fri & Sat 5pm-10:30pm; Sun 4pm-9pm.* $

Matsuya
3429 North Clark. 248-2677. This longtime Japanese restaurant is a refreshing favorite for fresh-fish lovers. Well-prepared broiled catch of the day as well as sushi and sashimi. Fried dump-

ling appetizers, tempura and chicken teriyaki too. Bargain dinner combinations. Japanese beers and saki; you may bring your own wine. Reserve for four or more. MC, V. *L, Sat & Sun only, noon-5pm. D, Mon & Wed-Sun 5pm-10:30pm. CLOSED Tues.* $

New Japan Oriental Café
45 West Division. 787-4248. Unpretentious, luncheonettelike little spot for good Japanese food on a shoestring. Ramen (noodle soup) is a good value choice. Tempura, teriyaki, yakisoba (Japanese-style chow mein), pot stickers (dumplings), and sushi. Counter service and seven tables. Bring your own wine or beer. No reservations. No credit cards. *L, Mon-Sat 11:45am-2:30pm. D, Mon-Thurs 5pm-10pm; Fri & Sat 5pm-11pm. CLOSED Sun.* $$

Ron of Japan Steakhouse
230 East Ontario. 644-6500. Attractive Japanese steakhouse with complete dinners prepared at your communal table by showmen/chefs. The hearty servings of beef will delight meat-lovers. It's fun (prime ribs served on a samurai sword) and filling. No denim, please. Reserve. AE, DC, MC, V. *OPEN Mon-Thurs 5pm-10pm; Fri & Sat 5pm-11pm; Sun 4:30pm-11pm.* $$$

Shiroi Hana
3242 North Clark. 477-1652. Mirrored and tiled setting for extremely fresh (the proprietor is in the wholesale fish business) and temptingly presented sushi, sashimi, and maki, in combination or individual. Also, tempura, teriyaki, sukiyaki dinners. Quite good daily specials. Reserve. AE, MC, V. Parking in the pm. *OPEN Mon-Thurs noon-10:30pm; Fri & Sat noon-11pm; Sun noon-10pm.* $

Yanese
818 North State. 337-9598. Downtown eatery for top-notch, but somewhat pricey, sushi. Limited menu. Well-priced dinners included with entrée, meso soup, salad, rice, fresh fruit, and tea. Also tempura, teriyaki, sukiyaki. Reserve. AE, CB, DC, MC, V. *L, Mon-Fri 11:30am-2:30pm; Sun noon-3pm. D, Mon-Sat 5pm-10pm.* $$

Jewish

(*See also* RESTAURANTS, Delicatessen.)

Ashkenaz Old World Deli
12 East Cedar. 944-5006. Jewish-style basics like corned beef, chicken soup, chopped liver, gefilte fish, but there's also a pizza bagel and barbecued salmon! Order six-foot sandwiches ahead of time for do-it-yourself party catering. No credit cards. *OPEN Mon-Sat 10:30am-7:30pm; Sun 9am-7pm.* $

The Bagel
3000 West Devon. 764-3377. Popular for very good Jewish-style meals—kugel, latkes, blintzes, brisket, sweet-and-sour cabbage as well as the deli usuals. Breakfast-anytime-choices include a lox and onion omelette or challah French toast. No alcohol served but you may bring your own

wine or beer. Braille menus available. Reserve for eight or more. No credit cards. Free dinner parking. Takeout too. *OPEN Sun-Thurs 6:30am-10pm; Fri & Sat 6:30am-11pm.* $

Bagel Nosh
1135 North State. 266-6369. Large cafeteria-style eatery features nine flavors of bagels (Grandmother just groaned) with or without something on them. Commendable chopped liver. Sunday am go for the cream cheese and lox, Governor Thompson did. *OPEN Sun-Tues & Thurs 7am-midnight; Wed 7am-1am; Fri & Sat 24 hours.* $

Frances'
2453 Norht Clark. 248-4580. Homey and homely. When your glasses unfog (from the steam table), you can read the signs that tell you to pick out your food and then go to your table, where the motherly waitress will tend to you. Abundant choices and portions. Saturday and Sunday mornings it seems as if the whole Lincoln Park neighborhood is filling the communal Formica tables. Good blintzes. *OPEN Tues-Sun 7am-10pm. CLOSED Mon.* $

Korean

Dae Ho
2741 West Devon. 274-8499. Good inexpensive Korean storefront eatery. Bulgogi—grilled marinated beef—is a standout. Spicy-food lovers won't be disappointed. Beer only, bring your own wine if you wish. Reserve. DC, MC, V. *OPEN Wed-Mon 11am-11pm. CLOSED Tues.* $

Gin Go Gae
5433 North Lincoln. 334-3895. Unique and tasty Korean specialties from a limited menu in pleasant, bright surroundings. Galbi—marinated barbecued beef short ribs; a hot spicy fish soup holds the catch of the day; tofu fish cakes; octopus with green chilis. Reserve for five or more. MC, V. *OPEN Mon, Tues, Thurs-Sun 11am-10:30pm. CLOSED Wed.* $

Poong Mee House
See RESTAURANTS, Late Night/24-Hour.

Seoul House
5346 North Clark. 728-6756. Longtime popular source for Korean pancakes, fried dumplings, raw skate, hot stew, and rice soup. No alcohol served, bring your own wine or beer. Reserve. MC, V. *OPEN Mon-Thurs 11am-10pm; Fri & Sat 11am-10:30pm; Sun noon-9 pm.* $

Shilla
5930 North Lincoln. 275-5930. Top-rated Korean restaurant draws a Korean clientele. Spacious setting, with private tearooms for cook-it-yourself Korean barbecue; beef and seafood are featured. Standouts: the sliced marinated beef (bulgogi) and the short ribs (kaibi). Spicy baby octopus, noodle dishes, spicy soups, and copious casseroles. Sushi, too. Reserve for the barbecue. AE, CB, DC, MC, V. *OPEN Tues-Sun 11:30am-10:30pm. CLOSED Mon.* $

Late-Night/24-Hour

(See also 24-HOUR CHICAGO, 24-Hour Eating.)
Mel Markon's
2150 North Lincoln Park West. 525-5550. Fresh-fruit daiquiris, an eclectic menu, wee hours, and the casual ambiance draw crowds. Especially for weekend breakfast and very late-night snacks. Good borscht as well as onion soup. French-fried ice-cream dessert. Favorite of local theater people. Reserve for early dining only. AE, MC, V. OPEN Mon-Fri 11am-4am; Sat 9am-5am; Sun 9am-4am. $
The Oak Tree
25 East Oak. 751-1988. Windows on the world of Rush at Oak at 3am may be the best show in town. The food is sustaining, period. Reserve for dinner. No credit cards. OPEN 24 hours a day, 7 days a week. $
Poong Mee House
3752 West Lawrence. 478-0217. No-frills store-front Korean restaurant open 24 hours a day for filling soups, Korean pancakes, short ribs, noodle dishes, seafood, marinated grilled beef (no pork or chicken). Language may be a problem. Reservations taken. No credit cards. OPEN 7 days, 24 hours. $
Ritz-Carlton Café
Ritz-Carlton Hotel, 160 East Pearson, 12th floor. 266-1000. Adjoining the lobby, a plush palm-bedecked oasis for sophisticated snacking on proper entrées, sandwiches, salads, or the Ritz Burger (refers to the price as well as the quality). No-smoking section. Reserve for breakfast and dinner. AE, CB, DC, M, V. OPEN 24 hours Sat-Thurs. CLOSED Thurs midnight-6:30am Friday. $$$
Scampi's
Hyatt Regency Chicago, East Tower, 151 East Wacker. 565-1000. Northern Italian cuisine and seafood on an island in the middle of a 4,000-foot lagoon! Part of the Hyatt Regency's Glass House atrium lobby. Recommended: the fileto carpaccio for raw-beef lovers. Live music daily from 7am to 4am. No-smoking section. No reservations. AE, CB, DC, MC, V. OPEN 24 hours a day, 7 days a week. $$

The following serve food at least until 11pm. See also RESTAURANTS, Bars & Burgers and Delicatessen; and NIGHTLIFE.
The Abacus (Chinese)
Abril (Mexican)
Ann Sather (Swedish)
Army & Lou Restaurant & Lounge (Soul)
Arnie's Cafe (Continental)
Atlantic Restaurant (British Isles)
Bacino's (Pizza)
Bagel Nosh (Jewish)
The B.A.R. Association (Middle Eastern)
Benihana of Tokyo (Japanese)
Beppino's (Italian)
Blackhawk on Pearson (American)
Bruna's Ristorante (Italian)
Café Angelo (Italian)

Café Azteca II (Mexican)
Cafe Ba-Ba-Reeba! (Spanish)
Café Bernard (French)
Cafe Royal (British Isles)
Caffè Pergolesi (Cappuccino & Espresso)
Cape Cod Room (Fish & Seafood)
Carson's—The Place for Ribs (American)
The Casbah (Middle Eastern)
Chestnut Street Grill (Fish & Seafood)
Chicago Pizza & Oven Grinder Company (Pizza)
Como Inn (Italian)
Courtyards of Plaka (Greek)
Cricket's (American)
Dae Ho (Korean)
Dianna's Oppa (Greek)
Dos Gringos (Mexican)
Dos Hermanos Cantina (Mexican)
El Criollo (Latin American)
Eli's, The Place for Steak (Steak)
El Jardin (Mexican)
Eugene's (American)
Febo Restaurant (Italian)
Fireplace Inn (American)
Frances' (Jewish)
Fritz, That's It! (American)
Geja's Café (Fondue)
Gene & Georgetti, Ltd. (Steak)
Gino's East (Pizza)
Giordano's (Pizza)
The Golden Ox (German)
Greek Islands (Greek)
Half Shell (Fish & Seafood)
Hard Rock Cafe (American)
Hashikin (Japanese)
Heartland Café (Vegetarian)
Hemingway's Movable Feast (Soups, Salads & Sandwiches)
Home Run Inn (Pizza)
Hong Min (Chinese)
House of Bertini (Steak)
Hunan Palace (Chinese)
Ireland's (Fish & Seafood)
Kennessey Wine Cellar (Cappuccino & Espresso; Hungarian)
La Canasta (Mexican)
La Choza (Mexican)
La Fontanella (Italian)
La Margarita Restaurant (Mexican)
Lawry's The Prime Rib (American)
Lee's Canton Café (Chinese)
The Magic Pan Creperie (Crêpes)
Mama Desta's Red Sea Restaurant (Ethiopian)
Maxie's (Rooms with a View)
Melvin's Café Garden/Outdoor Dining)
Mi Casa—Su Casa (Mexican)
Middle Eastern Gardens (Middle Eastern)
Miller's Pub & Restaurant (American)
Mini Max Tacos 'n Things (Mexican)
Morton's Steak House (Steak)
My Place For (Greek)
Nick's Fishmarket (Fish & Seafood)
The Ninety-Fifth (Rooms with a View)
No Exit Café (Cappuccino & Espresso)

On the Tao (Chinese)
Park Hyatt Hotel (Afternoon Tea)
Parthenon (Greek)
Philander's Oak Park (Fish & Seafood)
Pinnacle Restaurant & Lounge (Rooms with a View)
Pizzeria Uno & Pizzeria Due (Pizza)
Pronto (Italian)
The Pump Room (Continental)
Resi's Bierstube (German)
Ria's Pizzeria (Pizza)
Ricky's East (Delicatessen)
Ristorante Italia (Italian)
Ritz-Carlton Greenhouse (Afternoon Tea; Rooms with a View)
R. J. Grunts (American)
Rodity's (Greek)
Rosebud (Italian)
Sage's on State (American)
Salvatore's (Italian)
Sayat Nova (Middle Eastern)
Schullen's (German)
71-Club (Rooms with a View)
Spiaggia (Italian)
Stefani's (Italian)
Su Casa (Mexican)
Sweetwater (American)
Tamborine (American)
Tap Root Pub (Fish & Seafood)
That Steak Joynt (Steak)
Theater Café (Cappuccino & Espresso)
Three Happiness (Chinese)
Toscano's (Italian)
Trader Vic's (Polynesian)
Trattoria Pizzaria Roma (Italian)
Un Grand Café (French)
The Waterfront (Fish & Seafood)
Zum Deutschen Eck Restaurant (German)

Latin American

(See also RESTAURANTS, Mexican and Spanish.)
El Criollo
1706 West Fullerton. 549-3373. Hearty Argentinian specialties are featured in this cozy dimly lit hybrid (Argentinian/Mexican/Puerto Rican) restaurant, specifically grilled meat: short ribs, churrasco, Argentine steak, sweetbreads. Mexican beers, sangria. Reserve. AE, DC, MC, V. OPEN Mon-Thurs 4pm-10pm; Fri 4pm-midnight; Sat 1pm-12:30am; Sun 2pm-10pm. $
El Piqueo
5427 North Clark. 769-0455. Located in Andersonville (a Swedish area), this comfortable Peruvian storefront serves low-cost, savory five-course prix-fixe dinners. Hot food aficionados will be catered to. Bring your own wine or beer (there is a corkage charge). Reserve. AE, MC, V. OPEN Tues-Sat 5:30pm-10:30pm. CLOSED Sun & Mon. $$
La Llama
3811 North Ashland. 327-7756. A bright and cheerful dining room. The Peruvian food, on the

hot side, is interesting and authentic, albeit expensive. The wide array of appetizers will tempt you to go no further, but do. Broccoli fritters, chicken in walnut sauce, grilled beef tenderloin in vinegar marinade, paella, deep-fried fish. Reserve. AE only. OPEN Tues-Sun 5:30pm-10:30pm. CLOSED Mon. $$$

Mexican

(See also RESTAURANTS, Latin American and Spanish.)
Abril
2607 North Milwaukee. 227-7252. Deservedly popular, this is one of the best Mexican outposts in the city. Good food, potent margaritas, and a well-stocked jukebox. Reserve. AE, CB, DC, MC, V. OPEN Sun-Thurs 11am-midnight; Fri 11am-3am; Sat 11am-4am. $
Boca del Rio
917 West Belmont. 281-6698. Pleasantly decorated relaxed setting. The emphasis is on Mexican seafood preparations: grilled shrimp with fresh garlic, snapper Veracruzana, avocado stuffed with chopped eel. The usual enchiladas, burritos, and chimichangas, too. Reserve. AE, CB, DC, MC, V. Free parking. OPEN Tues-Fri 4pm-10:30pm; Sat & Sun 1pm-10:30pm. CLOSED Mon. $
Café Azteca II
215 West North Avenue. 944-9854. In Old Town, one of the city's oldest and best Mexican restaurants. Combinacio Azteca is a good sampler. Strolling musicians during dinner. Outdoor flower- and tree-filled garden in summer. Reserve, except on weekends during summer. AE, CB, DC, MC, V. OPEN 7 days noon-12:30am. $
Dos Gringos
1004 North Clark. 951-0988. Wonderful deep-fried flour tortillas, chimichangas, steak Mexican, and a host of regional dishes, all very inexpensive. Full service bar. Free parking Saturday and Sunday. Reserve. AE, MC, V. OPEN Mon-Thurs 11:30am-11pm; Fri 11:30am-midnight; Sat 3pm-midnight; Sun 3pm-11pm. $
Dos Hermanos Cantina
Water Tower Place, 845 North Michigan, 6th level. 280-2780. Mexican specialties and a 27-ounce margarita to fortify you for shopping. How about chimichangas for dessert? In a Mexican-villa setting. No reservations. AE, DC, MC, V. OPEN Mon-Thurs 11am-10pm; Fri & Sat 11am-11pm; Sun noon-9pm. $
E1 Jardin
3335 North Clark. 528-6775. Chili rellenos—stuffed green peppers dipped in egg batter; carne de pollo en mole—chicken in a tangy sauce; and vegetarian combinations. Garden in summer. Delivery. No reservations. AE, DC, MC, V. OPEN 7 days noon-11:30pm. $
Frontera Grill
445 North Clark. 661-1434. Classic Mexican sauces and preparations inspired by the cooks of Mexico; born of years of on-the-scene re-

search by chef/owner Rick Bayless. The results: interesting and extremely satisfying. For a good sample, begin with an appetizer platter; main courses include marinated fresh fish baked in banana leaves, chile rellenos. For dessert, fried plantains with thick cream, mango ice cream. Reserve for six or more only. AE, CB, DC, MC, V. *L, Tues-Fri 11:30am-2:30pm. D, Tues-Thurs 5:30pm-10pm; Fri & Sat 5:30pm-11pm. "Late breakfast," Sat 9am-2:30pm. CLOSED Tues.* $

La Canasta
1007 West Armitage, 975-9667. Casual Sheffield-area spot for authentic Mexican food: great guacamole, nachos, and enchiladas Indios at pleasing prices. *Very* popular. Mañana-paced service. Mexican beers, California wines. Carryout too. No reservations. AE, CB, DC, MC, V. *OPEN Mon-Thurs 4pm-11pm; Fri 4pm-midnight; Sat 3pm-midnight; Sun 3pm-11pm.* $

La Choza
7630 North Paulina. 761-8020; 465-9401. Tops for tacos and tortillas. Fiery authentic food and atmosphere too. Favored by Chicago's Mexican population. Bring your own beer or wine. Patio dining in summer. Free parking. Reserve for seven or more only. No credit cards. *OPEN Tues-Thurs 11am-11pm; Fri 11am-11:30pm; Sat 11am-midnight; Sun 11am-10:30pm. CLOSED Mon.* $

La Margarita Restaurant
868 North Wabash; 751-3434. And 6319 West Dempster, Morton Grove; 966-5037. Popular Mexican delight for moderate-priced food and drink. Very good paella and enchiladas. Strolling mariachi band Monday from 7pm to 2am and Tuesday to Sunday 6pm to 1am. Reserve. AE, CB, DC, MC, V. *L, Mon-Sat 11am-4pm; Sun noon-4pm. D, 7 days 4pm-4am.* $

Mi Casa—Su Casa
2524 North Southport. 525-6323. Comfortable, authentic, casual. Catering. Reserve. AE, CB, DC, MC, V. *OPEN Sun-Thurs 4pm-midnight; Fri & Sat 4pm-2am.* $

Mini Max Tacos 'n Things
1119 West Webster. 348-3493. One of those secrets that everyone knows. Buy your beer in the up-front grocery, then go to the rear of the store for satisfying, always reliable, well-priced Mexican food. Spicy enchiladas, good tacos and nachos, delicious queso fundido—fondue Mexican style. For breakfast, huevos ranchos. No reservations. AE, DC, MC, V. *OPEN Mon-Sat 7am-11pm; Sun 7am-10:30pm.* $

Su Casa
49 East Ontario. 943-4041. Attractive hacienda-style decor surrounds reliably satisfying mild Mexican fare (hot upon request). Chili rellenos; Mexican beef stew; shrimp Vera Cruz. Good bet: the deluxe combination of grilled steak, stuffed peppers, a taco, and guacamole. *Great* margaritas. Strolling guitarist 6pm to 12:30am. Reserve. AE, CB, DC MC, V. *OPEN Mon-Fri 11:30am-12:30am; Sat 5pm-12:30am. CLOSED Sun.* $$

Middle Eastern

The B.A.R. Association
1224 West Webster. 871-1440. Charming casual dining spot for Persian food. The cozy, romantic setting is enhanced by a fireplace. Wonderful outdoor garden in summer. AE, MC, V. *OPEN in winter: Tues-Thurs 5pm-11pm; Fri & Sat 5pm-midnight; Sun 11am-11pm. CLOSED Mon. In summer: 7 nights 5pm-midnight. Brunch, year-round Sun 11am-4pm.* $$

The Casbah
514 West Diversey. 935-7570. You won't find Peter Lorre here, but you will find pleasant service, candlelit atmosphere, and delicious Armenian and Middle Eastern food. Interesting selections include beorak—meat and onions in a filo pastry; kibbe'h—raw lamb and Bulgar wheat; maglubeh, lamb, cauliflower, and pine nuts (weekends only); couscous 7 days. Finish with strong Turkish coffee. Reserve on weekends. AE, CB, DC, MC, V. *OPEN 7 days 5pm-10:30pm.* $$

Middle Eastern Gardens
2621 North Clark. 935-3100. A variety of well-prepared Middle Eastern lamb dishes as well as vegetarian offerings. No smoking. No reservations. No credit cards. *OPEN 7 days 11am-midnight.* $

Sayat Nova
157 East Ohio; 644-9159. And 20 West Gulf Road, Des Plaines; 296-1776.* Armenian specialties distinguish this excellent Middle Eastern restaurant: raw kibbe'h, kiflah shish kebab. Reserve. AE, CB, DC, MC, V. *OPEN Mon-Thurs 11:30am-11pm; Fri & Sat 11am-1am; Sun 11am-10pm. *L, Mon-Sat 11:30am-2pm. D, Mon-Thurs 4:30pm-10:30pm; Fri & Sat 4:30pm-midnight; Sun 4pm-10pm.* $

No-Smoking Areas

The following have no-smoking areas:
The Berghoff (German)
Biggs (Continental)
Bread Shop Kitchen (Vegetarian)
Capt'n Nemo's (Soups, Salads & Sandwiches)
D. B. Kaplan (Delicatessan)
Frontera Grill (Mexican)
George's (Italian)
Heartland Café (Vegetarian)
La Tour (Breakfast/Brunch; Rooms with a View)
The Magic Pan Creperie (Crêpes)
Middle Eastern Gardens (Middle Eastern)
My Place For (Greek)
On the Tao (Chinese)
Ritz-Carlton Café (Late-Night/24-Hour)
Scampi's (Late-Night/24-Hour)
Theater Café (Cappuccino & Espresso)
The Walnut Room (Afternoon Tea)

Pizza

(See also RESTAURANTS, Italian.)
Bacino's
2204 North Lincoln. 472-7400. *The* stuffed pizza

by any other name. Lincoln Park-area favorite, formerly a Giordano's. Features their famous stuffed pizza, favorites being the spinach and the vegetarian. Thin also available; individual-size pizzas too. Homemade soups. Eat here and watch the "spinners" or take out. Call ahead at lunchtime only. No reservations. AE, MC, V. *OPEN Mon-Thurs 11am-10pm; Fri-Sun 11am-midnight; Sun 11am-10pm.* $

Chicago Pizza & Oven Grinder Company
2121 North Clark. 248-2570. Chicago-style deep-dish pizza by the pound! Sausage or vegetarian. Salads and grinders too. No carryout. No reservations. Patio for drinks while you wait to be seated. No credit cards. *OPEN Mon-Thurs 4pm-11pm; Fri 4pm-midnight; Sat noon-midnight; Sun noon-11pm.* $

Gino's East
160 East Superior. 943-1124. Popular bi-level graffitti-filled spot for Chicago-style deep-dish pizza—thick crust, layered with abundant quantities of cheese, filled with fresh peppers, sausage, onions, covered with tomato sauce. Two can easily share a small. Carryout too. Reserve weekdays only. AE, CB, DC, MC, V. *OPEN Mon-Thurs 11am-11pm; Fri & Sat 11am-midnight; Sun 2pm-10pm.* $

Giordano's
747 North Rush; 951-0747. And 3214 West 63rd; 436-2969. Also 5927 West Irving Park, 736-5553; 1840 North Clark, 944-6100; and 12 other locations. In this pizza town, this one is considered the best by the most. The double-crust soufflé-like pie is what's so special. Try the sausage or shrimp but especially the spinach. Call ahead to order. Beer and wine. Carryout too. North Rush: *OPEN Sun-Thurs 11am-midnight; Fri & Sat 11am-1am;* AE, DC; no reservations. West 63rd: *OPEN Mon-Thurs 11am-midnight; Fri & Sat 11am-1am; Sun noon-midnight;* MC, V; no reservations. West Irving Park: *OPEN Sun-Thurs 4pm-midnight; Fri & Sat 4pm-1am;* AE, MC, V. North Clark: *OPEN Sun-Thurs 11am-midnight; Fri & Sat 11am-2am;* AE, CB, MC, V. $

Home Run Inn
4254 West 31st. 247-9696. Another front-runner in "Where's the best pizza in Chicago?" sweepstakes. This is considered the best *thin*-crust pizza, choice of toppings. Also pastas and grilled sandwiches. All against a noisy backdrop of jukebox, pinball machines, and if you time it right, a Sox game on TV. Carryout too. *OPEN Mon-Thurs 11am-12:30am; Fri 11am-1:30am; Sat 11am-2am; Sun noon-midnight.* $

Pizzeria Uno & Pizzeria Due
Uno: 29 East Ohio; 321-1000. Due: 619 North Wabash; 943-2400. Another slice of Chicago history. Uno is credited with the invention, in 1943, of thick-crust (universally referred to as "Chicago-style") pizza. Overflow crowds use Due as backup. Phone ahead for takeout on weekdays. Uno: *OPEN Tues-Thurs 11:30am-midnight; Fri & Sat 11:30am-1am; Sun 1pm-8pm; Mon 4pm-midnight;* reserve for lunch only; AE, CB, DC, MC, V. Due: *OPEN Mon-Thurs 11:30am-* 1:30am; Fri 11:30am-2:30am; Sat 4pm-2:30am; Sun 4pm-11:20pm; no reservations; AE, CB, DC, MC, V. $

Ria's Pizzeria
3943 North Lincoln. 281-8949. Nondescript spot, but another favorite of thick-crust-pizza aficionados. The sausage is homemade and generously layered. Call ahead to reserve and order. AE, MC, V. *OPEN Tues-Thurs & Sun 4pm-midnight; Fri & Sat 4pm-2am. CLOSED Mon.* $

Polish

Arcadia
2943 North Milwaukee. 342-1464. Reliable Polish fare in a more polished than usual setting. Delicious homemade soups; roast pork tenderloin stuffed with prunes, pork cutlet with sauerkraut, roast duck with apples, red cabbage slaw. Also, blintzes, pierogi, kielbasa, bigos. Good value complete dinners, most under $10. Full service bar. Reservations accepted. No credit cards. *OPEN 7 days 10am-10pm.*

Old Warsaw Restaurant & Lounge
4750 North Harlem. 867-4500. As-much-as-you-can-eat Polish-style buffet. Fantastic pierogi and kolacky. Reserve. AE, DC, MC, V. *OPEN Tues-Sat 11:30am-10pm; Sun & holidays 11am-9pm. CLOSED Mon.* $

Patria
3201 North Long. 622-1300. Authentic *and* abundant Polish home cooking. Try the combination with pierogi, naleśniki (blintzes), chicken livers, and more; or the chicken Kiev. Salad bar. Homemade desserts. Polish beer. Reserve for four or more. No credit cards. *OPEN Thurs-Tues 11am-9pm. CLOSED Wed.* $

Senkowski Home Bakery
2931 North Milwaukee. 252-3708. A pleasant, old-fashioned bakery, grocery store, and small dining room purveying tasty and filling Polish delights. Wonderful soups, potato pancakes, apple-stuffed crêpes; daily specials. All extremely inexpensive. No alcohol, you may bring your own. No credit cards. *OPEN 7 days 10am-9pm.* $

Teresa
3938 West School. 286-5166. Polish Chicagoans favor this tiny, homey spot for simple Polish fare. Homemade soups, pierogi, cutlets. Table and counter service. No credit cards. *OPEN Sun-Thurs 11am-9pm; Fri & Sat 11am-10pm.* $

White Eagle
6845 North Milwaukee. 647-0660. Homemade mushroom-barley soup, pierogi, kolacky. Large, inexpensive family dinners feature these and other Polish specialties. Reserve for very large groups only. No credit cards. *L, Mon-Sun 11am-3pm. D, Tues-Sat 3pm-9pm; Sun 3pm-7:30pm.* $

Polynesian

Trader Vic's
Palmer House, 17 East Monroe. 726-7500, ext

385. Downtown, famed for South Seas motif and incredibly extensive menu. Most fun: dine on appetizers and revel in flower-filled rum-based drinks. Jacket preferred. Reserve. AE, CB, DC, MC, V. *L, Mon-Fri 11:30am-2:30pm. D, Mon-Thurs 5pm-11pm; Fri & Sat 5pm-midnight; Sun 4:30pm-11pm.* $$$$

Rooms with a View

Don Roth's River Plaza
See RESTAURANTS, American.

La Tour
Park Hyatt Hotel, 800 North Michigan. 280-2230. Swanky, sophisticated dining on classical and nouvelle cuisine in a setting to match. Floor-to-ceiling windows, affording a view of the castellated Water Tower, are aglow with little Tivoli lights in the pm. Extensive wine list; champagne bar with a choice of 39, also available with meals. Classical pianist, except at breakfast. No-smoking section. Reserve. AE, CB, DC, MC, V. *B, Mon-Sat 7am-10:30am. L, Mon-Sat 11:30am-2:30pm. D, 7 days 6pm-10:30pm. Brunch, Sun 10:30am-2:30pm.* (*See also* RESTAURANTS, Breakfast/Brunch.) $$$$

Le Ciel Bleu
Mayfair Regent Hotel, 181 East Lake Shore Drive. 951-2864. From this posh perch on the Mayfair Regent Hotel's roof (19th floor) you can view glittering Lake Shore Drive, the Lake, and much blue sky (*ciel bleu*) while leisurely dining on ofttimes ambitious French cuisine. The mirror-ceilinged setting is luxurious, so is the tariff. Jacket and tie required. If you're on a trainer budget go for breakfast or the sumptuous unlimited prix-fixe Sunday champagne brunch. Valet parking. Reserve. AE, CB, DC, MC, V. *B, Mon-Sat 7am-10am. L, 7 days 11:30am-2pm. D, 7 days 6pm-9:30pm. Brunch, Sun 11:30am-2pm.* $$$$

Maxie's
McCormick Center Hotel, Lakeshore Drive & 23rd. 791-1900. All four walls of this 23rd-floor club are made of glass, offering an unimpeded view in every direction. Meals are prepared in view as well, either on the grill in the center of the room or tableside. Seafood Bar in the evening. Jacket and tie required for dinner. Dance floor. Lunch, members only. Reserve. AE, CB, DC, MC, V. *OPEN Mon-Sat 5pm-midnight. CLOSED most Sun; call first.* $$$$

The Ninety-Fifth
John Hancock Center, 172 East Chestnut, 95th floor. 787-9596. Dine continental in the world's tallest bi-level (Images on 96, *see* Bars & Burgers) restaurant. The four-state view along Lake Michigan is nothing short of spectacular. Jacket and tie required. Reserve. AE, CB, DC, MC, V. *L, Mon-Fri 11:30am-2pm. D, Sun-Thurs 5:30pm-10pm; Fri & Sat 6pm-11pm. Sunset Dinner Specials Sun-Fri 5:30pm-6:15pm. Brunch, Sun 10:30am-2pm.* $$$

Pinnacle Restaurant & Lounge
Days Inn—Lake Shore Drive, 644 North Lake Shore Drive. 943-9200. See the skyline and the Lakefront from a slowly revolving (360° every hour) romantic restaurant on the 33rd floor or a lounge that wisely does not revolve. *Great* at sunset. No denim. Reserve. AE, CB, DC, MC, V. *OPEN 7 days, 5:30pm-11:30pm. Brunch, Sun 10:30am-2pm.* $$

Ritz-Carlton Greenhouse
Water Tower Place, 160 East Pearson, 12th floor. 266-1000. Have lunch, tea (*see* RESTAURANTS, Afternoon Tea) or cocktails in this 12th-floor greenhouse, just off the lobby, while enjoying a view to the north up Michigan Avenue. Piano music Monday to Friday from 5:30pm to 11pm. No denim, please. No reservations. AE, CB, DC, MC, V. *L, Mon-Sat 11:30am-2:30pm. Tea, Sun-Fri 3pm-5pm. Cocktails, Mon-Fri 11:30am-1am; Sat 11:30am-2am; Sun noon-1am.* $

71-Club
Executive House Hotel, 71 East Wacker. 346-7100. On the penthouse floor, the unmatched Chicago skyline provides the backdrop for good continental fare; seasonal specialties. In nice weather, outdoor terrace for dining or cocktails. During the day, it's a private luncheon club for members and hotel guests. Jacket requested. Reserve. *OPEN 7 days 7am-11pm.* $$$$

The Signature
Holiday Inn, 350 North Orleans, 15th floor. 836-5000. Atop the Apparel Mart, lovely tree-lined and mirrored dining room with a view to the south. Piano and vocalist during dinner. On opera nights, end of September to December, free transportation to and from opera (your car is parked here free) and special dinners featuring the cuisine of the opera's origin—France, Germany, or Italy. Jacket preferred. Reserve. AE, CB, DC, MC, V. *L, Mon-Fri 11am-2:30pm. D, 7 days 5pm-10:30pm.* $$$

Soul

(*See* also RESTAURANTS, Cajun/Creole.)

Army & Lou Restaurant & Lounge
420 & 422 East 75th. 483-6550. Heaping portions of soulful Southern soul food at rock bottom prices. Simply great fried chicken and ribs, deep-fried fish, Creole gumbo, greens seasoned with smoky bacon, fried sweet potatoes, and corn bread. Start with one of their wonderful soups. Reserve. AE, DC, MC, V. Parking. *OPEN Mon-Wed, Thurs & Sun 11am-10:30pm; Fri & Sat 11am-11:30pm.* $

Soups, Salads & Sandwiches

(*See also* RESTAURANTS, Delicatessen; Jewish; *and* Vegetarian.)

Big John's
1147 West Armitage. 477-4400. Popular Turkey Melt sandwich and bratwurst (from Gepperth's)

with Swiss cheese. Also, ½-pound burgers and an extensive selection of domestic and imported beers. Large beer garden in summer. No reservations. No credit cards. *OPEN Mon-Sat 11:30am-10pm; Sun noon-6pm.* $

Boudin Bakery
63 East Chicago Avenue. 329-1580. Bright back-of-the-bakery for sandwiches on sourdough bread or rolls. Also, pizza bread served hot or cold and a soup du jour. Soft drinks, tea, and coffee. Order ahead and take out or eat in. No reservations. MC, V. *OPEN Mon-Sat 7:30am-7pm; Sun 10am-5pm.* $

Capt'n Nemo's
7367 North Clark; 973-0570. And 3311 Marshfield; 929-7687.* This sub place is the exception to the rule: friendly, cheerful, and clean; a wide variety of fillings; homemade soups and desserts. Special feature: free soup du jour while you wait for your order. No-smoking section. *OPEN Mon-Sat 11am-8pm. CLOSED Sun. *OPEN Mon-Sat 11am-9pm; Sun 11am-7pm.* $

Carlyn Berghoff
Goodman Theater, 200 South Columbus Drive. 443-3820. Good-value European-style buffet offers salads, breads, pastries, cheese, and fruit. Reserve. AE, MC, V. *OPEN during Goodman Theater Main Stage season only, Wed-Sat 6:15pm-8pm.* $

Chapman Sisters Calorie Counter
444 North Michigan. 329-9690. Friendly serve-yourself spot for salads, soups, sandwiches. Vegetarian chili, quiche. Carrot cake too, *but* the caloric content of everything is posted. Conscience raising. *OPEN Mon-Fri 8am-3:30pm.*
$

Hemingway's Movable Feast
1825 North Lincoln. 943-6225. Deli restaurant with a variety of loaded sandwiches (with cute names) to go or stay. Service is slow, but you might not care if you sit in the outdoor café in good weather. Soda-fountain treats. Beer and wine available. Catering too. For eight or more a 15% gratuity is added to your check. No reservations. AE, MC, V. *OPEN Sun-Thurs 11:30am-11pm; Fri & Sat 11:30am-midnight.*
$

Jerry's
215 East Grand. 337-2500. For corned beef on rye with a side of verbal abuse, go here. The sandwiches are good. Jerry barks but has not bitten any customers—yet. Seating and takeout. *OPEN Mon-Fri 6:30am-6:30pm; Sat 6:30am-4pm. CLOSED Sun.* $

Out to Lunch
Seneca Hotel, 200 East Chestnut, lower level. 642-4649. Via Holland, a puffed yeast bun—a broodje—packed with your choice of filling, including wonderful salad mixtures: sardine and onion, roast beef and horseradish. So inexpensive (you get two) you needn't go Dutch. Terrific soups, salads, chili too. No credit cards. *OPEN Mon-Fri 8am-3pm; Sat 8am-2pm. CLOSED Sun.* Takeout and deliveries from 10:30am to 2pm, in

area bounded by Oak, Ontario, Lake, and State streets. $

Spanish

(See also RESTAURANTS, Latin American *and* Mexican.)

Cafe-Ba-Ba-Reeba!
2024 North Halsted. 935-5000. Lively authentic tapas bar atmosphere. The place is colorful and crowded, the food is quite good. Gazpacho; black bean soup; hot or cold tapas; paella for two. Over 40 sherries and Spanish wines. *Great* desserts include baked bananas with caramel sauce. Outdoors in summer in a large garden. Reserve. AE, CB, DC, MC, V. *L, Tues-Sat 11am-2:30pm. D, Mon-Thurs 5:30pm-11pm; Fri 5:30pm-midnight; Sun 5pm-10pm.* $

La Paella
2920 North Clark. 528-0757. Charming family-run storefront Spanish restaurant. Delicious paella specialty, served in the skillet; duckling in a sweet mango-and-brandy sauce. Tapas menu every night but Saturday. Pleasant flower-bedecked surroundings; cordial service. Free parking. Reserve. AE, CB, MC, V. *OPEN Tues-Sun 5:30pm-11pm. CLOSED Mon.* $

Steak

Eli's, The Place for Steak
215 East Chicago Avenue. 642-1393. Plush setting for excellent steaks and prime ribs. Complimentary chopped liver and vegetables. Highly rated cheesecake for a finale. Loyal following, including many Chicago celebrities and sports types. It can get hectic. Piano bar for drinks. Jacket required. Reserve. AE, CB. *L, Mon-Fri 11am-2:30pm. D, 7 days 4pm-11:30pm. CLOSED holidays.* $$$

Gene & Georgetti, Ltd.
500 North Franklin. 527-3718. Though it's an Italian restaurant, its reputation stems from the excellence of the aged prime steak, accompanied by crispy home fries. Merchandise Mart vicinity ensures crowds most times. Of the two floors, downstairs is only a *bit* quieter. Reserve for three or more. AE, DC. Free parking. *OPEN Mon-Thurs 11:30am-midnight; Fri & Sat 11:30am-1am. CLOSED Sun.* $$$$

House of Bertini
535 North Wells. 644-1397. A long-established (since 1930) Italian steak house for unpretentious good food and service. In addition to steak and cottage fries, well-prepared pastas. Reserve. Valet parking. AE, CB, DC, MC, V. *L, Mon-Fri 11:30am-2:30pm. D, Mon-Sat 5pm-11:30pm. CLOSED Sun.* $$

Morton's Steak House
1050 North State. 266-4820. An excellent choice for *always* good (and large) prime steak and

lobster. Delicious hash-brown accompaniment. Blackboard menu; open grill. Extensive wine list. Order-ahead dessert soufflé. Noise and smoke are the only drawbacks. Reservations taken until 7pm only, so expect a wait. AE, CB, DC, MC, V. *OPEN Mon-Fri 5:30pm-11pm; Sat 5:30pm-11:30pm. CLOSED Sun.* $$$$

The Palm
Mayfair Regent Hotel, 181 East Lake Shore Drive. 944-0135. *The* no-frills New York steak house comes to Chicago—ceiling fans and cartoons intact. So, too, the giant-sized, high-quality steaks, double-rib lamb chops, huge lobsters, and sky-high tab. *Great* and plentiful cottage fries. Imported (from the Bronx) cheesecake. Be forewarned: It's all à la carte. Reserve. AE, CB, DC, MC, V. *OPEN Mon-Fri 11:30am-10pm; Sat 5pm-10:45pm. CLOSED Sun.* $$$$

That Steak Joynt
1610 North Wells. 943-5091. In Old Town, where excellent steak is the specialty and they do it your way: charbroiled; with garlic or pepper; sautéed in butter with onions. Very good ribs too. Piano bar. Reserve. AE, CB, DC, MC, V. *OPEN Sun-Thurs 5pm-midnight; Fri 5pm-1am; Sat 5pm-2am.* $$$$

Swedish

Ann Sather
925 West Belmont. 348-2378. Charming long-time restaurant in former Swedish area serves "just good food." Fruit soup, Swedish pancakes, sautéed chicken livers, lamb stew with dumplings. Home-baked-daily pies and bread and banana, carrot, and fruit cake. Inexpensive, consistently good home cooking. No reservations. AE, MC, V. *OPEN Sun-Thurs 7am-11pm; Fri & Sat 7am-2am.* $

Villa Sweden
5207 North Clark. 334-1883. In the Andersonville area, a nice spot for smorgasbord featuring hot and cold dishes, smoked fish and meats; Thursday only: lingonberry pancakes for dessert. Full of families. Nice Sunday brunch alternative. Bring your own wine or beer. Reserve. No credit cards. *OPEN Mon-Sat 11am-8pm; Sun 11:30am-8pm. Smorgasbord Thurs 4pm-8pm; Fri & Sat 11am-8pm; Sun 11:30am-8pm.* $

Thai

Ananda
941 North State. 944-7440. More chic (and pricey) than the usual Thai restaurant but a consistently fine choice. Good salad choices, especially the yum ah ngoon with shrimps, grapes, and cashews, seasoned with coriander and ginger. Also, the cold but-oh-so-hot steak tartare, and the "drunken noodles." Extensive wine list. Reserve. AE, MC, V. *L, Tues-Thurs*

11:30am-2pm. D, Sun, Tues-Thurs 5pm-10pm; Fri & Sat 5pm-10:30pm. CLOSED Mon. $

Bangkok House
2544 West Devon. 338-5948. Spicy Thai food in plain surroundings. Bring your own wine. AE, MC, V. *OPEN Tues-Thurs & Sun noon-9pm; Fri & Sat noon-10pm. CLOSED Mon.* $

River Kwai
440 North State. 644-1144. Large plain storefront for satisfying Thai fare. Ground pork salad; coconut milk soup; chicken satay; spicy basil chicken; pad Thai; and, to finish, homemade coconut ice cream. Reserve. AE, CB, DC, MC, V. *OPEN Mon-Thurs 11am-10:30pm; Fri & Sat 11am-11pm.* $

Siam Café
4710 North Sheridan Road. 989-0157. New location accommodates 200 diners. Extensive menu. Whole fish with hot sauce, coconut milk curries, pad Thai, pork satay. On Monday, Wednesday, and Thursday from 11:30am to 2pm, they feature an all-you-can-eat buffet. Reservations for eight or more only. MC, V. *OPEN Wed-Mon 11:30am-9pm. CLOSED Tues.* $

Siam Square
622 Davis Street, Evanston. 475-0860. Seating only 36, this tiny Thai restaurant serves excellent appetizers. Also, chicken curry with sweet potatoes; sautéed seafood; thick rice noodles; interesting desserts. Bring your own wine or beer. Reserve. AE, DC, MC, V. *OPEN 7 days 11am-10pm.* $

Thai Little Home Café
4747 North Kedzie. 478-3944. The unpretentious favorite of most Chicagoans. Caveat for the uninitiated: spirited seasoning. Try the tom yum king, spicy soup; wonderful whole red snapper. AE, DC, MC, V. *L, 11:30am-2:30pm. D, Mon, Tues, Thurs & Fri 5pm-9:30pm; Sat & Sun 1pm-9:30pm. CLOSED Wed.* $

Thai Room
4022 North Western. 539-6150. *Very* extensive menu includes some unusuals. This is hot stuff. Service is pleasant but known to be slow. Reserve. MC, V. *OPEN Tues-Thurs & Sun 10am-10pm; Fri & Sat 10am-10:30pm. CLOSED Mon.* $

Thai Villa
3811 North Lincoln. 281-2323. Tiny storefront serves very fine authentic Thai, Vietnamese, and Mandarin specialties. Recommended: the Thai-style barbecued chicken. When not busy they will cook anything you specify. Bring your own wine or beer. Carryout as well. Reserve on weekends. AE, DC, MC, V. *OPEN Tues-Sun 4pm-10pm. CLOSED Mon.* $

Vegetarian

Bread Shop Kitchen
3400 North Halsted. 528-8108. A full service vegetarian deli, bakery, and grocery. All soups, salads, entrées, sandwiches, and desserts are made from all-natural ingredients. All are avail-

able for carryout. No smoking. No credit cards.
OPEN Tues-Sat 9am-8pm; Sun 11am-5pm.
CLOSED Mon. $
Heartland Café
7000 North Glenwood. 465-8005. A homey, laid-
back place for good salads, great corn bread,
daily vegetarian and fish specials. Baking done
on premises. Sidewalk café in summer. Potbelly
stove in winter. Smoking frowned upon. Bring
your own wine or beer. Reserve for eight or
more. No credit cards. *OPEN in summer: Mon-
Fri 7am-midnight; Sat 8am-midnight; Sun 8am-
11pm. In winter: Mon-Thurs 8am-11pm; Fri &
Sat 8am-midnight; Sun 9am-10pm.* $

Yugoslavian

Yugo Inn
2824 North Ashland. 348-6444. Charming old-
world neighborhood find: chicken paprika; stuffed
cabbage; pljeskavica—a coarsely ground beef
with onions; raznjici—a shish kabob of beef,
pork, or chicken. Inexpensive complete dinners
include starter, main course, vegetable, and a
choice of soup, salad, or dessert. Palacinke—
dessert crêpes filled with walnuts and jam. Strong
Serbian coffee. Yugoslavian wines. Reserve. No
credit cards. *OPEN Wed-Sun 5pm-midnight.
CLOSED Mon & Tues.* $

SHOPPING

The Century

LARGE STORES

Bonwit Teller
John Hancock Center, 875 North Michigan; 751-1800. And 35 Oakbrook Center; 573-6300.* Fine contemporary and classic clothing for women, men, and children. (No children's department at Oakbrook store.) The Safari shop for high-fashion designer duds, London's legendary Turnbull and Asser for men, and the exclusive Missoni and Hermès shops. AE, DC, MC, V, Bonwit charge. *OPEN Mon & Thurs 10am-8pm; Tues, Wed, Fri & Sat 10am-7pm; Sun noon-5pm. *OPEN Mon-Fri 10am-9pm; Sat 10am-6pm; Sun noon-5pm.*

Carson Pirie Scott & Company
1 South State; 744-2000. And Prudential Building. Also 15 suburban locations. Over 126 years old, housed in what is now a Chicago landmark (*see* HISTORIC & NEW CHICAGO, Historic Buildings & Areas). Full service including fine fashion selections for women, men, and children. They're old-fashioned enough to have a bride's consulting service in addition to the registry. AC, MC, V, Carson charge. *OPEN Mon & Thurs 9:45am-7:30pm; Tues, Wed, Fri & Sat 9:45am-5:45pm. Also first Sun of every month, open 11am-5pm for Super-Dooper Sunday sales.*

Chas A. Stevens
25 North State; 630-1500. And Water Tower Place, 835 North Michigan; 787-6800.* Also 18 suburban locations. In business for 94 years, but their fashion image is very *now*. A fine Designer Shop; the new Chas at Water Tower Place features youthful-life-style clothes and accessories; Executive Place for the career woman. Good shoe selections. AE, MC, V, Stevens charge. *OPEN Mon & Thurs 9:45am-7pm; Tues,*

*Wed, Fri & Sat 9:45am-5:45pm. *OPEN Mon-Fri 10am-7pm; Sat 10am-6pm; Sun noon-5pm.*

I. Magnin & Company
830 North Michigan; 751-0500. And Northbrook Court; 480-0500.* From the land of sunshine, a prestigious name in high-style, high-quality fashion. Strong in *au courant* status designs and designers; furs, jewelry, and cosmetics. Moderately priced clothing and accessories too. Specialized departments for contemporary juniors, children, executive women, and men. Bonus: nice view from the 2nd-floor Designer Salon. AE, CB, DC, MC, V, Magnin charge. *OPEN Mon & Thurs 10am-7pm; Tues, Wed, Fri & Sat 10am-6pm; Sun noon-6pm. *OPEN Mon-Fri 10am-9pm; Sat 10am-6pm; Sun noon-5pm.*

Lord & Taylor
Water Tower Place, 835 North Michigan. 787-7400. And six suburban locations. Contemporary classic clothes and accessories for women, men, and children on seven floors. Great emphasis on American designers. AE, Lord & Taylor charge. *OPEN Mon-Fri 10am-8pm; Sat 10am-7pm; Sun noon-6pm.*

Marshall Field's
111 North State; 781-1000. And Water Tower Place, 835 North Michigan; 781-1234.* The State Street store was founded in 1852, and they are still "giving the lady what she wants." Not to mention her husband and children. Go to the original for the store itself as much as for what's in it (*see* HISTORIC & NEW CHICAGO, Historic Buildings & Areas). It's full service on 2¼ million square feet! One could easily move in and want for nothing. "28 Shop" for elegant couture fashions, Espirit for juniors, Pacesetter for designer sportswear, Careers for professionals, and *so* much more. Emphasis on quality, service, and courtesy. AE, MC, V, Field's charge. *OPEN Mon*

& *Thurs 9:45am-7:30pm; Tues, Wed, Fri & Sat 9:45am-5:45pm; and first Sun of every month noon-5pm.* **OPEN Mon-Sat 10am-8pm; Sun noon-6pm.* (*See also* RESTAURANTS, Afternoon Tea: Walnut Room.)

Montgomery Ward & Co., Inc.
7601 South Cicero in the Ford City Shopping Center. 284-4800. The well-known name in catalog sales. Their full-line department store sells wearing apparel, home furnishings, and much more. Delivery service available. Good annual sales April, September, and October. AE, MC, V, Montgomery Ward charge. *OPEN Mon-Fri 10am-9pm; Sat 10am-5:30pm; Sun 11am-5pm.*

Neiman Marcus
Olympia Center, 737 North Michigan. 642-5900. The famed swank Texas retailing giant. This is the largest NM outside of that great state. On four floors, designer apparel, furs, and a food complex for Petrossian caviar and smoked salmon. Neiman-Marcus charge only. *OPEN Mon & Thurs 10am-8pm; Tues, Wed, Fri & Sat 10am-6pm; Sun noon-5pm.*

Saks Fifth Avenue
669 North Michigan. 944-6500. The always quality store for elegant designer clothes and a good selection of young sportswear—that's for both men and women. The price range is moderate to expensive (Revillon furs, Louis Vuitton, etc.). A fine children's department as well. AE, CB, DC, Saks charge. *OPEN Mon & Thurs 10am-7pm; Tues, Wed, Fri & Sat 10am-6pm; Sun noon-5pm.*

Wieboldt
1 North State. 782-1500. And 11 other stores. Moderately priced department store known to be reliable and helpful. Updating its fashion image on third and fourth floors. Also men's and children's apparel, furnishings, appliances, cosmetics, etc. AE, MC, V, Wieboldt's charge. *OPEN Mon-Sat 9:45am-5:45pm.*

SHOPPING MALLS

Chicago

The Atrium
100 West Randolph. 346-0777. Housed on the first three levels of the State of Illinois Center. Twenty-two shops in all, and on the lower level The Great State Fare (opens at 6:30am), a variety of fast, tasty foods in a pleasant cafeteria setting. *OPEN Mon-Fri 8am-6pm. From Thanksgiving to Christmas, Sat 10am-4pm.*

The Brickyard
6465 West Diversey. 745-8838. Approximately 120 stores comprise this enclosed mall, including J. C. Penney, K-Mart, and Montgomery Ward. Restaurant: York Steak House. Free parking. *OPEN Mon-Fri 10am-9pm; Sat 10am-5:30pm; Sun 11am-5pm.*

The Century
2828 North Clark. 929-8100. Approximately 55

stores in this architecturally fascinating seven-level New Town-area shopping center (*see* HISTORIC & NEW CHICAGO, Historic Buildings & Areas). Mall & stores *OPEN Mon-Fri 10:30am-9pm; Sat 10:30am-6pm; Sun noon-5pm.*

Ford City Shopping Center
7601 South Cicero. 767-6400. Approximately 155 stores in this enclosed shopping mall, including J. C. Penney, Montgomery Ward, Wieboldt. Restaurants: Harvest House, John's Garage, Rascal House. *OPEN Mon-Fri 10am-9pm; Sat 10am-5:30pm; Sun noon-5pm.*

Harper Court
5210-25 South Harper. 363-8282. Approximately 22 specialty shops and restaurants in four enclosed buildings. Restaurants: Café Coffee, Medici on Harper, Tentsuma (Japanese). Street parking only; city parking lot nearby. Most stores *OPEN Mon-Sat 10am-6pm; some open Sun. Restaurants OPEN 7 days lunch and dinner.*

Water Tower Place
835 North Michigan. 440-3165. This urban complex houses a seven-story atrium shopping mall with some of the choicest shops, including Marshall Field's and Lord & Taylor. Some swell restaurants too. It constitutes a major sightseeing attraction. Mall *OPEN 7 days 9am-midnight.* Stores *OPEN Mon & Thurs 10am-7pm; Tues, Wed, Fri & Sat 10am-6pm; Sun noon-5pm.*

Suburbs

Evergreen Plaza
9500 South Western Avenue, Evergreen Park. 445-8900. One hundred and fifty stores form this enclosed mall, including Carson Pirie Scott, Chas A. Stevens, Montgomery Ward. Restaurants: French Baker, M. C.'s Evergreen Inn. Free parking. *OPEN Mon-Fri 10am-9pm; Sat 10am-5:30pm; Sun noon-5pm.*

Golf Mill Shopping Center
Golf & Milwaukee roads, Niles. 699-1070. Ninety stores in this enclosed mall, including J. C. Penney, Sears, Main Street. Restaurants: Sbarro's, Wall Street Deli. Three theaters, including the Golf Mill Theater. Free parking. *OPEN Mon-Fri 10am-9pm; Sat 10am-5:30pm; Sun 11am-5pm.*

Northbrook Court
2171 Northbrook Court, Northbrook. 498-5144. An enclosed mall with 150 shops, including Neiman Marcus, Lord & Taylor, J. C. Penney, I. Magnin. Restaurants: James Tavern, Pomodoro, Vie de France, Claim Company. Free parking. *OPEN Mon-Fri 10am-9pm; Sat 10am-5:30pm; Sun noon-5pm.*

Oakbrook Center
Route 83 & Cermak Road, Oakbrook. 573-0250. This outdoor shopping complex contains 95 stores, including Bonwit Teler, Marshall Field's, Lord & Taylor, Sears, Saks Fifth Avenue, Neiman Marcus, and I. Magnin. Restaurants: Bristol Seafood Grill, Magic Pan, Houlihan's, The French

Baker, Annie's Santa Fe. Free parking. *OPEN Mon-Fri 10am-9pm; Sat 9:30am-5:30pm; Sun noon-5pm.*

Old Orchard
Skokie Boulevard & Old Orchard's Road, east of Edens Expressway, Skokie. 673-6800. Approximately 80 shops in this outdoor mall; includes Baskin's, Marshall Field's, Chas A. Stevens, Montgomery Ward, Saks Fifth Avenue, Lord & Taylor. Restaurants: Greener Field, Houlihan's, Szechwan Pavilion, The French Baker. Free parking. *OPEN Mon-Fri 10am-9pm; Sat 9:30am-5:30pm; Sun 11am-5pm.*

Plaza del Lago
1515 Sheridan Road, Wilmette. 256-4467. Approximately 38 specialty shops comprise this beautiful outdoor shopping mall. Restaurants: Convito Italiano, Melange. Free parking. *OPEN Mon-Sat 9:30am-5:30pm. CLOSED Sun.* Restaurants *OPEN for lunch and dinner Tues-Sun.*

Randhurst Shopping Center
999 Elmhurst Road, Mt. Prospect. 259-0500. Enclosed mall with approximately 120 stores, including Carson Pirie Scott, Montgomery Ward, Wieboldt. Restaurants: Bo-James, The Reunion. Free parking. *OPEN Mon-Fri 10am-9pm; Sat 10am-5:30pm; Sun 11am-5pm.*

Stratford Square
Army Trail Road & Gary. 351-9405. More than 165 specialty shops and restaurants, plus Marshall Field's, Carson Pirie Scott, Montgomery Ward, Wieboldt, Main Street. Restaurants: Houlihan's, Carlos Sweeney's, Sbarro Ristorante, Taverna. Enclosed mall. *OPEN Mon-Fri 10am-9pm; Sat 9:30am-5:30pm; Sun 11am-5pm.*

Woodfield Shopping Center
Golf Road at Route 53, Schaumburg. 882-0220. World's largest multilevel enclosed shopping mall—approximately 230 stores, including Marshall Field's, Lord & Taylor, J. C. Penney, Sears. Restaurants: Lucky's Diner, John's Garage. Free parking. *OPEN Mon-Fri 10am-9pm; Sat 9:30am-5:30pm; Sun 11am-5pm.*

Yorktown Shopping Center
Butterfield Road & Highland, Lombard. 629-7330. Approximately 130 stores make up this enclosed mall, including Carson Pirie Scott, J. C. Penney, Chas A. Stevens, Montgomery Ward, Wieboldt. Restaurant: Sbarro's. Free parking. *OPEN Mon-Fri 10am-9pm; Sat 10am-5:30pm; Sun noon-5pm.*

WOMEN'S CLOTHES

Contemporary

Ann Taylor
103 East Oak. 943-5411. And Old Orchard and Northbrook Court. Wonderful selection of contemporary clothes and footwear on two levels. Well stocked, well organized. AE, MC, V, Ann Taylor charge. *OPEN Mon-Sat.*

Apropos
3315 North Broadway. 528-2130. Fashionable in any season with their moderate to expensive, colorful contemporary separates. Lovely accessories—up to and including socks—for a total look. AE, MC, V. *OPEN 7 days.*

Arthur's
25 West Division. 787-2292. Fine selection of women's imported fashions. Good end-of-season sales. AE, MC, V. *OPEN Mon-Sat.*

August Max
Water Tower Place, 835 North Michigan, 6th level. 266-6416. Moderately priced contemporary looks for the contemporary woman. Features "bi-coastal" fashions. AE, MC. V. *OPEN 7 days.*

Avenue 540
540 North Michigan. 321-9540. Designer imports and moderately priced fashions for ladies of uncommon taste. Fashion-savvy owner. AE, DC, MC. V. *OPEN Mon-Sat.*

Banana Republic
Water Tower Place, 835 North Michigan, 4th level. 642-7667. These "safari and travel clothes" were available for years only through their catalog—yes, even before *Out of Africa,* the movie. The amusing and inviting environment is stocked to the rafters with natural fiber, earth-toned active and casualwear at moderate to high prices. Clothes, leather and canvas belts, bags, shoes, and boots for men and women. AE, DC, MC, V. *OPEN 7 days.*

Benetton
Water Tower Place, 835 North Michigan, 5th level; 337-3901. And 121 East Oak; 944-0434. Also Century Mall, 2828 North Clark, 972-7111; 608 North Michigan, 944-2904; 25 East Washington, 855-0775; and 2008 North Halsted, 871-4719. Extremely successful mass merchandiser of stylish Italian knit sportswear separates. Colorful, youthful, and affordable. AE, MC. V. *OPEN 7 days.*

Blake
2448 North Lincoln. 477-3364. Specializing in fashion-forward clothing. Katherine Hamnett, John Galliano, Go Silk (for men and women), Masanori, Satoh. All in a stark setting. AE, MC, V. *OPEN 7 days.*

Bottega
106 East Oak. 944-0981. The specialty is eveningwear. Dorothee Bis, Sophie Sitborn, Kbuki. In-house designing by Kontessa. Fabulous accessories—jewelry and hats too. AE, MC, V. *OPEN Mon-Sat.*

Caché
Water Tower Place, 835 North Michigan, 6th level; 480-9790. And Northbrook Court. Expensive designer fashions and accessories; sportswear; hats. AE, CB, DC, MC. V. *OPEN 7 days.*

Dégagé
2246 North Clark. 935-7737. A colorful, imaginative approach to dressing. Specializes in contemporary sportswear and clothes by newly discovered designers. Nice accessories too. AE, MC, V. *OPEN 7 days.*

Giovanni
Drake Hotel, 140 East Walton. 787-6500. Luxurious designer collections and *au courant* sportswear. Unique accessories. AE, CB, DC, MC, V. *OPEN Mon-Sat.*

Indulgence
2625 North Clark. 281-9009. Medium to high fashion; specialty is party clothing. Colorful, kicky accessories and gift items. Custom-made hats. AE, MC, V. *OPEN 7 days.*

Jacher
2419 North Clark. 327-7711. Local and renowned designers in women's fashions. Lovely environment. Accessories too. AE, DC, MC, V. *OPEN 7 days.*

Jean Charles
30 East Oak Street. 787-3535. Pricey European and Japanese designs for men and women— Adolfo, Therry Mugler. Flatware, china, and crystal by Castelbajac. Shoes via France and Italy. AE, CB, DC, MC, V. *OPEN 7 days.*

Kane's
1325 North State Parkway. 787-0700. *Au courant* designer fashions for women. Bags, belts, wallets, scarves, and other accessories. AE, MC, V. *OPEN Mon-Sat.*

Laura Ashley
Water Tower Place, 835 North Michigan, 6th level; 951-8004. And Oakbrook Center and Northbrook Court. Clothing for the young—and young at heart—woman. Like floral bouquets straight from the English countryside. Also, fabric, linens, china, wallpaper, and fragrances. AE, MC, V. *OPEN 7 days.*

Luv Boutique
2106-10 North Clark. 929-2330. Suits; sportswear. Day and night wear. Fun accessories. AE, MC, V. *OPEN 7 days.*

My Sister's Circus/Isis
38 East Oak. 664-7074. Sportswear and accessories in unusual designs by unusual designers, including one-size fits all California designs. Expensive. AE, MC, V. *OPEN 7 days.*

The New Source
1509 East Hyde Park Boulevard. 684-0888. Contemporary clothing and shoes. Some designer wear; accessories too. AE, MC, V. *OPEN 7 days.*

Nonpareil
2300 North Clark. 477-2933. Easy-to-wear clothes. Colorful whatnots. Creative jewelry and accessories; gifts too. AE, MC, V. *OPEN 7 days.*

North Beach Leather
Water Tower Place, 835 North Michigan, 3rd level. 280-9292. *Very* special leather fashions for women and men. Leather bathing suits and more. From the totally outrageous to the subdued. AE, CB, MC, V. *OPEN 7 days.*

Pompian
57 East Oak. 337-6604. Fine European sportswear; dresses, suits, and coats for women, on two levels. Accessories too. AE, CB, DC, MC, V. *OPEN Mon-Sat.*

Port of Entry
2032 North Halsted. 348-4550. Distinctive, one-of-a-kind fashions, mainly for women. Hand-knits,

crocheted, and woven. Jewelry and accessories, most of which are handmade. AE, MC, V. *OPEN Mon-Sun.*

Presence
2501 North Clark. 248-1761. Vibrant "now" fashions and accessories at affordable prices. AE, MC, V. *OPEN 7 days.*

Ringolevio
301 West Superior; 751-1850. And 2001 North Halsted; 642-4999. Spirited shop for upscale, contemporary sportswear for men and women. Paul Smith, Joan Vass, Axis, Bettina Riedell. Tony Barone makeup. Shoes, gifts, travel, desk, and more. AE, MC, V. *OPEN 7 days.*

Rodier Paris
Water Tower Place, 835 North Michigan, 3rd level; 337-0178. And Northbrook Court. Chic French sportswear classics in natural fabrics and a coordinated color range. AE, MC, V. *OPEN 7 days.*

Stanley Korshak
940 North Michigan; 280-0520. And Northbrook Court; 564-1650. Where Chicago's best-dressed clothes horses go to get outfitted. The best from the best American and European designers. Wonderful "now" accessories. In addition, this very special specialty store stocks handmade tableware, cosmetics, hosiery, dancewear, home accessories, and more! Plus, *terrific* windows. AE, MC, V. *OPEN Mon-Sat.*

Sugar Magnolia
110 East Oak; 944-0885. And 2130 North Halsted; 525-9188. Women's, men's, and children's fun and forward fashion clothing. American quilts; handmade clothing. Lots and lots of colorful accessories. AE, MC, V. *OPEN 7 days.*

Toshiro
3309 North Clark. 248-1487. Traditional woven Japanese clothing. Also vintage items from late 19th and 20th centuries all beautifully restored. AE, MC, V. *OPEN Wed-Sun.*

Traffick
3313 North Broadway. 549-1502. Casual unisex clothing for men and women made of natural fibers only. Gift items too. AE, MC, V. *OPEN 7 days.*

Ultimo
114 East Oak. 787-0906. Aptly named for the ultimate in one-stop deluxe shopping. *Très exclusive.* For men: Armani, Valentino, Yohji Yamamoto, Zegna. For women (sizes 4-12 only): Armani, OMO Kamali, Missoni, Rykiel, Zoran. Walter Steiger, Class A shoes. Antique accessories. Men's department complete with fireplace. Don't miss it. AE, CB, DC, MC, V. *OPEN Mon-Sat.*

Conservative

Careers
Marshall Field's, 111 North State, 6th floor. 781-3088. Professional wardrobe consultant for the busy career woman. Alterations. Corporate gift service too. AE, MC, V, Field's charge. *OPEN Mon-Sat.*

Jackie Renwick
65 East Oak. 266-8269. Geared toward the business person. Suits, dresses by local Chicago designers. Accessories, briefcases, attachés. Men's and women's wear. AE, MC, V. *OPEN Mon-Sat.*

Jaeger
Water Tower Place, 835 North Michigan, 3rd level. 642-6665. The conservative classics in beautiful fabrics for women. Accessories too. AE, DC, MC, V. *OPEN 7 days.*

Robert Vance, Ltd.
Water Tower Place, 835 North Michigan, 3rd level. 440-0993 (men); 440-1182 (women). Traditional and classic clothing for men and women. Ralph Lauren is featured. AE, MC, V. *OPEN 7 days.*

Discount

(*See also* SHOPPING, Specialty Shops & Services: Discount Merchandise.)
Handmoor
70 East Randolph; 726-5600. Also 495 Lake Cook Plaza, Deerfield; 564-8150. A Chicago must for smart shoppers. Designer fashions at 20-30% off (Calvin Klein, Harve Bernard among others). Sportswear, furs, dresswear, fashionable accessories, including Gucci watches. Patience—fortitude. AE, MC, V. *OPEN 7 days.*

Loehmann's
7118 Golf Road, Morton Grove; 966-1350. And Downers Grove and Matteson. In a class by itself, the Champ of the discount designer clothing business. Everything a bargain hunter could want and put up with: outrageously low prices (30-50% off), uneven selections, communal dressing room, and just a hint of the designer label still attached. *OPEN 7 days.*

Royal Knitting Mills Factory Outlet Store
2007 South California. 247-6300. Discounts 50-70% off men's, women's, and children's clothes; wool, acrylic, and cotton sweaters. Odds and irregulars. *OPEN Mon-Fri.*

Maternity

Dan Howard's Maternity
710 West Jackson Boulevard, 7th floor; 263-6700. And in the suburbs. Dan Howard Maternity fashions—irregulars and samples—sizes 4-26. Maternity bathing suits and lingerie at 20-50% off retail. AE, MC, V. *OPEN Mon-Sat.*

Lady Madonna
Water Tower Place, 835 North Michigan, 6th level; 266-2420. And 211 West Wacker; 372-6667. Also Oakbrook, Orland Park, and Wilmette. The pioneer in the well-dressed-though-pregnant idea. Everything everyone else wears but for the mother-to-be. AE, MC, V. *OPEN 7 days.*

Lady Madonna Outlet
Off Center Mall, 300 West Grand at Franklin. 329-0771. Their designer maternity fashions at 20-50% off regular retail. AE, MC, V. *OPEN 7 days.*

Mother's Work
Garland Court, 50 East Washington, 2nd floor. 332-0022. For fashionable clothing throughout your pregnancy. Business suits, dresses, lingerie, bathing suits, sportswear, exercise clothes. Catalog available. AE, MC, V. *OPEN 7 days.*

Recreations
Chestnut Street Galleria, 17 East Chestnut, 2nd floor. 664-1840. Very pretty, modestly priced maternity clothes. Career daytime suits to evening dresses. Maternity pantyhose and leotards. Mail order. AE, MC, V. *OPEN 7 days.*

Resale

(*See also* SHOPPING, Women's Clothes: Vintage.)
Entre-nous
21 East Delaware. 337-2919. Just between thee and me and any other smart shopper, these are previously owned designer fashions. Sizes 6-16. *OPEN Mon-Sat.*

Fashion Exchange
67 East Oak. 664-1657. They resell clothing, shoes, handbags, and accessories for the best-dressed women in Chicago. *OPEN Tues-Sat.*

Ultimately Yours
2941 North Broadway. 975-1581. Pragmatic snob appeal for fashionable though budget-conscious women and men. European and American designer fashions. Missoni, Albert Nippon, Calvin Klein, Ralph Lauren, Giorgio Armani; Gucci bags and Maude Frizon shoes; all previously, though in most cases gently, worn. AE, MC, V. *OPEN Thurs-Mon.*

Sportswear

(*See also* SHOPPING, Men's Clothes: Surplus/Sportswear, *and* Specialty Shops & Services: Sporting Goods.)
A Capriccio
47 East Oak. 787-9824. Via California and Europe—unusual and colorful activewear and dancewear for women. Ballet shoes. Sports and cruisewear too. Bathing suits stocked year-round. MC, V. *OPEN Mon-Sat.*

The Swinging Set
3223 Lake Avenue, Wilmette. 251-2255. Samples, overruns, and discontinued tennis and golf wear at 40-60% off retail. MC, V. *OPEN 7 days.*

Tennis Lady/Tennis Man
Water Tower Place, 835 North Michigan, 3rd level. 649-1110. Be well dressed on the court or while running. AE, MC, V. *OPEN 7 days.*

Unusual Sizes

Geneva Convention
1128 West Armitage. 975-6280. Good buys on sample women's separates. MC, V. *OPEN Mon-Sat. CLOSED Tues.*

Ladies at Large
3730 West Dempster, Skokie. 677-7447. Their

"ultimate"-woman sizes, 16½-26½, for stylish though "special"-sized. MC, V. *OPEN 7 days.*

Lane Bryant
9 North Wabash; 621-8700. And Oakbrook, Old Orchard, and Woodfield Mall. Sizes 14-28. Designer sportswear and lingerie too. Accessories, millinery. Shoe department for sizes 6-12 wide and 10-13 narrow (downtown only). AE, MC, V, Lane Bryant charge. *OPEN Mon-Sat.*

Rhoda's
148 Roosevelt Road, Villa Park. 832-8321. Large-size (14½-46) coats, suits, dresses, and sportswear. MC, V. *OPEN Mon-Sat.*

Tall Girls Shop
16 North Wabash. 782-9867. Businesswear, sportswear, dresses, and accessories for 5'8" and taller. MC, V. *OPEN Mon-Sat.*

Woman's World Shops
Orland Square; 349-1993. And Fox Valley; 851-7575. Also Vernon Hill, 362-0516; Southlake Mall, (1-219) 738-9025; The Brickyard, 889-5665; Yorktown Mall, 627-2030; Harlem-Irving Plaza, 452-9100. Clothing for women sizes 14½-24½. Some designer fashions. AE, MC, V. *OPEN 7 days.*

Vintage

(*See also* SHOPPING, Women's Clothes: Resale.)

Blair House
912 West Armitage. 528-5145. One of Chicago's earliest vintage shops (dating back to Sgt. Pepper look). Now the intimately cluttered shop stocks some lovely 30s and 40s dresses, nightwear, and smashing accessories. Savvy sophisticated owners. AE only. *OPEN 7 days.*

Chicago's Recycle Shop
5308 North Clark. 878-8525. For the intrepid. This one is referred to by the vintage-clothes cognoscenti as "the thrift shop in Andersonville with the great stuff in the basement." You must ask to go down, and bring your patience. There's more than enough to choose from. Tip: Look at the stuff in the daylight before you purchase. *OPEN Mon-Sat and the first Sun in every month.*

Clark Street Waltz
2360 North Lincoln. 472-5559. Beautiful vintage finds: dresses, 40s blouses, Victorian whites, silk kimonos. In addition, contemporary accessories, including hats, handcrafted silver jewelry, and 40s and 50s costume baubles. AE, MC, V. *OPEN Tues-Sat.*

Consuelo's
3931 North Ashland. 935-7943. In the Lake View area, a vintage setting for a nice selection of men's and women's vintage clothing from the 1890s to 1960s, all in wonderful condition. Lingerie and accessories too. No credit cards. *OPEN Wed-Sat 1-6pm; Sun 3-6pm.*

Flashy Trash
3521 North Halsted. 327-6900. Vintage clothes, 1860-1960s, much of it never worn. For men, there is an entire room devoted to eveningwear: tuxedos, top hats, suspenders. Large selection

of day and eveningwear for women. Jewelry, Victorian to 50s costume, and an impressive selection of restored vintage watches. Seasonal finds such as Hawaiian shirts and furs. AE, MC, V. *OPEN 7 days.*

Gloria's
1007 Webster. 327-9665. Formerly Kitch. Clothes are well displayed and organized and reflect excellent taste. Twenties through 50s men's and women's wear; Hawaiian and cowboy shirts, as well as gabardine. Lovely coats and dresses, plus some *very* special pieces, beautiful vintage furs. Alligator shoes and bags. Expensive, and everything but the as-is pieces is worth it. Full-moon 20%-off sales monthly, when the store is open till midnight and wine is served. (Get on the mailing list.) AE, MC, V. *OPEN 7 days.*

Kismet
2934 North Lincoln. 528-4497. Vintage clothing and accessories in a casbah setting. *OPEN Mon-Sat (loosely speaking).*

Modalisque
616 West Adams. 559-0107. Unusual shop off the beaten path showcases vintage fashions and accessories of the 20s, 30s, 40s, and 50s. Chicago fashions and some high-quality imports as well. No credit cards. *OPEN Tues-Sat.*

Silver Moon
3337 North Halsted. 883-0222. Owner Tari Costan obviously loves beautiful old things, and the clothing in her shop reflects the elegance of times past: Victorian and Edwardian pieces; Chinese shawls; 30s, 40s, and early 50s evening dresses as well as day dresses. Hats too. Men's dress tails, tuxedoes, white jackets, tuxedo shirts, and smoking jackets. All at good prices, considering the fabrics and workmanship. Some art deco and art noveau costume jewelry. AE, MC, V. *OPEN 7 days.*

WOMEN'S ACCESSORIES

Furs

Chicago Fur Outlet
7777 West Diversey. 348-3877. Discounts on new and used furs. Full service furrier. AE, MC, V. *OPEN 7 days.*

Evans
36 South State. 855-2000. And in the suburbs too. The nation's largest furrier, it's their specialty. Cloth, fur, and raincoats—fur-lined or -trimmed. Good values on accessories too. AE, CB, DC, MC, V. *OPEN Mon-Sat.*

Keim Furs, Inc.
1820 Foster. 561-8680. All coats are made on the premises in this longtime family operation. AE, MC, V. *OPEN Mon-Sat.*

Mysels Furs
108 North State, 10th floor. 372-9513. All new furs, discounted to the public. Five-year guarantees. AE, CB, DC, MC, V. *OPEN Mon-Sat; Oct-Jan, Sun too.*

Rosenthal Furs, Inc.
940 North Michigan, 3rd floor. 943-1365. Long-time family-owned business, well known for excellence. Designer furs, including Geoffrey Beene, Yves St. Laurent, Oscar de la Renta, and Ralph Lauren—for men and women. Coats and jackets as well as fur-lined, reversibles, and petites. AE, MC, V. *OPEN Mon-Sat.*

Thorpe Furs
Water Tower Place, 835 North Michigan, 6th level; 337-1750. And Northbrook Court. Furriers since 1890—fashionable furs for the whole family. Designer, too. Accessories also. AE, CB, DC, MC, V. *OPEN 7 days.*

Carol & Irwin Ware Fur Collection
I. Magnin & Co., 830 North Michigan. 337-4841. Exclusive designer furs in one of the country's largest luxury-fur collections. AE, CB, DC, MC, V, I. Magnin charge. *OPEN 7 days.*

—Resale Furs

Resale Fur Salon
108 North State, 9th floor. 346-3483. This kind of recycling really makes sense to the animals and you. Excellent-condition previously owned furs, many from the best salons. Designer furs too. AE, CB, DC, MC, V. *OPEN Mon-Sat; Oct-Jan, Sun too.*

Handbags

Bottega Veneta
107 East Oak. 664-3220. When your own initials are enough. Woven leather shoes and bags; luggage; sweaters and silk scarves, too. AE, MC, V. *OPEN 7 days.*

Chicago Trunk & Leather Works, Inc.
12 South Wabash. 372-0849. One of the best selections in Chicago of handbags (Pierre Cardin, Anne Klein, Whiting & Davis, Coach), also briefcases and luggage. AE, CB, DC, MC, V. *OPEN Mon-Sat.*

The Factory Handbag Store
1036 West Van Buren. 421-4589. Manufacturer to you. Factory overruns at wholesale prices: handbags, belts, wallets, leather goods, luggage. Special Sunday sale four times a year. MC, V. *OPEN Mon-Fri.*

Hermès of Paris
At Bonwit Teller, John Hancock Center, 875 North Michigan. 787-8175. The elegantly handsome, high-status, high-quality leather bags, wallets, and accessories. Ready-to-wear gifts; equestrian wear. AE, CB, MC, V, Bonwit charge. *OPEN Mon-Sat.*

Koro Bags
5 North Wabash, Suite 1015. 332-4169. Bags and wallets, including designer, as well as attaché cases, at this on-premises bag manufacturer, for 20% off retail. Fine custom work too. *OPEN Mon-Sat. CLOSED Sat in summer.*

Hats

All of the larger stores and most boutiques have a good selection of seasonal hats.

Lingerie

Enchanté
Water Tower Place, 835 North Michigan, 4th level. 951-7290. Feminine, mainly French underthings. Designers such as Sanchez, Papillon. AE, CB, DC, MC, V. *OPEN 7 days.*

Forget Me Nots
553 West Belmont. 871-1505. An elegant selection of lingerie and loungewear. MC, V. *OPEN 7 days.*

Frederick's of Hollywood
Woodfield Shopping Mall, Schaumburg; 882-4061. And Golf Mill Shopping Mall; 299-7686. Famed purveyor of risqué lingerie. The accoutrements of seduction. AE, CB, MC, V. *OPEN 7 days.*

Leo's Advance Theatrical Company
1900 North Narragansett. 889-7700. Danskin leotards and tights that have been discontinued, at 50% off; not all sizes and colors. Regular stock of Leo's own brand, Danskin and Freed of London for basic dance wear. MC, V. *OPEN Mon-Fri; Sat in fall.*

Lorraine Lingerie Outlet Store
4220 West Belmont. 283-3000. Aisles and aisles of nightgowns, p.j.s, slips, robes, panties (no bras or girdles), long johns, at straight-from-the-factory-to-you prices. *OPEN Mon-Sat.*

Schwartz's Intimate Apparel
945 North Rush. 787-2976. Impressive selection of undergarments in this friendly shop. Fine swimwear collection year-round from bikinis to hard-to-fit sizes. AE, MC, V. *OPEN Mon-Sat.*

Underthings
804 West Webster. 472-9291. Pretty, feminine lingerie. Designers such as Dior, Stillman, Sanchez. Special designer wear during holidays. Some loungewear. MC, V. *OPEN Mon-Sat.*

Whispers
2657 North Clark; 327-4422. And 528 Dempster, Evanston; 491-0011. Delicately sensuous intimate apparel. AE, MC, V. *OPEN Mon-Sat.*

Shoes

(See also SHOPPING, Men's Clothes: Shoes & Boots.)

Bally of Switzerland
919 North Michigan. 787-8110. The famed, finely crafted imports for men and women. AE, CB, DC, MC, V. *OPEN 7 days.*

Chandler's Shoe Store
27 North State. 263-8157. Reasonably priced shoes in fashionable styles. Handbags and hosiery too. Good annual sales January and December. AE, MC, V. *OPEN Mon-Sat.*

Charles Jourdan
Water Tower Place, 835 North Michigan, 3rd level. 280-8133. *The* French trend-setter in sensuous footwear. Now introducing a complete line of ready-to-wear clothes, also perfume, accessories, and jewelry. Men's shoes and accessories too. AE, CB, DC, MC, V. *OPEN 7 days.*

Chernin's
606 West Roosevelt Road; 939-4080. And Morton Grove, Downers Grove, Buffalo Grove, and Matteson. One of those places everyone in Chicago knows about. Famous brands, some designer styles, and imports at 30-60% off. Sales too. Shoes and boots: Nichols, Jazz, 9 West, Anne Klein, Florsheim, Garolini, Caressa. Sizes 5-11 AAA-EE. Best of women's handbags. Best athletic wear for men, women, and children. AE, MC, V. *OPEN 7 days.*

Florsheim Thayer MacNeil
727 North Michigan; 642-4762. And Water Tower Place, 845 North Michigan, 5th level; 944-6990. Also 41 North Wabash Avenue; 372-6684.* Fashionable footwear: Jacques Cohen, Garolini, Bass, and Frye. All at moderate prices. AE, CB, DC, MC, V. *OPEN 7 days. *OPEN Mon-Sat.*

The Four Cohns Shoes
2603 West Devon. 764-2311. Specializes in only wide-width and large-size shoes for women: 5-11, C, D, E, through EEE. Full line of men's shoes. MC, V. *OPEN Mon-Sat.*

Joseph Salon Shoes
679 North Michigan; 944-1111. And 50 East Randolph; 332-2772.* Also Oakbrook, Northbrook, and Old Orchard. Steiger, Pfister, Frizon, Bally, Amalfi, Jourdan, Martinique, Geller, Pancaldi, Anne Klein, Beene Bag, Casadei, Barefoot Originals. Magli, etc., etc., etc. With unique apparel, designer clothing, accessories, furs too. AE, MC, V. *OPEN 7 days. *OPEN Mon-Sat.*

Little Max's Shoes
1536 West Chicago. 421-8435. Wide-calf boots the specialty: medium: 10½-14; 5-13, wide; 5-12, extra wide. Will custom-tailor what you already have. Extra-wide and large shoes for tall women. AE, MC, V. *OPEN Mon-Sat.*

Lori's Discount Designer Shoes
808 West Armitage. 281-5655. Good source for designer and better women's shoes, boots, and accessories at 10-50% off retail. Sizes 5½-10. AE, MC, V. *OPEN 7 days.*

Niermann's
17 North State, 12th floor. 346-9797. Hard-to-find shoe types for tall girls: 5-12 EE; 5-13 D; 9½-14 AAA-C; 6-13 AAAAA-AAAA. AE, MC, V. *OPEN Mon-Sat.*

Parkway Shipper Box
2754 North Clark. 248-2235. Moderately priced shoes and boots. Frye, Bass, Capezio, Bandolino, Zodiac. AE, MC, V. *OPEN 7 days.*

Smyth Bros. Shoe Parlor
33 East Oak; 664-9508. And Water Tower Place, 835 North Michigan, 6th level; 642-7798. A wide variety of styles and prices. Emphasis on fine European imports: Jacques Cohen, Charles Jourdan, Anne Klein, Nickels, Joan & David, Garolini, Adriano Fosi. Wonderful windows. AE, MC, V. *OPEN 7 days.*

Take a Walk
2112 North Clark. 528-8510. These shoes are meant for walking. Comfort first. Rockport, Timberland, Bass. Books and magazines on walking. AE, MC, V. *OPEN 7 days.*

This Little Piggy
Water Tower Place, 845 North Michigan, 5th level. 943-7449. Stylish footwear for men, women, and children. Evan Picone, Le-Roi, Ralph Lauren. AE, MC, V. *OPEN 7 days.*

MEN'S CLOTHES

Contemporary

(*See also* SHOPPING, Women's Clothes: Contemporary and Vintage.)

ACA Joe
622 North Michigan; 337-0280. 2740 North Clark; 248-8802. And Woodfield Mall. Pre-washed, colorful, and casual 100% natural fiber sportswear for men and women. AE, CB, DC, MC, V. *OPEN 7 days.*

Bad Boys
3311 North Broadway. 549-7701. Contemporary sportswear and accessories by Henry Grethel, Generra, Calvin Klein, Union Bay, Merona. Silkscreened tees by Bruce Weber. AE, CB, DC, MC, V. *OPEN 7 days.*

Baskin Clothing Co.
137 South State: 346-3363. And Water Tower Place, Northbrook, Oakbrook, Old Orchard, Woodfield, and others. Fine specialty store on five floors. For men: contemporary and classic; Hart Schaffner & Marx, Hickey-Freeman, Christian Dior. Women's clothes too. Emphasis on personal service. AE, MC, V, Baskin charge. *OPEN Mon-Sat.*

Bigsby & Kruthers
Water Tower Place, 835 North Michigan, 7th level; 944-6955. And 1750 North Clark; 440-1750. Also La Salle & Madison, 236-6633; and Woodfield Mall. Traditional and international. Everything man could want in one spot: suits, shirts, trousers, ties, and shoes by, among others, Giorgio Armani, Hickey Freeman, Mani by Giorgio Armani, Kilgour French and Stanbury, Valentino. AE, DC, MC, V. *OPEN 7 days.*

Brittany, LTD.
999 North Michigan; 642-6550. And 29 South La Salle; 372-5985.* Also Northbrook Court. Contemporary and classic men's wear. Good tie selection at North Michigan. Norman Hilton, Southwick, Burberry, Alan Paine. AE, CB, DC, MC, V. *OPEN 7 days. *OPEN Mon-Fri.*

Brooks Brothers
74 East Madison; 263-0100. And Northbrook Court. The consummate classic men's store. Younger men have the choice of a slightly wider lapel. Women's wear too: shirts, sweaters, blazers, slacks, and coats. Moderate to expensive. AE, Brooks charge. *OPEN Mon-Sat.*

Burberry's of London
633 North Michigan. 787-2500. The famed plaid-lined trench coats (since World War I) plus their distinctive English country-weekend look for both men and women. AE, MC, V. *OPEN 7 days.*

Capper & Capper
1 North Wabash. 236-3800. Men's specialty shop on the conservative side. Countess Mara ties, Church of England shoes, custom-tailored Walter Morton suits. AE, MC, V. *OPEN Mon-Sat.*

Davis for Men
1547 North Wells. 266-9599. *Terrific* source for men's sportswear and suits: Claude Montana, Reporter, Baumler, Shamask, Della Spiga, Chester Barrie, Missoni, Pancaldi, Kansai, Yamamoto, Zanella. Custom-made shirts and suits. AE, CB, DC, MC, V. *OPEN 7 days.*

Dei Giovani
2421 North Clark. 549-4116. And Elmwood Park. High-fashion European clothes for men. AE, MC, V. *OPEN 7 days.*

In Rare Form
814 North Franklin. 944-0069. In River North, better European and American hand-knit sweaters (17 different styles). Forward-looking designer pants, shirts, leather jackets. Next-day alterations; free delivery. Champagne served on weekends. AE, MC, V. *OPEN Tues-Sun.*

Intrinsic
440 North Wells. 644-6212. Expensive forward fashions for men featuring such names as Versace, Montana, and Mario Valentino. Fine fabrics abound—much leather and silk. Flashy accessories and jewelry draw such women as Oprah Winfrey. AE, MC, V. *OPEN 7 days.*

Irv's Men's Clothing
2841 North Laramie; 286-7293. And Prospect Heights. Racks upon racks of men's suits, jackets, pants, shirts, sweaters. All first quality (no damages or irregulars). Current season designer wear—Pierre Cardin, Geoffrey Beene, Oscar de la Renta. Accessories; ties; shoe department. Women's jeans. All at 35-50% off retail. MC, V. *OPEN Mon & Wed-Sun. CLOSED Tues.*

Jaeger International
Water Tower Place, 835 North Michigan, 3rd level; 642-6665. And Northbrook Court. Superb line of the famed English tailored classics as well as sportswear. Beautifully made. AE, MC, V. *OPEN 7 days.*

Karoll's
32 North State; 263-0600. And the suburbs. Fine labels of distinction for men. Accessories too. AE, MC, V, Karoll's charge. *OPEN Mon-Sat.*

Polo by Ralph Lauren
One Magnificent Mile, 960 North Michigan. 280-1655. What Ralph calls the perfect environment for his Classic American collections for men, women, boys, and girls. He's right! AE, MC, V. *OPEN Mon-Sat.*

Russo
2209 North Halsted. 348-8588. Town house setting furnished in 50s collectibles for European designer clothing and accessories for men and women. Unusual, sophisticated, and expensive. (Shoes for men only.) AE, MC, V. *OPEN 7 days.*

Stuart Chicago
102 East Oak. 266-9881. Men's businesswear, casual sportswear, accessories, and shoes. Missoni, Cerruti, Zanella. Free alterations. AE, DC, MC, V. *OPEN 7 days.*

Ultimo Ltd
114 East Oak. 787-0906. Luxurious setting and selections. For men and women. AE, CB, DC, MC, V. *OPEN Mon-Sat.*

Versace
101 East Oak. 337-1111. Elegant bi-level shop for Italian designer, Gianni Versace's complete line of clothing and accessories for men and women. AE, MC, V. *OPEN Mon-Sat.*

Formal Wear

Buy-a-Tux
545 West Roosevelt Road. 243-5465. Why rent? New and used tuxedos (over 20,000 in 75 colors!) for sale. Great if you're contemplating marrying often or joining a band. AE, MC, V. *OPEN 7 days.*

Gingiss Formalwear Center
185 North Wabash. 263-7071. Tuxedos for rent or sale from the largest selection in Chicago. Traditional and designer names such as After Six, Pierre Cardin, Adolfo, YSL, Lord West, and Bill Blass. AE, CB, DC, MC, V. *OPEN Mon-Sat.*

Seno Formalwear
106 East Oak; 280-0800. And 6 East Randolph; 782-1115. Sale and rental formal wear. Same-day service. Givenchy, Adolfo, Pierre Cardin, Bill Blass, After Six, and Lord West. AE, CB, MC, V. *OPEN Mon-Sat.*

Shirts

Custom Shop
Water Tower Place, 835 North Michigan, 3rd level; 943-0444. And 38 South Michigan; 263-3816.* Also 8 La Salle, 372-1952**; and Northbrook Court and Oakbrook Center. Custom made-to-measure shirts at no extra charge (prices based on the cutting of four). Wide choice of fabrics (including imported) and styles. For women as well. Six- to 10-week delivery. AE, DC, MC, V. *OPEN 7 days. *OPEN Mon-Sat. **OPEN Mon-Fri.*

Riddle McIntyre
175 North Franklin. 782-3317. Custom shirts. A fitting is required. Four-week delivery. Extensive selection in 100% imported cottons. Pajamas and shorts too. Four-shirt minimum order. AE only. *ONLY Mon-Sat.*

Vart Tailors
604 Davis Avenue, Evanston. 475-0202. Made to measure. Work done on the premises. Large selection of poly-cottons and 100% cottons. Two-shirt minimum order. MC, V. *OPEN 7 days.*

Shoes & Boots

(*See also* SHOPPING, Women's Accessories: Shoes.)

Brass Boot Shoes
55 East Oak. 266-2731. Imported limited editions for men and women. Artioli and Moreschi for men; Casadei for women. Nocona Western boots. AE, CB, DC, MC, V. OPEN Mon-Sat (Occasional Sun).

Chernin's
606 West Roosevelt; 922-4545. And Morton Grove, Downers Grove, Buffalo Grove, and Matteson. A Chicago institution. Best athletic shoes for men, women, and children. Shoe fashion for less. Bally, Stacy Adams, Allen Edmonds, Timberland, Rockport, Bruno Magli. Discounted 30-60%. Sizes 6-15 AA-EEE. Socks, too. Bring the family, women's and children's too. AE, MC, V. OPEN 7 days.

Chicago Footwear, Inc.
654 West Diversey. 929-5060. Distinguished men's and women's footwear with a European flair. AE, CB, DC, MC, V. OPEN 7 days.

Chicago Shoe Outlet
4422 West Belmont. 736-1144. Men's and women's dress, sport, and work shoes; boots. MC, V. OPEN Mon-Sat.

Surplus/Sportswear

(See also SHOPPING, Specialty Shops & Services: Sporting Goods.)
Eddie Bauer
123 North Wabash; 263-6005. And Water Tower Place, Oakbrook Mall, and Old Orchard Mall. Pioneer in high-quality down-insulated garments. Men's and women's woolen gear too. Outdoor clothing and equipment. Backpacking and skiing outfitters. Knowledgeable source. AE, MC, V. OPEN 7 days.

Rowbottoms & Willoughby, Ltd.
72 West Hubbard. 329-0999. Famed for their classic outerwear, such as quail hunting coats, A-2 horsehide flight jackets designed for the Army Air Corps in 1931, as well as the safari jackets Willis & Geiger made for Hemingway. All-weather clothes and gear. Now, too, stylish cottons for women in summer, woolens in winter. AE, MC, V. OPEN Mon-Sat.

Uncle Dan's
2440 North Lincoln. 477-1918 or -1919. Army-Navy surplus store. Camping equipment is a standout. War memorabilia bought and sold. You can even rent an army uniform for your M*A*S*H party. They'll ship anywhere. MC, V. OPEN 7 days.

Unusual Sizes

Bigsby & Kruthers
1750 North Clark; 440-1750. And Water Tower Place, 835 North Michigan, 7th level; 944-6955. Also La Salle & Madison, 236-6633; and Woodfield Mall. Specially proportioned suits, jackets, shirts (start with 13-inch neck, 30-inch sleeve)

and coats, for men 5'7" and under, who wear sizes 36-44. AE, CB, DC, MC, V. OPEN 7 days.
M. Hyman & Son
Water Tower Place, 835 North Michigan, 4th level. 266-0060. And Homewood, Schaumburg, and Skokie. They suit guys who are big and tall: 46-60 regular and long; extra long 38-60, double extra long to 50; portlies to 60. AE, DC, MC, V. OPEN 7 days.
Rochester Big and Tall
149 East Ohio. 644-4848. Casualwear and Hart, Schaffner & Marx. Regular to double extra long. Accessories too. AE, CB, DC, MC, V. OPEN Mon-Sat.

SPECIALTY SHOPS & SERVICES

Adult Education

The city colleges offer a variety of language, vocational, cooking, auto and home repair, arts and crafts, dance, hobbies, sports, and exercise classes. Call the following schools for information:

Citywide City College
30 East Lake. 781-9430.
Daley College
7500 South Pulaski. 735-3000.
Gordon Technical High School
3633 North California. 539-3600.
Hyde Park Academy
6220 Stony Island. 947-7180 (weekdays).
Kennedy-King College
6800 South Wentworth. 962-3200.
Loop College
30 East Lake. 781-9430.
Malcolm X College
1900 West Van Buren. 942-3000.
Olive-Harvey College
10001 South Woodlawn. 568-3700, ext 292 (ext 320 for Spanish-speaking persons).
Truman College
1145 West Wilson. 878-1700.
Wright College
3400 North Austin. 777-7900.
The Learning Exchange
2940 North Lincoln. 549-8383. Matches people who want to learn a subject with those who teach it.
Learning for Living
Central YMCA, 211 West Wacker, and other locations. 984-8151. Classes in dance, communication, language, culinary and secretarial arts, creative writing, needlework, photography, and more.
Office of Continuing Education
5835 South Kimbark. 962-1722. Classes in three convenient locations: Hyde Park campus (Sat); 410 South Michigan; and 190 South Delaware. On a quarterly basis, courses in a variety of cultural and self-enriching subjects.

Temple Sholom J.C.C./OPEN University
3480 North Lake Shore Drive. 975-8375. Non-credit college standard courses for people over 55 years of age.

Antiques & Collectibles

Good antiques shopping areas: Belmont 1600-2600 West; Lincoln 2800-2900 North; Wells 700 North; Armitage 2000 North; Webster 2200 North; Halsted 800 West; Diversey 1200 West.

(See also SHOPPING, Specialty Shops & Services: Flea Markets; Furniture: Antique & Collectible; *and* Memorabilia. For antique clothes, see SHOPPING, Women's Clothes: Vintage.)

Abe Lincoln Antiques
3827 North Lincoln. 348-2392. An overwhelming selection of antiques: furnishings, rugs, some quilts; 20,000 square feet on three floors. The top floor—chairs! Carved-oak furniture, stained glass, art glass, paintings and sculpture, brass beds, small collectibles. *OPEN Mon-Sat.*

Anita's Rags to Riches
901 Sherman Avenue, Evanston. 864-2078. A kitch collector's haven—mainly 30s and 40s jewelry, dolls, vintage clothing, collectibles. Plan to spend time and bring your patience. MC, V. *OPEN Mon-Sat.*

Another Time, Another Place Antiques
1243 Chicago Avenue, Evanston. 866-7170. Quilts, oak and mahogany furniture, china. Antique kitchen appliances, picture frames, antique jewelry. *OPEN Tues-Sat.*

Antiques of Evanston
912 Chicago Avenue, Evanston. 869-3555. Wide range of collectibles, jewelry, glassware, and furniture—1700s to 1950s. MC, V. *OPEN Tues-Sat.*

Aunt Edie's Glass
3339 North Halsted. 528-1617. Specializes in antique stemware. Large stock of glass of all periods. Replacement service. *OPEN Wed-Sun.*

The Bell Jar Antiques
2117 West Touhy. 973-3077. Antiques: jewelry, postcards, books (lots of cookbooks), U.S. mint stamps. *OPEN Thurs-Sat.*

Clyde's Collection
1223 West Diversey. 871-0491. Antiques, collectibles, furniture; clocks, accessories, old trunks, some fireplace mantels. *OPEN Fri-Wed.*

Eureka! Antiques & Collectibles
705 West Washington, Evanston. 869-9060. Wonderful collectibles source: advertising tins and signs, coronation memorabilia, mechanical toys, art deco accessories, sheet music, antique clocks, some furniture. Effective search service. *OPEN Tues-Sat.*

Hollywood Antiques, Too
5657 North Clark. 275-0747. Three roomfuls of knickknacks, bric-a-brac, glassware, furniture, and Fiesta ware. MC, V. *OPEN Mon-Sat; the occasional Sun.*

Indigo
2262 North Clark. 348-1418. Primarily 19th- and 20th-century objects. Lacquer boxes, vases, kimonos. AE, MC, V. *OPEN Tues-Sun.*

Josie's
3323 North Broadway. 871-3750. Art deco delights: collectibles, jewelry, sterling curios, beaded bags. AE, MC, V. *OPEN Wed-Sun.*

La Bourse
67 East Oak. 787-3925. Decorative antiques: silver, porcelain, glassware. Proceeds to Chicago Medical School. AE, MC, V. *OPEN Mon-Sat.*

Legends Antiques
7023 North Clark. 761-1576. Unique glassware and knickknacks—Fiesta, cobalt. Some furniture 1920s-50s. Yesteryear costume jewelry; clothes, mainly 50s, hats too. No credit cards. *OPEN 7 days (1pm-6pm).*

Linda & Company
2727 West Touhy. 973-6030. Antiques and collectibles. *OPEN Mon-Sat.*

O'Hara's Gallery
707 North Wells. 751-1286. Decorative antiques, stained glass, fine European and American period furnishings; Oriental art. AE, MC, V. *OPEN Mon-Sat.*

Old World Antiques, Ltd.
3752 North Broadway. 248-6302. Late 18th- to early 19th-century American and European antiques; Victorian furniture also. Art nouveau posters featuring Mucha, Robbe, Icart. A design service too. MC, V. *OPEN Wed-Sun.*

Once Upon a Time Antiques
3012 North Lincoln. 477-9308. A nice selection of interesting pieces: furniture, glass, and china; primitives, at good prices. MC, V. *OPEN Tues-Sun.*

Romano Gallery
613 North State. 337-7541. Mainly Victorian and art deco antiques, collectibles, paintings, prints, and posters. AE, MC, V. *OPEN Tues-Sat.*

Salvage One
1524 South Sangamon. 733-0098. This warehouse under the railroad tracks is a unique source for architectural artifacts, stained and leaded glass, brass doorknobs, wrought-iron gates, fireplace mantels, moldings, doors, mirrors, etc., etc., etc. No credit cards. *OPEN Tues-Sat.*

State Street Collection
609 North State. 951-1828. Depression glass, art deco kitchenware and home furnishings. It's a collector's dream of a shop, with a nice selection of vintage duds as well. MC, V. *OPEN Mon-Sat.*

Steve Starr Studios
2654 North Clark. 525-6530. *The* place for decorative deco. MC, V. *OPEN 7 days. CLOSED Sun in summer.*

Turtle Creek Country Store
850 West Armitage. 327-2630. Antique wicker furnishings heavily featured in summer in this lovely quilt- and country-accessory-filled shop. American primitive furniture too. Machine caning repairs available. Antique linens and jewelry. MC, V. *OPEN Thurs-Sun.*

Victorian House Antiques
806 West Belmont. 348-8561. Chock-full of Victoriana. No credit cards. *OPEN 7 days.*

The Wicker Witch
2146 West Belmont. 528-5550. Expensive, unique antique wicker furnishings. Oak and walnut; rugs too. V only. *OPEN Thurs-Sun; Mon-Wed by appointment only.*

Art Stores

American Academy of Art
122 South Michigan, 10th floor. 939-3883. A limited supply of pads, markers, paints, and school art supplies. The only art supply store in the Loop area open in the evening (till 8:30 pm). *OPEN Mon-Sat.*

Favor Ruhl Company
23 South Wabash. 782-5737. Since 1888. Very well stocked store for fine-art, graphic-art, and drafting supplies. Framing supplies too. MC, V. *OPEN Mon-Sat.*

The Flax Company
176 North Wabash. 346-5100. Complete line of art and drafting materials; artists' papers, picture framing, and a wonderful selection of the finest writing instruments. AE, MC, V. *OPEN Mon-Sat.*

Rich's Art Supply & Framing Shop
3838 North Cicero. 545-0271. Everything an artist needs; silk-screen supplies; some handmade paper. Custom-made picture frames too. AE, MC, V. *OPEN Mon-Sat.*

Trost Hobby Shop
3111 West 63rd. 925-1000. Artists' materials and crafts supplies: brushes, paints, canvas. MC, V. *OPEN Mon-Sat.*

Baked Goods

Ann's Bakery
2158 West Chicago Avenue. 384-5562. Ukrainian bakery for wonderful rye and black bread. Rolls and cakes also. *OPEN 7 days.*

Augusta Bakery
901 North Ashland. 486-1017. Pound cakes, plain, chocolate, marble, or iced. But the standout: cheesecake-lined coffee cake. *OPEN 7 days.*

Boudin Bakery
63 East Chicago Avenue. 329-1580. San Francisco sourdough bread, baked fresh daily. (*See also* RESTAURANTS, Soups, Salads & Sandwiches.) *OPEN 7 days.*

The Bread Shop
3400 North Halsted. 528-8108. Fifteen varieties of organic whole-grain breads, cookies, cakes, and pies. Natural pizza too. Full service deli, salad bar, quiches. *OPEN Tues-Sun.*

Charlanne's Pastry Shop
1822 West Montrose. 561-9239. Old-fashioned bakery for German, Bohemian, and Polish goodies. *OPEN Mon-Sat.*

Chicago Baking Company
1003 West Armitage. 549-5800. Toscana recipe for wonderful bread; great pizza dough. Ring loaf, raisin croissants, coffee cake, and bread sticks. *OPEN 7 days.*

Cole's Bakery
3229 West Fullerton. 486-4205. Call and order in advance for large quantities of sweets. Batches of brownies, masses of muffins. Cookies, coffee cakes, rolls too. *OPEN Sun-Fri.*

Dinkel's Bakery
3329 North Lincoln. 281-7300. Large, third-generation bakeshop. Over 50 years of sweet temptation: stollen, coffee cakes, and decorated cakes for all occasions, chocolate-chip cookies, and the strudels—almond and apple, poppy seed and walnut. Sweet rolls and great rye too. MC, V. *OPEN Mon-Sat.*

Fong's Fortune
2850 North Clark. 348-5150. Chinese bakery. Incredible almond cookies. Meat pastries and vegetable buns. *OPEN Tues-Sun.*

The French Baker
26 West Madison; 346-3534. And Old Orchard. French baguettes baked before your eyes. Croissants, French pastries. Coffee, cheeses, wines too. *OPEN Mon-Sat.*

Gladstone Park Bakery
5744 North Milwaukee. 774-4210. Whipped- or butter-cream cakes with interesting fillings like white fudge, apricot, and banana cream. Decorated while you wait. *OPEN 7 days.*

George J. Jewel Catering
1110 West Belmont. 935-6316. Cakes the likes of coconut, devil's food, and lemon, filled, no less, with zabaglione, fresh strawberries, or mint, in a shape meaningful to someone's occupation or personality. *OPEN 7 days.*

Kaufman's Bagel Bakery
4905 Dempster Street, Skokie. 677-9880. Challah; bagels—onion, cinnamon-raisin, garlic, poppy, and sesame; pumpernickel and rye bread; rolls and cakes also. *OPEN 7 days.*

Let Them Eat Cake
948 North Rush; And 66 East Washington. Also 224 West Adams; 1701 West Foster; and Skokie. 728-4040 (all locations same phone number). Only the best ingredients, "cost be damned." Your favorite pet, car, or person in cake. Specializes in wedding cakes. *OPEN Mon-Sat.*

Lotus Bakery
2501 North Lotus. 237-4477. Polish babka (Friday and Saturday), cheesecake, pastries, and coffee cakes. *OPEN Mon-Sat.*

Lutz Continental Pastries
2458 West Montrose. 478-7785. Ten out of 10 Chicagoans with a sweet tooth will say this *kleine konditorei* has the city's best, certainly the richest, baked goods. Glorious Viennese pastries. *Great* Black Forest cake! *OPEN Tues-Sun.*

Maier's Bakery & Pastry Shop
706 Main Street, Evanston. 475-6565. Savory stone-ground wheat and caraway rye bread, pecan rolls, éclairs, hot cross buns, cookies. *OPEN Mon-Sat.*

Roeser's
3216 West North. 489-6900. German bakery with

good breads, rolls, pastries, and coffee cakes. Homemade ice cream too. *OPEN Tues-Sun.*

Swiss Pastries
7016 North Western. 465-5335. Miniature pastries, cakes, tortes, strudel. *OPEN Tues-Sat.*

Vie de France
Water Tower Place, 835 North Michigan, mezzanine; 266-7633. And Northbrook Court. Fragrant fresh-baked French rolls, crusty baguettes, croissants (almond, chocolate, and plain), brioches, and pain du chocolat. From unbleached flour, with nothing artificial. Continental breakfast available. *OPEN 7 days.*

Work of Art Cakes
642 West Diversey. 528-6507. Custom-made cakes for which they require three days' notice. Cookies, homemade candies, croissants, pastries. *OPEN Wed-Mon.*

Balloons

(*See also* SHOPPING, Specialty Shops & Services: Telegrams: Unusual.)

Balloon-ee Tunes
1316 Church, Evanston. 328-1108. A 28-balloon bouquet and a singing, costumed messenger for "any" occasion. Delivery 7 days a week, 24 hours a day. AE, MC, V. *OPEN Mon-Sat.*

The Balloonery
32 Valley Road, Highland Park. 432-9005. Twenty-four large helium-filled multicolored balloons delivered anywhere in the city, 7 days a week, day or night. Nice variation on flowers—they don't require water. Also party decorations. Call to order. AE, MC, V. *OPEN Mon-Sat.*

Balloons Above Chicago
625-0190. Bouquets of buoyant balloons tied with a pretty ribbon. AE. *OPEN Mon-Sat.*

Baskets

The Basket Case
203 East Butterfield Road, Elmhurst; 530-4114. And 1736 West Algonquin, Arlington Heights; 253-0040. Great selection of baskets in this all's-well-that's-wicker store. MC, V. *OPEN 7 days.*

Pier 1 Imports
651 West Diversey; 871-1558. And Evanston, Westmont, Arlington Heights, Glenview, and Matteson. An impressive array of imported baskets. AE, MC, V. *OPEN 7 days.*

Bath, Bathrooms & Hot Tubs

Bathwares
740 North Wells. 642-9420. Elegant imported bathroom fixtures and furnishings, including the showerheads custom-crafted for the Savoy Hotel in London. Door handles, furniture pulls, accessories too. No credit cards. *OPEN Mon-Sat.*

Caswell Massey
Water Tower Place, 835 North Michigan, 7th level. 664-1752. The folks who blended cologne for the Washingtons (yes, George and Martha), Lafayette too. A mind-boggling selection of soaps,

fragrances, and oils, all in an old-fashioned apothecary setting à la the original, still in New York (since 1752). Phone and mail orders; catalog available. AE, MC, V. *OPEN 7 days.*

Crabtree & Evelyn
Water Tower Place, 835 North Michigan, 5th level; 787-0188. And Woodfield Mall. England's famed all-natural toiletries and comestibles—beautifully presented and packed. Imported jams, cookies, honey, and other edible items. AE, MC, V. *OPEN 7 days.*

Clear Water Hot Tubs
15 West Hubbard. 527-1311. Custom cedar hot tubs, fiberglass spas, indoors or out. A tester on premises, rental by the hour by appointment. AE, MC, V. *OPEN 7 days.*

Beauty Specialists

(*See also* SHOPPING, Specialty Shops & Services: Hair.)

Brady C'est Bon Beauty Salons
Water Tower Place, 845 North Michigan, 8th level; 664-3600. Deep-pore cleansing facials with René Guinot products. Makeup too. Body wrap, body waxing, manicures, pedicures, and hairstyling. MC, V. *OPEN Tues-Sat by appointment only.*

Claudia Skin Care Center
Water Tower Place, 835 North Michigan, Suite 911E. 642-2118. Facials, body massage with steam; manicure, pedicure; eyebrow and eyelash tint; body wrap. Hair removal by electrolysis, Depilitron or wax. MC, V. *OPEN Mon-Sat by appointment only.*

Elizabeth Arden Salon
717 North Michigan. 266-5750. A mini-spa behind the red door: facials, massage, waxing, Scotch hose. AE, DC, MC, V. *By appointment only.*

Georgette Klinger
Water Tower Place, 835 North Michigan, 3rd level. 787-4300. The skin experts' soothing hour-long facials for men and women, as well as manicures, pedicures, massage, waxing. Skin care regimen. Makeup lessons or application. AE, CB, DC, MC, V. *OPEN Mon-Sat by appointment.*

Ilona of Hungary
45 East Oak. 337-7161. Full service skin care for women and men. Facials, body massage, manicures, pedicures, scalp treatments. AE, MC, V. *OPEN Mon-Sat by appointment.*

Janet Sartin
Marshall Field's, 111 North State; 781-5512. And Water Tower Place; 781-1280.* Also suburbs. Scientific cosmetology. (Ms. Sartin was formerly with Erno Lazlo.) Regimen programmed for you after analysis to help correct and maintain balance. AE, MC. V, Field's charge. *OPEN Mon-Sat. *OPEN 7 days.*

Mahogany Nails
155 North Harbor Drive. 856-1785. Nail sculpturing; body wrap, pedicure, manicure. *By appointment only.*

Nails by Ann Lombardi, Ltd.
65 East Oak, 2A. 642-4109. Manicure and pedicures. *OPEN Mon-Sat by appointment only.*

Books

—Books: Chain Stores

B. Dalton Booksellers
129 North Wabash; 236-7615. And 645 North Michigan; 944-3702. Also 175 West Jackson Boulevard; 922-5219.* Very large, well-known, well-stocked nationwide chain store on three levels. Over 15,000 paperbacks. One floor for bargains. Current fiction titles and often their authors to autograph them. AE, MC, V. *OPEN Mon-Sat. *OPEN Mon-Fri.*

The Book Market
6 East Cedar; 944-3358. And 4018 North Cicero; 545-7377. Small and fine for current best-sellers (including some autographed), paperbacks, and performing arts books. Great for magazines, newspapers, and periodicals, including foreign and out-of-town. Will mail anywhere. Personalized service. MC, V. *OPEN 7 days.*

Kroch's & Brentano's, Inc.
29 South Wabash. 332-7500. Established in 1907, *the* fine full-service Chicago bookstore occupying 80,000 square feet! One of the largest paperback stocks in the country. Excels in business and profession reference as well as art and photography. AE, MC, V, Kroch's charge. *OPEN Mon-Sat.*
Other Chicago branches: 105 West Jackson, 922-8056, *OPEN Mon-Fri;* 516 North Michigan, 321-0989, *OPEN Mon-Sat;* Water Tower Place, 835 North Michigan, 4th level, 943-2452, *OPEN 7 days.*

Kroch's & Brentano's Bargain Book Center
29 South Wabash. 332-7500. Bargains galore within this well-known book emporium. Remainders, promotional sales, overruns, reprints, imports, at 50-80% off. AE, MC, V, Kroch's charge. *OPEN Mon-Sat.*

Waldenbooks
200 East Randolph; 565-2489. And Brickyard, 6465 West Diversey; 745-8660.* Also 233 South Wacker; 876-0308. Largest national bookstore chain. Specializes in practical how-tos and consumer-oriented titles. AE, MC, V. *OPEN Mon-Fri. *OPEN 7 days.*

—Books: General

Barbara's Bookstore
1434 North Wells; 642-5044. And 2907 North Broadway; 477-0411. Also Oak Park Mall, 121 North Marion; 848-9140. Chicago's *very* special source for small- and alternative-press books. Excels in literature, politics, Black studies, science fiction, women's books, poetry, and the performing arts. Good kids' selection too. Periodic readings and autograph parties. Knowledgeably staffed. AE, MC, V. *OPEN 7 days.*

Great Expectations
911 Foster Street, Evanston. 864-3881. A book person's delight. Scholarly works on philosophy, science, poetry, mathematics, world literature and academic reference, history, critical theory, and music. MC, V. *OPEN Mon-Sat.*

Marshall Field's
111 North State, 3rd floor. 781-1000. *Excellent.* America's premier department-store bookstore. Adjacent antiquarian section: antique first editions and prints. Good cookbook and children's-book sections. Autographing events are frequent. Literary book club and magazine subscription. They mail anywhere. AE, MC, V, Field's charge. *OPEN Mon-Sat and first Sun of every month.*

Oak Street Bookshop
54 East Oak. 642-3070. Inviting small shop excels with theater/film book section. Children's art, fiction, and nonfiction. Chicago writers are featured. MC, V. *OPEN 7 days.*

Rizzoli International Bookstore & Gallery
Water Tower Place, 835 North Michigan, 3rd level. 642-3500. A beautifully dignified setting for fine-art books (and a graphics gallery); foreign-language books, magazines, newspapers; classical and international records and tapes; as well as the usuals. AE, MC, V. *OPEN 7 days.*

Seminary Cooperative Bookstore, Inc.
5757 South University, basement, 752-4381. And 1301 East 57th; 684-1300. It has 18,000 co-op owners; 50,000 titles: theology, political science, social sciences, humanities, and philosophy—indeed, any academic area. MC, V. The South University store's emphasis is on academics. The East 57th location is a general bookstore with a large selection of children's books. MC, V. *OPEN Mon-Sat.*

University of Chicago Bookstore
970 East 58th. 962-8729. General books on 1st floor, texts on the 2nd:* sociology, medicine, philosophy, poetry, and reference. AE, MC, V. *OPEN Mon-Sat. *OPEN Mon-Fri.*

—Books: Antique, Old & Used

Aspidistra Bookshop
2630 North Clark. 549-3129. A well-used used-book-lovers' paradise—shelves and shelves and shelves and. . . . New arrivals weekly. Hardcover and paperback; review copies occasionally. Great for drama, fiction, mystery, and occult. MC, V. *OPEN 7 days.*

Bill's Book Nook
6132 West Belmont. 725-1545. Buys, sells, and trades used paperbacks. A little of everything old and new—25,000 in tight stock. No credit cards. *OPEN Mon-Sat.*

Booksellers Row
2445 North Lincoln. 348-1170. Nice source for out-of-print and used books. Rare and fine books, too. Good Chicago book selection. MC, V. *OPEN 7 days till 10:30pm.*

Hamill & Barker, Inc.
400 North Michigan, 26th floor. 644-5933. Very

fine antiquarian book source. Rare books in all fields. No credit cards. *OPEN Mon-Fri. CLOSED July & Aug.*

Harry L. Stern, Ltd.
1 North Wacker, Suite 206. 372-0388. Antiquarian books, maps, and prints. *By appointment only.*

John Rybski
2319 West 47th Place. 847-5082. Out-of-print American-history books. *By appointment only.*

Kenneth Nebenzahl, Inc.
333 North Michigan, 28th floor. 641-2711. Rare books, manuscripts, and maps. Rare and antiquarian prints too. MC, V. *OPEN Mon-Fri.*

O'Gara and Wilson, Ltd. Booksellers
1311 East 57th. 363-0993. Long-established. One of the best selections of used books, especially fiction. Some science, military, American history, psychology, religion, Midwest, film, and kids. MC, V. *OPEN 7 days.*

Powell's Bookshop
1501 East 57th. 955-7780. Over 200,000 used books—Chicago's largest and most chaotic selection. MC, V. *OPEN 7 days.*

Powell's Warehouse
1020 South Wabash, 4th floor. 341-0748. Over 300,000 new and used books and scholarly remainders. Some foreign-language materials. MC, V. *OPEN Mon-Sat.*

Titles, Inc.
1931 Sheridan Road, Highland Park. 432-3690. Antiquarian and rare first editions: juvenile books, photograhica, private press, limited editions, Americana. Good Chicago collection. Search-and-find service. Leatherbound volumes. *OPEN Mon-Sat.*

—Books: Special Interest

Abraham Lincoln Bookshop
18 East Chestnut. 944-3085. American Presidential history; the Civil War and Lincoln manuscripts; autographs, prints. MC, V. *OPEN Mon-Sat.*

Astrologer's Medium
2615 North Halsted. 935-3033. Astrology and occult books. Astrologers' supplies too. Computer to do charts. Tarot lessons, basic and advanced. Staff readers. No credit cards. *OPEN Mon-Thurs, also by appointment.*

Barbara's Bookstore Performing Arts Annex
2907 North Broadway. 477-0411. Theater, dance, music, film. Reference books, production scripts. AE, MC, V. *OPEN 7 days.*

Chicago Hebrew Bookstore
2942 West Devon. 973-6636. Jewish books, hardcover and paperback. Gifts too, imported from Israel or New York. MC, V. *OPEN Sun-Fri.*

China Books & Periodicals
37 South Wabash, Suite 600. 782-6004. Books from and about the People's Republic. General politics and history. Children's books from Third World countries; gifts, crafts, soap. MC, V. *OPEN Mon-Fri, but call first.*

Europa Book Store
3229 North Clark; 929-1836. And 915 Foster Street, Evanston; 866-6262. French, German, and Spanish literature, texts, dictionaries and children's books. Catalog available in each language. MC, V. *OPEN 7 days.*

Guild Books
2456 North Lincoln. 525-3667. Good selections on music, film, drama, literature, current events, and history. Specialty magazines. Records and sale books. Also Spanish-language literature, Chicago art, and reference books. Calendars and posters as well. AE, MC, V. *OPEN 7 days till 10:30pm.*

I Love a Mystery Bookstore
55 East Washington. 236-1338. Agatha Christie and Co. Pure escapism; mainly new. Paperback murder mysteries, domestic and British imports. MC, V. *OPEN Mon-Sat.*

J. Toguri Mercantile Company
851 West Belmont. 929-3500. Books devoted to Oriental culture and art; records and tapes, furniture; calligraphy and origami supplies; clothes and dolls. AE, MC, V. *OPEN Mon-Sat.*

Kazi Publications
3023 West Belmont. 267-7001. Islamic books. MC, V. *OPEN Mon-Sat.*

Logos Bookstore
2423 North Clark. 935-4540. Mainly ecumenical and inspirational books and records. Social-justice books. NY *Times* best-seller-list hardcovers. Greeting cards. AE, MC, V. *OPEN 7 days.*

London Bookshop & Gallery
P.O. Box 10115, Chicago 60610. 642-8417. Scholarly source for used, rare, and out-of-print British culture, history, and literature books. Prints, etchings, and autographs. *OPEN by appointment only.*

Modern Bookstore
1642 South Blue Island Avenue. 942-0800. Hardcover and paperback. Socialist publications: politics, economics, labor. American and European periodicals. *OPEN Mon-Sat.*

Occult Bookstore
3230 North Clark. 281-0599. Claims to be America's oldest occult bookstore (1918). Paraphernalia too. On-premises astrologer Wednesday to Saturday by appointment. MC, V. *OPEN 7 days.*

Owen Davies, Bookseller
200 West Harrison, Oak Park. 848-1186. Transportation, including new and used railroad books; naval and maritime history. Railroadiana, including timetables, buttons, and menus. *OPEN Tues-Sat.*

Prairie Avenue Bookshop
711 South Dearborn. 922-8311. One of America's largest architectural-book stores, stocking over 4,000 titles. Architecture, urban planning, interior design. New, old, and out-of-print. Architectural exhibits on display. MC, V. *OPEN Mon-Sat.*

Rand McNally
23 East Madison; 332-4627. And the suburbs;

973-9100. *The* store for travel books. No matter what direction you're going in, they have a map or a guide book to help you get there. Books of all publishers. AE, MC, V. *OPEN Mon-Sat.*

The Savvy Traveller
Garland Court, 50 East Washington, second floor. 263-2100. Travelers' aids including money belts, portable coffee makers, card games to play in the car, diaries, and every manner of printed guide and map to near and faraway places. AE, MC, V. *OPEN Mon-Sat.*

Seoul Books & Records
3450 West Peterson. 463-7756. Korean books, magazines, records, and tapes. MC, V. *OPEN 7 days.*

Stuart Brent Books
670 North Michigan. 337-6357. A special, highly individual spot. Specializes in psychology and psychiatry textbooks; literature and art too. Fine selection of children's books; the Book Club for Kids. MC, V. *OPEN 7 days.*

Thomas More Association
223 West Erie. 951-2100. Catholic publisher: books, records, tapes. MC, V. *OPEN Mon-Fri.*

Ukrainian Bookstore
2315 West Chicago. 276-6373. Ukrainian books, magazines, newspapers, and records. Gifts from Canada, the U.S., and the Ukraine. Transfer embroideries and materials. *OPEN 7 days.*

Women & Children First
1967 North Halsted. 440-8824. "Her-story," culture, self-help. Specializes in feminist and non-sexist, nonracist children's books. Over 10,000 titles are stocked. Fiction and poetry by women authors. Posters, records, cards. AE, MC, V. *OPEN 7 days.*

Brass

Brass Works
2142 North Halsted. 935-1800. Restores (on premises) and sells antique brass lighting fixtures and architectural hardware. Good rehaber's source. Also authentic old barber chairs. MC, V. *OPEN 7 days.*

Brown Beaver Antiques
2600 West Devon. 338-7372. Large and small original brass beds built between 1820 and 1915, refurbished. Some elaborately embellished with onyx, porcelain, or mirrors. Iron with brass as well; bird cages, hall trees. MC, V. *OPEN Tues-Sat.*

Top Brass
Water Tower Place, 835 North Michigan, 7th level. 280-7709. Solid-brass hardware and accessories, as well as a good variety of decorative gifts. AE, MC, V. *OPEN 7 days.*

Cameras

See SHOPPING, Specialty Shops & Services: Photographic Equipment.

Candles

Marshall Field's has a good candle department. (*See also* SHOPPING, Specialty Shops & Services: Gifts.)

Wicks 'n' Sticks
Water Tower Place, 835 North Michigan, 7th level; 944-7777. And The Brickyard, 6465 West Diversey; 889-0110. Also Vernon Hills and Schaumburg. Great selection of candles for every occasion; holders and oils too. AE, MC, V. *OPEN 7 days.*

Candy

Affy Tapple, Inc.
7110 North Clark. 338-1100. Taffy apple seconds at 50% off; frozen bananas too. *OPEN Mon-Sat.*

Aunt Diana's Old Fashioned Fudge
Water Tower Place, 835 North Michigan, 5th level. 664-1535. Fudge! Homemade; nine mouthwatering flavors. Mail orders. AE, MC, V. *OPEN 7 days.*

Cupid Candies
3230 West 95th; 636-4433. And 4709 West 95th; 423-2729. Also 7637 South Western; 925-8191 (candy kitchen only).* Old-fashioned soda fountain for 20 flavors. Homemade boxed chocolate too. *OPEN 7 days.* *CLOSED Sun.*

Delicatessen Meyer
4750 North Lincoln. 561-3377. Classic old-world German shop and at Easter time, one of the best imported filled-chocolate-egg collections: kirsch, marzipan, nougat, truffle. *OPEN 7 days.*

Dove Candies and Ice Cream
6000 South Pulaski. 582-3119. Since 1939, hand-dipped chocolate and homemade, all-natural ice cream, which the rest of the world has recently discovered. That's right, the Dove Bar. Soda Fountain. *OPEN 7 days.*

Fannie May
1137 West Jackson; 243-2700. And 433 North Michigan; 751-8512.* Chicago's own for over 70 years and still going strong. Over 100 types of chocolate including fudge, peanut brittle, and assorted nuts. There are 75 outlets in Chicagoland. These are the reject shops for bags of less-than-perfect-looking but still fine-tasting candy: mints, (battered) butter creams, (creased) caramels, or (chipped) nut clusters. *OPEN Mon-Sat.* *OPEN 7 days.*

Gayety Candy & Ice Cream
9211 Commercial. 933-9867. Since 1920, hand-dipped candy and homemade ice cream. *OPEN 7 days.*

Godiva
Water Tower Place, 845 North Michigan, 7th level. 280-1133. The ultimate in sweet indulgence. AE, MC, V. *OPEN 7 days.*

House of Fine Chocolates
3109 North Broadway. 525-8338. Butter creams, nuts, and fruits. Assorted filled chocolates. *OPEN Tues-Sun.*

Ideal Candy Shop
3311 North Clark. 327-2880. Sinfully rich hand-dipped chocolates made on premises from an old family recipe. Old-fashioned soda fountain for homemade nut-fudge topping, homemade ice-cream sundaes. No smoking. *OPEN Wed-Sun.*

Land O' Sweets
4347 West Fullerton. 252-4310. Full line of homemade chocolates. Mints, cherry cordials, solid chocolate, hard candies too. Holiday specialties: solid-chocolate bunnies and Santas, cream eggs, etc. *OPEN Mon-Sat.*

Margie's Candies
1960 North Western. 384-1035. A family business for 70 years. Fountain creations as well as hand-dipped (in view in the window) chocolates. "World's largest sundae" with a half gallon of fresh homemade ice cream topped with homemade fudge. *OPEN 7 days.*

Marshall Field's
State Street at Randolph, 1st floor. 718-4657. Frangos, a Field's and Chicago staple treat, made on the premises since 1921. The original mint has been joined by almond, coffee, lemon, orange, raspberry, rum, and the newest, peanut butter. Related specialties too. Imports as well. AE, MC, V, Field's charge. *OPEN Mon-Sat.*

Martha's Candy Shop
3257 North Broadway. 248-8733. Personalized chocolates; favors for every occasion. From chocolate Snoopys to infinitely edible pianos. *OPEN 7 days.*

Thornton's English Chocolate Shop
Water Tower Place, 845 North Michigan, 5th level. 266-3415. English creams, truffles, nuts, toffees, and yummy pecan treacle. Lovely fanciful packaging available. AE, MC, V. *OPEN 7 days.*

Universal Candies
5056 South Ashland. 778-9580. Hand-dipped chocolates. Soda fountain too. Wholesale and retail. *OPEN 7 days.*

Caterers

(*See also* SHOPPING, Specialty Shops & Services: Gourmet *and* Party: Party Help.)

Bagel Nosh
1135 North State. 266-6369. Hearty party fare: a do-it-yourself catering with a "Big Wheel" oversized bagel (serves 12) stuffed with meats, fish, or salad. Free delivery. *OPEN 7 days.*

Cook's Tour
447-2738. Cooks fine meals *at your place*—they leave before your guests arrive. Shhh! Regular catering also.

Gaper's Caterers
340 West Evergreen. 332-4935. Private office parties, plant openings; custom-tailored menus. Unusual sites for your party (Wrigley Field, Navy Pier). Exclusive caterers at Rivinia. Products to purchase without fully catered party. No credit cards. *OPEN Mon-Sat.*

Mitchell Cobey Cuisine
100 East Walton. 944-3411. Imaginative French or Northern Italian cuisine, for a buffet or a sit-down dinner, or very special hors d'oeuvres. MC, V. *OPEN Mon-Sat.*

The Mixing Bowl, Ltd.
1341 North Sedgwick. 644-6900. Catering—business, box lunches, breakfasts, barbecues, tent weddings, and clambakes. *OPEN Mon-Sat.*

Ceramic Tiles

Hispanic Designe
6125 North Cicero. 725-3100. Portuguese, Mexican, Dutch, and Italian tiles in a wide variety of designs and prices. MC, V. *OPEN Mon-Fri.*

Peerless
3028 North Lincoln. 525-4876. Ceramic, quarry, and mosaic tiles. Large selection of imports from Spain, Italy, Mexico, Portugal. Do it yourself or professional installation. AE, MC, V. *OPEN 7 days.*

China, Glassware, Porcelain & Pottery

C. D. Peacock
101 South State. 630-5700. And Old Orchard, Oakbrook Center, Northbrook, Woodfield, Hawthorne, River Oaks, Skokie. Well-respected source for fine china and crystal. AE, MC, V. *OPEN Mon-Sat.*

Crate & Barrel
850 North Michigan. 787-5900. And Plaza del Lago, Oakbrook Center, Hawthorne, Northbrook, Woodfield, Old Orchard, Washington, Wabosh. Dinner and glassware, stemware, including Marinekko, Kosta, Pilgrim. AE, MC, V. *OPEN 7 days.*

Crate & Barrel Warehouse Store
1510 North Wells. 787-4775. Every day is sale day at Crate & Barrel's Warehouse Store. Seconds, closeouts, and special-purchase items. Some first-quality too. AE, MC, V. *OPEN 7 days.*

The Crystal Cave
1141 Central Avenue, Wilmette. 251-1160. Large selection of very fine crystal. AE, MC, V. *OPEN Mon-Sat.*

The Crystal Suite
Water Tower Place, 835 North Michigan, 7th level. 944-1320. The exquisite crystal designs of Baccarat, Daum, Lalique, Orrefors, Saint Louis, Val St. Lambert, Waterford. From $40 to $40,000! AE, MC, V. *OPEN 7 days.*

Distinctive Interior Designs
2322 North Clark. 248-0738. Wedgwood, Spode, Rosenthal, Orrefors, Royal Worcester, Val St. Lambert. MC, V. *OPEN 7 days.*

Lill Street Studios
1021 West Lill. 477-6185. Ceramic workshop where pottery is available, or design your own pattern; dinner plates, platters, soup tureens, cannister sets, mugs, cups, goblets. AE, MC, V. *OPEN Mon-Sat.*

Table of Contents
446 North Wells. 644-9004. Visual and practical delights for the table. Classic, contemporary, and just plain classy. AE, MC, V. OPEN Mon-Sat.

Wedgwood
636 North Michigan. 944-1994. The famed English bone china, plus Jasperware and leaded crystal. AE, MC, V. OPEN Mon-Sat.

—China: Restorers & Repairers

K. Matsumoto
226 South Wabash, 7th floor. 922-4110. They'll fix anything "worth fixing"—porcelain, crystal, Jade, Ivory. OPEN Mon-Fri.

Mort Jacobs Restoration
6549 North Whipple. 764-8602. Restores and replaces missing or broken parts on porcelain, ivory, china, bronze, white metal. OPEN by appointment only.

Sierra Studios
807-809 Garfield Street, Oak Park. 848-2020. Preservation and restoration of fine porcelain, structural and visual. OPEN Tues-Sat.

Clocks

(See also SHOPPING, Specialty Shops & Services: Watches: Antique & Contemporary.)

Guaranty Clock Company
6422 West Belmont. 282-6730. Decorator wall clocks including cuckoos and grandfathers at discount. AE, MC, V. OPEN Mon-Sat.

Joy's Clock Shop
Water Tower Place, 835 North Michigan, 7th level. 664-1531. Fashionable, functional, or whimsical watches and clocks. AE, DC, MC, V. OPEN 7 days.

Coins

Archie's Coins
5516 West Devon. 774-1433. U.S. gold and silver coins, some paper money. MC, V. OPEN 7 days.

Jake's Marketplace Inc.
2955 North Central. 725-1344. U.S. and foreign, modern. AE, MC, V. OPEN Mon-Sat.

Marshall Field's Stamp & Coin Department
111 North State, 3rd floor. 781-4231. U.S. coins, gold, ancient and limited medals. AE, MC, V, Field's charge. OPEN Mon-Sat.

Rarcoa Coins
31 North Clark. 346-3443. U.S. and foreign, Gold bullion, currency; autographs. MC, V. OPEN Mon-Fri.

Costumes

(See also SHOPPING, Specialty Shops & Services: Women's Clothes, Vintage.)

Beverly Record, Costume & Novelty Shop
11628 South Western. 779-0068. Large selection of costumes for children and adults. Mostly rental, some for sale. AE, MC, V. OPEN Mon-Sat.

Broadway Costumes, Inc.
932 West Washington. 829-6400. Over 200,000 costumes in stock. Largest selection in Midwest, the fourth largest in the country. AE, MC, V. OPEN Mon-Sat. CLOSED Sat in summer.

Crafts

(See also SHOPPING, Specialty Shops & Services: Needlework and Quilts.)

Artisan Shop
Plaza del Lago, 1515 Sheridan Road, Wilmette. 251-3775. Incredible variety of unusual handcrafted items—pottery, macramé, patchwork, batik, jewelry, woodcarvings. MC, V. OPEN 7 days.

The Artistree Gallery & Studio
10431 South Kedzie. 445 5880. America handcrafted gifts and country decor. Designs in clay, fiber, and glass by midwestern crafts people. MC, V. OPEN Tues-Sat.

Beverly Arts Center
2153 West 111th. 445-3838. Classes in textile arts, stained glass, jewelry making, batik, calligraphy, and dance.

Illinois Artisans Shop
State of Illinois Center, 100 West Randolph, 2nd floor. 917-5324. The work of over 200 Illinois craftspeople. Ethnic, folk, traditional, and contemporary: prints, jewelry, ceramics, sculpture, clothes, carvings, quilts, wall hangings, baskets. All high-quality juried pieces on consignment. Prices range from $1 to $15,000. AE, MC, V. OPEN Mon-Fri.

Old Town Triangle Art Center
1763 North North Park. 337-1938. Classes for kids and adults in drawing, sketching, mixed media. Ten-week sessions, day or evening.

Cutlery & Gadgetry

(See also SHOPPING, Specialty Shops & Services: Housewares.)

Brookstone
Water Tower Place, 835 North Michigan, 4th level, 943-6356. And Oakbrook, Woodfield, and Hawthorne malls. Products for the home, garden, auto care and repair, all practical, attractive, and guaranteed for life. AE, MC, V. OPEN 7 days.

Corrado Cutlery
26 North Clark. 368-8450. Began in the Loop as a grinding shop 81 years ago. Great source for the world's best knives from Swiss army to stag-handled pocket; cheese knives, boning knives, and, if you're with the circus, knives to throw. AE, MC, V. OPEN Mon-Sat.

Hammacher Schlemmer
618 North Michigan; 664-5292. And 212 West Superior; 664-8170. The famed store for gadgets, conveniences, and indulgences for every room in the home, the car, the sauna, the boat,

the plane, and elsewhere. AE, CB, DC, MC, V. OPEN Mon-Sat.

Hoffritz for Cutlery
634 North Michigan. 664-4473. Cutlery raised to a fine art. AE, DC, MC, V. OPEN 7 days.

Discount Merchandise

With these stores, it's easy to go broke saving money. (See also SHOPPING, Women's Clothes: Discount, and Specialty Shops & Services: Flea Markets.)

The Buyer's Market
4545 West Division. 227-1889. New jeans, vintage records, new and used appliances, antiques, and fresh produce, all at pretty hard-to-beat prices, at this indoor-outdoor (it depends on the weather) flea market. Free parking. OPEN year-round every Sat & Sun 8am-5pm.

Cooley's Corner
5211 South Harper Court. 363-4477. Housewares, linens, kitchenware, at 20% off retail. AE, MC, V. OPEN 7 days.

Sears Catalog Surplus Store
5555 South Archer. 284-3200. Sears overstock from their catalog sales division, returns, and some seconds: clothing, accessories, housewares, at 20–80% off. Sears charge only. OPEN 7 days.

Ethnic

Chicago's ethnic museums (see MUSEUMS & GALLERIES) all have shops selling imported giftware.

The Alaska Shop
104 East Oak. 943-3393. Eskimo art, including soapstone, scrimshaw, whalebone, ivory, antler, and jade sculpture; jewelry and, as expected, very warm clothing. MC, V. OPEN Mon-Sat.

American Indian Gift Store
1756 West Wilson. 769-1170. Indian arts and crafts. Jewelry, beadwork, relics, Kachina dolls, baskets, and bone carvings. OPEN Tues-Sat.

Asiana Company
3312 West Lawrence. 539-6664. Korean furniture, traditional clothing, jewelry, pottery and gift items. AE, MC, V. OPEN Mon-Sat.

Erin Isle
2246 North Clark. 975-6616. Step into a very personal world of all-natural fabrics and materials, housed in a lovely setting. Art, clothes, and handicrafts all lovingly chosen and imported from Ireland. Including hats, yarn, bedspreads, sweaters, shawls, carvings, jewelry, dolls, toys, rugs, baskets woven from Shannon River rushes, crystal, stoneware, Jimmy Hourihen designer fashions for women, soap, fragrances, potpourri. MC, V. OPEN 7 days. CLOSED Sun in Jan & Feb, July & Aug.

Eye on Design
35 South Washington Street, Ainsdale. 986-5228. Upstairs, a treasure house of primitive art, fabric, jewelry, ceremonial masks from Indonesia, Mex-ico, Afghanistan, Peru, Guatemala, Italy, China, and Africa. AE, MC, V. OPEN Mon-Sat.

Japan Books & Records
3450 West Peterson. 463-7755. Japanese records and books. MC, V. OPEN 7 days.

Mexican Folk Arts
2433 North Clark. 871-1511. A clutter of colorful handcrafted decorative items such as papier-mâché fruit, folk pottery, weavings, tins, candle holders, wonderful masks, as well as jewelry, clothes, serapes, and fabric—all from south of the border. AE, MC, V. OPEN 7 days.

Panellinion Imports
2411 West Lawrence. 784-7066. Greek-language books, newspapers, magazines, records, and tapes. Jewelry and antiquity repros. AE, MC, V. OPEN Mon-Sat.

The Polonia Bookstore
2886 North Milwaukee. 489-2554. Polish-language books, magazines, newspapers, and records. No credit cards. OPEN Mon-Sat.

Roxy Records & Book Co.
215 West 23rd Street. 225-6683. Chinese records. AE, MC, V. OPEN 7 days.

Scandinavian Design
875 North Michigan; 664-9232. And 548 West Diversey; 248-8229. Also the suburbs. Home furnishings and decorative accessories from Denmark, Sweden, Norway, and Finland. Great place for imported wooden and straw Christmas decorations. MC, V. OPEN 7 days.

The Sweden Shop
3304 West Foster. 478-0327. Swedish cookware, china, dinnerware, and accessories, including Dansk, Orrefors, Royal Copenhagen, as well as jewelry. Also crystal and clocks. Not to mention clogs for the whole family. Bridal registry. MC, V. OPEN Mon-Sat.

Uma Sarees
2535 West Devon. 338-6302. Traditional silk saris and sari fabric as well as help with the donning. MC, V. OPEN Wed-Mon.

Ethnic Foods

Erikson's Delicatessen
5250 North Clark. 561-5634. In Chicago's Swedish neighborhood, Andersonville, a smorgasbord of delights. Herring, Scandinavian cheeses including Norway's clove-studded nokkelost; limpa and flat breads. OPEN 7 days.

Happy Garden
2358 South Wentworth. 225-2730. Bakeshop and Chinese snack foods. OPEN 7 days.

Hellas Pastry
2627 West Lawrence. 271-7500. Greek bakery: filo rolls filled with cheese or spinach; baklava and custard pastries. OPEN 7 days.

Indian Gifts & Food
1031 West Belmont. 348-4393. Pakora, samosa, chutney, as well as Indian spices and nuts. OPEN Tues-Sun.

Kuhn's Delicatessen
3053 North Lincoln; 525-9019. And Deerfield

and Des Plaines. Teutonic taste treats: wursts, herrings, salamis, chocolates, wines, and 150 kinds of German beer! *OPEN 7 days.*

Meyer Delicatessen
4750 North Lincoln. 561-3377. Over 6,000 items stocked, mainly German: liver sausage, salads, herrings, wine, cakes, and candies. *OPEN 7 days.*

Mikolajczyk Sausage Co.
1737 West Division. 486-8870. Polish foods, including good sausages. *OPEN Mon-Sat.*

Oriental Food Market
2801 West Howard. 274-2826. Great egg rolls. *OPEN Mon-Sat.*

Paulina Market
3501 North Lincoln. 248-6272. Swedish-style smoked meats and fish, including ham, salmon, lake trout, and goose breast. *OPEN Mon-Sat.*

Ramune's Restaurant
2547 West 69th. 476-7975. Lithuanian deli for headcheese, meat blintzes, spice cookies. *OPEN Tues-Sun.*

Riviera Italian Imported Foods
3220 North Harlem. 637-4252. Wide selection of Italian meats, cheeses, salads, and breads. *OPEN 7 days.*

Star Market
3349 North Clark. 472-0599. Excellent Japanese grocery store features sashimi to go. *OPEN 7 days.*

Exercise

Jazzercise
Seven locations in Chicago. Also Des Plaines, Glenview, Norridge, Skokie, and Franklin Park. Jazz dance fitness program. Continual classes, day and evening, for men and women. For information call 774-7119 in Chicago and the north suburbs; 397-7230 in the west suburbs; and 429-7722 in the south suburbs. *OPEN Mon-Fri.*

The Workout, Ltd.
22 East Elm Street. 280-9166. Combination of ballet, yoga, calisthenics and weight resistance, for women and men. *OPEN Mon-Sat by appointment only.*

Fabric

Fishman's Fabrics
1101 South Des Plaines. 922-7250. Three floors, with hundreds of fine imported fabrics as well as bolts and remnants direct from designer (Cardin, Blass, Adolfo) houses. Notions and patterns too. MC, V. *OPEN 7 days.*

Laura Ashley
Water Tower Place, 835 North Michigan, 6th level. 951-8004. Famed for her charming English country print fabrics; wallpaper to match. AE, MC, V. *OPEN 7 days.*

Liberty of London
845 North Michigan Avenue, 7th level. 280-1134. A touch of London. Straight from the famed fabric house on Regent Street—fabrics, apparel,

ties, scarves, and gift items, all with that unmistakable Liberty look and feel. AE, MC, V. *OPEN 7 days.*

Loomcraft
6343 Gross Point Road, Niles. 647-6647. Good prices on remnants, seconds, overruns, and discontinued fabrics for upholstery and drapery, including silks and velvets. By the yard or bolt. *OPEN Mon-Sat. CLOSED Sat in July & Aug.*

Pierre Deux
113 East Oak. 642-9657. Choose from over 1,000 Soleiado ("sunny day") Provençal cotton print fabrics (50-by-36-inch widths) in a French-country setting. Desk accessories, handbags, pillows, and fashions. Custom orders taken for bed and table linens as well as yacht sails. AE, MC, V. *OPEN Mon-Sat.*

Vogue
732 Main Street, Evanston. 273-2025. Block-long selection of clothing fabrics, upholstery and drapery materials. Buttons, patterns, and other supplies also. MC, V. *OPEN Mon-Sat.*

Fish

Burhops
745 North La Salle. 642-8600. And Plaza del Lago, Wilmette. Highland Park, Glenview, Lombard, and Hinsdale. Purveyors and importers of prime seafood. Seasonal species. *OPEN Mon-Sat.*

Chicago Fish House
1250 West Division. 227-7000. From this fish house two live 2-pound lobsters to go in a wooden crate with tools, bibs, and lemons (three days' notice). *OPEN Mon-Sat.*

Pick Fisheries
702 West Fulton Market. 226-4700. Savings of 25% on over 500 different varieties of fresh and frozen seafood. Filleting and cleaning extra. *OPEN Mon-Sat.*

Flea Markets

The Great American Flea Market
1333 South Cicero. 780-1600. New and used "miscellany" at over 250 booths in this indoor market. Small admission charge, lower for children and senior citizens. *OPEN year-round; Sat & Sun 8am-4pm.*

Maxwell Street Market
Maxwell near Halsted. Outdoors year-round (brrr in winter). A few antiques, collectibles, and a great deal of junk. Colorful to say the least. Sunday morning is the time to go. (*See also* HISTORIC & NEW CHICAGO, Historic Areas & Buildings.)

Swap-O-Rama
7400 Waukegan, Niles. 774-3900. The maximum 250 sellers, of everything from fine antiques to the weathered contents of a garage, are here in winter, slightly fewer in spring and fall. Nominal admission, lower for children and senior citi-

zens. Indoors. *OPEN Sept-Apr, Sat & Sun 7am-4pm.*

Flowers

Amlings Flowerland
8900 West North Avenue, Melrose Park; 344-0770. And Hyatt Regency, 151 East Wacker; 861-1790.* Also 625 North Michigan; 787-6300. In business since 1890, and thought by many to be Chicago's best florist. Large selection of flowers and plants. Delivery anywhere. AE, CB, DC, MC, V. *OPEN Mon-Sat. *OPEN Mon-Fri.*

The Clay Pot
Illinois Center, 111 East Wacker, concourse. 565-0114. Fresh and *faux* flowers; plants, pots, hostess gifts. AE, CB, DC. *OPEN Mon-Sat.*

Fischer's Flowers
852 West Armitage. 248-1900. Flowers, plants, and accessories. AE, MC, V. *OPEN Mon-Sat.*

Floral Designs
3021 North Southport, 2353 North Clark,*540 North Michigan. 528-9800. A sophisticated "less is more" approach to floral arrangements. Specializing in a creative, *very* natural look. Greenhouses at North Southport. AE, CB, DC, MC, V. *OPEN Mon-Sat. *OPEN 7 days.*

The Flower Cart
3819 North Broadway. 477-7755. Unique fresh floral arrangements with unusual choices of flowers. Accessories and giftware in a range of prices. AE, CB, DC, MC, V. *OPEN Mon-Sat.*

Flowers by Bygone
5900 North Ridge. 769-5424. Imaginative seasonal and special-occasion centerpieces. AE, MC, V. *OPEN Mon-Fri; Sat by appointment.*

Orchids by Hausermann, Inc.
2N134 Addison Road, Villa Park. 543-6855. A bloomin' heaven of blooming orchid plants. *Thousands* of varieties. Delivery to Chicago. AE, MC, V. *OPEN Mon-Sat.*

Randolph Street Flowers
59 East Lake. 263-8228. Bouquets of fresh flowers brighten up this Loop street. AE, MC, V. *OPEN 7 days.*

Villari
Merchandise Mart (east lobby); 822-9595. And 820 West Randolph; 738-1600.* Freshly cut flowers, pots, plants, dried flowers, trees, and shrubs. AE, MC, V. *OPEN Mon-Fri. *OPEN 7 days.*

Zuverink
1 East Erie. 751-2290. They never wilt: silk and dried flowers—beautifully arranged. Expensive. MC, V. *OPEN Mon-Sat.*

Framing

Billy Hork Framing
3033 North Clark. 935-9700. Metal moldings, wood frames, museum-quality mats at this good frame source. MC, V. *OPEN 7 days.*

Chicago Picture Supply Company
1210 West Fry. 829-5240. Fine work at low cost. No credit cards. *OPEN Wed-Sat.*

Frameway Studios, Inc.
319 West Ontario, 2nd floor. 751-1660. Complete custom-framing service including photo and specialty mounting and, for your important works of art, conservation framing. No credit cards. *OPEN Mon-Fri.*

Frederic's Frame Studio
1230 West Jackson. 243-2950. Custom framing. Specializes in gold leaf and leafing, antique frames, and Plexi boxes. Mounting also. AE only. *OPEN Mon-Fri.*

The Great Frame Up
2905 North Broadway; 549-3927. Also in the suburbs. Frugal framing—the frame-it-yourself store. Step-by-step instruction. Good selection of frames, moldings, and mats. Dry mounting too. AE, MC, V. *OPEN 7 days.*

Hellman Studio and Gallery
953 West Webster. 525-7757. A friendly little custom frame shop. MC, V. *OPEN Mon-Sat.*

Furniture

—Furniture: Antique & Collectible

(*See also* SHOPPING, Specialty Shops & Services: Antiques & Collectibles *and* Brass.)

Adam Monroe Antiques
1358 West Belmont. 525-1133. Antique furniture and accessories from the U.S., England, and the Continent. Also repair and refinishing. NOTE: The Lake View area is rich in antique shops and you can pick up a free guide to them here. AE, MC, V. *OPEN Tues-Sun.*

Aged Experience
2034 North Halsted. 975-9790. Like wandering through someone's house—but here, if you like something, you may buy it. Nice prices on mainly oak furnishings. Country accessories. No credit cards. *OPEN Tues-Sun.*

Bell, Book & Candle
2409 West Lunt. 973-2858. Furniture, antiques, collectibles. Repair and refinishing too. No credit cards. *OPEN Tues-Sun.*

Collector's Nook
1714 North Wells. 642-4734. Eighteenth- and 19th-century American, English, and French period and country furnishings. Accessories too. *OPEN Tues-Sat, or by appointment.*

Donrose Galleries
751 North Wells. 337-4052. One of the largest. French and English furnishings, crystal and porcelain objets d'art, paintings; Oriental art. MC, V. *OPEN 7 days.*

Frantz Antiques
2323 West Belmont. 327-6676. American Victorian walnut and oak furniture. Lace curtains, needlework, tablecloths. Restoration services available. AE, MC, V. *OPEN Wed-Sun.*

Gloria
1007 West Webster. 327-9665. Primarily vintage fashions but also art deco and art moderne furniture and "objets de kitsch." AE, MC, V. *OPEN 7 days.*

Griffins & Gargoyles
2140 West Lawrence. 769-1255. Large selection

(7,000 square feet!) of European imported antique furniture; country pine, oak, and walnut armoires, buffets. Some architectural pieces, farm tables, light fixtures. MC, V. *OPEN Thurs-Mon.*

International Antiques
2907 North Clark. 528-4602. Large pieces of Edwardian and Victorian furnishings, mainly at good prices. Large selection of armoires. Importers; they will find what you're looking for. Brass (old and new) beds, accessories too. AE, MC, V. *OPEN 7 days.*

Jay Roberts Antique Warehouse
149 West Kinzie. 222-0167. A warehouseful, on three floors, of antique armoires, brass beds, mantels, clocks, tables, bedroom furnishings, brass and copper accessories, stained glass. MC, V. *OPEN Mon-Sat.*

Lost Eras
1511 West Howard. 764-7400. Wonderful place for period furnishings: Victorian, art nouveau, art deco, art moderne—furniture, rugs, paintings, art glass, and pottery. Some vintage duds and books too. Antique jewelry. AE, MC, V. *OPEN 7 days.*

Malcolm Franklin, Inc.
56 East Walton. 337-0202. Seventeenth- and 18th-century English furniture and accessories. No credit cards. *OPEN Mon-Sat. CLOSED Sat in summer.*

Manifesto
200 West Superior. 664-0733. River North shop for furniture and decorative accessories by Alvar Aalto and Josef Hoffman. Also lighting, textiles, and collectibles, ca. 1890-1940. MC, V. *OPEN Tues-Sat; Mon by appointment only.*

Marshall Field's
111 North State, 8th floor Decorating Galleries. 781-5714. A fine collection of 17th-, 18th-, and 19th-century American, English, and European antique furniture and accessories. AE, MC, V, Field's charge. *OPEN Mon-Sat.*

Old Chicago Antiques
2336 West Belmont. 935-1200. Refurbished oak furniture and country accessories, including rolltop desks and brass beds. No credit cards. *OPEN Wed-Sun.*

Russ's Pier W
2833 North Lincoln. 1227 West Diversey; 1213 West Diversey. 327-5718. Turn-of-the-century oak and walnut desks, rockers, tables, chests. No credit cards. *OPEN Tues-Sun.*

—Furniture: Contemporary

Butcher Block & More
1600 South Clinton; 421-1138. And Downers Grove and Glenview. Save on manufacturers' solid-oak or maple butcher-block tables, shelves, benches, bowls, and boards. Discount of 20-40%! MC, V. *OPEN Mon-Sat.*

City
213 West Institute Place. 664-9581. Affordable, adaptable, *au courant*, high-tech home furnishings; lighting for that uncluttered, highly functional look. AE, MC, V. *OPEN 7 days.*

Colby's
129 East Chestnut. 266-2222. And Northbrook and Oakbrook. America's most prestigious furniture makers—Drexel, Heritage, Siffel, Baker, Henredon. MC, V. *OPEN 7 days.*

D & L Office Furniture
30 West Hubbard. 527-3636. Midwest's largest inventory of business furnishings and accessories. AE, MC, V. *OPEN Mon-Fri.*

D & L Office Furniture Outlet
4336 West Addison; 286-5025. Subterranean Sale Showroom, 30 West Hubbard; 527-3636. New, used, one-of-a-kinds, and odds and ends at 30% discount. At Sale Showroom at least 50% off of floor samples, discontinued, close outs. AE, MC, V. *OPEN Mon-Sat.*

H. Brian Convertible Sofas
2840 North Halsted; 281-7650. And Schaumburg, Lombard, Burbank, and Niles. Wide selection of convertible sofas. MC, V. *OPEN 7 days.*

The House Store
620 West Shubert. 525-7771. A no-frills furniture supermarket on two floors. Attractive affordable contemporary "life-style" home furnishings that leave the store with you. Some of the high-tech and modular systems need assembly, and a clever "Rating System" indicates how much intelligence and/or friends are needed to accomplish the task. AE, MC, V. *OPEN 7 days.*

J & D Brauner Butcher Block
1735 North Ashland; 276-1770. And Lombard, Wilmette, and Palatine. Where the solid, sturdy butcher block is translated into contemporary furnishings. AE, MC, V. *OPEN 7 days.*

New Town Interiors
824 West Diversey. 248-4181. Over 50 different styles of convertible sofas. AE, MC, V. *OPEN 7 days.*

Noelwood Handmade Furniture
1524 South Peoria. 942-1031. Custom-built fine hardwood furniture. Your design, their skill. No credit cards. *By appointment only.*

Phoenix Design
733 North Wells; 951-7945. And 5908 South Kedzie; 436-0600. The familiar staple of "life-style" furnishings at affordable prices. MC, V. *OPEN 7 days.*

Scandinavian Design
875 North Michigan; 664-9232. And 548 West Diversey; 248-8229. Also in the suburbs. Imported teak and rosewood furniture, accessories, textiles, ceramics, wood, brass, and china including Royal Copenhagen and Rosenthal. MC, V. *OPEN 7 days.*

Winston Bartlett
748-4410. Fine American and European antique furniture restoration. Also creates impeccable repros of the same. *By appointment only.*

Workbench
158 West Hubbard. 661-1150. In a bi-level former fishery, their prizewinning contemporary furniture designed for today's life-style. Modular seating, storage systems, and more at moderate prices. MC, V. *OPEN 7 days.*

—Furniture: Refinishing

Speedy Strippers
2546 North Halsted. 528-9550. Inexpensive expert furniture stripping *only*—you do the rest. MC, V. *OPEN Tues-Sat.*

—Furniture: Rental

Mr. Rents
222 West Hubbard. 943-4500. Rental as well as sales, in a variety of styles for home and office. Accessories too. MC, V. *OPEN Mon-Sat.*

Games

Devon Hobby Models, Inc.
2358 West Devon. 262-2136. Source for handheld games. AE, MC, V. *OPEN 7 days.*

Gamers' Paradise
The Century, 2828 North Clark. 549-1833. Video games and tapes; board games, electronic games, chess and backgammon. AE, MC, V. *OPEN 7 days.*

Gamesters
Water Tower Place, 835 North Michigan, 7th level. 642-0671. An adult game store. Monopoly, Scrabble, English pub dart boards, chess and backgammon, video computer and card games. AE, DC, MC, V. *OPEN 7 days.*

Gifts

(See also SHOPPING, Specialty Shops & Services: Crafts.)

A.D.O.P.T. an Animal
Lincoln Park Zoological Society, P.O. Box 96141, Chicago, IL 60690. 935-6700. Animals Depend on People Too! Give someone an African crested porcupine, an Addra gazelle, or a Bengal tiger. They continue to reside at the zoo in quarters hopefully upgraded, with your donation *(see* PARKS & GARDENS, Zoos & Aquariums: Brookfield Zoo). You and your adoptee can visit—during regular zoo hours, of course. Call Monday to Friday 9am to 5pm for information.

Art Institute Gift Store
South Michigan & East Adams. 443-3534. Prints and books; gifts; reproductions, jewelry, art glass, AE, MC, V. *OPEN 7 days.*

Courtesy Neon Sales
2014 West Belle Plaine. 525-2666. Always wanted your name in lights? Well, here's your chance. Your design or his. Plastic signs also. No credit cards. *OPEN Mon-Fri.*

Elaine Fisher
831-4028. Custom-designed dolls, "Lil' charmers" personalized to suit any occasion and any personality. *By appointment only.*

Findables
2050 North Halsted. 348-0674. An eclectic gift shop for old and new treasures handcrafted here, there, and everywhere. AE, MC, V. *OPEN 7 days.*

He Who Eats Mud
3247 North Broadway. 525-0616. Unique, colorful, whimsical giftware. Cards, candles, soap, costume jewelry. MC, V. *OPEN 7 days.*

Nonpareil
2300 North Clark. 477-2933. A toy store for adults, though the stock varies from easy-to-wear clothing to creative jewelry to imported rugs to Bonnie Katz pottery. Oh, there are handmade kids' toys too. AE, MC, V. *OPEN 7 days.*

Omiyage
2482 Lincoln. 477-1428. *Omiyage* is Japanese for "gift." It's a charming shop for "people accessories." Literally hundreds of items—toys, pillows, stationery and cards, kites, jewelry, rubber stamps, baskets, ceramics, purses—much of them made by Chicago artisans, with prices starting at 5¢. MC, V. *OPEN Tues-Sun.*

Rocket 69
3180 North Clark. 472-7878. A true 80s emporium: whimsical gifts and novelties galore; cards; well-priced vintage and new clothes; American Indian jewelry. Great postcard collection. AE, MC, V. *OPEN 7 days.*

Sky Pies
O'Hare International Airport, 686-6700. On upper departure levels of terminals two and three. A practical gift from Chicago! Packed to go Chicago deep-dish pizza; stays frozen for 12 hours. MC, V. Available *7 days 8am-9pm.*

Tuscany Studio, Inc.
601 North Wells. 664-7680. A landmark of sorts. Looking for a gift for your mother-in-law? Bring a truck. One or all of the Seven Dwarfs, a white elephant, or perhaps a gargoyle? No credit cards. *OPEN Mon-Sat.*

Wine & Roses
893-WINE. A handpicked rose and a bottle of champagne stylishly delivered the next day within a 25-mile radius of Chicago. AE, MC, V. *Available 24 hours.*

Glasses

For Eyes
2564 North Clark. 929-5553. It's the name that catches the eye; but the prices are great for prescription lenses, with your choice from over 100 frames. MC, V. *OPEN Mon-Sat.*

Glasses, Ltd.
49 East Oak. 944-6876. Optometrist. Designer frames as well as lorgnettes, 40s and 50s vintage frames for that Hollywood look. AE, DC, MC, V. *OPEN Mon-Sat.*

Gourmet

(See also SHOPPING, Specialty Shops & Services: Caterers *and* Ethnic Foods.)

Conte-di-Savoia European Specialties
555 West Roosevelt Road. 666-3471. International foods bazaar—Russian, Polish, English, French, Italian, German. Barrels of spices, grains, and olives; imported oils, vinegars; dried fruits;

coffees, teas, homemade pastas, cheese. MC, V. *OPEN 7 days.*

Food Works
935 West Armitage; 935-6800. And 1002 West Diversey; 348-7801. Also 1527 West Morse; 465-6200. Delicious gourmet items, like 50 varieties of cheeses; coffees, homemade pastas, salads, quiches, vegetarian pâtés, croissants. Home-baked chocolate-chip cookies and delicious apricot-chocolate torte. Jams, jellies, spices. Freshly baked bread on Saturday. Expensive. No credit cards. *OPEN 7 days.*

La Salle Street Market
745 North La Salle. 943-7450. Choose from 200 varieties of cheese (large selection of goat cheese), pâtés, terrines, caviars. Lunchbox year-round; menu available. Fall grape stomp in the parking lot next to the Chicago Avenue police station. MC, V. *OPEN Mon-Sat.*

Mitchel Cobey Cuisine
100 East Walton. 944-3411. Gourmet shop for pâtés, cheeses, salads, and home-baked pastries specializes in imaginative menus for small and large gatherings. One of the best. MC, V. *OPEN Mon-Sat.*

Stop & Shop
233 East Wacker; 853-2160. And 445 East Ohio; 853-2165. Also 1313 North Ritchie Court, 853-2150; and 260 East Chestnut, 853-2155. Well-respected gourmet foods source; extensive selection. Wines and liquors too. MC, V. *OPEN 7 days.*

Treasure island
75 West Elm. 440-1144. Other locations. Famed cooking expert Julia Child calls it "the best grocery in the nation." You be the judge. MC. *OPEN 7 days.*

Hair

(See also SHOPPING, Specialty Shops & Services: Beauty Specialists.)

Charles Ifergan Salon
106 East Oak, 4th floor. 642-4484. Full service hair salon where the chic take their *cheveux;* men and women; makeup consultations too. *OPEN Tues-Sat by appointment only.*

Cheveux Hair Shop
908 West Armitage. 935-5212. A friendly place and talented too! Winner of the national salon-of-the-year award. Manicure, pedicure, makeup. *OPEN Tues-Sat by appointment only.*

Gayle Johnson's Salon
46 East Oak. 2nd floor. 642-8395. For *all* of you. Hairstyling, private makeup lessons (using Il Makiage products), and wardrobe planning. *By appointment only.*

Paul Glick & Assocs.
701 North Michigan, 3rd floor. 751-2300. Often recommended. Complete salon services for women and men. Makeup and skin care too. Facials, body massage. *OPEN Tues-Sat by appointment only.*

Vidal Sassoon Salon
Water Tower Place, 835 North Michigan, 3rd floor. 751-2216. For both men and women. "If you don't look good, they don't look good." Manicure and pedicure. *OPEN Mon-Sat by appointment only.*

Health Clubs

(See also SHOPPING, Specialty Shops & Services: Exercise.)

Chicago Health & Racquet Club
1 Illinois Center, 111 East Wacker, 31st floor; 861-1220. And 230 West Monroe; 263-4500.[a] Geared to executives. Racquetball, gyms, whirlpool, saunas, steam, massage; aerobic dance and gymnastics classes. Juice bar and lounge area. *Seventy-foot swimming pool. Membership for men and women. *OPEN Mon-Sat.*

Downtown Court Club
441 North Wabash. 644-4880. Aerobic dance classes, racquetball, squash, tennis, track, swimming, whirlpool, sauna. Membership. *OPEN Mon-Fri 6am-11:30pm; Sat & Sun 7am-11pm.*

East Bank Club
500 North Kingsbury Court. 527-5800. Handball, racquetball, squash, tennis, track, basketball court, game room. Nautilus equipment; indoor and outdoor pools; massage; whirlpool, sauna, steam, sun rooms. Membership for men and women. *OPEN 7 days.*

Lakeshore Center
1320 West Fullerton. 477-9888. Exercise classes (dance and yoga); Eagle equipment; indoor and outdoor tennis, swimming, track, racquetball; sun deck; steam, sauna, whirlpool. Membership for men and women. *OPEN Mon-Fri 5am-midnight; Sat & Sun 6am-11pm.*

McClurg Court Sports
333 East Ontario. 944-4546. Handball, indoor and outdoor tennis, racquetball, pool, weight lifting; massage, sun deck; sauna, steam, whirlpool. *Membership. OPEN 7 days.*

Health Foods

All the Best Natural Foods
3008 West Devon. 274-9478. Sandwiches, groceries, herbal teas. Kosher products including Freeda Natural Vitamins. MC, V. *OPEN 7 days.*

The Bread Shop
3400 North Halsted. 528-8108. Fifteen varieties of fresh bread available daily, as well as whole-grain pastries and pastas. Some organic produce; grains in bulk, tofu, and cheeses. Carryout vegetarian deli (everything made on premises); hot soups too. No credit cards. *OPEN Tues-Sun.*

Central Health Foods
5713 West Belmont. 889-5408. Bulk herb teas, whole grains and pastas, vitamins, minerals, cosmetics, and books. Juice and sandwiches too. No credit cards. *OPEN 7 days.*

Chicago Nutrition Center
4758 West Belmont. 286-8808. Whole grains and flours, dairy products, vegetables; vitamins at a 10% discount, minerals. Books and pamphlets. No credit cards. *OPEN Mon-Sat.*

Golden Carrot, Inc.
60 East Chicago. 787-3463. Organic fruits, juice, unrefined oils, whole grains, herbs. Sandwiches and whole-wheat pizza. MC, V. *OPEN 7 days.*

Great Earth Vitamin Stores
59 East Chicago Avenue. 642-7961. Their own natural vitamins and minerals. PH cosmetics and shampoos. MC, V. *OPEN 7 days.*

Heartland
7000 North Glenwood. 465-8005. General store and café *(see RESTAURANTS, Vegetarian).* Teas, grains, cosmetics. AE only. *OPEN 7 days.*

Life Spring
3178 North Clark. 327-1023. Health foods, juice bar, sandwiches, ice cream. MC, V. *OPEN 7 days.*

Sherwyn's Health Food Stores
645 West Diversey. 477-1934. Dairy, whole grains, flours, nuts, herbs, in bulk; some organic produce; decaffeinated coffee. MC, V. *OPEN 7 days.*

Sunflower Seed Health Foods
5210 South Harper. 363-1600. Dairy products, herb teas, freshly ground peanut butter; vitamins and minerals. No credit cards. *OPEN Mon-Sat.*

Herbs & Spices

Dr. Michael's Herb Center
1223 North Milwaukee; 276-7186. And 5109 North Western; 271-7738. Long established (1928). Stocks over 400 varieties of herbs. No credit cards. *OPEN Mon-Sat.*

Monk's Herb Center
2928 North Milwaukee. 772-6595. Many, many prepackaged herbs. No credit cards. *OPEN Mon-Sat.*

Village Green Plant & Garden Center
1952 North Halsted. 472-2800. In spring, fresh herbs and spices. AE, MC, V. *OPEN 7 days.*

Housewares

(See also SHOPPING, Specialty Shops & Services: Cutlery & Gadgetry.)

Cose
750 North Franklin. 787-0304. Unmistakably Italian objects and housewares in River North. Work by Moretti, Alessi, Rossi, and Sabattini. AE, CB, DC, MC, V. *OPEN 7 days.*

Crate & Barrel
850 North Michigan; 787-5900. And 101 North Wabash; 372-0100. Also 1510 North Wells, 787-4775*; and the suburbs. A wonderful source for Chinese baskets, French cutlery, Italian chairs, German heaters, Finnish fabric, as well as copper cookware and nylon luggage. Seconds room on the lower level for 30-70% savings. *The outlet store (30-70% savings). AE, MC, V. *OPEN Mon-Sat.*

William-Sonoma
17 East Chestnut. 642-1593. Renowned kitchen outfitter from the basic to the esoteric—it's all here. AE, MC, V. *OPEN Mon-Sat.*

Jewelry: Antique and Contemporary

(See also SHOPPING, Specialty Shops & Services: Antiques & Collectibles.)

C. D. Peacock Jewelry
101 South State. 630-5700. Since 1837, a source for exquisite jewelry, including Cartier's Les Musts. AE, MC, V. *OPEN Mon-Sat.*

Fischer Jewelers
2461 North Clark. 525-4999. Specializes in antique jewelry. Watch and jewelry repair and restoration. *OPEN Mon-Sat.*

Gia Originals
Water Tower Place, 845 North Michigan, 9th floor. 944-5263. Designers of handcrafted gold jewelry to order. AE, MC, V. *OPEN Tues-Sat.*

The Goldsmith, Ltd.
Water Tower Place, 835 North Michigan, 2nd level. 751-1986. Handmade contemporary jewelry from original designs. AE, DC, MC, V. *OPEN 7 days.*

Great Lakes Jewelry
104 East Oak. 266-2211. A tiny shop with a wide selection of sterling silver and art deco jewelry. AE, MC, V. *OPEN Mon-Sat.*

Henry Kay Jewelers
547 North Michigan; 467-6515. And Water Tower Place, 835 North Michigan, 3rd level; 266-7600.* Carries a complete line of Du Pont accessories, including the famed lighters. AE, CB, DC, MC, V. *OPEN Mon-Sat.* *OPEN 7 days.*

H. Horowitz Co.
Water Tower Place, 845 North Michigan Avenue, 9th floor. 337-3500. Diamond importers since 1899. AE, MC, V. *OPEN Mon-Sat. CLOSED Sat in July & Aug.*

Jan Dee
2308 North Clark. 871-2222. Creative designs in gold and silver. AE, MC, V. *OPEN Tues-Sat.*

Jewels by Stephanie
46 South Clark. 782-6300. Investment-sized rings, as well as Hummel, Seiko clocks, Royal Doulton figurines, Orrefors crystal. AE, CB, DC, MC, V. *OPEN Mon-Fri.*

Lebolt & Company
35 North State; 263-5500.* And Water Tower Place, 835 North Michigan, 2nd level; 649-1000. Also, Northbrook Court. Fine jewelry since 1899. AE, DC, MC, V. *OPEN 7 days.* *CLOSED Sun.*

Little Gems
Inge Parks. 871-7017. Nicely priced antique jewelry. Victorian pins, lockets, brooches, and rings. No credit cards. *By appointment only.*

Supreme Jewelers
1452 East 53rd. 643-0599. Large selection of 14-karat gold chains. AE, CB, DC, MC, V. *OPEN Tues-Sat.*

Tiffany & Co.
715 North Michigan. 944-7500. The prestigious treasure house for jewelry, including the designs

of Elsa Perretti, Angela Cummings, and Paloma Picasso. Diamonds, china, and crystal (including Baccarat); silver flatware. Stationery and playing cards too. Don't be intimidated, there are reasonably priced items among them all. AE, DC, MC, V. *OPEN Mon-Sat.*

Lamps/Lighting

(See also SHOPPING, Specialty Shops & Services: Antiques & Collectibles *and* Furniture.)
New Metal Crafts
812 North Wells. 787-6991. Antique as well as custom-designed lighting; imports too. No credit cards. *OPEN Mon-Sat.*
Sarah Bustle
821 Dempster, Evanston. 869-7290. Antique, mainly Victorian, lighting ca. 1860-1910. Art nouveau and art deco accessories. Unusual antique gift items, silver, china. AE, MC, V. *OPEN Tues-Sat. 10am-6pm.*
Stanley Galleries
2118 North Clark. 281-1614. Antique lighting specialist—gas, electric, chandeliers, desk, table, floor—as well as architectural hardware, stained glass, fretwork, and terra cotta. AE, MC, V. *OPEN 7 days.*

Leather Goods/Luggage

(See also SHOPPING, Women's Accessories: Handbags.)
Chicago Trunk & Leather Works
12 South Wabash; 372-0845. And Sears Tower, Jackson Street Concourse; 993-9822. An extensive selection of luggage, trunks, business cases, handbags, and accessories. Free initialing. AE, CB, DC, MC, V. *OPEN Mon-Sat.*
Deutsch Luggage
111 East Oak; 337-2937. And 39 West Van Buren; 939-2935. Most national brands of luggage, small leather goods. Repairs too. AE, CB, DC, MC, V. *OPEN Mon-Sat.*
Gucci
713 North Michigan. 664-5504. World-renowned snob appeal leather goods, luggage, handbags, and travel accessories with or without the status initials. Clothing in luxurious fabrics for men and women too. AE, CB, DC, MC, V. *OPEN 7 days.*
The Leather Shop
191 West Madison. 782-5448. Excellent selection of travelware, luggage, handbags, attaché cases, and smaller leather goods. Wallets and belts too. AE, DC, MC, V. *OPEN Mon-Sat.*
Schultz & Mark
25 East Washington, Room 908. 236-1156. Expensive, albeit expert, luggage repair. Handbags and briefcases too. No credit cards. *OPEN Mon-Fri.*

Limousines

Al & Harold Golub Limousine Service
188 West Randolph. 726-1035. Cadillacs and limousines, complete with bar and moon roof. "All legal requests for extras are filled."
Carey Limousine
663-1220; (1-800) 336-4646. Chicago's largest fleet of chauffeur-driven sedans.
Lake Shore Limousines
334-2343. Elegant limousine service including the "longest most luxurious, Lincoln Presidential stretch limo."

Linens

Crate & Barrel Warehouse Store
1510 North Wells. 787-4775. Discontinued and closeout Marimekko linens and comforters, 40-50% off. AE, MC, V. *OPEN 7 days.*
Franklin-Bayer
612 North Michigan. 944-4737. A gracious shop for the finest table linens; bed and bath too. AE, MC, V. *OPEN Mon-Fri.*
Linens Plus
8760 Dempster Plaza, Niles. 296-5330. And Oakbrook Center, Arlington Heights, and Matteson. Sheets, towels, comforters, bedspreads. Up front, a broad selection of quality brands; in the rear, Linen Mill outlet at 30-60% discount. MC, V. *OPEN 7 days.*
Pass the Salt & Pepper
3337 North Broadway. 975-9789. Specialty shop. Table boutique: salt and pepper shakers, place mats, napkins, candle holders, mugs. AE, MC, V. *OPEN 7 days.*
Private Lives
1506 Sherman Street, Evanston. 869-8920. *Haute* bed and bath boutique for the Chicago area's largest collection of bed linens. Bath coordinated accessories. Stocks satin sheets. Very personal service. Will make things to order. AE, MC, V. *OPEN Mon-Sat.*
Shaxted
940 North Michigan. 337-0855. The finest of fine linens for bed, bath, and table. Custom orders. Unique and imported accessories. Monogramming. Great annual spring sale. AE, MC, V. *OPEN Mon-Sat.*

Makeup

Aloe Vera
8301 South Ashland. 881-1994. Cosmetics from the aloe plant—retail and wholesale. Facial beauty kits available. Distributed privately. *OPEN 7 days.*
Bravco, Inc.
43 East Oak. 943-4305. Professional makeup from this beauty and health supply shop at low, low prices. *OPEN Mon-Sat.*
Marilyn Miglin
112 East Oak. 943-1120. Devoted exclusively to making you more beautiful. Her complete line of wonderful makeup and skin-care products and applicators. Well worth the price. *OPEN Mon-Sat.*
Merle Norman Cosmetic Studios
4202 North Harlem. 456-1718. Well-known name

in cosmetics. Free personalized make-over. Best by appointment. AE, MC, V. *OPEN Mon-Sat.*

The Paint Shop
49 East Oak. 642-7115. Makeup consultation and application, as well as cosmetics, brushes, and whimsical fashion accessories. MC, V. *OPEN Tues-Sat.*

Maps

(See also SHOPPING, Specialty Shops & Services: Memorabilia.)

The Chicago Map Society
Newberry Library, 60 West Walton. 943-9090. Established in 1976 and based here at the Newberry. Publishes a *World Directory of Dealers in Antiquarian Maps,* available at the Newberry bookstore.

Graton & Graton
866-7096. Broad selection of antique maps, rare sea charts, and luminated manuscripts from the 13th to the 19th century. *By appointment only.*

Kenneth Nebenzahl
333 North Michigan, 28th floor. 641-2711. Well-known and respected Chicago map dealer for 30 years.

Rand McNally
23 East Madison. 332-4627. Mapmakers for more than a century. In this lovely old shop you will find maps of every kind, including some antique. Knowledgeable staff. AE, MC, V. *OPEN Mon-Sat.*

Memorabilia

(See also SHOPPING, Specialty Shops & Services: Antiques & Collectibles.)

Accent Chicago
Water Tower Place, 835 North Michigan, 7th level. 944-1354. In a city of boosters (remember this is where "windy" came from) this shop puts its *raison* where its heart is. Wonderful collection of all things Chicago—from your very own neon skyline to key rings, posters, umbrellas, and books. Very wide price range. AE, MC, V. *OPEN 7 days.*

Chicago Gift Shop
200 North La Salle. 580-6900. Operated by the Chicago Association of Commerce and Industry. Small shop of Chicago books, mementos, memorabilia. All very affordable. MC, V. *OPEN Mon-Fri.*

Chicago Historical Society Gift Shop
Clark at North Avenue. 642-4600. Reproductions of antique posters among other Chicago-related memorabilia. *OPEN 7 days.*

Collector's World, Inc.
Water Tower Place, 835 North Michigan, 6th level. 266-0499. From the Gorham Norman Rockwell collection: limited editions. Also, Hummels, Royal Doulton, and Mickey Mouse. AE, MC, V. *OPEN 7 days.*

Ginkgo Tree Book Shop
951 Chicago Avenue, Oak Park. 848-1606. For

the architect on your list. Frank Lloyd Wright memorabilia and books, gift items. *OPEN 7 days.*

Golden Age Nostalgia Book Shop
534 North Clark. 751-9163. Movie posters, Old Chicago; marbles, old records and sheet music, vintage books, toys. AE, MC, V. *OPEN Mon-Sat.*

Larry's Comic Book Store
1219 West Devon. 274-1832. New and used comics. Science fiction too. *OPEN Mon-Sat.*

Metro Goldwyn Memories
5425 West Addison. 736-4133. Tune in to a simple time. Tapes of old favorite radio shows. From the 30s to 50s, original movie stills and posters, books, magazines, vintage comics. Vintage television shows and movies. MC, V. *OPEN 7 days.*

The Sport Collector's Store
95 South La Grange Road, La Grange. 354-7970. Old sports collectibles, baseball cards, programs, yearbooks, pennants. Baseball, football, basketball, hockey. MC, V. *OPEN Mon-Thurs & Sat.*

Sullivan Sporting Books
3748 North Damen. 472-2638. A hobby that grew. Baseball, football, and boxing programs, scorecards, and guides for collectors. Buys and sells. *By appointment only.*

Yesterday
1143 West Addison. 248-8087. A treasure trove, near Wrigley Park, of hundreds of old baseball cards, scorecards, and other baseball mementos. Movie posters, old newpapers and magazines. No credit cards. *OPEN 7 days.*

Music Boxes

(See also SHOPPING, Specialty Shops & Services: Antiques & Collectibles.)

Collector's World
Water Tower Place, 835 North Michigan, 6th level. 266-0499. Music boxes, some antique. AE, MC, V. *OPEN 7 days.*

Needlework

(See also SHOPPING, Specialty Shops & Services: Crafts.)

Bunka Embroidery
5518 West Devon. 763-7880. "Bunka Shi Shu"—cultural embroidery of Japan. Classes and supplies. Also direct embroidery on wearables. No credit cards. *OPEN Tues-Sat.*

Franklin Knit Shop
1656 North Wells. 280-8244. Free instruction with purchase of their almost exclusively imported yarns. MC, V. *OPEN Mon-Sat.*

Midwest Discount Yarns
3157 West Irving Park Road. 588-3120. A bargain source for wool or acrylic yarn by the skein or hank or cone. Cones for machine knitting and weaving. Outlet for senior citizens' handiwork on consignment. No credit cards. *OPEN Mon-Sat.*

The Shepherd's Harvest
1930 Central Avenue, Evanston. 491-1353. Yarn in beautiful hues of spun natural fibers, cotton,

silk, wool. Sacks of fleece; carded wool. New Zealand spinning wheels. Spinning, weaving, knitting, and basketry lessons. MC, V. *OPEN Mon-Sat.*

Weaving Workshop
916 West Diversey. 929-5776. Great selection of imported and domestic yarns; paraphernalia too. Weaving and knitting classes year-round. AE, MC, V. *OPEN 7 days.*

We'll Keep You in Stitches
67 East Oak, 4th level. 642-2540. Elegant knit and needlepoint emporium. Tempting selection of yarns, canvas, needles, patterns, and books. Instruction and personalized service. Knit it yourself or they'll knit it for you. AE, MC, V. *OPEN Mon-Sat.*

Newspapers & Magazines

Chicago & Main Newsstand
Evanston. 864-2727. Fifty out-of-town papers including the *New York Times* and the Sunday *Los Angeles Times.* Books, paperbacks, magazines. No credit cards. *OPEN 7 days.*

Eastern Newsstands
1 North Dearborn. 782-2990. Local papers, magazines, paperbacks. No credit cards. *OPEN Mon-Fri.*

Kiosque
Mayfair Regent Hotel, 181 East Lake Shore Drive. 787-8500. Foreign and domestic newspapers and magazines as well as books. MC, V. *OPEN Mon-Sat.*

Loyola News Stand
6524 North Sheridan. 465-3204. Local papers, *New York Times,* and limited supply of magazines. *OPEN 7 days.*

Nuts & Seeds

(See also SHOPPING, Specialty Shops & Services: Health Foods.)

Georgia Nut Company
3325 North California. 539-0240. Filberts, pecans, peanuts, walnuts, pistachios, cashews. Dried fruit too. No credit cards. *OPEN Mon-Fri.*

Ricci & Company
162 West Superior. 787-7660. Since 1919. Importers, shellers, salters. Discount nut outlet. Roasting on premises. No credit cards. *OPEN Mon-Sat.*

Party

—Party Help

(See also SHOPPING, Specialty Shops & Services: Caterers.)

Banqueteers
1440 West North Avenue, Melrose Park. 6101½ West North Avenue, Oak Park. 848-9778. Will supply everything but the reason to have the party. Can find the facility, food, drink, music, staff, and scenery for theme parties. No credit cards. *OPEN 7 days.*

Gapers
340 West Evergreen. 332-4935. Part of the long-established and well-respected Stop & Shop concern. Consultation for a luncheon for 15 or a fully catered theme party for 1,500 (high tea or Wild West). No credit cards. *OPEN Mon-Sat.*

George Jewel Catering
1110 West Belmont. 935-6316. Jewel stores' catering arm. Lovely simple meals to extravagant banquets. Minimum order, depending on when and what it is. No credit cards. *OPEN 7 days.*

Master Caterers
2110 West Grand. 226-5545. Luxury social catering for intimate dinners and parties. Highly flexible. They supply silver, china, linens, flowers, candles, maids and waitresses, etc. *OPEN Mon-Fri.*

The Mixing Bowl, Ltd.
1341 North Sedgwick. 664-6900. Less expensive than you would expect for nicely prepared party food and party help. Full service: butlers, bartenders, etc. No credit cards. *OPEN 7 days.*

Out to Lunch
200 East Chestnut. 642-4649. Complete party service, starting with the invites. From a stylish picnic for 500 to an elegant sit-down dinner. Custom-designed menus.

Plunkett Catering
5222 West Belmont. 725-4848. From the simple to the sublime—a catered picnic, perhaps. Done with imagination and flair. *OPEN Mon-Sat.*

River Entertainment, Inc.
230 East Ontario, Suite 1004. 642-3278. Anyone can have a yacht party; how about a party on a 100-foot stern-wheel riverboat with the Chicago skyline as the backdrop as you cruise the Lake? Catering too. *OPEN Mon-Fri.*

R.S.V.P. Party Services
715 West Diversey. 327-8506. Enthusiastic party planners, from food to entertainment. Tables to china. Custom-designed themes. No credit cards. *OPEN 7 days.*

Susie Snyder Executive Catering
1838 South Canalport. 525-7500. Contrary to the name, it's film and art community people who use her services most. Creative small parties or elaborate meals for a crowd. Feeds anyone, anything, anyplace, anytime. Including breakfast in bed.

—Party Music

Bert Rose
272-2637. Longtime music man with a wide repertoire. Disco to polkas.

Bill Scott Orchestra
998-0792. Middle-of-the-road, easy-to-dance-to Broadway show tunes, Cole Porter classics. Six-to eight-piece band. Very versatile.

Dance All Night
940-9788. DJ, light show, and endless sound right in your own home. Call for details.

Dance Trax
966-9197. Mobile entertainment for any type of

party. Disco, country & western, rock & roll, nostalgia. Fog too.

Ircari & Stephens Orchestra
966-9197. Live music and entertainment. Known for their creativity and ingenuity; they were cited by the *Chicago Tribune* as one of Chicagoland's top society bands.

Steve Miles Orchestra
973-4480. Lori Brittin & the Miles Group, a very versatile six- to twelve-piece band. Jazz and pop (with a little blues and swing thrown in), but they will tailor their repertoire to meet your requests (even Bach if you wish). They have appeared in major jazz clubs in Chicago.

—Party Paraphernalia

Hall Rental Service
3950 West Devon Avenue, Lincolnwood. 982-9200. *The* place for rental: china (six different patterns), glassware, silverware, pewter, silver punch bowl, coffee and tea service. No credit cards. *OPEN Mon-Sat.*

HDO Productions, Inc.
237 Melvin Drive, Northbrook. 564-1700. "Rent a tent for an event"—largest supplier of tents in the world. Artificial turf, dance floors, heating, and lighting. Consultation too, on your tented event. No credit cards. *OPEN Mon-Fri.*

Roosevelt Chair & Supply Co.
1717 West Belmont. 248-3700. One or 50,000 chairs. Tables, china, silver service, glassware too. No credit cards. *OPEN Mon-Sat.*

Pets

—Pet Shops

And Feathers Bird Studio
1015 West Webster. 549-6944. Amazon parrots, finches, parakeets, canaries, love birds, macaws, and cockatoos. Cages, accessories, feed. MC, V. *OPEN Tues-Thurs & Sat. CLOSED Fri & Mon.*

Animal Kingdom
2980 North Milwaukee. 227-4444. Tigers, lions, birds, and monkeys from all over the world. Also, pets, supplies, food, and accessories for sale. FREE admission. *OPEN 7 days.*

Feline Inn
1445 North Wells. 943-2230. Cats, cat statues, and paraphernalia; gifts. No credit cards. *OPEN Mon & Wed-Sat. CLOSED Tues & Sun.*

Park View Pet Shop
2222 North Clark. 549-6341. Birds and fish mainly; seminars on dog training. Grooming, supplies, gift items. AE, MC, V. *OPEN Tues-Sun.*

World Wide Aquarium
2852 North Clark. 525-6093. Over 200 species of fresh- and saltwater fish. Pet accessories and supplies. Birds too. AE, MC, V. *OPEN 7 days.*

—Pets: Adoption

The Anti-Cruelty Society
157 West Grand. 644-8338. Adoption center run by the Anti-Cruelty Society. They have pets,

food, supplies, and accessories. Fee includes spaying or neutering, as well as shots. It's all for a good cause. *OPEN 7 days.*

Tree House Animal Foundation
1212 West Carmen. 784-5488. Nonprofit humane organization. Adoption program, low-cost neutering/spaying, emergency care, and counseling. Rescues abandoned strays. No credit cards. *OPEN Wed-Sun.*

—Pets: Boarding

Collar & Leash
3541 West Columbus. 737-1323. Kennel will board your pet for any length of time. Dogs must be vaccinated against parvo, para-influenza, rabies, and distemper. You must pick up and deliver your own pet. Rates vary with size of dog. *OPEN Mon-Sat.*

—Pets: Information

D.I.A.L. P.E.T.
342-5738. The Chicago Public Library. Fortyone 5- to 7-minute tapes, written by vets and humane society officers, with general information pertaining to cats, dogs, birds, fish, horses, snakes, rodents, and lizards. Brochure available at your vet or local library. *OPEN Mon-Sat.*

Tree-House Pet Owner Telephone Counseling Service
784-5488. Pet experts answer your questions. *Call Wed-Sun.*

—Pets: Treatment

Chicago Veterinary Emergency Service (North)
3123 North Clybourn. 281-7110. *OPEN Mon & Tues, Thurs & Fri 7pm-8am; Wed noon-8am; Sat noon-Mon 8am continuous.* Call first.

Emergency Veterinary Care (South)
13815 South Cicero. 388-3771. *OPEN Mon-Fri 7pm-8am; Sat 1pm-Mon 8am continuous.* Call first.

Lake Shore Animal Hospital
225 West Division. 787-5080. Vet on duty *Mon-Fri 9am-6pm; Sat 9am-5pm. CLOSED Sun.* Call before going.

Photographers

Bachrach Studios
104 South Michigan. 236-1991. Since 1868, famed portrait photographers. Black-and-white and color. Weddings, family groups, candids. MC, V. *OPEN Mon-Fri by appointment.*

Stuart Rogers Photography
70 East Walton Place; 787-8696. And 2504 Green Bay Road, Evanston; 864-7322. Long established (40 years). Kids, weddings, candids—debs to annual reports. Black-and-white and color. *By appointment only.*

Photographic Equipment

Central Camera
230 South Wabash. 427-5580. Chicago's oldest

(since 1899) complete camera store. Discount prices. MC, V. *OPEN Mon-Sat.*

Helix
325 West Huron. 421-6000. Photographers' heaven. Equipment on three floors with over 11 departments. Special darkroom department; used equipment. Ask to be put on their catalog mailing list. MC, V, Helix charge. *OPEN Mon-Sat.*

Shutan Camera
312 West Randolph. 332-2000. Since 1918, new and used photographic equipment. They buy, sell, trade, repair. Accessories too. MC, V. *OPEN Mon-Sat.*

Solar Cine Products, Inc.
4247 South Kedzie. 254-8310. Long-established source for the latest-model cameras. Darkroom equipment, some audio. Low prices. MC, V. *OPEN Mon-Sat.*

Wolk Camera
Two Illinois Center. 565-5901. Video and audio equipment. Discount prices, helpful service. MC, V. *OPEN Mon-Fri.*

Picnics

See SHOPPING, Specialty Shops & Services: Gourmet.

Plants

(*See also* SHOPPING, Specialty Shops & Services: Flowers.)

Amlings—Plant Rental
789-6400. Commercial rental only. Long-term plant rentals in the Hinsdale location. Other Amlings rent at the discretion of the manager for short periods. AE, MC, V. *OPEN Mon-Fri.*

Farmer's Market Garden Center
4110 North Elston. 539-1200. Tools and bulbs. July to September, fresh fruits and vegetables. MC, V ($25 minimum). *OPEN 7 days.*

Plants, Inc.
2457 West Montrose. 478-8208. A design service for home or office. Greenhouse for retail. City and suburban delivery. MC, V. *OPEN Mon-Sat.*

Potpourri Flower Shop
3409 North Broadway. 472-7228. Lovely spot for cut flowers, European silk flowers, imported dried flowers, and plants. Your container or theirs. AE, DC, MC, V. *OPEN 7 days.*

Village Green
1952 North Halsted. 472-2800. Outdoor garden and indoor plant center. AE, MC, V. *OPEN 7 days.*

Plastic

American Acrylics
4868 North Clark. 784-7400. Lucite in sheets, cut to size. No credit cards. *OPEN Mon-Fri.*

Great Ace Hardware
2818 North Broadway, 2nd floor. 348-0705. Good selection of acrylic accessories for the home. AE, MC, V. *OPEN 7 days.*

Quilts

Many antique shops have a few quilts among their stock; see also SHOPPING, Specialty Shops & Services: Antiques & Collectibles.

Wild Goose Chase
1524 Chicago Avenue, Evanston. 328-1808. Mint-conditions quilts ca. 1820-1930; mainly midwestern, some Pennsylvania Amish. Some contemporary. No credit cards. *OPEN Tues-Sat.*

Records & Tapes

Dr. Wax
2529 North Clark. 549-3377. Popular for used and never-used records. Jazz, pop, blues, shows, folk, classical. MC, V. *OPEN 7 days.*

Rose Records
1122 North State; 943-8530. And 3259 North Ashland; 880-0285. Also 214 South Wabash, 987-9044; and 13 suburban stores. Chicago's oldest dealer. Claims to have one of the largest and most complete inventories. It's big. Incredible selection of pop, jazz, classical, and country records, tapes, and video cassettes. The annual sale is a must. AE, MC, V. *OPEN Mon-Sat.*

Spirit Record Shop
1444 East 57th. 684-1505. Classical, jazz, and rock records. MC, V. *OPEN 7 days.*

—Records: Specialized

Beverly Costumes, Records & Novelty Shop
11612 South Western. 779-0066. Collectors' hard-to-find 33s, 45s, and 78s. Educational and foreign current records too. AE, MC, V. *OPEN Mon-Sat.*

Empire Records
4350 North Cicero. 545-2005. Fine selection of new and used LP's. Jazz, classical, rock, country, folk, bluegrass. Buy, sell, trade. No credit cards. *OPEN 7 days.*

Gibson's Music Store
1956 West 51st. 776-0700. Midwest's largest selection of country & western records, old and new. MC, V. *OPEN Mon-Sat.*

Jazz Record Mart
11 West Grand. 222-1467. Anything that has to do with jazz, old and new. Collectors' source. AE, MC, V. *OPEN 7 days*

Record Hunt
5951 West Lawrence. 685-7113. Used pop, rock, jazz, classical, country, Broadway. Buy, sell, trade. No credit cards. *OPEN Mon-Sat.*

Second Hand Tunes
2550 North Clark; 929-6325. And 1375 East 53rd; 684-3375. Also 818 Dempster Street, Evanston, 491-1690; and Oak Park and Milwaukee. Buy and sell used records. Jazz, classical, folk, blues, rock, soul—and any other music ever recorded. MC, V. *OPEN 7 days.*

Vintage Vinyl
925 Davis, Evanston. 328-2899. From the new to the obscure, they claim to have it. Vintage and imports. New Wave, reggae, Broadway,

blues, rhythm & blues. No credit cards. *OPEN Mon-Sat.*

Wax Trax
2449 North Lincoln. 929-0221. Punk-rock imports, new and used. Fifties and 60s oldies; soul. AE, MC, V. *OPEN 7 days.*

Rubber Stamps

National Rubber Stamp Company
1919-21 West Irving Park Road. 281-6522. They stock stamps, pads, and accessories. Custom-made rubber stamps also. No credit cards. *OPEN Mon-Sat.*

Rugs

Caravans Awry
318 West Grand. 644-5395. All handmade imports from Pakistan, Afghanistan, China, India, and Persia at great savings. A few old kilims, dhurries as well. Old and antique rugs. They buy direct and pass the savings on to you. AE, MC, V. *OPEN 7 days.*

Caspian Oriental Rugs
700 North La Salle. 664-7576. Knowledgeable importers will help you choose from over 5,000 new, antique, and used Oriental rugs. AE, MC, V. *OPEN 7 days.*

Joseph W. Fell, Ltd.
3221 North Clark. 549-6076. Collectors' rugs, kilims, geometrics; restoration; appraisals too. No credit cards. *OPEN Tues-Sat, by appointment.*

Leon Beloian Rug Company, Inc.
6241-43 North Broadway. 743-5700. Rug specialists since 1906. *Hand* cleaning and expert repair of Oriental rugs. No credit cards. *OPEN Mon-Sat.*

Minasian Oriental Rugs
1244 Chicago Avenue, Evanston. 491-0985. Longtime reliable source for hand-knotted Oriental rugs. Cleaning and repair too. AE, MC, V. *OPEN Mon-Sat.*

Nahigian Brothers, Inc.
645 North Michigan. 943-8300. Since 1890, fine establishment for antique, modern Aubusson, and Chinese rugs. AE, MC, V. *OPEN Mon-Sat.*

Peerless Rug Company
3028 North Lincoln. 525-4876. Everything but flying carpets: Oriental, Navajo, grass, flokati; wood, ceramic, and vinyl tiles. AE, MC, V. *OPEN 7 days.*

Sol Hakimian & Company
2727 West Touhy. 973-6030. Antique and semi-antique Chinese, Caucasian, domestic. No credit cards. *OPEN Mon-Sat; Sun by appointment.*

Silver

(*See also* SHOPPING, Specialty Shops & Services: Antiques & Collectibles.)

Arthur Reiffel & Company
2700 West Van Buren. 638-0142. In business for 80 years—repair and refinishing of silver plate. No credit cards. *OPEN Mon-Fri.*

Barnett's Chicago
33 East Madison. 332-7460. Sterling by Reed & Barton, Gorham, Heirloom, Towle, International, Fraser. AE, DC, MC, V. *OPEN Mon-Sat.*

Char Crews, Inc.
101 West Chestnut, Hinsdale. 920-0190. And Plaza del Lago, Wilmette, Barrington, and Park Ridge. Sterling silver and silverplate, pewter, and stainless flatware at 20% discount. Gorham, International, Kirk-Steif, Lunt, Oneida, Reed & Barton, Towle, Wallace. China and crystal too. Mail and phone orders accepted. Very friendly help. MC, V. *OPEN 7 days.*

Forsberg & Hoover
5 North Wabash. 332-1352. Jewelry and sterling silver. Silverplate too. No credit cards. *OPEN Mon-Sat.*

—Silver: Repairs

Ciske & Dresch
1125 Paramount Parkway, Batavia. 879-7818. Long-established gold and silver repair firm. Missing parts supplied; plating work also. No credit cards. *OPEN Mon-Fri.*

House of Williams
37 South Wabash. 236-6320. Stocks of silver pieces as well as custom silver work. Quality workmanship in brass, gold, copper, and silver-plating. Retinning of copper pots. Awards, trophies. No credit cards. *OPEN Mon-Fri.*

Sporting Goods

Athlete's Foot
2140 North Halsted; 477-1200. And The Century, 2828 North Clark; 327-7333. Also in the suburbs. For the serious runner. Every type of running shoe for men, women, and children. Also a line of jogging accessories. AE, MC, V. *OPEN 7 days.*

Chicago Yachting & Navigation, Ltd.
1661 North Elston. 227-7900. Boating supplies, marine equipment. Mostly sails and clothing. MC, V. *OPEN 7 days.*

Eddie Bauer
123 North Wabash; 263-6005. And six suburban stores. One of the very best for sporting goods, camping equipment, woolen and down winter wear. AE, MC, V. *OPEN 7 days.*

Erewhon Mountain Supply
414 North Orleans. 644-4411. Cross-country ski equipment, in season. Camping, canoeing, and mountaineering supplies. Clothes too. AE, MC, V. *OPEN 7 days.*

Herman's World of Sporting Goods
4052 North Cicero; 545-5858. And 111 East Chicago; 951-8282. Also in the suburbs. A top sporting-goods source. Stocks all the famous brands. AE, CB, DC, MC, V. *OPEN 7 days.*

Land's End
2317 North Elston. 384-4170. Clothing, accessories, soft luggage. Catalog available. AE, MC, V. *OPEN 7 days.*

Land's End Men's Outlet
2241 North Elston. 276-2232. Discounts of 20-80% on luggage, clothing, and accessories from the Land's End catalog warehouse. Also one-of-a-kind samples, discontinueds, and seconds. AE, MC, V. *OPEN 7 days.*

Morrie Mages Sports
620 North La Salle; 337-6151. And in the suburbs. *Very* well stocked sporting-goods mecca on eight floors. Huge 18-hour sale three times a year (February, August, November), plus a blockbuster just before Christmas. AE, CB, DC, MC, V. *OPEN 7 days.*

Port Supply
2245 South Michigan; 842-2704. Also 111 North Elston; 276-0330. Everything marine: accessories, supplies for repair and refinishing of wood and fiberglass boats. Fine line of foul-weather gear. MC, V. *OPEN Mon & Tues, Thurs-Sat. CLOSED Wed & Sun.*

Sportif
5225 West Lawrence. 685-0240. Over 100 different styles of athletic shoes, including Adidas, Puma, Nike. Odd sizes too. Some 850 bikes on display, 10,000 in stock, 40 top brands. AE, MC, V. *OPEN Mon-Sat.*

Trout & Grouse
1147 Wilmette Avenue, Wilmette. 251-8090. Rods, reels, flies. Outdoor gear. Fly-casting lessons by appointment only. Fly-fishing weekend school mid April to August. MC, V. *OPEN Mon-Sat.*

Viking Ski Shop
3422 West Fullerton. 276-1222. Chic ski duds and accessories. MC, V. *OPEN 7 days. Irregular hours, best to call.*

Stamps

Carson Pirie Scott & Co. has quite a good stamp and coin department.

Archie's
5516 West Devon. 774-1433. Buys and sells stamps. Appraisals. MC, V. *OPEN 7 days.*

John G. Ross
12 West Madison. 236-4088. Buys and sells. MC, V. *OPEN Mon-Fri.*

Liberty Stamps
140 South Dearborn. 332-4464. Buys and sells. MC, V. *OPEN Mon-Sat.*

Stationery

Printers Row Printing Museum
715 South Dearborn. 987-1059. From the place where a traditional art and craft is being kept alive. Original 19th-century presses do the printing. You pick the typeface and paper for personalized notes, stationery, Christmas cards. *OPEN Sat & Sun only.*

The Stationery Station, Ltd.
640 Central Avenue, Highland Park. 432-3044. Custom designing and printing. Some stock of stationery and invitations. MC, V. *OPEN Mon-Sat.*

The Watermark
109 East Oak. 337-5353. "Elegance on paper": custom-designed stationery, invitations, announcements. Personal and business writing paper. Greeting cards. Distinctive desk accessories; photo albums too. AE, MC, V. *OPEN Mon-Sat.*

Write Impressions, Ltd.
42 East Chicago Avenue. 943-3306. Custom stationery, printed party supplies, business cards, gifts. Desk accessories, Mont Blanc pens, antique inkwells, rolls of stickers. All in a charming, friendly atmosphere. MC, V. *OPEN Mon-Sat.*

Stereo & Sound Systems

Audio Consultants
1014 Davis, Evanston. 864-9565. Friendly consultation on components and custom-designed audio units. AE, MC, V. *OPEN Mon-Sat.*

Musicraft
48 East Oak. 337-4150. And Oak Park, Villa Park, Morton Grove, Palatine, Evergreen Park, Homewood. Very well stocked with over 50 name brands. Knowledgeable. MC, V. *OPEN Mon-Sat.*

Paul Heath Audio, Ltd.
2036 North Clark. 549-8100. Finest stereo equipment—Bang & Olufson, Mark Levinson. Designer equipment. MC, V. *OPEN Tues-Sat.*

Radio Shack
Water Tower Place, 835 North Michigan, 5th level; 642-2851. And 200 South Michigan; 786-1407. Also 4359 South Archer, 847-1434; 328 West Madison, 332-7683; 5440 West Belmont, 725-8900; 5918 West Lawrence, 736-4411; 2923 North Ashland, 929-3360; 1453 East 53rd, 667-5050; 3219 West 63rd, 434-4666; 6455 West Diversey, 622-7006; 4821 West Irving Park Road, 685-8040; 7601 South Cicero, 582-6070; and 212 North Michigan, 236-1485. Good values at this supermarket of sound. AE, MC, V. Hours vary store to store; some *OPEN 7 days.* Call ahead.

United Audio
6181 North Lincoln; 478-7505. And The Century, 2825 North Clark; 525-7005. Home and car stereos. Portables too. AE, MC, V. *OPEN 7 days.*

Victor's Stereo
8 East Erie. 642-6349. Bang & Olufson, Mission, Onkyo, and more. AE, MC, V. *OPEN Mon-Sat.*

Tattoos

Permanent body art. Best when sober and sure.

Chicago Tattooing Company
922 West Belmont. 528-6969. Traditional American (Mom, apple pie) or Oriental designs. Minimum age, 21. *OPEN Wed-Sat.*

Southwest Tattoo Emporium
3747 West 63rd. 582-4500. One of theirs or one of yours. Minimum age, 21. *OPEN 7 days.*

Tea & Coffee

Coffee & Tea Exchange
3300 North Broadway. 528-2241. Aromatic. Cof-

fee in bulk, ground to order. Good assortment of teas. Mail order. AE, MC, V. *OPEN 7 days.*

The Coffee Bean Limited
248 Old MacHenry Road, Long Grove. 634-3101. Coffee, tea, and spices. A different coffee brewed each day for sampling. AE, MC, V. *OPEN 7 days.*

Coffee Corner
1700 North Wells. 951-7638. Coffees, teas, nuts, spices; tea and coffee makers. Small packages of tea for sampling new brews. AE, MC, V. *OPEN 7 days.*

Something's Brewing
958 West Diversey. 871-7475. Fresh roasted and ground coffee; tea; espresso machines; teapots, mugs, coffee pots, grinders. Sit-down or stand-up coffee-and-tea bar. MC, V ($10 minimum). *OPEN 7 days.*

Telegrams: Unusual

(*See also* SHOPPING, Specialty Shops & Services: Balloons.)

Eastern Onion
636-0264. Clowns and balloons, gorillagram; bellygram: 5-minute "act" by an entertainer gets your message across. Deliveries 7 days a week, 24 hours a day. AE, MC, V. *Call Mon-Fri 9am-6pm; Sat 10-3pm. CLOSED Sun.*

Hey! Wires
351-1234. Singing and dancing telegrams for any occasion, including the Fantasygram; "anything legal, not harmful to life and limb, nor in *incredibly* bad taste." Singing and dancing gorillas, belly dancers, and funny doctors are among the cast of characters.

Sgt. Yukon Singing Messenger
334-4441; 951-8400. Move over Nelson Eddy, this Canadian Mountie will sing your Indian love call to a fair maiden. Advance notice needed for foreign languages. AE, MC, V. *OPEN 7 days till midnight.*

Tele-Tune
Highland Park. 831-2000. A "singing" balloon in a box mailed anywhere in the country; five days' notice. Or the pipes in person. All original tunes; delivered via telephone as well. AE, MC, V. *OPEN 7 days.*

Theatrical

(*See also* SHOPPING, Specialty Shops & Services: Memorabilia.)

Capezio Dance-Theater Shop
50 East Washington, 3rd floor. 236-1911. Foot, leg, and body wear for dancing. Bags also. AE, MC, V. *OPEN Mon-Sat.*

Dance & Mime Shop
2402 North Lincoln, 2nd floor. 477-1928. Tights, leotards, costumes, shoes, makeup, dance bags. Children's and men's also. Books, records, and postcards. MC, V. *OPEN Mon-Sat.*

The Goodman Theater Store
200 South Columbus, off lobby. 443-3800. Theatrical items including autographed scripts and plays, T-shirts from past and present productions, as well as posters, coloring books, mugs. The store is open one hour before, during, and half an hour after performances. AE, MC, V. *OPEN, during the season, Wed-Sun.*

Leo's Advance Theatrical Company
1900 North Narragansett. 745-5600. Put on their dancing shoes, as well as their tutus, leotards, top hats, and castanets (but *not* all together). All for sale. MC, V. *OPEN Mon-Sat.*

Tobacconists

Alfred Dunhill of London, Inc.
Water Tower Place, 835 North Michigan, 2nd level. 467-4455. The renowned tobacconists for custom-blended tobacco; impecably carved briar pipes, humidors, cigars, and gifts, including their famed expensive lighters. Also men's clothes and leather accessories. AE, MC, V. *OPEN Mon-Sat.*

Cellini Pipe Company
5630 West Dempster, Morton Grove. 966-7111. Longtime family operation (60 years). Custom-made pipes of natural aged briar, no fills, varnish, or lacquer. Over 100 custom tobacco blends. Collectors' source and trading post. Repairs too. MC, V. *OPEN Mon-Sat.*

Iwan Ries & Company
19 South Wabash. 372-1306. Chicago's oldest family-run company—since 1857. "World's largest selection of pipes and accessories." Antique too. Tobacco, loose and in tins. Imported and domestic cigars. Catalog available. AE, CB, DC, MC, V. *OPEN Mon-Sat.*

Logan Square Cigar Store
2541 North Kedzie. 278-4554. Large selection of imports as well as domestic cigars and tobacco. Carries Nat Sherman loose cigarette tobacco. Cigars for births. No credit cards. *OPEN 7 days.*

Pittsfield Building Cigar Shop
55 East Washington. 263-2478. Specializes in handmade cigars. MC, V. *OPEN Mon-Sat.*

Rubovits Cigars
320 South La Salle. 939-3780. Pipes, cigars, cigarettes, imported and domestic. Tobacco: loose, packaged, or in tins. Smokers' accessories. AE, MC, V. *OPEN Mon-Fri.*

The Tinder Box
Water Tower Place, 835 North Michigan, 4th level. 943-4475. Cigars, imported and domestic; cigarettes; loose tobacco; pipes, lighters and smokers' gift items. AE, MC, V. *OPEN 7 days.*

The Up Down Tobacco Shop
1550 North Wells. 337-8505. Loose cigarette tobacco and over 250 brands of cigars, including many imports. The world's largest (40-foot) "humidor" for cigar storage. AE, MC, V. *OPEN 7 days.* (*See* ANNUAL EVENTS, April: Chicago Pipe-Smoking Contest.)

Wallpaper

Laura Ashley
Water Tower Place, 835 North Michigan, 6th level. 951-8004. English floral coordinated wallpaper, fabric, and linens. *OPEN 7 days.*

The Paper Place
1844 West 95th. 233-1421. A traditional wallpaper store that goes by the book. MC, V. *OPEN 7 days.*

Sandy's Wallpapers
939 West Armitage. 935-5350. Imported and domestic wallpapers. Paint, fabric, window shades, mini-blinds, and vertical blinds. MC, V. *OPEN Mon-Sat.*

Thybony
5440 North Clark; 561-2275. And Glen View and Evanston. Choose from over 500 wallpaper patterns, including fabric wall coverings. Window treatments, paint, and paraphernalia. MC, V. OPEN 7 days.

Watches: Antique & Contemporary

(See also SHOPPING, Specialty Shops & Services: Clocks.)
Flashy Trash
3521 North Halsted. 327-6900. This vintage clothing store carries a large selection of men's art deco watches. AE, MC, V. *OPEN 7 days.*

Lester Lampert
701 North Michigan. 944-6888. Excellent selection of watches. Every April a spectacular sale of the Swiss ones. AE, CB, DC, MC, V. *OPEN Mon-Sat.*

Nonpareil
2300 North Clark. 477-2933. Reconditioned vintage watches—ca. 1915-55. *OPEN 7 days.*

Smart Jewelers
3350 West Devon, Lincolnwood. 673-6000. Chicago area's largest selection of watches: Omega, Rolex, Seiko, Patek Philippe. Bands, straps, and bracelets too. AE, CB, DC, MC, V. *OPEN Mon-Sat.*

Watchworks
Water Tower Place, 835 North Michigan, mez-

zanine. 266-9377. New, often unusual watches—wrist and pocket. Repairs too. AE, CB, DC, MC, V. *OPEN 7 days.*

Wines & Spirits

(See also SHOPPING, Specialty Shops & Services: Gourmet.)
Armanetti's
7324 North Western; 764-6425. And 2307 North Clark; 525-3223. Also in the suburbs. One of the largest liquor stores in Chicago. MC, V. *OPEN 7 days.*

Chalet Wine & Cheese Shops
444 West Fullerton; 871-0300. And 405 West Armitage; 266-7155. Also 3000 North Clark, 935-9400; and 1525 East 53rd, 324-5000. Wine tastings on Sunday at 53rd; every week on Clark Street. Call for schedule. MC, V. *OPEN 7 days.*

Connoisseur Wines, Ltd.
77 West Chestnut. 642-2375. Knowledgeable, helpful owners. Stock runs from budget to brilliant. Wine tastings; call for schedule. Delivery. AE, MC, V. *OPEN Mon-Sat.*

Sam's Liquors
1000 West North. 664-4394. The best. Though from the outside it looks like *the* place to buy pints in brown bags, inside is a sensational selection of fine wines. Chicago's largest wine selection with over 300,000-plus bottles and you'll be surprised at the low prices of many of them. Very knowledgeable staff. AE, MC, V. *OPEN 7 days.*

Sandburg Super Mart Wine Shop
1525 North Clark. 337-7509. Good selection of classic French and German wines as well as the best of California and Oregon. No credit cards. *OPEN 7 days.*

Say Vino
729-8466. Schedules of wine tastings and other wine-related news. Updated every Monday at 3pm.

Zimmerman's Cut Rate Liquor Store
213 West Grand. 332-0012. Excellent selection of French, Italian, and German wines. MC, V. *OPEN 7 days.*

24-HOUR CHICAGO

Marshall Field Clock

24-HOUR EATING

Unless otherwise noted, everything listed is OPEN 24 hours a day, 7 days a week.

Bagel Nosh
1135 North State. 266-6369. *OPEN Sun-Tues & Thurs till 11pm; Fri & Sat 24 hours; Wed till 1am.* (*See also* RESTAURANTS, Jewish.)

Belden Corned Beef Center
2315 North Clark. 935-2752. (*See also* RESTAURANTS, Delicatessen.)

BOSA Donuts
3358 West Belmont. 463-6630.
5301 West Belmont. 736-7743.
2471 North Clark. 472-8466.
6034 North Clark. 761-8627.
39 West Division. 664-9868.
4000 West Fullerton. 342-4734.
208 West North. 649-0862.

Dunkin' Donuts
7171 West Irving Park Road. 794-1050.
6738 West Archer. 586-5969.
3132 West Devon. 262-4561.
5821 West Diversey. 745-9767.
10150 Grand Avenue, Franklin Park. 455-0319.
5000 West Irving Park Road. 545-0515.
1743 West Lawrence. 334-0554.
5448 South Pulaski Road. 767-2055.
4045 West Lawrence. 725-2806.
6336 West North. 637-9477.
4667 West 79th. 585-2432.
8661 South Pulaski. 767-5745.
10401 South Western. 881-3410.

El Presidente
2531 North Lincoln; 528-8121. And 2558 North Ashland; 525-7938.

Express Grill
1316 South Halsted.738-2112.

Five Faces Ice Cream Parlor
10 West Division. 642-7837. (*See also* RESTAURANTS, Ice Cream.)

Golden Nugget Pancake House
3953 West Diversey. 227-4346.
3243 West Irving Park Road. 267-1987.
2720 North Clark. 929-0724.
3001 North Central. 725-5510.
6349 North Clark. 338-5551.
4229 West Irving Park Road. 777-7107.
4747 North Ravenswood. 769-6700.
4340 North Lincoln. 583-6969.

Granny's Waffle House
501 West Diversey. 348-6626. *OPEN Sun-Thurs 5am-1am; Fri & Sat 24 hours.*

Harris Restaurant
3150 West Irving Park Road. 539-0300.

Izola's
522 East 79th. 846-1484.

Jeff's Laugh Inn
1800 North Lincoln. 751-0434.

Jim's Original Hot Dog Stand
1320 South Halsted at Maxwell. 666-0533.

Korean Restaurant
2659 West Lawrence. 878-2095.

Lawrence Fisheries
2120 South Canal. 225-2113.

Mel Markon's
2150 North Lincoln Park West. 525-5550. *OPEN Mon-Fri 11am-4am; Sat 9am-5am; Sun 9am-4am.* (*See also* RESTAURANTS, Late-Night/24-Hour.)

McDonald's
600 North Clark. 664-7940. The world's busiest Big-Mac-ery. Served with a healthy dose of 50s and 60s nostalgia.

Miller's Pub & Restaurant
23 East Adams. 922-7446. *OPEN 7 days 10:30am-4am.* (*See also* RESTAURANTS, American.)

New York Bagels & Bialys
4714 West Touhy, Lincolnwood. 677-9388.

The Oak Tree
25 East Oak. 751-1988. (*See also* RESTAURANTS, Late-Night/24-Hour.)

Poong Mee House
3752 West Lawrence. 478-0217. (*See also* RESTAURANTS, Late-Night/24-Hour.)

Scampi's
Hyatt Regency Chicago, 151 East Wacker. 565-1234. (*See also* RESTAURANTS, Late-Night/24-Hour.)

Tempo
1 East Chestnut. 943-4373.

24-HOUR SERVICES

Credit Cards Lost

American Express: (1-800) 528-2121.
Carte Blanche: (1-800) 525-9150.
Diners' Club (1-800) 525-9150.
MasterCard (1-800) 826-2181.
Visa: (1-800) 336-8472.

Food Stores

Dominick's
OPEN 24 hours; CLOSED only Sun midnight-Mon 7am.
5253 North Lincoln. 728-4100.
4700 South Kedzie. 247-1400.
7000 South Pulaski. 581-6700.
6009 North Broadway. 769-2300.
3300 West Belmont. 588-7740.
3012 North Broadway. 549-6100.
3350 North Western Avenue. 929-8910.
3145 South Ashland. 247-2633.
5829 South Archer. 284-1228.
Jewel
3120 North Pulaski. 685-7550. OPEN Mon-Sat 24 hours; Sun till midnight.
3400 North Western. 929-4313. OPEN 7 days till 1am.
White Hen Pantry
All are OPEN 24 hours a day, 7 days a week.
6425 South Archer. 586-6182.
7600 North Ashland. 761-2565.
600 North McClurg Court. 649-9671.
10657 South Pulaski Road. 233-1696.
2600 West 51st. 925-9898.
3500 West 63rd. 737-0346. 7 days till 1am.
2900 West 87th. 778-3988.
2421 West 103rd. 445-9215.

Locksmiths

All will require identification and proof of residency before they help you get into an apartment, proof of ownership with a car.
A-AAABAL Lock
664 North Michigan. 266-0189.
A-AAAmes Emergency Road & Locksmith Service
5151 West Diversey. 637-7700.
Amazing Lock Service
739 West Belmont. 935-8900.
Don's Lock & Key Service
11353 South Bell. 239-3511.
J D's Key & Lock Shop
2547 West 51st. 436-8200.

The Lock Works
3789 South Archer. 523-7338.

Newsstands

At Clark & Diversey (2800 North & 600 West).
At Lincoln, Halsted & Fullerton (800 West & 2400 North).
Magazines, newspapers & candy 24 hours a day, 7 days a week.

Pharmacies

Alco Drug Store
347 East 35th. 225-4660. Prescriptions filled 24 hours.
Health Rite
8401 North Crawford Avenue, Skokie. 673-5940. OPEN Sun-Fri 7am-11pm; Sat 7am-midnight.
Modern Rexall Pharmacy
600 West 31st. 842-5131. OPEN Mon-Fri 9am-midnight; Sat, Sun & holidays 9am-10pm.
Northwestern Pharmacy, Inc.
1576 North Milwaukee. 486-0987. Prescription service 7 days 8am-midnight.
Walgreen's
Prescriptions 24 hours a day, 7 days a week.
757 North Michigan. 664-8686.
3302 West Belmont. 267-2328.
7501 South State. 224-1211.
6310 North Nagle. 774-2225.
1554 East 55th. 667-1177.

Plumbers

Evans Plumbing Company
7443 South Exchange; 10305 South St. Louis. 779-8437.
Rooter King
3439 West 63rd. 585-3200.

Post Office

Self-Service Postal Service
433 West Van Buren. 765-3210. Stamps and scale available 24 hours a day, 7 days a week.

TRAVEL
&
VACATION
INFORMATION

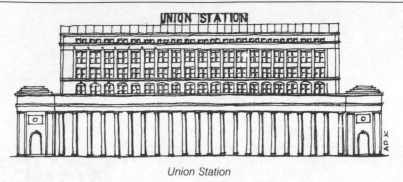

Union Station

PASSPORTS

During peak travel times, apply at least three weeks in advance of scheduled departure. Definitely call before going, as certain information and documentation are necessary. Some renewals can be done through the mail. There are 30 designated post offices and outlying Clerk of Court offices that will process passports. Call for information.

United States Passport Agency
230 South Dearborn. 353-5426 (recording); 353-7155 (questions, information). *OPEN Mon-Fri 8:15am-4pm.*

Passport Photographs

Two identical photos are needed. These can be done by any photographer as long as they fit the required specifications. For details, call 353-7155.

American Passport Studios
25 West Jackson, main floor. 939-2524. Quite near the passport office. Color or b/w photos while you wait. *OPEN Mon-Fri 8:30am-5:30pm; Sat 9am-1pm.*

U.S. Passport Photo Service
27 West Jackson Boulevard, ground floor. 922-1234. Across from the passport agency. Color and b/w while you wait. *OPEN Mon-Fri 8am-5pm; Sat 9am-1:30pm.*

OTHER IMPORTANT NUMBERS

Immigration & Naturalization Service
219 South Dearborn. 353-7334 (information 24 hours).

U.S. Customs Service, Public Information
610 South Canal. 353-6100; 353-6115 (tourist information). *OPEN Mon-Fri 8:30am-5pm.*

CURRENCY EXCHANGE

Most Chicago banks do not as a policy exchange foreign currency, so it is best to arrive with some American dollars. At the O'Hare International Terminal, ground level, there is a Foreign Currency Exchange open 7 days a week 8am-8pm. If you are going abroad, it's best to buy some foreign currency. You can purchase the currency at the following exchange offices.

Continental Illinois National Bank & Trust
209 South La Salle. 828-7654. International services. Buy and sell foreign currency, American Express foreign traveler's checks. *OPEN Mon-Fri 8:30am-5:30pm.*

Deak-Perera
17 North Dearborn, main floor. 236-0583. One hundred kinds of currency, a dozen foreign traveler's checks. *OPEN Mon-Fri 9am-5pm.* Branch at O'Hare in the International Terminal; 686-0626; *OPEN 7 days 8:30 am-8:30pm.*

First National Bank of Chicago
1 First National Plaza, Clark & Monroe, plaza level. 732-5198. The currency of 23 major countries and American Express foreign traveler's checks. *OPEN Mon-Fri 8:30am-4pm.*

TRAVELER'S CHECKS

Banks and almost all stores accept traveler's checks with proper identification.

American Express Company Travel Service
Lost or stolen American Express Travelers Cheques: call (1-800) 221-7282, 24 hours a day, 7 days a week.
625 North Michigan. 435-2570. *OPEN Mon-Fri 9am-5pm.*
20 South Michigan. 435-2595. *OPEN Mon-Fri 9am-5pm.*
Marshall Field's, 111 North State. 781-4477. *OPEN Mon-Sat 9:45am-5:45pm.*
1515 Sheridan Road, Wilmette. 251-7530. *OPEN Mon-Fri 9am-5pm; Sat 9am-12:30pm.*

Woodfield Mall, Schaumburg. 884-1606. *OPEN Mon-Fri 10am-7:30pm; Sat 9:30am-5:30pm.*

Barclay's Traveler's Checks
Listed below are two banks at which they may be purchased:

Pathway Financial Savings & Loan
100 North State. 346-4200. *OPEN Mon-Fri 8:30am-5:30pm.*

Citi Corp Savings of Illinois
1 South Dearborn. 977-5000. *OPEN Mon-Fri 8:30am-4:30pm.*
For other information and refund inquiries, call (1-800) 221-2426, 24 hours a day, 7 days a week.

Thomas Cook Travel
For information and refund inquiries, call (1-800) 233-7373, 24 hours a day, 7 days a week.
435 North Michigan. 828-9750. *OPEN Mon-Fri 9am-5pm.*
1900 East Golf Road, Schaumburg. 884-1414. *OPEN Mon-Fri 9am-5pm.*

LOST PROPERTY

Railroads

Randolph Street Station: 322-7819.
Union Station: 207-6571 (except Amtrak); Amtrak, 930-4390.

Long-Distance Buses

Greyhound: 74 West Randolph. 781-2907.
Trailways: 20 East Randolph. 726-9500.

CTA/RTA Buses & Trains

Chicago Transit Authority Buses & Rapid Transit: 664-7200.
Regional Transit Authority Buses & Rapid Transit: 917-0734.

Taxicabs

To report any items left in a cab, call City of Chicago, Department of Consumer Services, Public Vehicles Operations, 54 West Hubbard. 744-7502 or -6227. *OPEN Mon-Fri 9am-4:30pm.*

Airports

Property lost on a plane would be held by the airline. If loss occurred on airport grounds, call:
Meigs Field: 744-4787.
Midway: 767-0500.
O'Hare International: 686-2200.

TRAVELER'S AID

Traveler's Aid/Immigrants Service
Tourist information, lodging referrals, counseling and financial assistance, referrals for community and social services.

Greyhound Station, 74 West Randolph. 435-4537. *OPEN Mon-Fri 8:30am-5pm.*
Union Station, 210 South Canal. 435-4543. *OPEN Mon-Fri 8:30am-5pm.*
O'Hare International Airport, TWA Terminal. 686-7562. *OPEN Mon-Fri 8:30am-5pm.*
Weekends and evenings, call 686-7562.

Lost Anywhere

Contact the nearest police station (*see* HELP!, Emergency: Police Stations).

Lost Child

The police: 911.

Lost Pets

Animal Welfare League
10101 South Ridgeland, Chicago Ridge. 636-8586. *OPEN Mon-Sat 11am-4:30pm.*

The Anti-Cruelty Society
157 West Grand. 644-8338. *OPEN Mon-Fri noon-7:30pm; Sat 10:30am-6pm; Sun noon-5:30pm.*
Also, put up notices in shops in the area of the loss, with a description of the pet and your phone number *only*. Ads in local neighborhood publications are also helpful.

TOURIST OFFICES (INTERNATIONAL)

For literature and helpful travel information.

Andorra Bureau for Tourism
1923 West Irving Park Road. 472-7660.

Austrian National Tourist Office
500 North Michigan. 644-5556.

Bahamas Tourist Office
875 North Michigan. 787-8203.

British Tourist Authority
875 North Michigan. 787-0490.

Canadian Government Office of Tourism
310 South Michigan. 427-1888.

Cayman Islands Department of Tourism
333 North Michigan. 782-5832.

German National Tourist Office
104 South Michigan. 263-0850.

Greek National Tourist Organization
168 North Michigan. 782-1084.

Haiti Tourist Office
919 North Michigan. 337-1603.

Hong Kong Tourist Association
333 North Michigan. 782-3872.

Government of India Tourist Office
230 North Michigan. 236-7869.

Irish Tourist Board
230 North Michigan. 726-9356.

Israel Government Tourist Office
5 South Wabash. 782-4306.

Italian Government Travel Office (E.N.I.T.)
500 North Michigan. 644-0990.

Jamaica Tourist Board
36 South Wabash. 346-1546.
Japan National Tourist Organization
333 North Michigan. 332-3975.
Korea National Tourism Corporation
230 North Michigan. 346-6660.
Mexican Government Tourist Office
233 North Michigan. 565-2785.
Netherlands National Tourist Office
225 North Michigan, Suite 326. 819-0300.
Philippine Ministry of Tourism
30 North Michigan. 782-1707.
Polish National Tourism Office (ORBIS)
333 North Michigan. 236-9013.
Puerto Rico Tourist Department
11 East Adams. 922-9701.
Quebec Government Office
35 East Wacker. 726-0681.
Spanish National Tourist Office
845 North Michigan. 944-0216.
U.S. Virgin Islands Division of Tourism
343 South Dearborn. 461-0180.
Zimbabwe Tourist Board
35 East Wacker, Suite 1778. 332-2601.

SOME DOMESTIC TOURIST OFFICES

Chicago Tourism Council
163 East Pearson. 280-5740.
Hawaii Visitors Bureau
180 North Michigan. 236-0632.
Illinois Travel Information Center
160 North La Salle. 793-2094.
Indiana Department of Tourism
(1-800) 292-6337.
Kentucky Travel Information
(1-800) 225-8747.
Las Vegas Convention & Visitors Authority
230 North Michigan. 951-8655.
Minnesota Office of Tourism
(1-800) 328-1461.
Wisconsin State Division of Tourism
75 East Wacker. 332-7274.

DOMESTIC AUTO TRAVEL

Mail Service

Map with suggested routings can be obtained from the following by mail. Advise destination, time of year, and length of time to travel. Allow several weeks for reply.
   Exxon Touring Service
   Box 10210, Houston, TX 77206.
   Mobil Travel Service
   Box 25, Versailles, KY 40383.
   Texaco Travel Service
   Box 1459, Houston, TX 77001.

TRAVEL SHOPS

Rand McNally & Company
23 East Madison. 332-4627. Impressive selection of maps and guides for the traveler's aid in a lovely old store. *OPEN Mon-Sat.*
Savvy Traveller
50 East Washington, Garland Court, 2nd floor. 263-2100. Maps and guides and a stock of practical and interesting traveler's aids. AE, MC, V. *OPEN Mon-Sat.*

ANIMALS IN TRANSIT

Check with commercial carriers for their requirements. Some states require a health certificate for your pet. A veterinarian will issue that and advise you of the care and feeding of your pet while traveling.
   For information on international travel with animals, contact the United States Department of Agriculture, Animal and Plant Health Inspection Service, Veterinarian Service, 3166 Des Plaines Avenue, Des Plaines. 298-0320. *OPEN Mon-Fri 8am-4:30pm.*

CAR HIRE

Drive Yourself

Avis
Domestic: (1-800) 331-1212. *24 hours a day, 7 days a week.*
O'Hare International Airport: 694-5600. *OPEN 24 hours a day, 7 days a week.*
Midway Airport: 471-4495. *OPEN Mon-Fri 7am-10pm.*
Downtown: 200 North Clark. 782-6825. *OPEN Mon-Fri 7am-9pm; Sat 7am-8pm; Sun 9am-9pm.*
Budget
Out-of-town reservations: (1-800) 527-0700. *24 hours a day, 7 days a week.*
O'Hare International Airport: 968-6661. *OPEN 24 hours a day, 7 days a week.*
Downtown: 1025 North Clark. 664-9800. *OPEN Mon-Fri 7am-10pm; Sat 7am-9pm; Sun 8am-8pm.*
Hertz
Worldwide reservations: (1-800) 654-3131. *24 hours a day, 7 days a week.*
O'Hare International Airport: 686-7272. *OPEN 24 hours a day, 7 days a week.*
Midway Airport: 735-7272. *OPEN Mon-Fri 7am-10pm; Sat 7am-7:45pm; Sun 8am-7:45pm.*
Downtown: 9 West Kedzie. 372-7600. *OPEN Mon-Fri 7am-9:45pm; Sat 7am-7:45pm; Sun 8am-7:45pm.*
Rent-A-Wreck
6600 North Western Avenue. 274-5599. Lower-priced alternative: 1981-86 American cars in pretty good shape. Daily, weekly, and monthly rates. *OPEN Mon-Fri 8:30am-7pm; Sat 9am-6pm.*

Chauffeur-Driven

(See also SHOPPING, Specialty Shops & Services: Limousines.)

Carey Limousine
663-1220; (1-800) 336-4646. Blue or black Cadillacs. Stretches on request. 24-hour service.

Chicago Limousine Service
726-1035; (1-800) 621-7307. Lincoln and Cadillac limousines with chauffeurs. Special white limo with moon roof and bar on request. Hourly rates. 24-hour service.

Metropolitan Limo
751-1111; (1-800) 922-0343. Lincoln town cars, Lincoln stretch limos, and Mercedes standard limos. Can accommodate any request. Hourly rates. 24-hour service.

COACH & BUS HIRE

Charter Greyhound
840 North Michigan. (1-800) 528-0447.

Chicago Motor Coach Company
5601 North Sheridan. 989-8919. Rent a double-decker bus.

Chicago Transit Authority
Merchandise Mart Plaza. 664-7200, ext 3398. Rent a bus or an el train.

Trailways Charter Service
1718 South Clark. 726-5238. "Big Red" buses.

BUS STATIONS

Greyhound Terminal
74 West Randolph. 781-2900. Greyhound, Indiana Motor Bus, Indian Trails, Peoria & Rockford Transit. Food available 24 hours. Pinball machines. Traveler's Aid.

Trailways Depot
20 East Randolph. 726-9500. Continental Trailways buses. Food available 7am-7pm.

TRAIN STATIONS

La Salle Street Station
La Salle & Van Buren. 836-7000.

Randolph Street Station
151 North Michigan. 836-7000.

Union Station
South Canal & West Adams. Amtrak: from Chicago, call 558-1075; nationwide, call (1-800) USA-RAIL.

AIRPORTS

Chicago Midway Airport
5700 South Cicero. 767-0500. Ten miles south of, and extremely convenient to, downtown Chicago. Domestic and private flights.

Meigs Field
15th Street & the Lake. 744-4787. One mile east of downtown Chicago. Private flights.

O'Hare International Airport
Mannheim Road & Kennedy Expressway. 686-2200. Seventeen miles northwest of downtown Chicago. It's the world's busiest airport: arrivals and departures every 30 seconds. Domestic and international flights.

AIRLINES

Aer Lingus
(1-800) 223-6537.

Aerolineas Argentinas
875 North Michigan. 951-1944.

Aero Mexico
(1-800) 237-6639.

Aero Peru
297-0026.

Air Afrique
875 North Michigan. 440-7908.

Air Canada
300 North State. 686-0288.

Air France
875 North Michigan. 440-7922.

Air India
36 South Wabash. 782-6263.

Air Jamaica
(1-800) 523-5585.

Air New Zealand
644-2650; (1-800) 262-1234.

Air Panama International
5550 North Elston. 631-7803.

Air Wisconsin
O'Hare Airport. 569-3000.

Alaska Airlines
(1-800) 426-0333.

ALIA (Jordan)
104 South Michigan. 236-1702.

Alitalia
138 South Michigan. 781-0540.

Allegheny Commuter
O'Hare Airport. 726-1201.
4 East Monroe (Continental).

American
41 South La Salle. 372-8000.
203 North La Salle.
17 East Monroe (Palmer House).
500 North Michigan (Amtrak Ticket Office).
140 East Walton Place (Drake Hotel).

Avianca
(1-800) 327-9899.

Braniff
(1-800) 272-6433.

British Airways
67 East Madison. (1-800) 247-9297.
2 North Michigan. 332-7744.

Britt Airways
O'Hare Airport. (1-800) 652-7488.

Canadian Pacific
(1-800) 426-7000.
China Airlines
312 South Michigan. 427-2920.
Continental
4 East Monroe. 686-6500.
203 North La Salle.
Delta
346-5300. 540 North Michigan (Chicago Marriott
   Hotel).
172 West Adams (Midland Hotel).
62 East Monroe.
Eastern
21 East Monroe. 467-2900.
875 North Michigan (John Hancock Center).
Ecuadoriana Airlines
10 North Michigan. 332-0063.
El Al Israel
174 North Michigan. 236-7264.
Ethiopian Airlines
505 North Lake Shore Drive. 663-4100.
Finnair
3158 Des Plaines Avenue, Des Plaines. 296-
   1144; (1-800) 223-5700.
Iberia Airlines of Spain
180 North Michigan. 332-0694.
Icelandic Air (Lofteidir)
c/o American, 2 South La Salle. (1-800) 223-
   5500.
Japan
225 North Michigan. 565-7000.
KLM
225 North Michigan. 861-9292.
O'Hare Airport. 686-6070.
Korean Airlines
230 North Michigan. 558-9300.
LAB Airlines (Lloyd Aereo Boliviano)
8 South Michigan. 782-1143.
LAN-Chile
333 South Michigan. 332-5885.
LOT Polish Airlines
333 North Michigan. 236-3388.
Lufthansa
875 North Michigan. 751-0111.
Mexicana
55 East Monroe. 346-8414.
Mid State Airlines
O'Hare Airport. (1-800) 826-0522.
Midway Airlines
Midway Airport. 767-3400.
Midwest Express
(1-800) 452-2022.

Mississippi Valley
O'Hare Airport. 686-7400.
Northwest
75 East Monroe. 346-9860.
Olympic Airways
168 North Michigan. 329-0400; (1-800)
   223-1226.
Ozark
104 South Michigan. 726-4680.
Pakistan International
104 South Michigan. 263-3082.
Pan American
(1-800) 221-1111.
41 South La Salle.
Philippine Airlines
104 South Michigan. 332-7477; (1-800) 435-9725.
Piedmont
O'Hare Airport. 263-3656.
1717 South Naper Boulevard, Naperville. 357-
   0258.
Qantas
(1-800) 227-4500.
Royal Air Maroc
8 South Michigan. 782-7956.
Scandinavian
O'Hare Airport. 686-5900; (1-800) 221-2350.
Singapore Airlines
6 North Michigan. 332-6780.
Thai Airways International Ltd.
36 South Wabash. 332-5733; (1-800) 426-5204.
Trans World Airlines (TWA)
Domestic: 75 East Monroe. 558-7000.
International: 875 North Michigan (John Hancock Center), 332-1118; 233 North Michigan, 558-7000.
United Airlines
35 East Monroe. 569-3000.
540 North Michigan (Chicago Marriott Hotel).
875 North Michigan (John Hancock Center).
151 West Wacker (Hyatt Regency Hotel).
208 South La Salle.
U.S. Air
O'Hare Airport. 726-1201.
4 East Monroe (Continental).
UTA French Airlines
875 North Michigan. (1-800) 237-2747.
Varig Brazilian
233 North Michigan. 565-1301.
Viasa Venezuelan
(1-800) 327-5454.
Yugoslav Airlines
180 North Michigan. 782-1322.

HELP!

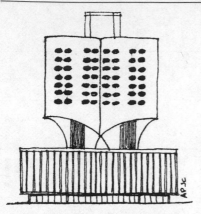

Prentice Women's Hospital

EMERGENCY

Emergency services 24 hours a day, 7 days a week.

Abused Child
(1-800) 252-2873.

Alcohol Helpline
577-1919.

Alcoholics Anonymous
346-1475.

Crisis Hot Lines
462-1700; 769-6200; 908-8100.

Dental Emergency Service
726-4321.

Desperate/Suicidal
644-4357.

Drug Abuse Hotline
278-5015; 722-2273.

Fire/Police Emergency
Dial 911.

Parental Stress Hotline
975-3221.

Poison
942-5969.

Rape
744-8418.

Runaway Switchboard
(1-800) 621-4400.

Police Stations
Emergency: Dial 911.
  Below is a listing of Chicago police precincts and their direct numbers for questions and help.
1st Precinct
11 East 11th. 744-6230.
2nd Precinct
5101 South Wentworth. 744-8366.
3rd Precinct
7070 South Cottage. 744-8201.
4th Precinct
2255 East 103rd. 744-8205.
5th Precinct
727 East 111th. 744-8210.
6th Precinct
819 West 85th. 744-8214.
7th Precinct
6120 South Racine. 744-8220.
8th Precinct
3515 West 63rd. 744-8224.
9th Precinct
3501 South Lowe. 744-8227.
10th Precinct
2259 South Damen. 744-8246.
11th Precinct
3151 West Harrison. 744-8386.
12th Precinct
100 South Racine. 744-8396.
13th Precinct
937 North Wood. 744-8350.
14th Precinct
2150 North California. 744-8290.
15th Precinct
5327 West Chicago. 744-8300.
16th Precinct
5430 West Gale. 744-8286.
17th Precinct
4461 North Pulaski. 744-8347.
18th Precinct
113 West Chicago. 744-8230.
19th Precinct
2452 West Belmont. 744-5983.
20th Precinct
1940 West Foster. 744-8330.
21st Precinct
300 East 29th. 744-8340.
22nd Precinct
1830 West Monterey. 744-6381.
23rd Precinct
3600 North Halsted. 744-8320.
24th Precinct
6464 North Clark. 744-5907.

25th Precinct
5555 West Grand. 744-8605.

Police Services

Available 24 hours a day, 7 days a week. For location of nearest precinct and general information concerning police services: 744-4000.

Ambulance

In emergency dial 911 and a city ambulance will respond free of charge to the patient. The ambulance will take the patient to the nearest emergency room according to geographic location. If a specific, nonpublic ambulance is preferred, this list provides private 24-hour ambulance services on a fee-pay basis:
Abby
Northwest Side and northern suburbs. 283-7766.
Advance Ambulance
Northwest Side and suburbs. 252-7800.
Ambulance Service Corporation
Anywhere in the city and northern suburbs. 248-2712.
Roberts Ambulance Service
North Side and northern suburbs. 561-5430.

Hospital Emergency Rooms

Augustana
2035 North Lincoln. 975-5000.
Barclay
4700 North Clarendon. 728-7100.
Belmont Community
4058 West Melrose. 736-7000.
Bethany Brethren—Garfield Park
3425 West Van Buren. 265-7700.
Bethany Methodist
4950 North Ashland. 271-9040.
Bethesda
2451 West Howard. 761-6000.
Booth Memorial
5040 North Pulaski Road. 725-7441.
Central Community
5701 South Wood. 737-4600.
Chicago Lake Shore
4840 North Marine Drive. 878-9700.
Chicago Maternity Center
250 East Superior. 908-7300.
Chicago Osteopathic
5200 South Ellis. 947-3000.
Chicago-Read Mental Health Center
4200 North Oak Park. 794-4000.
Children's Memorial
700 West Fullerton Parkway. 880-4000.
Columbus-Cuneo-Cabrini Medical Center
2520 North Lake View. 883-7300.
Cook County
1835 West Harrison. 633-6000.
Edgewater
5700 North Ashland. 878-6000.
Englewood
6001 South Green. 962-5000.

Forkosh Memorial
2544 West Montrose. 722-2273.
Frank Cuneo
750 West Montrose. 883-8300.
Franklin Boulevard Community
3240 West Franklin. 722-3020.
Garfield Park Mental Health Center
4651 West Madison. 261-5010.
Grant
550 West Webster. 883-2000.
Henrotin
920 North Clark. 440-7700.
Holy Cross
2701 West 68th. 297-1800.
Hyde Park Community
5800 South Stony Island. 643-9200.
Illinois Eye & Ear
1855 West Taylor. 996-7000.
Illinois Masonic Medical Center
836 West Wellington. 975-1600.
Illinois Psychiatric Institute
1601 West Taylor. 996-1000.
Jackson Park
7531 South Stony Island. 947-7500.
La Rabida Children's
East 65th & Lake Michigan. 363-6700.
Loretto
645 South Central. 626-4300.
Louise Burg
255 West Cermak Road. 225-4500.
Martha Washington
4055 North Western. 583-9000.
Mary Thompson
140 North Ashland. 666-7373.
McGaw Medical—Northwestern
339 East Chicago Avenue. 908-8649.
Mercy Medical Center
Stevenson Expressway & Martin Luther King, Jr., Drive. 567-2000.
Michael Reese Medical Center
Lake Shore Drive & 31st. 791-2000.
Mount Sinai Medical Center
1500 South Fairfield. 542-2000.
Northwest
5645 West Addison. 282-7000.
Northwestern Memorial
250 East Superior. 908-2000.
Norwegian-American
1044 North Francisco. 278-8800.
Passavant Pavilion—Northwestern
303 East Superior Street. 908-2000.
Provident
426 East 51st. 285-5300.
Ravenswood
4550 North Winchester. 878-4300.
Rehabilitation Institute
345 East Superior. 908-6000.
Resurrection
7435 West Talcott. 774-8000.
Ridgeway
520 North Ridgeway. 722-3113.
Roseland Community
45 West 111th. 995-3000.
Rush Presbyterian—St. Luke's
1753 West Congress. 942-5000.

Schwab Rehabilitation
1401 South California. 522-2010. *OPEN 7 days 1-8pm.*
Sheridan Road—Rush Presbyterian
6130 North Sheridan Road. 743-2600.
Shriners Crippled Children
2211 North Oak Park. 622-5400.
South Chicago Community
2320 East 93rd. 978-2000.
South Shore
8015 South Crandon. 768-0810.
St. Anne's
4950 West Thomas. 378-7100.
St. Anthony
2875 West 19th. 521-1710.
St. Bernard
326 West 64th. 962-3900.
St. Elizabeth's
1431 North Claremont. 278-2000.
St. Francis Xavier Cabrini
811 South Lytle. 883-4300.
St. Joseph
2900 North Lake Shore Drive. 975-3000.
St. Mary of Nazareth
2233 West Division. 770-2000.
Swedish Covenant
5145 North California. 878-8200.
Thorek Medical Center
850 West Irving Park Road. 525-6780.
University of Illinois
1740 West Taylor. 996-7000.
Veterans Administration (West Side)
820 South Damen. 666-6500.
Veterans Administration Research
333 East Huron. 943-6600.
Walther Memorial
1116 North Kedzie. 227-3100.
Weiss Memorial
4646 North Marine Drive. 878-8700.
Wesley Pavilion—Northwestern
250 East Superior. 649-2000.
Woodlawn
6060 South Drexel. 752-3000.

ASSISTANCE

These organizations help and advise anyone in need—the ill, the lonely, the victimized, the desperate, and those people who simply need solutions to problems. Remember, of course, that 24 hours a day, 7 days a week, there is police assistance.

Booklet with Useful Information

Guide for Senior Citizens
Community resources for the older person in the Chicago and metropolitan area. Write: Department on Aging and Disability, 121 North La Salle, Room 703, Chicago, IL 60602.

General Services

American Red Cross
43 East Ohio. 440-2000 (24-hour hotline). Disaster services—food, clothing, and shelter. Also courses in first aid, water safety, and health; nontechnical aid at hospitals and blood banks.
Board of Education
1819 West Pershing. 890-8000. Pupil personnel services and special education. Medical, mental, and school health services. Recreation. *OPEN Mon-Fri 8am-4:30pm.*
Catholic Charities
126 North Des Plaines. 236-5172. Information and referrals for children, families, individuals, and the aged. Emergency assistance. Addiction prevention services. English- and Spanish-speaking. *OPEN Mon-Fri 8:30am-4:30pm.*
Citizens' Information Service
67 East Madison, Room 1406. 236-0315. Nonpartisan information about government and civic concerns. Classes in how to organize, to lobby, to be effective. Telephone information service and pamphlets. Referrals. English and Spanish. *OPEN Mon-Fri 9am-5pm.*
City of Chicago Department of Human Services
744-4045 (information 24 hours). Emergency service for shelter and assistance. Senior-citizen services, referrals and assistance. Social-service counseling and referrals. Family and individual referrals.
Community Referral Service
104 South Michigan. 580-2850. Referrals for alcoholism, blind services, child abuse and neglect, consumer protection, day care, drug abuse, health care, legal aid, recreation, runaways, senior citizens, veterans, women's services, youth services. Collect calls accepted. *OPEN Mon-Fri 8:30am-5pm. After 10pm answering service.*
Jewish Family & Community Service
1 South Franklin. 346-6700. Legal services, homemaker services, family-life education, senior-citizen services. *OPEN Mon-Fri 9am-5:30pm.*
Mayor's Office of Inquiry and Information
744-5000. *24 hours a day, 7 days a week.*
Metro-help
2210 North Halsted. 929-5150. Referrals for child abuse and neglect, drug abuse, legal aid, suicide prevention, women's services, and youth services. *OPEN Mon-Fri 8:30am-5pm.*
Parental Stress Services
407 South Dearborn. 463-0390 (24-hour hotline). Community outreach and referral program. Thirty-three Parents Anonymous chapters throughout the city. Counseling for parents having problems.
Salvation Army of Chicago & Northern Illinois
800 West Lawrence. 275-9383 (24-hour hotline). Disaster services, information and referral for alcohol and drug counseling, family services.
State of Illinois Department for Public Aid
17 North State. 793-3033. Child support, medical services, public assistance, financial, medi-

cal, and social services for those who qualify. OPEN Mon-Fri 8:30am-5pm.

Voluntary Action Center
580-2581. Recruitment and referral service for volunteers willing to work in day care, old-age homes, hospitals, and rehabilitation centers. OPEN Mon-Fri 8am-4:30pm.

Abortion & Birth Control

Community Referral Service
580-2850. (See HELP!, Assistance: General Services.)

Health & Evaluation Referral Service (HERS)
248-0166. Feedback and referral on Chicago abortion clinics. OPEN Mon-Fri 9am-5pm.

In-Touch Hotline
996-5535. Crisis intervention; unwanted pregnancy, suicide, family counseling, alcoholism. Open 7 days 6pm-3am.

Planned Parenthood Association
17 North State, 15th floor. 781-9550. Birth-control clinic, exams, lab work, VD testing, pregnancy testing, sterilization information, teen clinic, counseling, and community education in reproductive health care. OPEN Mon-Fri 9am-4:45pm.

AIDS

U.S. Public Health Service Hotline
(1-800) 324-AIDS.

Crime Victims

Crime Victims Division Office of the Attorney General
174 West Randolph. 793-2585. Compensation for victims of crime. Applications and information. OPEN Mon-Fri 9am-5pm.

Victim-Witness Assistance Program
2600 South California; 890-7209. And 2452 West Belmont; 871-0247. Provides assistance and support to victims and witnesses of crimes.

Disaster Relief

American Red Cross
440-2000. Emergency food, clothing, and shelter. OPEN 24 hours a day, 7 days a week.

City of Chicago Department of Human Services
744-4045. Emergency disaster unit assists with transportation, food, relocation, and temporary shelter. OPEN 24 hours a day, 7 days a week.

Salvation Army
275-9383. On-the-scene first aid and temporary housing. OPEN 24 hours a day, 7 days a week.

Drug Abuse

Community Referral Service
580-2850. (See HELP!, Assistance: General Services.)

Metro-help
929-5150. (See HELP!, Assistance: General Services.)

Legal Assistance

Chicago Volunteer Legal Services
332-1624. Free legal aid. OPEN Mon-Fri 9am-5pm.

Medical Assistance

Chicago Board of Health
744-3558. Clinic referral Mon-Fri 8:30am-4:30pm.

Medical Referral Service
670-2550. Private-doctors referral Mon-Fri 8:30am-4:30pm.

Rape

City of Chicago Department of Human Services
744-4045. Emergency counseling, emotional support, assistance in securing medical and legal help. OPEN 24 hours a days, 7 days a week.

Loop Center YWCA
37 South Wabash. 372-6600, ext 301. Counseling for raped and abused women. Referral for post-mastectomy and problem solving. Program times and cost vary. OPEN Mon-Fri 9am-5pm.

Women in Crisis Can Act
2114 West Belmont. 528-3303 or -3304. Hotline and drop-in crisis service for abused women, rape victims, sexual harassment on the job, abused children, and suicide. OPEN Mon-Fri 6pm-10pm for rape, referral & crisis intervention.

Senior Citizens

(See also HELP!, Assistance: General Services: Catholic Charities; Community Referral Service; Jewish Family & Community Service; and Metro-help.)

Department on Aging and Disability
121 North La Salle, Room 703. 744-4016. Senior citizens' meals at 101 sites in the city, nutrition information, limited home delivery of meals. Referral service. OPEN Mon-Fri 8:30am-5pm.

Little Brothers of the Poor
1658 West Belmont. 477-7702. Home-delivered meals, some emergency food service. Near North, North, and West sides of the city. OPEN Mon-Fri 9am-5pm.

Retired Senior Volunteer Program
Hull House, 118 North Clinton. 726-1526. Gives older citizens (60 and up) a chance to share

their talents, skills, and experiences. *OPEN Mon-Fri 8:30am-4:30pm.*

Tenants' Rights

Chicago Volunteer Legal Services
332-1624. Free legal service. *OPEN Mon-Fri 9am-5pm.*
City of Chicago
922-7922 or 7925. Housing discrimination complaints.
City of Chicago Buildings Department
744-3420 or -5000 (night). For building complaints. *OPEN Mon-Fri 8am-4:30pm.*

City of Chicago Department of Neighborhoods
744-5000. Referral Service. *24-hour hotline.*
Heating Complaints
744-5000 (24 hours a day).

Women

Women's Midwest Center
663-4163. Referrals for legal help, day care, employment, resources, health, networking, sexual harassment, shelters, older-women networks, women's centers. *OPEN Mon-Fri 9am-5pm.*

INDEX

The I LOVE city guides
by Marilyn J. Appleberg

America's most acclaimed urban travel books—
in new, updated editions

I Love Boston
I Love Chicago
I Love Los Angeles
I Love New York
I Love Washington